100 Years of NCVO and Vo

Justin Davis Smith

100 Years of NCVO and Voluntary Action

Idealists and Realists

Justin Davis Smith
Cass Business School
City, University of London
London, UK

ISBN 978-3-030-02773-5   ISBN 978-3-030-02774-2   (eBook)
https://doi.org/10.1007/978-3-030-02774-2

Library of Congress Control Number: 2018961480

This Palgrave Macmillan imprint is published by the registered company Springer Nature Switzerland AG
The registered company address is: Gewerbestrasse 11, 6330 Cham, Switzerland

For Julia

FOREWORD

Civil society needs to look to the future, and through the *Civil Society Futures Inquiry* we have spent time looking at the major changes taking place and presenting us with challenge and opportunity in equal measure. But to look forward we need to look back, and the historic arc of the voluntary sector illuminates many of our current dilemmas and choices.

Civil society has developed and changed in response to seismic social change—from the industrial revolution through the horrors of two world wars, political upheavals, and enormous, seemingly overwhelming social challenges. Understanding where we have come from is a vital part of understanding where we decide to go.

The National Council for Voluntary Organisations (NCVO) in its various forms over the last century faced challenges, dilemmas, and opportunities. Now in 2019 we live in a time when many institutions across public life are questioned. How can NCVO, formed in the wake of the First World War, find new-found relevance in the wake of the internet revolution, Black Lives Matter and #metoo?

Three themes in Justin Davis Smith's fascinating history might hold the answers.

First, the tension between the local and the national has been felt since the very start of the National Council. Recognising the crucial importance of local voluntary action and impulse has always been in tension with the desire for a national presence.

The need to rediscover deep and effective connections with local communities arises again and again—what does that rediscovery look like now?

Second, the 'insider' status of a sector able to have the ear of government and business, negotiating on equal terms and representing the power and capability of wider civil society, is in constant tension with the need to stand with and for the dispossessed and overlooked, recognise and express their anger, and challenge the seat of power.

Through every era people rightly ask: whose side are you on?

And equally, thirdly, the tension between leading and representing. All umbrella bodies in all sectors face the choice between serving their members, going at their pace and ensuring that their needs are met—and, from time to time, leading and challenging the very sector they exist to serve.

What does leadership in a new century mean, and how does it differ from the past?

Justin reveals these perennial tensions and demonstrates the different ways they have been reconciled. At the same time, he reminds us of the changing context in which we always operate. The impact of austerity—after the war and again more recently. The changing levels of trust in politicians and the political process. The different ways in which voluntary action manifested itself.

In doing so he shows us how civil society has always been affected by broader trends—but crucially has also had the power to influence them. He illustrates the complex choices that need to be made, and the tricky decisions that need to be navigated. Reading this excellent history I was struck time and time again by the continued power of civil society to challenge and disrupt other sources of power, to mobilise money and effort to solve major social problems. And our capacity for connecting people, bringing people together to maximise their own power, and at the same time ensuring that those voices are heard throughout the country, remains our enduring purpose.

We must not be naive of course. Understanding where we have come from does provide us with a powerful set of tools for navigating our increasingly uncertain future. But history is never a completely accurate guide, and it clearly tells us that we can take nothing for granted—and change is our constant companion.

What is the history of the next 100 years that we want to write?

Chair of Independent Inquiry into the
Future of Civil Society; CBE   Julia Unwin
York, UK

Acknowledgements

Thanks are due to many people for assistance with this project. To Emily Russell and colleagues at Palgrave Macmillan, for publishing the book and support during the production process. To members of the advisory group—Nicholas Deakin, Pat Thane, Diana Leat, and Peter Grant—who acted as critical friends, offering invaluable advice on content and structure and providing much appreciated personal support and encouragement. To colleagues at the Centre for Charity Effectiveness, Cass Business School, especially Stephen Lee and Paul Palmer, for reading draft chapters and providing expert feedback. And to a number of other colleagues and friends who have offered advice and guidance, notably Irene Hardill of Northumbria University.

A big thank you goes to those interviewed as part of the oral history strand, namely, Tesse Akpeki, Margaret Bolton, Ian Bruce, Sir Stephen Bubb, David Clark, Dame Julia Cleverdon, Nicholas Deakin, David Emerson, Sir Stuart Etherington, Adam Gaines, Richard Gutch, Richard Harries, Oliver Henman, Deborah Hinton, Bharat Mehta, Sir Graham Melmoth, Janet Morrison, Sara Morrison, Foster Murphy, Baroness Pitkeathley, Baroness Prashar, Andrew Purkis, Campbell Robb, Bill Seary, Marilyn Taylor, Judy Weleminsky, and Perri 6. Space dictates that I haven't been able to do full justice to your contribution, but I hope I have given a flavour of your insights and wisdom.

Thanks to the staff at the London Metropolitan Archives (LMA), who dealt with my numerous requests for assistance with good grace and professionalism. This book draws heavily on the catalogued National Council for Voluntary Organisations (NCVO) collection within the archives, which provides a thorough record of the administrative work of the Council from the early 1920s through to the late 1970s. It is unfortunate that the foundation records of the Council were destroyed in a fire during the Second World War, but I have been able to fill in some of the gaps by reference to the records of the Charity Organisation Society (one of the bodies that came together to create the Council), which are also located at the LMA. For the later period in the Council's history, I have drawn on the uncatalogued collection housed at the

LMA and the organisation's own, largely digitised records. Thanks also go to the staff at other libraries and archives whose resources I have utilised, including the London School of Economics, Senate House Library, British Library, the National Archives, and my own institution, City, University of London. I should like to give particular thanks to Iona Birchall for granting me privileged access to the Birchall family archives, which include private and very poignant correspondence between Edward and his family and friends while on the front line in France during the First World War.

Many staff members at NCVO have been incredibly helpful over the course of the project, but special mention should be made of Tracy Kiernan and Michelle McErlean, who shared their extensive knowledge of the organisation's records, ordered up boxes from the archives at short notice, and provided me with space to work. Thanks also go to successive heads of research at the Council, Nick Ockenden, Ruth Driscoll, and Veronique Jochum, for supporting the advisory group and giving valuable feedback on draft chapters, and to Stuart Etherington and the Board at NCVO for commissioning the project and resisting the urge to interfere. Thanks also to Julia Unwin for writing such a thoughtful foreword.

Three final thanks are due. To all staff and volunteers involved with the Council over the past 100 years, who contributed so much to the health and vitality of the voluntary movement and provided the raw material and inspiration for the project. To my parents, who have embodied the spirit of voluntary action during their lives. And to my wife, Julia, who has supported and encouraged me throughout. This book is dedicated to her with much love.

Prologue: Edward Vivian Dearman Birchall

Edward Birchall has rightly been credited as the *founding father* of the National Council for Voluntary Organisations.[1] It was his legacy of £1000 to his close friend and colleague S.P. (Percy) Grundy that enabled the organisation to get started and keep going for its first few years, when few alternative funds were available. But more than this, Birchall can lay claim as its ideological inspiration, or at least co-inspiration, along with Grundy and a small group of individuals in the voluntary movement at the turn of the twentieth century.[2] Despite his death in France in 1916 at the age of 32, it was the ideas that Birchall and others had mulled over in the years leading up to the outbreak of the First World War that led directly to the formation of the new organisation. Birchall did not live to see them come to fruition, but his vision and generosity allowed others to realise his dream.[3]

Birchall was born on 10 August 1884 at Bowden Hall, Upton St Leonards. His mother died when he was 3 weeks old. His family, originally from Quaker stock, made its fortune in the textile industry in Leeds before moving to Gloucestershire in the latter half of the nineteenth century, where it quickly shed its Quaker roots for the established church.[4] Birchall (known as Thomas to the family) was one of five children, three boys and two girls, and after attending Eton where he was awarded school colours at football, he took an honours degree in chemistry at Magdalen College, Oxford. Like many of his Oxbridge contemporaries, Birchall was attracted by the idea of community service. But in contrast to most, who saw a year or two volunteering as a stepping stone to a career in politics or business (one of his older brothers John, for example, went to Eton and Oxford, volunteered at Oxford House Settlement in London, fought in France, and entered Parliament as Conservative MP for North East Leeds), Birchall decided at an early age he wanted to make a career in the voluntary movement. A contemporary later recalled how at university he had thrown himself into social work with 'most intense humility and great reticence' and had pursued causes with 'a supreme contempt for "money grubbing" and all forms of speculation'.[5]

After graduating from Oxford in 1907, he went to Birmingham where, following a short spell at the Juvenile Police Court, he joined the Birmingham Civic Aid Society, which was pioneering new approaches to the relief of poverty. Set up in 1906, the Society sought to establish a closer relationship with the local authority than most charitable endeavours. In doing so it was in keeping with the newly emerging guild of help movement, which was establishing itself as the pre-eminent charitable coordinating body, and at odds with the long-established Charity Organisation Society (COS), which called for a distance to be maintained between the community and the state.[6] Before long Birchall, who had risen to the post of honorary secretary at the Civic Aid Society, was playing a key role in the guild movement, a regular attendee at its annual conferences and one of the prime movers behind plans to set up a national body to oversee the numerous individual guilds that were emerging. In 1911 he became the first honorary secretary of the National Association of Guilds of Help (NAGH), a position he held until 1914 when he volunteered for action at the outbreak of war.[7] It was during his time with the guilds that Birchall began, in cooperation with Grundy and a small number of other close associates, to sketch out ideas for a new organisation to bring together the three separate traditions dominant at that time within the voluntary movement. In 1911 he wrote to a colleague in Newcastle outlining his vision for a new organisation that 'would combine all the very important and specific advantages of a Charity Organisation Society, a Guild of Help, and a Council of Social Welfare, and would at the same time to a great extent avoid the disadvantages which are inherent in each type', although he acknowledged that he wasn't yet ready to 'admit it on a public platform'.[8]

In 1911 he resigned his post with the Civic Aid Society and moved to London, where he helped establish another new group aimed at mobilising voluntary action. The Agenda Club, set up in February 1911, was to close in failure after a couple of years; but it was a novel undertaking and reinforced in Birchall's mind the need for greater coordination of charitable endeavour and difficulties inherent in bringing it about. The club was established as 'an association of men and women undertaking, or anxious to promote, voluntary service for the benefit of the community, and to inspire others to undertake such service'.[9] It styled itself as a club for English Samurai and members proclaimed respect for 'these Samurai, careless of material gain', even inviting a Japanese official to the first annual meeting.[10] Its main focus was on encouraging people to undertake short, intensive bursts of community service in pursuit of a common idea or 'Agendum', decided by members. In 1912, for example, the chosen topic was public health and a week of activities was organised in May aimed at supporting health-related groups. It also pioneered an early version of a volunteer bureau by establishing a signposting service directing those wanting to volunteer 'to the work where they will be best suited, and where their services are most needed'.[11] The club was undoubtedly elitist; the cost of membership was one guinea a year, although cheaper rates (for reduced benefits) were available. But in other respects, it was relatively enlightened for its age. Its Board of Control was elected by the membership; women were allowed as full members; it was keen to expand beyond public school and Oxbridge elites; and it was committed to developing its work outside London. It was these lofty ideals that set it against another similar club established at the time, the Cavendish Club, and ultimately led to its demise. The Cavendish Club aimed to do much the same things as the Agenda Club, but targeted public school, Oxbridge graduates. It was also male only. By the spring of 1913 it was clear the two clubs risked overlapping and diluting their resources and merger discussions were started. They came to nothing. The ideological divide between the two groups was unbridgeable, particularly the issue of women membership, and they agreed to continue down their separate paths.[12] For the Agenda Club, however, the end of the road was in sight, and in September 1913 the Board of Control recommended to its members that it should be dissolved, admitting it had achieved little of lasting value.[13]

The closure of the club appears to have impacted less on Birchall (who had resigned several months before the decision was taken by the Board) than the failure to reach agreement with the Cavendish over merger: 'I have a very strong feeling', he wrote to a member setting out his reasons for resigning, 'that neither club can succeed without the help of the other and that any failure in this field means the end of all inspirational work of the sort for years to come.'[14] The episode appears to have jolted Birchall's enthusiasm for social work, although it didn't stop him applying unsuccessfully for the job of secretary at the Cavendish Club. His private letters suggest a man uneasy with the way the voluntary movement was developing and unsure what to do next. For the time being he was 'luxuriating in freedom', it was the first break he had had since Oxford, although he admitted he didn't know 'how long it will last' and that 'sooner or later' he would 'probably be entrapped into the meshes' of some similar work. His frustrations led him to consider going into 'business of some sort or other', 'for the desire to see results which I believe you can get in business, and never see in any sort of social work', although he admitted he would not 'feel free to do so' unless he could take his 'conscience out one dark night and drown it'.[15] Birchall was not alone in holding these frustrations. His close colleagues within the guild, such as Grundy and Frederic D'Aeth, and leading figures within the council of social welfare movement and the COS, were also coming to the view that the overlapping of voluntary groups was a serious impediment to progress and rationalisation was required.[16]

After leaving the Agenda Club, Birchall was offered a role 'superintending the Relief Committee and Municipal Work' in the parish of St Martin-in-the-Fields by his close friend Dick Sheppard who had recently taken over as vicar, but he turned it down, taking a position instead with the Juvenile Branch of the Labour Exchange at the Board of Trade in Bristol.[17] He was not there long. Soon after the outbreak of war, he volunteered for action with the Oxfordshire and Buckinghamshire Light Infantry Regiment and, after seven months of training, was posted to France in February 1915.[18] Birchall had a long-standing attachment to the regiment, having volunteered for the Buckinghamshire Battalion Territorial Force in 1906, and was to have a distinguished military career. He was appointed captain in 1913 and led his battalion at the Battle of the Somme.[19] During one incursion on 23 July 1916 he was seriously wounded leading a successful attack on a German trench. He was transferred to the Liverpool Merchants' voluntary mobile hospital at Etaples, near Boulogne, and died from his wounds on 10 August 1916, his birthday. He was 32.[20] His other older brother, Arthur Percy, was killed the previous year during the second Battle of Ypres. For 'conspicuous gallantry and devotion to duty in action', Birchall was awarded the Distinguished Service Order, the telegram reaching him the day before he died.[21] He was buried at Etaples military cemetery and awarded a mention in despatches in July 1917.[22] Birchall was not married and had lived with his sister Violet 'Bay' at Saintbridge House in Gloucester since 1901. Both Violet and his surviving brother John attended his funeral. A tribute to Birchall published soon after his death described his final resting place as being one of several hundred graves 'situated in a hollow of the sand dunes close by the sea, surrounded by Scotch firs and scrub – just such a spot as he might have chosen'.[23] The tributes following his death were fulsome and made mention of his courage, unselfishness, and humanity. One guild of help secretary wrote that they had 'hoped in all the plans that we had laid for the uncertain future' to be able to draw upon 'the assistance of his unique qualities', and highlighted 'his absolute unselfishness and idealism, combined with a practical ability in handling all kinds of men and women', which gave him 'an influence over us all that we can never hope to get from anyone else'.[24]

In his will, he left money to his regiment, Oxford college, and hospitals in Leeds and Gloucestershire. He also left £1000 to his friend Grundy 'in trust for the National Association of Guilds of Help or some such similar Association'.[25] It was this money that was used to fund the establishment of the National Council of Social Service in 1919. Birchall informed Grundy of his plans in August 1915 from France. The letter offers both a poignant reflection on war and a clear indication that his pre-war interests were never far from his mind.

As to future of the war – I give it till end of October and then a sort of status quo (with what difference) ending: no sudden dramatic victory either way, but by the exhaustion of men and money, we may make war impossible for 20 years and by the deadlock we may even prove what everyone out here would swear with his hand on his heart (or rather that small minority who have actually heard a gun fire) that war is absolutely the most futile undertaking ever invented.

Re NAGH [National Association of Guilds of Help] here is a cheque – I should prefer to be anonymous: the one thing you do at this job is to save money. By the way if I get scuppered (tears all round and shouts of God forbid) I've left some money to be used for NAGH or any other old purpose in your absolute discretion: £1000 I think it is but don't mention it till I'm tuning my harp please.

Regarding a Secretary why not Bourdillon?[26] *I should have thought it a good notion but failing that of course you're the man and I don't see any real fundamental reason against it – run it as your main job and retain a sort of consulting practice in Manchester: we could raise the money on a five year guarantee. As for myself in the unlikely event of me surviving in any form but that of a fragrant memory (fragrant I said not flagrant) I don't think I shall ever do anything again but lie in a deckchair and give myself thrills by causing the cook to burst enormous paper bags at the end of the garden while four small boys shall imitate shell screams and the gardeners will throw spadefulls of earth at me. If that wears thin after a year or two I suppose I'll be asking the Board of Trade to rehabilitate me but not in exactly the same job as before.*

I am so sorry to hear you lost a brother too – I had not seen his name. So long now: keep cheerful and damn Northcliffe.[27]

On 15 August 1917 Dorothy Keeling, acting general secretary of the NAGH, wrote to Violet expressing 'sincere gratitude' for Birchall's 'devoted services to the guild of help movement and for his generous legacy in furtherance of its work'. She also expressed delight that Violet had been elected to the executive committee of the association.[28] Keeling went on to make a major contribution to the work of the Council.[29] In 1920 John Birchall financed the building of a village hall in Upton St Leonards in memory of his brothers, Edward and Arthur. It provided another link with the new Council as the village hall movement proved to be among its most enduring successes.[30] And some 20 years later there would be a further family connection when John's son, Peter, Edward's nephew, took a job with the Council for a few years.[31]

How are we to assess Birchall's contribution to the Council? On one level he was just one of a number of influential figures who saw the establishment of a new national agency as crucial to bringing greater coordination to a fragmented movement. He was not even the leading light among this group. Certainly in terms of intellectual clout two of his closest colleagues, Grundy and D'Aeth, had a greater impact on public debate. Indeed, if it hadn't been for his legacy, or the compelling story of a young man cut down in the prime of his life, who used his wealth to fund the establishment of an organisation that lasted 100 years, his contribution would be a footnote in this centenary history. Without his money a new national body would have been set up at some time, although whether it would have survived its first couple of years when funding was so tight is open to question. And without him, the vision of the organisation would have been much the same; Grundy, D'Aeth, Keeling, and the others would have ensured this was the case. But none of this matters and is just conjecture. What is important, and the reason Birchall deserves his place as the Council's *founding father*, is that it was his legacy, along with his pioneering work in Birmingham and London, that led directly to its establishment in 1919. The story of the Council takes in many men and women who have made a significant contribution to its work in many different ways. None though has made a bigger contribution than Edward Vivian Dearman Birchall.

Notes

1. See, for example, Etherington, 2016.
2. The contribution of Grundy and Birchall's other colleagues, such as Frederic D'Aeth, to the development of the Council are discussed in Chap. 2.
3. This chapter draws on a range of published and unpublished material relating to the life of Edward Birchall, including his entry in the Dictionary of National Biography, Laybourn, 2004, and a tribute published soon after his death as an addendum to his local parish magazine, Upton St Leonards Parish Magazine, 1916. Much of the information comes from unpublished correspondence and papers held by the Birchall family.
4. On Edward's parents, see Verey, 1983.
5. Upton St Leonards Parish Magazine, 1916, p. 1.
6. The battle for the soul of the voluntary movement between the COS and guilds is discussed in Chap. 2.
7. Laybourn, 2004.
8. Letter from Edward Birchall to A.S. Fryer, Newcastle-Upon-Tyne, 25 September 1911; Private papers, Birchall family archive.
9. Agenda Club, 1912, p. 1.
10. Laybourn, 2004.
11. Agenda Club, 1912, p. 4.
12. Letter from Edward Birchall to Clara setting out his reasons for leaving the Agenda Club, 14 April 1913; Private papers, Birchall family archive.
13. Agenda Club, 1913, pp. 3–4.
14. Letter from Edward Birchall to 'Clara', 14 April 1913; Private papers, Birchall family archive.
15. *Ibid.*
16. Efforts to bring together the different traditions within the voluntary movement are discussed in Chap. 2.
17. Correspondence between Birchall and Sheppard, May to July 1914; Private papers, Birchall family archive. On the friendship between Sheppard and Birchall, see Roberts, 1942. Sheppard was vicar of St Martin's during the First World War and gave refuge to soldiers on their way to France. He saw St Martin's as 'the church of the ever open door'. They have remained open ever since. See, St Martin in the Fields, no date.
18. The Regiment existed from 1881 to 1958 and fought in the Second Boer War and the First and Second World Wars. In 1958 it was renamed the 1st Green Jackets (43rd and 52nd), part of the Green Jacket Brigade.
19. The Battle of the Somme, the largest battle on the western front in the First World War, took place between 1 July and 18 November 1916 and resulted in one million wounded or killed.
20. For a description of Birchall's military career, see Murray, 2016, pp. 41–43. The Liverpool Merchants' voluntary mobile hospital, also known as No. 6 Hospital British Red Cross, was constructed and equipped from funds raised by members of the Liverpool Chamber of Commerce and staffed by volunteers from Liverpool. It is estimated that it treated over 20,000 casualties during the four years it was open. See www.merseyside-at-war.org
21. 'Deeds of valour in the field', The *Manchester Guardian*, 26 August 1916, p. 5.

22. Etaples military cemetery, designed by Sir Edwin Lutyens, holds over 11,500 dead from the First and Second World Wars.
23. Upton St Leonards Parish Magazine, 1916, p. 3.
24. Upton St Leonards Parish Magazine, 1916, p. 7. See also tribute in *The Times*, 14 August 1916, p. 9.
25. Epitome of the Will of Captain Edward Vivian Dearman Birchall, 10 July 1915; Private papers, Birchall family archive.
26. F.B. Bourdillon was secretary of the Reading Guild of Help and took over from Birchall as honorary secretary of the National Association of Guilds of Help at the outbreak of war in 1914. He was succeeded by C. Norris, secretary of the Sunderland Guild, in 1916 and then by Dorothy Keeling in 1917.
27. Copy of letter from Percy Grundy to Edward Birchall, 19 August 2015; Private papers, Birchall family archive. The reference is to Lord Northcliffe (Alfred Charles William Harmsworth), owner of the *Daily Mail* and *Daily Mirror* and later director of propaganda in Lloyd George's wartime government.
28. Letter from Dorothy Keeling to Violet Birchall, 15 August 1917; Private papers, Birchall Family Archive.
29. Keeling's contribution to the Council is discussed in Chap. 5. See also her own account of her career in Keeling, 1961.
30. Murray, 2016, p. 43. On the Council's support for village halls, see in particular Chap. 3.
31. Correspondence between John Birchall and his wife Adela, April 1936; Private papers, Birchall family archive. See also Chap. 4.

References

Agenda Club. (1912). *Constitution of the Agenda Club*. London: Agenda Club.
Agenda Club. (1913, September 26). *Memorandum to the members of the Agenda Club*. London: Agenda Club.
Etherington, S. (2016, August 10). Edward Birchall: The world war one soldier behind today's NCVO. *NCVO Blog Post*. https://blogs.ncvo.org.uk/2016/08/10/birchall/
Keeling, D. (1961). *The Crowded stairs*. London: NCSS.
Laybourn, K. (2004). Birchall, Edward Vivian Dearman (1884–1916). *Oxford Dictionary of National Biography*. Oxford: Oxford University Press.
Murray, I. (2016). Edward Birchall DSO, soldier and philanthropist. In S. Jenkins (Ed.), *Bugle & sabre IX: The military history of Oxfordshire and Buckinghamshire*. The Friends of the Oxfordshire & Buckinghamshire Light Infantry, in association with the Oxfordshire Yeomanry Trust.
Roberts, R. (1942). *HRL Sheppard: Life and letters*. London: John Murray.
St Martin in the Fields. (no date). *The Story of St Martin-in-the-Fields*. London: St Martin-in-the-Fields.
Upton St Leonards Parish Magazine. (1916, October). Tribute to Edward Vivian Dearman Birchall, born 10 August 1884, died of wounds, 10 August 1916, issued as a supplement to the *Upton St Leonards Parish Magazine*.
Verey, D. (1983). *The Diary of a Victorian squire: Extracts from the diaries and letters of Dearman and Emily Birchall*. Stroud: Alan Sutton.

CONTENTS

ABBREVIATIONS

ACENVO	Association of Chief Executives of National Voluntary Organisations
ACEVO	Association of Chief Executives of Voluntary Organisations
ACRE	Action with Communities in Rural England
AGNA	Affinity Group of National Associations
BOND	British Overseas NGOs for Development
CAB	Citizens' Advice Bureaux
CAF	Charities Aid Foundation
CBI	Confederation of British Industry
CEDAG	European Council for Voluntary Organisations
COS	Charity Organisation Society
CVS-NA	Councils for Voluntary Service – National Association
ENNA	European Network for National Associations
GLC	Greater London Council
ICSW	International Council on Social Welfare
LMA	London Metropolitan Archives
MDU	Management Development Unit
MSC	Manpower Services Commission
NACAB	National Association of Citizens' Advice Bureaux
NACRO	National Association for the Care and Resettlement of Offenders
NACVS	National Association of Councils for Voluntary Service
NAGH	National Association of Guilds of Help
NAVCA	National Association for Voluntary and Community Action
NCSS	National Council of Social Service
NCVO	National Council for Voluntary Organisations
NFCA	National Federation of Community Associations
NOPWC	National Old People's Welfare Committee/Council
NUWM	National Unemployed Workers' Movement
ODU	Organisation Development Unit
SSFA	Soldiers' and Sailors' Families Association (later SSAFA, Soldiers', Sailors' and Airmen's Families Association)
TSEN	Third Sector European Network

TUC	Trades Union Congress
WEA	Workers' Educational Association
WGPW	Women's Group on Public Welfare
WVS	Women's Voluntary Service

CHAPTER 1

Introduction

Anyone faced with a commission such as this is confronted with a number of choices. First, what style of book to write, chronological or thematic? Both have advantages and disadvantages, but I decided on the former because it better suits a major anniversary. The National Council for Voluntary Organisations (NCVO) has a good story to tell, and I felt I would more likely do it justice if I told it from start to finish. However, 100 years is a long time and institutional histories can easily become repetitive and internally focused, so I introduced a thematic element within each chapter to expand upon major issues. Inevitably this is something of a compromise, and whether I have been successful is for the reader to judge. In any case, I have no doubt there is another book about the Council to be written, by someone else, organised around key themes.

The second question was how critical to make it. The book adopts a narrative style and tells the story of the Council from its origins, in fact pre-origins, through to its centenary in 2019. I wanted it to be read as a continuous story so that a general reader, interested in the development of the voluntary sector in the UK, finds something in it of value. To this end I have tried to bring to life some of the main characters, from Edward Birchall onwards, who played a significant part in its work, and give enough internal detail to trace its development over the course of the century. But telling the story isn't sufficient. The Council holds a privileged position at the heart of the voluntary sector in this country and has been at the forefront of many debates, some of them highly contested. It has loyal supporters and fierce detractors, and I have tried to be even-handed in discussing these opposing points of view, albeit within the context of an anniversary publication, which has a flavour of the celebratory. It is not a warts-and-all critique, but I would not have been doing justice to the commission, or the Council, if I hadn't explored the failings as well as successes.

That the book has been commissioned by NCVO will inevitably raise questions about objectivity. All I can say is that I have not at any stage felt constrained

© The Author(s) 2019
J. Davis Smith, *100 Years of NCVO and Voluntary Action*,
https://doi.org/10.1007/978-3-030-02774-2_1

in what I can write, and the presence of an external advisory committee, composed of leading historians not renowned for their timidity, served as an important check. The issue of independence, in the face of a close funding relationship with the commissioner, mirrors one of the main themes in the book, namely the extent to which the Council has navigated the pressures of an increasingly close funding relationship with the state without compromising its integrity. My conclusion is that the Council has dealt with this pretty well throughout its history, and I hope I have too.

There is a further issue to do with the author to address, which finds a parallel in the history of the Council, that of insider status. There is a significant body of academic literature about the respective merits and constraints of different campaigning styles, in particular insider versus outsider status.[1] The Council was a classic insider body from the outset and used the privileged access this position conferred to bring significant policy change for the voluntary sector. Critics suggest this status can all too easily tip into compliance and point to several occasions in the Council's history when it was slow to challenge government or timid in its advocacy. This debate is explored throughout the book and an attempt made in chap. 11 to reach a balanced judgement.

In a similar vein, critics might suggest that my own 'insider status', having worked for the Council for three years from 2013 to 2016, following the merger with Volunteering England, and with many of the individuals detailed in the book over the past 25 years, must inevitably dampen my critical edge. My response is that no history is completely objective and that my detailed insider knowledge, rather than a drawback, is an advantage, enabling me to focus on key debates confronting the Council over its long history without getting bogged down in administrative detail. Again, the external advisory committee has been there, to comment on chapter drafts, question my interpretations, and suggest alternative, competing literature.

The book comprises ten substantive chapters, charting the history of the Council from the work of the dedicated band of social entrepreneurs at the turn of the twentieth century who brought about its establishment, to the *Big Society* experiment of the Coalition government in the second decade of the twenty-first century. In addition, there is a short prologue, which examines the pivotal role played by the *founding father* of the Council, Birchall. The chapters follow a broadly similar structure. Each deals with a particular time period, largely chosen with reference to well-established chronological divisions, rather than specific internal developments within the Council. After chapters on its establishment and early years, there are chapters on the inter-war depression, the Second World War, the post-war period, the 1960s and 1970s, the Thatcher years, New Labour, and the *Big Society* and beyond. Each starts with a brief introduction to give a flavour of developments within the wider voluntary movement, and each covers the main areas of work of the Council, grouped under key themes such as volunteering, relations with government, charity law, membership, and professionalisation. A conclusion at the end of each chapter draws the themes together and points the way to the next period.

A word on definitions. Brian Harrison has suggested that the term 'voluntarism', in the sense of 'denoting the involvement of voluntary organisations in social welfare', dates only from 1957 according to its first citation in the Oxford English Dictionary.[2] Before that, academics and policy makers, where they referred to the concept at all, favoured terms such as volunteer, volunteer (or voluntary) movement, and charity. The *voluntary sector*, according to Perri 6 and Diana Leat, was invented in the late 1970s by leading voluntary agencies, including the Council, to bolster the movement's influence with government.[3] Similarly, Pete Alcock has suggested the Council was active in the development of the *third sector* in the 1990s as a way of strengthening relations with the New Labour government.[4] For most of its early history, the Council favoured the term *voluntary movement* to describe the arena in which it was operating, and I have therefore adopted this terminology for the majority of the book, although I switch to *voluntary sector* towards the end to bring it in line with common parlance. Civil society, a much broader, though equally elusive term, makes the occasional appearance, as does citizenship.[5] Volunteering, where used, is largely self-explanatory, although I appreciate it is not an uncontested term. In line with Margaret Brasnett, who wrote the previous history of the Council for its 50th anniversary, I adopt *voluntary action* as an all-encompassing concept to describe both the individual act of volunteering and the organisational base where it takes place.[6]

When referring to the subject of the book, I have favoured the *Council*, or occasionally, the *National Council*, rather than National Council of Social Service (NCSS) or NCVO, for its immediacy and informality. In terms of geographic scope, the book concentrates primarily on developments in England, reflecting the Council's own focus of operation, especially from the Second World War. The Council started as a UK-wide body, but its reach outside England was always rather limited (apart from in Wales during the depression of the inter-war years), and with the establishment of independent councils in the home countries in the 1940s, it concentrated almost exclusively on England and its wider international ambitions. Relations with the other councils remained harmonious throughout its history, and until the transfer of government policy on the sector to the devolved administrations later in the century, it retained responsibility for leading on the development of UK-wide policy.[7]

The 100 years covered by the history of the Council has been a momentous period for the voluntary movement. For some commentators, it has been one of struggle and decline against the forces of the state.[8] But, although reliable comparative figures over time about levels of volunteering and voluntary organisations are difficult to come by, the available evidence does not support such a declinist narrative.[9] Pat Thane argues there is no evidence that the *Big State* has crowded out the voluntary sector. Voluntary action, she suggests, is not declining 'in the long or the shorter run', but should be viewed as part of the long history of a mixed economy of welfare involving both the state and the voluntary sector that 'reinforced and complemented each other, if sometimes in tension and with continually shifting boundaries'.[10] The period saw a decline in some traditional forms of civic engagement, such as church attendance and membership of political parties and trades unions, but levels of volunteering appear to be relatively constant and there has been a significant growth from the 1960s in the number of voluntary organisations and paid staff working within the sector.[11]

Of the themes explored in the book, three are of particular importance. First, shifting relations between government and the voluntary movement, what Geoffrey Finlayson refers to as the 'moving frontier'.[12] Jane Lewis, writing at the turn of the twentieth century, suggests there have been three major shifts in this relationship over the past 100 years, beginning with the *separate spheres* ideology of the latter years of the nineteenth century, moving through the *New Philanthropy* after the First World War, and arriving at the market-led, contracting revolution of the 1980s and 1990s.[13] Jeremy Kendall, also adopting a three-stage classification, suggests that policy discourse on the sector since the Second World War has moved from incremental 'charity-centric' institution building in the immediate post-war period to 'voluntary sector' orientated incremental consolidation, influenced by the Wolfenden report of 1978, to hyperactive mainstreaming of the sector after New Labour's arrival in office in 1997.[14]

My contention is that the Council played a crucial role in the development of the idea and practice of partnership with the state that has delivered significant benefits for voluntary action and society. However, I argue we have recently moved into a fourth stage of this shifting frontier, *strategic decoupling* by government, which can be traced somewhat ironically to the election of the Coalition government in 2010 and its pursuance of David Cameron's *Big Society* agenda. Relations between the state and the voluntary movement, and with it the Council's influence, is at its lowest since the immediate post-war period. Not everyone views this development in negative terms, and the history of the Council is closely linked to the fierce debate, which has taken place over the course of its 100 years, about the potential downside of too close an association with the state. For some the Council has been complicit in bringing about the movement's co-option with government and eroding its independence. The move away from a partnership discourse, they suggest, provides an opportunity for the Council to rediscover some of the pioneering spirit of its early years, with roots in citizenship and civil society rather than service delivery.[15]

The second major theme in the book concerns the equally contentious issue of professionalisation. For much of its history, the Council saw its responsibility, even its duty, to improve the performance of the voluntary movement. This was particularly the case after the appointment of Nicholas Hinton as director in the late 1970s, whose mission was to raise the status of the movement to compete with other providers as part of a radical new *welfare pluralism*. Such dreams ended in disappointment, but the Council's preoccupation with effectiveness and efficiency remains to this day. For many, it is right the sector does all it can to maximise the return on investment. For others, the growing emphasis on professional and organisational development risks the sector compromising its values and losing its distinctiveness.[16] The Council, as the standard-bearer for the professionalisation of the sector for much of its history, has been singled out for particular criticism.

Thirdly, the book explores the issue of organisational structure, charting the Council's shift away from federal support for a range of disparate groups and networks to a centralised structure, providing services to the voluntary sector as a whole. The argument advanced is that, although federalism was perhaps unworkable into the latter half of the twentieth century, something special was lost with its abandonment. The Council, which in its early history claimed legitimacy for its leadership through its thousands of associated groups and millions of volunteers, was forced to fall back on its professional expertise, a position which looks increasingly uncomfortable at the beginning of the twenty-first century. Looking to the future, the book argues that if the Council is to retain its leadership and connect with the informal, networked voluntary movement, which the *Civil Society Futures* project suggests is likely to be the dominant form of social organisation in the coming decades, it will need to rediscover some version of its federal roots.[17].

The Council was formed out of the unique set of circumstances of the First World War that raised the profile of the voluntary movement and ushered in a new commitment to partnership between civil society and state. From its inception, it combined an idealistic vision of the contribution the voluntary movement could make to human advancement, with a realisation of its limitations and of the compromises that would be required along the way. This *idealism* and *realism* underpins the work of the Council throughout its history and is the theme of this book.

NOTES

1. This issue is explored in Chap. 11. See, for example, Craig et al., 2004, and Maloney et al., 1994.
2. Harrison, 1988.
3. 6 and Leat, 1997.
4. This issue is examined in Chap. 9. See, in particular, Alcock, 2010a, and Alcock and Kendall, 2011.
5. Harris, 2003, especially pp. 1–12.
6. Brasnett, 1969.
7. On transfer of voluntary sector responsibility to the devolved administrations, see Alcock, 2010b.
8. See, for example, Prochaska, 1988, Harris and Seldon, 1987, and Whelan, 1999.
9. See, for example, Hilton et al., 2012.
10. Thane, 2012, p. 409.
11. Thane, 2012; Hilton et al., 2012.

12. Finlayson, 1990, 1994.
13. Lewis, 1999.
14. Kendall, 2000.
15. See, for example, Rochester, 2013.
16. This issue is discussed in Chaps. 9, 10 and 11.
17. Civil Society Futures is an independent inquiry into the future of civil society. Funded by a number of charitable foundations, it is chaired by Julia Unwin, previous chief executive of the Joseph Rowntree Foundation. It began work in 2017 and reported in 2018. For a summary of its findings, see Civil Society Futures, 2018.

REFERENCES

6, P., & Leat, D. (1997). Inventing the British voluntary sector by committee: From Wolfenden to Deakin. *Non-Profit Studies, 1*(2), 33–47.

Alcock, P. (2010a). A strategic unity: Defining the third sector in the UK. *Voluntary Sector Review, 1*(1), 5–24.

Alcock, P. (2010b). Devolution or divergence? Third sector policy across the UK since 2000. In G. Lodge & K. Schmuecker (Eds.), *Devolution in practice: Public policy difference within the UK*. London: Institute for Public Policy Research.

Alcock, P., & Kendall, J. (2011). Constituting the third sector: Processes of decontestation and contention under the UK labour governments in England. *Voluntas: International Journal of Voluntary and Nonprofit Organizations, 22*(3), 450–469.

Brasnett, M. (1969). *Voluntary social action*. London: NCSS.

Civil Society Futures. (2018). *The story of our times: Shifting power, bridging divides, transforming society*. London: Civil Society Futures.

Craig, G., Taylor, M., & Parkes, T. (2004). Protest or partnership? The voluntary and community sectors in the policy process. *Social Policy and Administration, 38*(3), 221–239.

Finlayson, G. (1990). A moving frontier: Voluntarism and the state in British social welfare, 1911–1949. *Twentieth Century British History, 1*(2), 183–206.

Finlayson, G. (1994). *Citizen, state, and social welfare in Britain, 1830–1990*. Oxford: Clarendon Press.

Harris, J. (Ed.). (2003). *Civil society in British history: Ideas, identities, institutions*. Oxford: Oxford University Press.

Harris, R., & Seldon, A. (1987). *Welfare without the state: A quarter-century of suppressed public choice*. London: Institute of Economic Affairs.

Harrison, B. (1988). Historical perspectives. In B. Harrison & N. Deakin (Eds.), *Voluntary organisations and democracy: Sir George Haynes lecture, 1987*. London: NCVO.

Hilton, M., Crowson, N., Mouhot, J., & McKay, J. (2012). *A historical guide to NGOs in Britain: Charities, civil society and the voluntary sector since 1945*. Basingstoke: Palgrave Macmillan.

Kendall, J. (2000). The mainstreaming of the third sector into public policy in England in the late 1990s: Whys and wherefores. *Policy and Politics, 28*(4), 541–562.

Lewis, J. (1999). Reviewing the relationship between the voluntary sector and the state in Britain in the 1990s. *Voluntas, 10*(3), 255–270.

Maloney, W., Jordan, G., & McLaughlin, A. (1994). Interest groups and public policy: The insider/outsider model revisited. *Journal of Public Policy, 14*(1), 17–38.

Prochaska, F. (1988). *The voluntary impulse: Philanthropy in modern Britain.* London: Faber.

Rochester, C. (2013). *Rediscovering voluntary action: The beat of a different drum.* Basingstoke: Palgrave Macmillan.

Thane, P. (2012). The "big society" and the "big state": Creative tension or crowding out? *Twentieth Century British History, 23*(3), 408–429.

Whelan, R. (Ed.). (1999). *Involuntary action: How voluntary is the 'voluntary' sector?* London: Institute of Economic Affairs.

CHAPTER 2

Setting Up

INTRODUCTION

In early 1919 a new organisation, the National Council of Social Service (NCSS), was launched. The *Manchester Guardian* reported on its establishment under the heading 'Promotion of social work: Co-ordination of existing agencies', while the *Daily Herald* described it as 'The corporate citizen effort to improve social conditions.'[1] It was the culmination of many years' work by a small group of individuals from the voluntary movement, drawn from the three main coordinating agencies active in the years leading up to the First World War: the Charity Organisation Society (COS), the Guild of Help, and the Council of Social Welfare. In this work they were supported by senior civil servants, who shared their vision of a more unified movement that would improve effectiveness and assist in forging a stronger partnership with the state. Attempts to develop closer ties were not easy, as differences over values and organisational rivalry remained at the fore, and progress was slow in the years up to 1914. It was the experience of war that finally persuaded them to put their differences to one side and bring together the different voluntary traditions under one over-arching umbrella.[2]

To understand the factors that led to the formation of the Council we need therefore to examine briefly the antecedents of these three separate movements and the steps taken to achieve greater collaboration. It would be a mistake, however, to assume that the goal of greater unity was a purely twentieth-century phenomenon. The explosion of voluntary action in the previous century led to several demands for greater common purpose. In the 1850s there was a call for a 'circle of moral and philanthropic movements' to lead individuals active 'in seeking the welfare of his fellow-men [sic]' in a 'step by step' progression from one cause to another, linking together such radical movements as free trade, temperance, peace, and housing reform.[3] In 1868 there was a proposal to establish a Central Board of Charities to provide a national focus for action, although it failed when the charities who would have

© The Author(s) 2019
J. Davis Smith, *100 Years of NCVO and Voluntary Action*,
https://doi.org/10.1007/978-3-030-02774-2_2

constituted the membership, rejected calls to fund it.[4] We should also not assume that the three lead organisations were the only players in the move to greater coordination. Margaret Brasnett, who wrote a history of the Council to mark its 50th anniversary in 1969, suggests that other bodies, although less influential, played a part in its formation, including the National Association for the Promotion of Social Science, founded in 1857 to promote information and research on social issues, the Agenda and Cavendish clubs, with which Edward Birchall was involved, and the British Institute of Social Service, established in 1904 to promote civic action and the exchange of information between organisations.[5] The institute, in particular, can claim a significant influence. Its journal, *Progress*, provided a template for the Council's later move into the publishing world and its focus on developing a library and information centre was adopted by the Council as an early priority.[6] There was an even closer connection when the Council in its early days, without premises and with few funds, took up shared residency with the institute and the two organisations nearly merged.[7]

The story of the formation of the Council also needs to take account of the unique experience of the war. This gave a significant boost to voluntary action and raised its standing.[8] But paradoxically, it further demonstrated its limitations and thus quickened up the process of statutory involvement in social welfare that had developed during the second half of the previous century and taken shape most markedly in the reforms of the great pre-war Liberal government. In 1919 the voluntary movement was in good shape and viewed as crucial to post-war reconstruction, but its future was seen as inextricably linked to the emerging statutory services. Notions of partnership were very much in the air, providing just the conditions necessary for a new idea like the Council to take root. In such an analysis, however, we should avoid falling into the *Whiggish* trap of seeing a linear historical progression from voluntary action to the welfare state. As Geoffrey Finlayson has reminded us, the history of state/voluntary sector relations has been characterised by fluidity and change and, what he terms, a 'moving frontier'.[9] The war did not represent a rigid break between the voluntary response of the past and the statutory response of the future. The past was full of examples of partnership and the relationship was never the complete *separate spheres* often portrayed. Similarly, the future did not herald the ushering in of a monolithic state. Voluntary action would prove remarkably resilient and stake a claim as a partner alongside the state, albeit for most of the next century a junior one, in the design and delivery of social services. This *moving frontier*, and the attempt to carve out a central role for the voluntary movement alongside the state, was the focus of the Council throughout its first 100 years and is the subject of this book. But, alongside an examination of its constituent members, and the part played by the war in forging closer collaboration between voluntary groups and between the voluntary movement and the state, the story of the Council is also one of individuals and ideas. No history can be told without an understanding of the men and women who had the vision and energy to push for its development and of the philosophies that inspired them to action. This story is as much about them as it is about institutions.

Just to correct one misconception at the outset. Richard Flanagan argues that the Council was a product of government, while Rodney Lowe claims it was a 'government-inspired creation'.[10] This is not the case. Certainly, the government was interested in greater cohesion within the voluntary movement and could see value in having a national agency to deal with in the period of post-war reconstruction. And certainly key statutory agencies and civil servants played a part in its establishment and getting it up and running. Simon Adderley argues that it grew from the Joint Committee of charitable organisations and government agencies that had been set up to organise wartime philanthropy in 1915 by the Local Government Board, and he suggests that the Council was happy to be co-opted by government as the 'relationship was useful to all parties'.[11] But, while the Joint Committee was an important staging post in its development, its establishment came from the movement. It had its origins in pre-war discussions between the Guild of Help, the Council of Social Welfare, and the COS, led by key figures within the movement such as Birchall, Frederic D'Aeth, Thomas Hancock Nunn, and Percy Grundy.[12] As for the claim that it was happy to be 'co-opted', this presupposes that it was co-opted, which is by no means a given and raises the issue of independence, which has been the subject of debate for almost its entire history. Rather than try and answer this question now, we will examine it over the course of the history and return to it in chap. 11.

CHARITY ORGANISATION SOCIETY

Of the three organisations that came together to found the Council, the COS was the oldest, largest, and best known. By the outbreak of war in 1914, however, its reputation had begun to founder and it was the target of increasing criticism.[13] Its values and methods were seen at odds with the spirit of the age and it was at risk of being overtaken as the pre-eminent charitable coordination body by the newly established, and rapidly expanding, guild of help movement.[14] The COS was founded in 1869 to facilitate greater coordination of charity to minimise waste and duplication. Two values underpinned its work: a belief in *scientific philanthropy*, based on the system of detailed casework led by volunteer visitors to root out scroungers and improve efficiency; and support for the notion of the *deserving* and *undeserving* poor and the *separation of spheres* between the state and the voluntary movement this implied. For the COS it was the role of charity to deal with deserving individuals who could be put back on the straight and narrow with a short burst of aid or non-financial support. The state's minimal contribution, through the poor law and the workhouse, was to deal with those who had brought about their own misfortune through profligacy or low morals and for whom personal salvation was out of the question.[15] The COS retained throughout this period a suspicion of the state and a firm belief in the primacy of the voluntary response, although

Finlayson suggests key individuals within the movement, such as Samuel and Henrietta Barnett, began to take a less hard-line approach from the turn of the century.[16] In 1909 it set up an internal committee to examine the reasons for its growing unpopularity and its recommendations called for greater collaboration with the guilds and other bodies, although it ruled out closer working with the state.[17] The climate, however, was moving towards increased statutory intervention, and by 1914 the COS was in danger of being swept away on a tide of progress. The experience of the war reinforced the demand for closer partnership between statutory and voluntary bodies and pushed the COS closer towards collaboration.[18]

GUILDS OF HELP

If the COS was the *Grande Dame* of the voluntary movement, the guilds of help were its *Young Turks*. It was the guilds that were the driving force behind the demand for greater collaboration that would lead eventually to the establishment of the Council. The first guild was set up in Bradford in 1904 to deal with the sharply rising levels of poverty in the town.[19] It was strongly influenced by the Elberfeld system for relief, which had been established in the German textile town in the late nineteenth century, and the historian of the guilds, Keith Laybourn, suggests many of the leading lights in the development of the Bradford Guild were German immigrants.[20] The Elberfeld system had much in common with the COS, in that both favoured detailed casework as an essential pre-requisite for efficient administration. However, Elberfeld advocated closer cooperation between the state and the voluntary movement, and it was this philosophy that chimed with the guilds and set them apart. It was not the only difference. For the guilds there was something increasingly unpalatable about the philosophy of the COS with its emphasis on individual failing as the root cause of poverty. Individual weakness was seen as only part of the cause. Far more important were deemed to be the external factors that lay beyond the capacity of individuals to influence. *Not alms but a friend* was the motto of the guilds, which deliberately set out to differentiate themselves from the ethos of the COS and emphasise personal support rather than financial aid.[21]

The guilds were also critical of what they saw as a top-down approach to relief, where middle-class women volunteers presided over the fate of the poor. The response to poverty, they argued, should be community-wide, and they set about trying to involve people from all classes, although the extent to which they were successful has been questioned.[22] We should, however, be wary about overstating the differences. Despite the clear philosophical departure between the two traditions, there was significant overlap, and it was this common ground that was crucial in bringing about greater collaboration. Both the guilds and COS favoured a casework approach based on teams of volunteer helpers and both were anxious to reduce overlap between charities. But it was the guilds that were on the rise. From the first experiment in Bradford, the movement spread quickly and by 1911 there were 70 guilds boasting a membership of 8000. The vast majority were in the north of England, although they were active in parts of London and the South East, with early organisations in Lewisham, Croydon, and Newport on the Isle of Wight.[23] Within a few years, the guild, according to Laybourn, had 'become the largest and most important voluntary organisation in England, outstripping the Charity Organisation Society'.[24]

The creation of a national organisation to bring together local guilds, however, was slow in development. National conferences were held annually from 1908 and discussions on the need for a national association took place as early as the Bolton conference in 1909. But it wasn't until the conference in Sheffield in 1910 that concrete steps were taken towards the setting up of a national association with the establishment of a provisional committee, which finally came into being after the conference the following year in Birmingham.[25] That it was the Birmingham conference that heralded this development is significant in the story of the Council, as it was in this city that Birchall made his name as secretary of the Birmingham Civic Aid Society. And it was Birchall who took on the responsibility for leading the new National Association of Guilds of Help (NAGH) as its first part-time honorary secretary, a post he held until the outbreak of war.[26]

The NAGH was not an immediate success. Local identity was strongly entrenched and by 1915 scarcely more than half of all guilds were affiliated to the national agency, which functioned more as an information exchange than a strategic body.[27] This local autonomy was reflected in the variety of names adopted by individual guilds, which included 'City League of Help', 'Guild of Social Services', 'Guild of Personal Services', and 'Civic Aid Society'. According to Laybourn, the guilds 'remained a collection of autonomous bodies whose emphasis upon civil consciousness might be regarded as almost inimical to national organisation'.[28] If Birchall had lived to see his dream fulfilled, this early experience in running a national representative body would have generated some useful learning, as the Council also faced the challenge of building a strong central presence in the face of entrenched local interest. In 1916 C.S. Norris, secretary of the Sunderland Guild, was appointed first full-time secretary of the NAGH, and in 1917 he was succeeded by Dorothy Keeling, who later played an important role in the work of the Council.[29] Indeed as Adderley points out, many of the early staff of the Council learnt their trade in the guild movement and were imbued with its values, particularly in relation to closer working with the state.[30]

COUNCILS OF SOCIAL WELFARE

The third institutions central to the formation of the Council were the councils of social welfare. Although less attention has been paid to them than the guilds and the COS, this shouldn't mask the critical nature of their contribution.[31] Nunn can be credited as the founder of the movement.[32] He was also a key figure in the COS, having served as honorary secretary of the Stepney COS and vice-chair of the Hampstead society. Nunn, a resident of Toynbee Hall for ten years, was also a member of the Poor Law Commission and wrote a glowing report on the work of the councils as an addendum to the *Majority Report* in 1909.[33] He served on the Executive Committee of the Council in its early years. Nunn's importance in relation to the founding of the Council lies in his experiment in Hampstead in London that led to the establishment of the first council of social welfare in 1902. Although having cut his teeth in the COS, by the turn of the century he saw collaboration with statutory bodies as essential to the success of the voluntary movement. In Hampstead he pioneered a new integrated approach to the provision of relief that linked the poor law and local charities. Moore suggests that the councils served as community organisation agencies, linking the voluntary movement to local authorities and, that of the three bodies involved in the formation of the National Council, they were the most interested in partnership work.[34] The movement spread quickly, especially in London, and in Hampstead it took over the local guild, although nationally the guilds grew faster. The councils were instrumental in the foundation of the London Council of Social Service in 1910, which predated the setting up of the National Council by almost a decade, and the pattern of local coordinating councils, based on the Hampstead model, proved influential in the development of what became the council of social service movement championed by the new national body after 1919.[35]

COMING TOGETHER

Relations between the three main charitable coordinating bodies before the war were strained. On the ground there was considerable overlap of function and personnel and local mergers were not uncommon, but philosophical differences ran deep. Laybourn has described a battle for the soul of the voluntary movement between the proponents of the *Old Philanthropy*, in the shape of the COS, and the *New Philanthropy*, characterised by the guilds.[36] The term *New Philanthropy* gained currency following the book of the same name by Elizabeth Macadam in the 1930s, which emphasised the distinction between the old and new.[37] Nowhere was the difference more marked than in attitudes towards the role of the state. The guilds enthusiastically welcomed the introduction of the National Insurance Act in 1911, while the COS bitterly opposed it on the grounds that it would undermine charity, although both welcomed the *Majority Report* of the Poor Law Commission in 1909, which praised the guilds and recommended the establishment in each town of a Voluntary Aid Council to better coordinate voluntary relief.[38] The *Minority Report*, the work mainly of Beatrice Webb, saw little role for voluntary associations in the breakup of the Poor Law and was opposed by all the charitable movements.[39] Jane Lewis, however, argues against the simplistic view of seeing the *Majority Report* representing the COS and the *Minority Report* the guilds and councils of social welfare and suggests there was far more convergence of views than sometimes acknowledged.[40] There was some take up of the new Voluntary Aid councils, for example, in Liverpool and Bolton, but progress towards coordination was slow.[41]

Nunn was particularly critical of the competition between the COS and guilds. In a special memorandum to the *Majority Report*, he argued that 'what each community needs is a co-operative civic body which will secure the organisation which makes all casework effective'.[42] By 1913 collaboration was in the air. At the sixth conference of the NAGH held in Halifax, Grundy from the Manchester Guild called for greater alliance between the guilds, COS, and councils of social welfare. In a paper, prepared in collaboration with Birchall and D'Aeth, *Case Work and Policy: A Synthesis*, Grundy argued that in all localities 'we find both a confusion of thought and a confusion of method' that results in groups 'groping in the dark towards further activities, for which their constitution may or may not fit them'.[43] He was particularly critical of the separation in some organisations between direct action and policy, believing both necessary for an effective response:

> To attempt the elaborate organisation of a Council of Social Welfare unless the Guild has obtained the confidence of the public by good sound casework would be to court disaster; to keep the helpers at an endless round of casework, with never the least influence on the causes of the troubles with which they are dealing, is to run the certain risk of losing the keenest and most enterprising among them.[44]

Grundy's warning was prophetic. This connectivity between policy and practice was an important feature of the Council's work for its first 70 years. When later the two elements were separated once more, the weakness would become apparent.[45] In response, L.V. Shairp from Leeds COS said he hoped means could be found to cooperate 'to make voluntary social service a really national movement', a view echoed by Nunn, although he cautioned against a monolithic response, arguing 'that our fundamental unity would be nothing were it not enveloped in variety'.[46]

Later the same year at the COS' annual conference, the call for greater unity was echoed by the grand old man of the society, Charles Loch, when he admitted that the COS was 'of close kinship with the Guilds' and that 'probably the lines of our several movements are likely to approach nearer to one another rather than to go apart'.[47] D'Aeth explored the idea of collaboration further in an article in *The Economic Review* in 1914. In it he argued for a coming together of the three movements, suggesting they were not only 'closely related' but 'inextricably entangled'.[48] He argued that what all towns needed was an agency to organise relief, which might be achieved by a merger of the guilds and COS, and a more general coordinating agency to organise local 'institutions', drawing on the experience of the councils of social welfare in London and Liverpool. Such an agency would fulfil a number of functions, including the coordination of voluntary groups, initiating of new projects, provision of information and advice, and, crucially, the linking of voluntary and statutory agencies.[49] Its role should extend beyond relief and take in all aspects of civic life, including music, exercise, and youth work, precisely the activities the Council would prioritise in its early years. In some small towns both functions—the organisation of relief and more general coordination work—might be delivered by the same organisation, although in larger areas separate groups would probably be needed.[50] Such an agency, he suggested, would 'stand for the creation of a district atmosphere, and of a district life and sentiment, which will enable the residents of the district to understand the meaning of citizenship and fellowship in a way at present impossible in our huge unplanned centres of population'.[51] Although the focus of D'Aeth's article was the need for local coordination, he concluded that 'the development of district organisation' was a matter 'which follows rather than precedes central organisation'.[52] In other words, without the establishment of a new national coordinating agency to bring together the different traditions within the voluntary movement, there was unlikely to be change locally.

In June 1914 the first joint conference between the COS, guilds, and councils of social welfare was held in Newcastle with the 'dominating theme', according to Laybourn, being one of 'unity', with calls going out for greater collaboration and mutual registration, but falling short of an outright merger.[53] Mutual registration was seen as essential to avoid overlap and joint schemes were established in a number of areas. A Joint Committee was formed to move the discussions forward.[54] The outbreak of war catalysed these attempts to forge closer relations. In 1915 a joint conference was held on *War Relief and Personal Services*, bringing together not only the guilds, the councils, and the COS but a range of other charities and statutory bodies, including the Local Representative Committees set up by government to coordinate wartime relief efforts. The 1915 conference was an important staging post on route to the establishment of the Council.

Wartime Developments

The context for the conference was the rapid growth in voluntary action and the growing call this had given rise to for better coordination. Some 18,000 new charities were formed during the war, and it is estimated that an additional £100 million was raised for charitable causes and as many as 2.4 million volunteers mobilised.[55] Voluntary action not only provided much-needed relief to those in need but might have contributed to victory. Peter Grant, for example, claims that the explosion of voluntary action, by generating social capital and breaking down class barriers, helped build legitimacy for the war and provided Britain with a distinct advantage over Germany, where more rigid state control stifled voluntary action.[56]

Some historians have suggested that the war massively increased state control over all aspects of public life, including charities.[57] We need to be careful not to overstate this point. Partnership between the state and voluntary groups had been present in many aspects of social provision in the years leading up to the war and well back into the nineteenth century.[58] The war, however, added extra impetus to partnership work, enhancing 'sharply', as Rex Pope has argued, 'the state's role in relation to the individual'.[59] The government moved quickly to coordinate charitable relief. On 4 August 1914 a Cabinet Committee was established under Herbert Samuel, president of the Local Government Board, 'to advise on the measures necessary to deal with any distress that may arise in consequence of the war'.[60] A National Relief Fund was launched on 6 August 1914 by the Prince of Wales with a *call to service*, anticipating an even more influential role he would play in the history of charity some two decades later when he launched a similar call at an event organised by the Council to deal with the crisis of unemployment.[61] Two days later the Local Government Board issued a circular to all mayors and local authorities inviting them to set up Local Representative Committees to oversee the relief work.[62] In total more than 300 committees were established and played an important role in collecting and administrating relief funds.

More important for this story was the contribution to the push for greater coordination. Although government inspired, the leadership of these committees took on different forms in different areas, with some being led by guilds, some by the COS, some by the Soldiers' and Sailors' Families Association, which played a crucial part in the wartime relief efforts, and some by local authorities.[63] In nearly all cases the result was greater collaboration, between individual charities and the voluntary movement and public bodies. In some areas mergers took place. For example, in Poole, Dorset, the local guild linked closely with the Local Representative Committee and virtually ceased to exist as an independent organisation for the duration of the war.[64] A clear sign of growing state involvement was the appointment in 1915 by the government of Sir Edward Ward as Director General of Voluntary Organisations, although the title is somewhat misleading as his role was mainly confined to coordinating the supply and distribution of *comforts* provided by voluntary groups for troops on the front line.[65] Greater regulation of charities was also considered. In 1916, following an initial abortive bill in 1914, the War Charities Act was passed to deal with what was seen as a growing problem with fundraising abuse by war charities, although there is some evidence that the problem was magnified by lurid press coverage, anticipating future fundraising scandals in which the press would also be accused of playing a key role.[66] The state did not take control of the voluntary movement during the war. However, it did significantly increase its reach and in doing so speeded up the developments that had been taking place before 1914 towards greater collaboration.

THE 1915 CONFERENCE

The pivotal conference in the journey that led to the establishment of the Council took place in June 1915 in London at Caxton Hall, Westminster. It was organised to consider the impact of the war on the voluntary movement and included 600 delegates, representing all main charities.[67] Much of the focus was on the need for greater collaboration and the scene was set with a paper from D'Aeth on *The Future of the Local Representative Committee*, which he had prepared with input from Grundy.[68] In the paper he acknowledged the steps taken towards greater collaboration before the war, but argued that the outbreak of hostilities and the setting up of the Local Representative Committees had given added impetus to the unity discussions: 'Provided that the various local situations are handled with sufficient skill', he suggested, the legacy of the 'terrible war' could be the 'foundation of a Voluntary Social Service on a civic basis which will be one of the greatest events of our day'.[69] D'Aeth was referring to the need for a network of local voluntary coordinating committees, but he also called for a new 'permanent Government Intelligence Department' to advise voluntary bodies on regulations and the establishment of a parallel 'permanent Advisory Committee representing local organisations' to liaise with government. D'Aeth referred to the standing Joint Committee, which had been formed following the Newcastle conference the previous year, and suggested it might serve as the blueprint for such a body. There was broad support for D'Aeth's proposal, but concerns were raised that anticipated future debates. Morris, from the London COS, for example, accepted that some measure of coordination was required, but said the trick would be 'how to control it without touching its independence, without impairing its efficiency, without touching its volition, and without in any sense destroying it'.[70] Saint, president of the NAGH, argued that 'if we spend Government or State money, we shall inevitably be more or less under the control of each' and asked 'how far will that hamper our work and our thought?'[71] And Matheson, from Birmingham Women's Settlement, commented on the constant demand being placed on voluntary groups to drive down administration costs. Such calls, she argued, were 'a scandal to charitable work', 'if we sweat the people whom we entrust to organise our national charities by underpaying them, by undervaluing them', how 'are they to raise the status of the voluntary worker'.[72]

A New Organisation

Following the conference, an expanded Joint Committee on Social Service was established to take forward the discussions and liaise with government.[73] The key individuals from the voluntary movement were involved, including D'Aeth, Grundy, Saint, and Keeling from the guilds and the Rev. John Pringle from the COS, along with representatives from the Charity Commission and various government departments.[74] Keeling and Pringle were appointed joint secretary to the group. At the national conference of guilds of help in Sheffield in 1916, Grundy spoke of the 'need for a co-ordinating agency, in touch with all the bodies and institutions, official and voluntary, that have to do with social help'.[75] In the same year, the guilds agreed to adopt the structure of the social welfare councils.[76] From 1917, the Joint Committee met quarterly and agreed on the need for a permanent national body to coordinate voluntary service. The national organisation was to be mirrored by local committees, which would 'work in co-operation with the central Joint Committee on Social Service'.[77] It was suggested these local groups might be called 'Citizen

Service'.[78] At a meeting on 1 February 1917, Lord Rhondda, president of the Local Government Board, gave the government's approval to the idea.[79]

The momentum towards the establishment of a new national body was unstoppable. However, not all three organisations were wholeheartedly committed. Papers in the files of the COS suggest that, although it continued to play an active part in the unity discussions, and ultimately signed up to the establishment of the new Council, it was also late in the day considering setting up a parallel national body. In July 1918, less than a year before the launch of the Council, the COS administrative committee considered a proposal to establish a new 'Central Association' to represent volunteers. The association would be made up of representatives of the voluntary movement and public bodies and charged with keeping a 'watch' on 'the action of the state in its attitude towards voluntary work', giving voice to 'the point of view and experience of voluntary workers', and helping to improve the effectiveness of voluntary work by 'urging the importance of training on those who offer their services'. In contrast to the plans being developed for the Council, it was envisaged it would be national only, although it was accepted that local groups might be set up later.[80] The proposal, which bears an uncanny resemblance to the aims of the Volunteer Centre, which was established in 1973 against the wishes of the Council, was not pursued, but it suggests an organisation only partially committed to the plans taking shape for the creation of a unifying national council.[81] The Council and the COS worked together on a number of initiatives in the future, but relations remained 'friendly but aloof'.[82] In early 1919 a small group, representing each of the three main voluntary traditions, met to agree on the final details, and in March the National Council of Social Service was launched. A handbook of information for voluntary workers was distributed to 11,000 organisations.[83]

One mystery remains unsolved: the identity of the individuals who met in early 1919 to decide on the final structure of the new organisation. Brasnett sparked the intrigue when, in her history of the Council, she cryptically referred to six significant players, five social workers and one civil servant, but without naming them.[84] Adderley, playing detective, suggests that the five social workers were Grundy and D'Aeth from the guilds, Nunn from the council of social welfare, Pringle from the COS, and Captain Lionel Ellis.[85] For the civil servant he names W.G.S. Adams. Drawing on a range of sources, we can conclude that Adderley is only partially correct. The most compelling evidence comes from the reminiscences of one of the group, Nunn. In 1934 he wrote:

The War was hardly over before Mr. S. P. Grundy, the pioneer of this third stage in our movement and a recognised leader of the Guilds of Help, drew to a little wayside inn those who were to play a leading part in the launching of the new Council. The party was made up of the founders of the Hampstead and Liverpool councils, the chief officer of the C.O.S., another leading member of the Guilds of Help movement, and last but not least, representatives of a high official at the Local Government Board. The significance of this addition to Mr. Grundy's week-end party was borne out by the first steps that were taken. The chairmanship of the Provisional National Committee, now formed, was accepted by an Assistant Secretary of the Board; the Committee's meetings were held at the Board; and the first circular issued early in 1919 to the chairmen of all the principal local authorities throughout the country was dated from the Local Government Board.[86]

From this account it is clear that Grundy, D'Aeth, Pringle, and Nunn himself were present. Grundy, a close friend of Birchall and the recipient of his £1000 legacy, was, apart from Birchall and D'Aeth, perhaps the most important figure in the establishment of the Council. After attending Balliol College, Oxford, where he graduated with a first-class honours degree in natural science, he became resident warden of Manchester University Settlement and secretary of the Manchester City League of Help, where he pioneered new approaches to working with the state. It was through his work with the NAGH, however, that he led the movement for greater unity. Brasnett suggests he 'had perhaps done more than anyone else to bring the NCSS into being' and in 1919 he became the new organisation's first honorary secretary.[87] He remained connected to the Council for many years and died in 1942.[88] D'Aeth is clearly the individual named by Nunn as founder of the Liverpool council. Born in 1875, he also went to Oxford University, to study theology, but after a short stint as a curate in Burnley and Leytonstone, Essex, he abandoned a career in the church in favour of social work.[89] He was involved in the new school of social work at Liverpool University and in establishing the Liverpool Council of Voluntary Aid in 1909. Like Grundy, he played a leading part in the development of the NAGH and in sketching out plans with Birchall for what eventually became the Council. He published widely and, according to one tribute, 'was the bringer-together, the enthuser, the provider of impeccable factual and statistical evidence, the catalyst'.[90] It was also in Liverpool under his tutelage that a young man, George Haynes, would cut his teeth in the voluntary movement and go on to lead the Council for over 25 years.[91] D'Aeth, like Grundy, joined the Executive Committee of the Council and later became its vice-chair. However, he soon withdrew from public life and died in 1940 after many years of ill health.[92] Adderley's case for Pringle is also watertight and is supported by Nunn's account. He took over as secretary of the COS after Loch and was appointed co-chair of the Joint Committee on Social Service.[93] His presence in the discussions ensured the new venture had the public support of the still influential COS, even if in private it was less than wholehearted in its commitment. Pringle remained deeply resistant to the development of the *New Philanthropy* and this antipathy ensured much of the COS at a local level was slow in getting behind the new organisation.[94] According to Finlayson, Pringle saw himself as the disciple of Loch and 'remained deeply suspicious of any form of aid which might erode self-reliance'.[95] It could be argued that the reluctance by the COS to fully engage with the Council was something of a blessing. Certainly, their reputation was fading and Robert Humphreys has suggested that after the war they 'again became a social leper, largely shunned by other charities and by government agencies'.[96]

So four of the individuals identified by Adderley as being involved in the secret retreat that led to the establishment of the Council are clearly identifiable: Grundy, D'Aeth, Nunn, and Pringle. The case for Ellis is harder to make. As with Birchall, he fought in France and occupied significant positions in the voluntary movement, in his case the COS rather than the guild. But, although he returned from the Front to take up the position of first paid secretary of the Council, a post he held with great distinction until 1936, he doesn't appear to have played a significant role in its establishment.[97] If we identify from Nunn's account D'Aeth as being the representative of the Liverpool council, then the fifth individual needs to be another figure from the guild, to go alongside Grundy. This rules Ellis out. The strongest claims are for F.B. Bourdillon of the Reading Guild, who replaced Birchall as honorary secretary of the NAGH at the beginning of the war, Henry Saint, of the Newcastle Guild, president of the association during the war, or Keeling, assistant secretary of the Bradford Guild from 1913 to 1917, acting general secretary of the NAGH in 1917, and co-secretary, with Pringle, of the Joint Committee on Social Service.[98] Brasnett, however, refers to 'the six men' involved in the discussions, so if we accept her version of events Keeling must be ruled out, although she was on the appointment panel that recruited Ellis as the Council's first paid member of staff and the Executive Committee in its early years.[99]

Adderley is also wrong in identifying Adams as the civil servant identified, but not named, by Brasnett. Like Ellis, Adams was involved in the Council from its inception and played a hugely significant role in its development, serving as chair for its first 30 years.[100] But like Ellis, there is no evidence to suggest he was involved in the discussions that led to its creation. A stronger claim can be made for Aubrey Vere Symonds, assistant secretary at the Local Government Board during the war and first chair of the Council, who chaired several of the Joint Committee of Social Service meetings in the run up to 1919 and put his name to the first memorandum issued by the new organisation. According to a tribute from Ellis, Symonds was 'one of the group of Civil Servants who took a leading part in the Council's formation'.[101] He handed over the chair of the Council to Adams soon after its establishment, as his time was increasingly taken over by the demands of transforming the Local Government Board into the Ministry of Health, where he became second secretary.[102] But there is one other possibility. In 1950 Ellis wrote a letter to *The Times* commenting on the obituary of Sir Adair Hore.[103] In it he drew attention to the 'part he played in the founding of the National Council of Social Service'. Hore, who had been a senior civil servant during the war, first at the Local Government Board and then at the Ministry of Pensions, had been impressed, Ellis noted, by the scale of voluntary relief and the close relations that had been formed with statutory agencies. 'His quick mind', Ellis wrote, 'saw here a principle of cooperation in social service which should hold good, nationally and locally, in peace as well as in war' and he helped to form a small group alongside Grundy, D'Aeth, and Pringle to work out 'proposals for a permanent National Council of Social Service'. It was Hore, according to Ellis, who recruited Symonds as the

Council's first chair and was responsible for drafting the memorandum in March 1919 announcing its establishment. 'If its history is ever written', Ellis concludes, 'Adair Hore's name should be one of the very first to be mentioned.'[104]

CONCLUSION

In March 1919 the NCSS came into being. Despite claims to the contrary, it was most definitely a creation of the voluntary movement. There was close involvement from government in the discussions that led to its establishment, and the setting up of the Local Representative Committees in 1915 provided a spur to action. The first address of the Council was the Local Government Board (soon to become the Ministry of Health) and the department was given a seat on the Executive Committee, along with several other government offices.[105] Peter Grant suggests its establishment may have been influenced by the office of the Director General for Voluntary Organisations, citing the fact that Ward worked closely with the Social Welfare Association for London before the war on the employment of ex-soldiers.[106] However, although government was a key player in the discussions and provided temporary accommodation for the new organisation, the stimulus came from the voluntary movement.

But if the Council was a creation of the movement, what does its emergence tell us about relations with the state? Some historians have seen the setting up of the Council as a sign of a loss of independence. Gordon Phillips, for example, has argued that the experience of war led to a more compliant post-war voluntary movement that was less willing to challenge the state.[107] Lowe agrees, arguing that the loss of independence was summed up by the emergence of the 'more accommodating' Council as the pre-eminent umbrella body for the movement in place of the 'fiercely independent' COS.[108] In contrast, Alan Kidd argues that the formation of the Council, in the face of increasing encroachment by the state, represented an attempt to give a more cohesive voice to the 'disparate parts of an emerging "voluntary sector"'.[109] Grant suggests the war changed voluntary organisations for the good, replacing the COS 'with its outdated concept of poverty and the state' with the Council, which was 'far more open to both cooperation with government and the adoption of modern management principles'.[110] The debate over whether the Council was too close to government continued for most of its history. While some accused it of being 'co-opted', the evidence points to an organisation committed to working in partnership with the state, but ready to challenge it in the interests of its members. In this respect, perhaps, it was no different from other coordinating bodies that emerged out of the experience of the war, such as the Federation of British Industries formed in 1916 and the National Confederation of Employers' Organisations set up in 1918. Both would seek in the future to work closely with the state, but both would see first loyalty to their members.[111]

The new organisation did not have an easy time establishing itself. G.D.H. Cole suggested its emergence, from the coming together of such different founding bodies, meant the Council was 'in many ways a queer mixture', and at times it would struggle to reconcile these different ideological strands.[112] Its reach at local level remained fragile. According to Laybourn, 'localism slowed down the pace of development of the NCSS' and it took almost a decade before all the guilds were fully integrated.[113] The same was true of the COS, many of whose local branches remained only partially committed to the new body.[114] Despite these challenges, the Council entered the post-war world with an air of optimism. The voluntary movement had performed well during the war, and there was general agreement it would have an important role to play in the reconstruction to follow. And, as Macadam later suggested, the Council had one major advantage: that even if not everyone knew what it was set up to do, it was 'blessed with a name' that did 'not arouse the same antagonism and prejudice' as the Charity Organisation Society.[115]

NOTES

1. *Manchester Guardian*, 29 March 1919, p. 10; *Daily Herald*, 12 May 1919.
2. On developments in the voluntary movement at the beginning of the twentieth century, see, for example, Harris, 2010, and Thane, 2012.
3. Quoted in Harrison, 2003, p. 82.
4. Quoted in Brasnett, 1969, p. 2.
5. Ibid., pp. 2–4. On the Agenda and Cavendish clubs, see the prologue. The National Association for the Promotion of Social Science, also known as the Social Science Association, was founded by Lord Brougham to advance public health, industrial relations, penal reform, and female education. It closed in 1886. See Goldman, 2002.
6. On the British Institute of Social Service, see Harris, 1992, p. 121.
7. Brasnett, 1969, pp. 27–28.
8. See, for example, Grant, 2014.
9. Finlayson, 1994. The term was first coined by William Beveridge in his 1948 report, *Voluntary Action*. Beveridge, 1948.
10. Flanagan, 1991, p. 202; Lowe, 1995b, p. 373.
11. Adderley, 2015, p. 21.
12. The contribution made by these individuals to the establishment of the Council is discussed below.
13. For a range of views on the COS and its work, see Finlayson, 1994, pp. 141–3.
14. On the history of the guilds, see Laybourn, 1994.
15. On the philosophy of the COS, see Lewis, 1995.
16. Finlayson, 1994, pp. 141–3. McBriar, 1987, p. 369, says that the COS later amended their construct of the deserving and undeserving poor to 'helpable' and 'unhelpable' in face of criticism that they were putting the blame on the victims rather than looking at what character traits would help them escape their situation. Samuel and Henrietta Barnett are perhaps best known for their role in establishing the first university settlement at Toynbee Hall in the east

end of London in 1884 and Hampstead Garden Suburb in the early twentieth century.

17. Lewis, 1996, p. 172.
18. Finlayson, 1994, pp. 172–3, and Moore, 1977, p. 97.
19. On the establishment of the Bradford Guild, see Cahill and Jowitt, 1980.
20. Laybourn, 1994, p. 4. On the Elberfeld system, see also Moore, 1977, p. 90.
21. Laybourn, 1994, p. 1.
22. Ibid., p. 49. See also Laybourn, 1993, pp. 54–58.
23. Laybourn, 1994, p. 6.
24. Ibid., p. vii.
25. Ibid., p. 73.
26. Ibid.
27. Ibid., pp. 73–74.
28. Ibid., p. 20.
29. Keeling's contribution to the Council is discussed more fully in Chap. 5.
30. Adderley, 2015, p. 49.
31. On the Council of Social Welfare movement, see Lewis, 1996.
32. On Nunn, see Moore, 1977 and Davis Smith, 2004.
33. Nunn, 1909.
34. Moore, 1977, pp. 98–99.
35. On the life and work of Nunn, see Anonymous, 1942.
36. Laybourn, 1994, p. 22.
37. Macadam, 1934.
38. Lewis, 1996, p. 173. The 1911 Act, part of the wider social welfare reforms of the Liberal government, 1906–15, introduced two independent contributory schemes of health and unemployment insurance.
39. The Royal Commission on the Poor Laws and Relief of Distress, 1905–09, established to advise on changes to the poor law, produced two conflicting reports, known as the *Majority* and *Minority* reports. Beatrice Webb, 1858–1943, a socialist, academic, and social reformer, is perhaps best known for her work in founding the Fabian Society and the London School of Economics.
40. Lewis, 1996, p. 174.
41. Brasnett, 1969, p. 9.
42. Quoted in Brasnett, 1969, p. 11.
43. Grundy, 1913, p. 10.
44. Ibid., p. 18.
45. See the conclusion for a discussion of this issue.
46. National Association of Guilds of Help, 1913, p. 60.
47. *The Helper*, Bolton Guild, Vol. 7, no. 3, March 1913, pp. 33–8, quoted in Laybourn, 1994, p. 195. Charles Loch, 1849–1923, was secretary of the COS from 1875 to 1914. According to one obituary, 'He made the COS; he was the COS', *The Times*, 25 January 1923, p. 13.
48. D'Aeth, 1914, p. 404.
49. Ibid., pp. 405–7.
50. Ibid., pp. 407–8.
51. Ibid., p. 414.
52. Ibid., p. 414.
53. Laybourn, 1994, p. 25.
54. Ibid.

55. Grant, 2014, p. 144; Finlayson, 1994, p. 205.
56. Grant, 2014, p. 18.
57. For example, Stevenson, 1984, p. 58.
58. For example, Thane, 2012.
59. Pope, 1991, p. 31. See also Lowe, 1995a.
60. Quoted in Grant, 2014, p. 23.
61. On the Prince's *call to service* in 1932, see Chap. 4.
62. Laybourn, 1994, p. 127.
63. Ibid., p. 127.
64. Ibid., pp. 135–7.
65. See Grant, 2014, for a detailed analysis of the role played by Ward during the war.
66. Ibid., p. 89. On later concerns over poor fundraising practice, see Chaps. 7, 8, and 10.
67. Laybourn, 1994, p. 148, and Moore, 1977, p. 103.
68. *Conference on war relief and personal service*, 1915, p. 107.
69. Ibid., p. 107.
70. Ibid., pp. 114–5.
71. Ibid., p. 116.
72. Ibid., p. 151.
73. For a summary of the work of the committee, see *A scheme for central and local committees on social service*, paper presented to the COS Council, 4 February 1918. Charity Organisation/Family Welfare Association Archives; London Metropolitan Archives (LMA): LMA/A/FWA/C/A/01/016.
74. Brief biographies of these key figures are given below.
75. Reported in *Help*, the Journal of the Bradford Guild, Vol. 12, no. 1, November 1916; quoted in Laybourn, 1994, p. 149.
76. Moore, 1977, p. 103.
77. See *Draft constitution of Joint Committee on Social Service*, paper discussed by the COS Administrative Committee, 17 January 1918. Charity Organisation Society/Family Welfare Association Archives; LMA/A/FWA/C/A3/53/1.
78. Ibid.
79. Moore 1977, p. 104. David Thomas, First Viscount Rhondda, 1856–1918, was a Liberal politician and businessman who served in Lloyd George's wartime Coalition government. He became president of the Board of Trade in 1916.
80. See *The place of organisation in voluntary effort in the future*, paper discussed by the COS administrative committee, 25 July 1918. Charity Organisation Society/Family Welfare Association Archives; LMA/A/FWA/C/A3/53/1.
81. On the establishment of the Volunteer Centre in 1973, see Chap. 7.
82. Rooff, 1972, p. 118.
83. Brasnett, 1969, p. 17.
84. Ibid., p. 1.
85. Adderley, 2015, pp. 64–65.
86. Anonymous, 1942, p. 173.
87. Brasnett, 1969, p. 22.
88. For a good review of the life and work of Grundy, see Sephton, 2009. For a tribute to Grundy by W.G.S. Adams, see *The Village*, Vol. 35, Spring 1943, p. 2.

89. On the life and times of D'Aeth, see Simey, 2005.
90. Poole, 1961, pp. 156–159.
91. Jenkins, 2001, p. 159. On Haynes' tenure at the Council, see Chaps. 5, 6, and 7.
92. Simey, 2004 and 2005. See also Poole, 1961, p. 158.
93. For a tribute to Pringle, see Astbury, 1963.
94. The London COS also decided to remain outside the new Council. See Humphreys, 2001, p. 143.
95. Finlayson, 1994, p. 246.
96. Humphreys, 2001, p. 143.
97. On Ellis, see Chap. 3.
98. See Keeling, 1961.
99. Brasnett, 1969, p. 2.
100. Adams' contribution to the Council is covered in Chaps. 3, 4, 5, and 6.
101. Ellis, 1931.
102. Symonds was knighted in 1919 and died in 1931. 'Sir Aubrey Symonds' *The Times*, 25 March 1931, p. 16.
103. *The Times*, 7 February 1950, p. 9.
104. Ibid.
105. NCSS, 1919.
106. Grant, 2014, p. 172.
107. Phillips, 1995, p. 140.
108. Lowe, 1995a, p. 42.
109. Kidd, 1999, p. 108.
110. Grant, 2014, p. 183.
111. See Harrison, 2003.
112. Cole, 1945, p. 26.
113. Laybourn, 1994, p. 153.
114. Humphreys, 2001.
115. Macadam, 1934, p. 68.

REFERENCES

Adderley, S. (2015). *Bureaucratic conceptions of citizenship in the voluntary sector (1919–1939): The case of the National Council of Social Service.* Unpublished PhD thesis, Bangor University.

Anonymous. (1942). *Thomas Hancock Nunn: The life and work of a social reformer, written by his friends for his friends.* London: Baines and Scarsbrook Ltd.

Astbury, B. (1963). John Christian Pringle. *Social Service Quarterly, 37*(1), 25–28.

Beveridge, W. (1948). *Voluntary action: A report on methods of social advance.* London: George Allen & Unwin.

Brasnett, M. (1969). *Voluntary social action: A history of the National Council of Social Service 1919–69.* London: NCSS.

Cahill, M., & Jowitt, T. (1980). The new philanthropy: The emergence of the Bradford City Guild of Help. *Journal of Social Policy, 9*(3), 359–382.

Cole, G. D. H. (1945). A retrospect of the history of voluntary social service. In A. Bourdillon (Ed.), *Voluntary social services: Their place in the modern state.* London: Methuen.

Conference on war relief and personal service. (1915, June 10–12). *Conference on war relief and personal service*. Organised by charity organisation societies and guilds of help, Caxton Hall, Westminster. London: Longmans.

D'Aeth, F. (1914). The social welfare movement. *The Economic Review, 24*(4), 404–414.

Davis Smith, J. (2004). Thomas Hancock Nunn. In *Oxford dictionary of national biography*. Oxford: Oxford University Press.

Ellis, L. (1931). Sir Aubrey Vere Symonds. *The Social Service Review, 12*(4), 67.

Finlayson, G. (1994). *Citizen, state, and social welfare in Britain 1830–1990*. Oxford: Clarendon Press.

Flanagan, R. (1991). *'Parish-fed bastards': A history of the politics of the unemployed in Britain, 1884–1939*. Westport: Greenwood Press.

Goldman, L. (2002). *Science, reform, and politics in Victorian Britain*. Cambridge: Cambridge University Press.

Grant, P. (2014). *Philanthropy and voluntary action in the First World War: Mobilizing charity*. London: Routledge/Taylor & Francis Group.

Grundy, S. (1913, June 5–7). *Case work and policy: A synthesis*. Paper prepared for the sixth annual conference of the National Association of Guilds of Help, Halifax, Guilds of Help.

Hancock Nunn, T. (1909). *A council of social welfare. A note and memorandum on the report of the royal commission on the poor law and relief of distress as to the functions and constitution of the new public assistance authority and its local committees*. London: Council of Social Welfare.

Harris, J. (1992). Political thought and the welfare state 1870–1940: An intellectual framework for British social policy. *Past and Present, 135*, 116–141.

Harris, B. (2010). Voluntary action and the state in historical perspective. *Voluntary Sector Review, 1*(1), 25–40.

Harrison, B. (2003). Civil society by accident? Paradoxes of voluntarism and pluralism in the nineteenth and twentieth centuries. In J. Harris (Ed.), *Civil society in British history – Ideas, identities, institutions* (pp. 79–96). Oxford: Oxford University Press.

Humphreys, R. (2001). *Poor relief and charity, 1969–1945: The London Charity Organisations Society*. Basingstoke: Palgrave.

Jenkins, J. (2001). The organization man: George Haynes at the National Council of Social Service. In L. Black et al. (Eds.), *Consensus or coercion? The state, the people and social cohesion in post-war Britain* (pp. 151–168). Cheltenham: New Clarion Press.

Keeling, D. (1961). *The crowded stairs: Recollections of social work in Liverpool*. London: NCSS.

Kidd, A. (1999). *State, society and the poor in nineteenth-century England*. London: Macmillan.

Laybourn, K. (1993). The Guild of Help and the changing face of Edwardian philanthropy. *Urban History, 20*(1), 43–60.

Laybourn, K. (1994). *The Guild of Help and the changing face of Edwardian philanthropy: The Guild of Help, voluntary work and the state 1904–1919*. Lampeter: The Edwin Mellen Press.

Lewis, J. (1995). *The voluntary sector, the state and social work in Britain: The Charity Organisation Society/Family Welfare Association since 1869*. Aldershot: Edward Elgar.

Lewis, J. (1996). The boundary between voluntary and statutory social service in the late nineteenth and early twentieth centuries. *The Historical Journal, 1*, 155–177.

Lowe, R. (1995a). Government. In S. Constantine, M. Kirby, & M. Rose (Eds.), *The First World War in British history* (pp. 29–50). London: Edward Arnold.

Lowe, R. (1995b). Welfare's moving frontier. *Twentieth Century British History, 6*(3), 369–376.

Macadam, E. (1934). *The new philanthropy: A study of the relations between the statutory and voluntary social services.* London: Allen & Unwin.

McBriar, A. (1987). *An Edwardian mixed doubles: The Bosanquets versus the Webbs, a study in British social policy 1890–1929.* Oxford: Clarendon Press.

Moore, M. (1977). Social work and social welfare: The organisation of philanthropic resources in Britain, 1900–1914. *The Journal of British Studies, 16*(2), 85–104.

National Association of Guilds of Help. (1913, June 5–7). Report of the sixth annual conference, Halifax, NAGH.

NCSS. (1919, March). *Memorandum.* London: NCSS.

Phillips, G. (1995). The social impact. In S. Constantine, M. Kirby, & M. Rose (Eds.), *The First World War in British history* (pp. 106–140). London: Edward Arnold.

Poole, H. (1961). Frederic D'Aeth 1875–1940. *Social Service Quarterly, 34*(4), 156–159.

Pope, R. (1991). *War and society in Britain 1899–1948.* Harlow: Longman.

Rooff, M. (1972). *A hundred years of family welfare: A study of the Family Welfare Association (formerly Charity Organisation Society), 1869–1969.* London: Michael Joseph.

Sephton, R. (2009). *S.P. Grundy: A life of social service in Manchester and North Berkshire.* Radley: Radley History Club.

Simey, M. (2004). Frederic George D'Aeth. In *Oxford dictionary of national biography.* Oxford: Oxford University Press.

Simey, M. (2005). *From rhetoric to reality: A study of the work of F.G. D'Aeth, social administrator* (D. Bingham, Ed.). Liverpool: Liverpool University Press.

Stevenson, J. (1984). *British society, 1914–1945.* Harmondsworth: Penguin.

Thane, P. (2012). The "big society" and the "big state": Creative tension or crowding out? *Twentieth Century British History, 23*(3), 408–429.

CHAPTER 3

Early Years

INTRODUCTION

The post-war world into which the Council was thrust was one of opportunity and challenge. Looming over the period was the spectre of depression and mass unemployment, which as we shall see in the next chapter served as the backdrop for much of its work. But the period was also characterised by significant political and social change, including universal suffrage, finally achieved for men in 1918 and women in 1928; continued agricultural decline and rural depopulation; a huge inner-city rehousing programme, coupled with the development of new towns and municipal housing estates; and an explosion of leisure opportunities that tapped into the increased living standards and reduced working hours for many of those in employment. And overshadowing the period was the growing threat as the decade wore on of a new international crisis. The Council cannot be accused of lacking ambition in its early days, despite its lack of resources, and it set out to mobilise the voluntary movement to contribute to all the big issues of the day. There were some significant successes, particularly in rural areas and on the new estates and, more controversially, in the arena of unemployment. But there were failures and frustrations as well, and there was a sense that the Council was trying to find its way in a challenging environment. According to Brasnett, the first decade was marked by 'steady growth and progress', but 'no spectacular developments'.[1] The rapid growth in unemployment, especially as the decade came to an end, transformed the work of the Council and raised its profile to unprecedented levels. It also set the course for a far closer relationship with government, which remained a feature of its work for much of the rest of the century.

The period was one of the mixed fortunes for the voluntary movement. For A.J.P. Taylor, volunteers sustained 'the public life of England' between the wars and 'provided the groundswell of her history'.[2] Other historians, such as Geoffrey Finlayson and David Owen, have pointed to the struggle faced by charities in securing sufficient funds and members in a time of rising inflation,

© The Author(s) 2019
J. Davis Smith, *100 Years of NCVO and Voluntary Action*,
https://doi.org/10.1007/978-3-030-02774-2_3

high taxes, mass unemployment, and greater involvement by the state in activities previously seen as the preserve of the voluntary movement.[3] Such a *declinist* narrative is difficult to sustain. Constance Braithwaite in *The Voluntary Citizen* found little evidence to support the idea that the increase in the role of the state had dampened charitable giving, although she acknowledged that growth in income had failed to keep pace with rising prices.[4] If some existing organisations faced tough times, the period also witnessed the emergence of a range of new agencies, from youth groups to leisure and hobby clubs. Many were linked to single issues and looked to take advantage of the widening of the franchise by encouraging new voters to support their cause, such as the National Council for the Unmarried Mother and her Child set up in 1918.[5] Helen McCarthy has claimed that the inter-war years were marked by an increasing democratisation of social and political life, brought about in part by voluntary agencies, that in turn led to a reconfiguring and democratisation of the 'world of voluntary action'.[6]

The contribution played by voluntary action in developing active citizens and schooling people in the ways of democratic life was a recurrent theme of the period, advanced by such establishment figures as the Conservative prime minister, Stanley Baldwin, and future Archbishop of Canterbury, William Temple.[7] And it was to be a central plank of the Council's emerging agenda, underpinning much of its work, especially in the countryside and on the new estates. If there is truth in McCarthy's assertion that voluntary action played a role in breaking down some of the barriers of class and gender between the wars, then the Council can be held to have contributed to this process through its support for the democratic control of community associations and village halls and its advocacy of mixed-gender membership within some of the new organisations it helped establish, such as the Youth Hostels Association and the National Association of Young Farmers' Clubs.[8] We must not, however, overstate such advances. Society remained deeply divided between the wars and some of the voluntary networks supported by the Council remained largely the preserve of the elite.[9] Ross McKibbin has argued that voluntary associations, rather than contributing to a more equal society, served to reinforce divisions and unite a diverse middle class in anti-Labour hostility.[10] McCarthy herself is keen to play down the extent of the transformation concluding, perhaps wisely, that the changes brought about by voluntary action during this period are perhaps best seen as leading to 'a more equitable distribution of social esteem', rather than 'greater social equality'.[11]

The link between voluntary action and democracy was not only of domestic interest. As international tensions grew, there was a growing sense that Britain's democratic strength could be explained partly by its voluntary tradition, in contrast to the weakness of the voluntary movement under totalitarian regimes. Voluntary action was seen as an essential component of a free and democratic society and a resource that Britain was perhaps uniquely placed to export to build international cooperation.[12] Such internationalism can be seen in the rapid growth of voluntary movements such as the League of Nations Union, but it was also present in the ambitions of the Council, which was keen to establish itself as a centre of international expertise and exchange. With fascism and communism on the march in Europe, Britain, the Council asserted in 1938, is a third system with state power 'tempered by democratic processes and traditions' of which voluntary action was a crucial component.[13] Helen McCarthy and Pat Thane have argued that the growing political influence of voluntary organisations between the wars contributed to the 'avoidance of crisis' that affected many other countries. 'Any account that seeks to explain the peculiar stability of modern British politics', they conclude, 'must consider the role of voluntary associations as they became closer partners of the state whilst remaining important vehicles for social and political activism.'[14] This belief in the power of voluntary action to build citizenship and democracy, at home and overseas, was a recurring theme of the Council's work throughout its early history.

The period was also one of growing partnership between the voluntary movement and the state, encapsulated in Elizabeth Macadam's description of the *New Philanthropy*.[15] Although collaboration between statutory and voluntary agencies was not new, there was a greater focus on joint working, building on forces unleashed at the end of the previous century and given a significant boost during the war.[16] It was this growing sense of partnership that defined much of the Council's early work, particularly in the area of unemployment, and set the foundation for its future direction. We need to be careful, however, not to overstate the break with the past. Reconstruction, which had been much in vogue towards the end of the war and in which the voluntary movement had been identified to play a significant part, had been largely abandoned by the early 1920s, although it was revised later by non-governmental agencies such as the Next Five Years Group and Political and Economic Planning.[17] Indeed the Council's own interest in research and study on the role of voluntary action in national renewal can be seen as part of this wider movement, identified by Arthur Marwick as a non-party political, 'middle opinion' approach to solving major social issues.[18] Frank Prochaska has argued that Macadam overstated the degree of convergence between the state and the voluntary movement during this period, and Finlayson has concluded that social policy 'tended to look in both directions: forward to Welfare State collectivism and backward to orthodox economic individualism, of which voluntarism in its most classic form was part'.[19]

But if the notion of partnership was generally viewed favourably, there was the more difficult question as to the appropriate role for voluntary action during austerity. The Council argued that in time of economic hardship the voluntary movement had a critical role to play. 'Voluntary social service, apart from other considerations', it stated in 1920, 'saves the country annually a vast amount of public expenditure, and at the present time it is only through a large extension of such voluntary service that the demands for economy and for social betterment can both be met.'[20] A similar argument would be advanced 90 years later when austerity was once again the dominant political narrative.[21]

On both occasions, the position adopted by the Council would bring censure from critics who argued that it was providing a cover for government inaction and for those using austerity as an excuse to roll back the state. It was an issue that bookended the Council's history and proved one of the most controversial and divisive it faced.

ESTABLISHING THE ORGANISATION

The Council was formally constituted in March 1919 and issued its first public notice the same month. It was sent with a covering letter from the inaugural chair, Sir Aubrey Symonds of the Local Government Board, to all mayors and chairs of local authorities outlining the case for social service.[22] In December the same year, the Council issued a further memorandum setting out its view on the relationship between the voluntary movement and statutory bodies. It identified two major contributions that voluntary action could play in support of the state: extending the work of statutory services 'by means of unpaid workers and voluntary societies' and acting 'as a pioneer force exploring new grounds and testing new methods of social reform'.[23] These dual ambitions—complementing the work of statutory services and pioneering new solutions to social need—underpinned the Council's approach to partnership in its early years. This did not mean, however, it took the view that the sole, nor indeed primary, purpose of the voluntary movement was to support the work of the state. For the Council, voluntary action had a value and purpose that transcended the work of statutory bodies. Indeed, such a purpose was hinted at in the December memorandum, with the claim that the voluntary movement had 'a very real value as a socialising force' in terms of 'developing a truer sympathy between groups', anticipating debates later in the century about the role of voluntary action in building social capital.[24] As to the specific role to be played in support of these aims, the Council's first annual report identified four functions for the new national body: to 'promote the systematic organisation of voluntary social work, both nationally and locally' and secure coordination with statutory agencies; to stimulate the development of local councils in each local government area 'representative of both voluntary and statutory administration'; to 'collect, register and disseminate information relating to all forms of social service'; and to 'encourage international co-operation in social service'.[25] These aims, reworded several times over the following years, served as the *leitmotif* for the Council for most of the century, until the separation of the local councils in the 1980s and 1990s necessitated a refocusing onto an almost exclusive national agenda.

The first priority for the new organisation was accommodation. The Local Government Board provided space for the first few months but, when this was reclaimed to meet the needs of the rapidly expanding Ministry of Health, the Council found itself homeless. A temporary room was rented at No. 8a New Cavendish Street for the summer of 1919, but there was a need for a longer-term solution.[26] For a short period, it set itself up in Oxford at Barnett House, which was a convenient base from which to organise its first major national conference, planned for the city in 1919, but put back to spring 1920 due to a rail strike.[27] Incidentally, this was to be the only time in its history that it was to base its headquarters outside the capital, although it seriously considered the option on several future occasions and established a network of regional offices as its work expanded. In 1920 an opportunity arose to share premises with the British Institute of Social Service, which had recently moved into the large London residence of the late Sir Richard Stapley.[28] There were several points of connection between the two organisations. Both had similar aims, the institute had an impressive library and information service on social service, which the Council was keen to acquire, and they shared the same president in the Speaker of the House of Commons, the Rt Hon. James Lowther.[29] In fact, co-location was seen as the first move towards an eventual merger of the two organisations. Early signs were encouraging and the first annual reports from the Council were issued in the name of both organisations. But the merger plans came to nothing partly, Brasnett says, because of concerns by the Institute whether the Council would survive.[30] Gradually the two agencies drifted apart, although Stapley House, 33 Bloomsbury Square, London, remained the Council's head-quarters until 1928.

Lack of accommodation wasn't the only problem. Funds for the new organ-isation were extremely tight. Apart from the Birchall legacy, there was a 'gift' of £400 from the National Association of Guilds of Help (NAGH), which had agreed to cede its assets to the Council, a small donation from a private bene-factor and a small sum of money generated from membership fees. The first annual report noted a bank overdraft of £32, which had grown to £400 the following year.[31] In 1925 members of the Executive Committee agreed to pro-vide personal guarantees for the overdraft with the bank in order to keep the organisation solvent.[32] From the outset, concerns were expressed about the impact the lack of funds was having on the Council's ambitions. 'Already the work has seriously out-grown the Council's financial resources', the annual report for 1919–20 noted, 'and its development is being hindered for lack of funds.'[33] An economy drive was launched almost immediately and plans were put in place for a national fundraising appeal, although it was admitted that 'it is impossible to base a popular or emotional appeal on the Council's work'.[34] This cycle was to reoccur throughout its history: periodic funding shortages, followed by economy drives and external appeals for funds, coupled with a realisation that its work would never lend itself to mass public appeals. In 1923 the Council applied for incorporation as a company limited by guarantee, and in 1928 it was granted charitable status.[35]

Membership of the Council in the early days was small but varied. At the end of its first year it was representing 15 councils of social service and a num-ber of local charity organisation societies (COSs) and guilds of help; 35 national voluntary agencies, including the NAGH, the Church of England, the Catholic Church, various friendly societies, Barnett House in Oxford, the Borstal Association, and the National Federation of Women's Institutes; 7 local authorities and associations, including the Poor Law Unions' Association and the County councils Association; and 6 central government departments.[36] The governance arrangements reflected this diversity with members of the ruling *Council* being appointed by four discrete groups: councils of social service, national voluntary agencies, local government authorities and associations, and central government departments, although in the latter case in an advisory capacity only. The day-to-day running of the agency was delegated to an Executive Committee chaired by Dr. W.G.S. Adams, who replaced Symonds within a couple of weeks of the launch. Also on the Executive Committee were two figures who played a significant role in the Council's formation: Percy Grundy, who became honorary secretary, and Frederic D'Aeth, who later became vice-chair. Two of the other founding fathers, Thomas Hancock Nunn and the Rev. John Pringle, also joined the Committee within a few years.

The first paid member of staff was Captain Lionel Ellis, who was appointed secretary in 1919. Ellis, like Edward Birchall, fought in France with distinction (he was a captain in the Welsh Guards and awarded the Distinguished Service Order and the Military Cross) and also had a background in the voluntary movement, having been secretary of the Southwark COS before the war. Given the COS' residual suspicion towards the new organisation, and its ongoing concern about the direction the voluntary movement was taking in seeking closer cooperation with the state, this appointment might be seen as surprising. But it was an inspired choice. Ellis was secretary for 17 years, overseeing the development of the Council into an efficient and effective organisation and skilfully marshalling it through the depression years of the 1930s. The appointment also sent out a clear signal that the Council was a broad church, seeking to reach out to all traditions within the voluntary movement.[37]

The Council held its first conference in Manchester in 1919 on the topic of leisure, out of which a standing committee was formed with the British Music Society and British Drama League to keep the issue on the agenda.[38] But it was the Oxford conference in April 1920 that provided its first significant national exposure. The title of the conference gave a clear indication of the Council's priorities: 'Reconstruction and Social Service: The Relation of the Voluntary Worker to the Public Authorities'.[39] Of nearly 400 delegates who attended, there was good representation from the COS, guilds, councils of social service, and national voluntary organisations, but also a strong contingent from local government. About 235 of the 394 representatives were women and 370 were from England, with just 9 from Wales, 8 from Ireland, and 6 from Scotland.[40] The issue of UK representation was a contentious one for much of the Council's early history, and its failure to shed its predominantly English profile would precipitate moves towards devolution in later years and the establishment of separate UK-country councils. The four main themes of the conference were public assistance, health, education, and the crucial issue of the relationship between voluntary and statutory bodies. The overwhelming mood of the event was positive, with speakers calling for the voluntary movement to play an important part in the country's reconstruction plans, alongside the growing statutory services. Partnership was very much the order of the day with one delegate, the mayor of Stepney and future prime minister, Clement Attlee, warning against a return to the 'pre-war' sentiments based on a 'fundamental fallacy' that people could look after their families without the need for public assistance. A second national conference was held the following year and a third in 1924, attended only by voluntary representatives, a clear indication, even at this early stage, as to where the Council's main focus in the future would lie.[41]

IDEALISTS AND REALISTS

The story of the formation of the Council can be told through the key institutions and individuals that came together in pursuit of a national body. But we also need to acknowledge the importance of ideas circulating at the time that had a significant influence on those who steered it during its formative years. Simon Adderley argues that the Council 'reflected an attempt to implement at a practical, "on the ground", level the Idealist conceptions of citizenship and community present throughout "progressive circles" from the mid-nineteenth century onwards'. He describes this fusion as 'bureaucratic citizenship'.[42] Idealism as a philosophy had taken hold in Britain in the latter quarter of the nineteenth century in the universities of Oxford and Scotland but remained influential in the post-war period.[43] Its leading exponent was T.H. Green, who during his time at Balliol College, Oxford, developed ideas of what it meant to be a good citizen. Drawing heavily on the classical writings of Aristotle, he argued that citizenship demanded an active commitment to social service and a readiness to get involved in practical community action.[44] Green's ideas and those of other Idealists, such as Henry Jones, W.H. Hadow, F.H. Bradley, and J.A. Hobson, influenced a number of academics who became leading figures in the voluntary movement, including Samuel Barnett, who pioneered the first university settlement at Toynbee Hall in London, and Ernest Barker, A.D. Lindsay, and J.L. Stocks who after the war played a key role in the Council's development.[45] According to Sandra Den Otter, 'the idealists powerfully responded to contemporary concern about the fragmentation of urban life' and translated this in 'a call to public service'.[46]

Perhaps of most significance for the Council, was the influence of Idealism on Adams, who led the organisation for its first 30 years. Adams was himself a Balliol graduate and a great admirer of Barnett and was largely responsible for establishing Barnett House in Oxford in 1914 as a memorial to his work.[47] It was set up as a library and training centre for social service, but at the end of the war, largely under Adams' influence, began to focus more on adult education and rural affairs. Barnett House played an important part in the early development of the Council, not only as its temporary headquarters in 1919 but as the birthplace of the rural community council movement.[48] After graduating from Balliol, Adams lectured in Manchester and Chicago before taking up a position within the Department of Agriculture and Technical

Instruction in Ireland from 1905 to 1910, where he came under the influence of Sir Horace Plunkett, whose ideas on the rural economy were to exert a big influence.[49] He returned to Oxford in 1910 and in 1912 took up the post of Gladstone professor at Balliol where he created the new course of Politics, Philosophy, and Economics and established the *Political Quarterly* journal. In 1914 he wrote an influential report for the Carnegie UK Trust on library services, another interest he took with him to the Council. Carnegie became a major supporter of the Council and Adams later joined the trust's board.[50] During the war he worked at the Ministry of Munitions, before accepting an invitation from the prime minister Lloyd George to head up his personal secretariat.[51] Adams returned to Oxford after the war and became warden of All Souls from 1933 to 1945 and pro-vice-chancellor of the university from 1939 to 1945. Alongside his marathon stint as chair of the Council, he was also a member of the Development Commission from 1923 to 1949, another body which provided significant funding to the Council for much of its early work, especially in rural areas. Inspired by his work with Plunkett in Ireland, Adams was especially interested in the contribution voluntary action could play in the revitalisation of rural life. He ran a farm and for many years was chair of the National Federation of Young Farmers' Clubs, which the National Council helped establish.

For Adams and the other Idealist leaders within the Council, such as Barker who led the work on the new housing estates and Lindsay who chaired the influential unemployment committee, voluntary action was far more than the delivery of services alongside the rapidly expanding state. First and foremost, it was an exercise in citizenship and democracy, providing an opportunity for individuals to take control of their lives and learn the skills and craft of democratic life. Voluntary social service could have significant economic and social benefits, but these were secondary to the democratic benefits. Such Idealist sentiments exerted a significant influence over the work of the Council between the wars, from its focus on adult education and 'useful leisure', to its support for community associations, village halls, and social service clubs for the unemployed. 'The special task of voluntary social service', the Council declared in 1931, 'is to develop constructive citizenship and an art of self-government that is expressed not only, or mainly, in the action of elected representatives and public authorities, but no less truly by personal action in voluntary associations with others.'[52]

The post-war period saw a growth in popular leisure pursuits driven by higher living standards and reduced working hours for significant parts of the population. Cinemas, music halls, rambling clubs, camping holidays, and the like spread rapidly as working people explored their new-found freedom after the constraints of the war. Nowhere was this trend more keenly felt than in the countryside, which became an increasingly popular destination for town folk looking to escape urban life for a few days.[53] For the Council it was crucial that this increase in free time was put to good use, on such socially uplifting activities as voluntary action, adult education, music, history, and drama, rather than wasted on frivolous pursuits. There was a long history to such demands, hark-ing back to the 'rational recreation' of the middle of the nineteenth century and embracing more recent movements such as the settlements and Workers Educational Association.[54] In 1930 the Council convened a conference to look at establishing a national body to support the emerging hostels set up to cater for young walkers and cyclists. The fledgling Youth Hostels Association was nurtured through the provision of administrative support and free accommo-dation until it was deemed able to stand alone as a fully independent organisa-tion. This was a process that defined the early work of the Council.[55] Robert Snape has argued that the period saw a switch from leisure being seen as a moral issue to a social act that would build citizenship and community, and the Council undoubtedly played a role in this transformation. Ultimately, it would prove only partially successful due to the allure of more commercial and popu-lar forms of leisure.[56] But a moral dimension remained that was embraced by the Council and its leadership. Barker, for example, felt that education 'should be a training in the right way of using leisure, which without education may be misspent and frittered away'.[57] The Council made a similar point in its annual report for 1929–30, arguing that 'commercialized recreation tends to induce contentment with passive amusement'.[58]

Such attitudes have led some commentators to accuse the Council of being at heart a conservative body. Snape, for example, argues that 'while the rhetoric of conference speakers and contributors to its bulletins often exhibited radical and idealist notions, the NCSS was inherently conservative, led by establish-ment figures including W.G.S. Adams, government adviser and Chairman from 1920 to 1949; the Eton educated Viscount Bledisloe as President and the Prince of Wales as Patron'.[59] This is only partially correct. Certainly in its early days it can be seen as part of the establishment, in that many of its leading fig-ures were drawn from the upper reaches of academia and the public sector, and it is true that some of the views it espoused had an elitist flavour. But there was also a radical strand to the Council's vision that was more in tune with tradi-tions of active citizenship, mutual aid, and self-advancement espoused by Liberal Idealists and Leftist thinkers such as William Morris and John Ruskin. Lindsay, for example, was a member of the Workers' Educational Association (WEA) and the Independent Labour Party in Scotland, and Dorothy Keeling had links to the Communist Party. Jose Harris has argued that Idealism, although often equated with conservatism, transcended political positions and had among its adherents liberals and socialists. This was certainly true of the Council in its early days.[60]

URBAN ACTIVITIES

The Council was founded in large part to bring greater coordination to the work of urban voluntary agencies, and establishing a representative council of social service in each town to oversee this work was seen as the number one priority for the new organisation.[61] Although some progress was made towards this goal, the results overall were disappointing. This was partly due to a lack of funding. In contrast to the support given by the Development Commission and the Carnegie UK Trust to the Council's rural activity, there were no obvious sources of funding to support its urban work. But it was more than this. In rural areas there was a strong sense of common purpose and the rural community councils, notwithstanding local variations, broadly followed a unified course. This was not true of the councils of social service, many of whom retained their old allegiance (and name) to the guilds of help or COS. In 1926 the Executive Committee noted that if the various local groups were 'to form part of one movement' there was a need for 'a real understanding of its ultimate goal and true harmony of outlook'.[62] Many councils, unlike their counterparts in the countryside, were slow in adapting to their new development role and continued to act almost as Edwardian relief agencies. The Council was also engaged in activities more redolent of the pre-war voluntary movement. In 1922 it agreed at the request of the Ministry of Health to carry out a pilot programme in Reading, Halifax, and Liverpool to log all relief provided over a four-week period to determine what more could be done to prevent overlap and duplication.[63] Progress towards building a network of councils of social service was also hampered by opposition from some local authorities. Hopes for better relations had been raised when, following a government inquiry into the coordination of statutory services involved in the delivery of public assistance called by the prime minister Bonar Law in 1923, official encouragement was given to the establishment of a network of councils. Central support, however, wasn't always matched at local level.[64] In 1929 Sir Wyndham Deedes, who later became vice-chair of the Council, toured the country and reported back on developments.[65] Relations with local authorities varied greatly and were found to be especially bad in Labour-controlled areas. Opinion on the value of councils of social service was mixed, with some commentators seeing them as a 'bulwark against the reds', while others viewed their work as demeaning and demoralising and responsible for weakening 'class consciousness'.[66] Relations with the church were also found to be difficult in some areas. Such rivalry, as Laybourn has pointed out, went back a long way with some church-based organisations before the war complaining about the guilds of help 'straying' onto their patch.[67] In the future the Council would seek to heal these rifts by establishing a Churches group to strengthen relations between the main faiths and the voluntary movement.[68]

Although overall the growth of councils of social service was disappointing, there were some important developments. Some councils set up 'poor man's lawyer' services, in association with local Law Societies, to provide free legal advice, others experimented with car schemes, blood donation banks, play centres and camps for young people.[69] In a number of areas 'citizen's friend' services were established, as the early prototypes of what would become the citizens' advice bureaux movement some 20 years later, and early examples of credit unions were trialled, offering loan finance at moderate rates to avoid people having to access money-lenders.[70] By 1938, councils of social service were in existence in about 120 towns. Attempts were also made to set up regional councils with the aim of bringing together councils of social service and rural community councils to provide a unified support service, but despite success in some areas such as Kent and Tyneside little headway was made.

RURAL WORK

The Council had more success in its early years in rural areas. On one level this was surprising, as it had no track record in the countryside. But on another, it was precisely this lack of a past that helped to bring about success. In the towns the different voluntary traditions that had come together to form the Council were still trying to find a way to live together. In rural areas the absence of existing networks of coordinating agencies offered a fertile environment for the new rural community councils to grow.[71] The Council's rural work tapped into widely held concerns about rural poverty, depopulation, and the decline of rural industry and new enthusiasm for the countryside as a place of leisure and escape for city dwellers. But there was also a nostalgic feel to the work, a longing after a vision of the countryside perhaps gone for good, which Stevenson has described as 'Deep England' and Burchardt as 'an example of sentimental, backwards-looking rural nostalgia'.[72] For the Council, the countryside, and more particularly the village, offered the perfect environment for the development of citizenship, and it was this vision of the countryside as a training ground for active community that underpinned its rural policy. Villages, the Council wrote in 1931, were important, not only for proving a 'closer contact with nature' that was deemed essential for human happiness but in offering 'training in self-government' and providing 'a school of democracy'.[73] In 1937 the Council went further in articulating its rural vision:

> The rural village provides, perhaps, the ideal setting for a community life in which all may have an opportunity of playing some active part. In the villages it is still possible to think of the whole community in terms of individuals who are known to us. In the village, as in no other community, it should be possible to ensure that no natural or man-made beauties are thoughtlessly destroyed, that no avoidable suffering or anxiety is allowed to cloud the life of any member of the community, that no talents and abilities are needlessly wasted, that those organisations which can contribute something of value to the community receive general support and encouragement in their work, and finally that the centres of social life – for instance, the village hall and the playing field – are the joint responsibility of all organised village interests.[74]

The origins of the rural community council movement have been described in detail elsewhere and can be summarised briefly here.[75] It began in Oxford at Barnett House under the dynamic leadership of Grace Hadow, who was appointed by Adams in 1920 as its new secretary.[76] Hadow, a lecturer at Lady Margaret Hall, Oxford, vice-chair of the National Federation of Women's Institutes, and a civil servant in the Ministry of Munitions, was one of the leading lights in the post-war voluntary movement and most inspirational speakers.[77] She later joined the Council's Executive Committee and, along with Adams, was the driving force behind its rural work. The Oxford Rural Community Council was established in 1920 and other councils quickly followed in the East Midlands and Kent.[78] Growth was rapid. By 1928 there were 18 councils and by 1939 there were 26. There was a fairly good distribution in England, but only patchy representation in Wales and none in Scotland.[79]

Funding was provided in the early years from the Development Commission, which was established by Lloyd George in 1909 to promote rural development, and from the Carnegie UK Trust.[80] Both institutions had close links to the Council. Lord Bledisloe, who was president of the Council from 1935 to 1938, was a trustee of Carnegie and Adams was a development commissioner from 1923 to 1949 and later also a trustee of the trust. According to Burchardt, 'what we have here then is a small group of powerful individuals, closely linked through shared membership of a network of statutory and voluntary organisations concerned with rural development'.[81] The rural work of the Council was coordinated centrally by a rural department, under Sir Henry Rew, chair of the Village Clubs Association.[82] A new quarterly newsletter, *The Village*, was launched to promote the Council's work and the first Rural Life conference was organised in 1921, a tradition that would continue for the next 60 years. The councils had a broad remit. Key activities included the promotion of adult education, drama, music, and local history. A Joint Committee for Music and Drama was established to disburse funds made available by the Carnegie UK Trust. The councils also supported rural industry through funding secured from the Development Commission and the Rural Industries Bureau.[83] Traditional industries such as blacksmiths, wheelwrights, and saddlers were provided with a mix of grants and loans to help with the modernisation of equipment or diversification into new areas of work. Support was also given to local tradespeople to form craft cooperatives. In Kent, for example, funding was provided to the Kent Rural Industries Cooperative Society to enable members to buy tools on favourable terms. Valuable though this support was for individual communities, it was ultimately doomed to failure and, as Burchardt has concluded, 'in the long run it proved impossible to stem the decline of the rural craft industries'.[84]

More successful was support for village halls. There was a strong Idealist strand to this work, with halls seen as having an important contribution to make to education, leisure, and local democracy. By 1939 councils had supported the building of over 1200 halls, covering about one in ten villages in England.[85] Many of the halls in the 1920s were built as war memorials, such as the one dedicated to Birchall and his brother in their home parish of Upton St Leonards. Self-management was seen as a priority to build leadership and local democracy. The Council provided only partial funding, with grants requiring matching by local fundraising. And to give a further push to self-ownership, funding was dependant on local people being involved in the management committees.[86] Women were well represented, partly due to the influence of the Women's Institute. The Council ran a village hall advisory service, provided a model trust deed for use by villages, and, in association with the Royal Institute of British Architects, drew up 'specimen' architectural plans to ensure good design was followed in construction. Brasnett concludes that 'some beautiful halls were built, even in quite small villages'.[87] Certainly, the impact could be profound, even in the smallest of places. A letter received by the Council from a remote island community with a population of 160 stated that 'This hall is one of the greatest boons our little community has enjoyed since the building of the bridge to the mainland.'[88] Another letter, sent by the residents of the village of Glanvilles Wootton in Dorset, with a population of 300, reported on how much the hall was being used and how 'the village have really acquired the right spirit of responsibility and ownership towards it'.[89]

The Council was also concerned with supporting local democracy more directly. In the early years, it experimented with support for village community councils, which it saw as important for encouraging social action and linking the community and local authority.[90] The experiment, however, was unsuccessful, and the Council turned its attention to the next layer of local democracy, the parish council, which was moribund at the time. For the next 20 years it expended much energy and resource in bolstering the work of parish councils.[91] In 1935 it set up a specialist advice unit delivered through the rural community councils, which by the end of the period was being used by over 700 parish councils.[92] In 1946, a National Association of Parish councils was established, which moved to independence in 1951.[93]

By 1938 there were 29 rural community councils in place, a central advisory council had been formed to strengthen governance, and the Council could look upon progress in the development of the movement with some pride. It had also been active in the emerging rural conservation movement and helped support the establishment of the Council for the Preservation of Rural England in 1926.[94] But there was no room for complacency. Large swathes of the countryside remained untouched by community councils and the sustainability of those already in existence was by no means guaranteed. Success depended very much on the presence of good relations with local authorities and this varied enormously from region to region. Several councils were forced to close due to lack of funds, including Dorset, Hampshire, West Sussex, and Hertfordshire. For some on the ground this was evidence that the Council wasn't doing enough to support its local affiliates. At the 1933 Rural Life conference in Oxford, there was 'considerable criticism' and an attempt to set up a new national organisation. Although nothing came of this venture, it was an early indication of the difficulties the Council faced later in the century in satisfying the needs of its varied and diverse membership, particularly at a local level.[95]

New Estates

Apart from its rural activity, perhaps the most significant area of the Council's work during this period was on the new estates. After the war, many hundreds of thousands of families were rehoused from inner cities to new towns and estates, under Addison's Housing and Town Planning Act of 1919 and the Wheatley Act of 1924.[96] While on the whole the quality of this accommodation was vastly superior to what existed before, there was increasing concern about the paucity of community provision. As one contemporary account noted, 'the first settlers on new estates everywhere found them bleak and comfortless, lacking most facilities for social life'.[97] The Council set about trying to fill this gap, focusing attention in particular on the development of community associations and centres. These independent networks, rooted in the settlements, tenants, and residents associations, were seen as the primary vehicle for the development of community life. According to Snape, 'the creation of an associational culture on estates' was 'inspired by the self-governing communities of garden cities such as Letchworth and Welwyn'.[98] In 1928 a New Estates Community Committee was set up to oversee this work, later reconstituted as the Community Centres and Associations Committee. The chair of the committee from 1931 to 1942 was Barker, another committed Idealist.[99] Barker, like Adams, had lectured at Oxford University, but made his name as principal of King's College London. In 1927 he became the first professor of political science at Cambridge University from where he developed much of his thinking on citizenship and the crucial role to be played by voluntary action. The new estates were seen as training grounds for active citizenship and lessons were drawn from the involvement of citizens in the *polis* of the Ancient Greek city-states. In his autobiography, Barker emphasised this heritage:

> I had always believed in voluntary effort and the value of voluntary societies, and I had always felt that much of what was great and fine in the history of my country ... was ultimately based on my countrymen's habit of doing things together for themselves in voluntary co-operation. What I learned of community centres and associations, as I saw them with my own eyes, and saw them actually at work, confirmed, with a visible and tangible evidence, the thoughts that had simmered in my brain as a result of my reading of history.[100]

From the late 1920s associations and centres were established on estates as far afield as Dagenham, Becontree, and Watling in London; Norris Green in Liverpool; and Wilbraham Road in Manchester.[101] Watling Community Centre in Middlesex, opened in 1932, is generally held to be the first purpose built community centre. A boost for this work came in 1930 when the Carnegie UK Trust agreed to fund a five-year pilot programme to develop community associations and by 1939 220 were in existence.[102] Independence was seen as paramount. The associations were to be self-governing and run by local residents. 'To place it in the charge of a statutory official', the Council wrote in 1937, 'would be to rob it of nine-tenths of its value as the focus of community life.'[103] Diversity of styles and structures was encouraged, and the Council made it clear it was not interested in controlling the movement from the centre.[104] In 1938 a National Consultative Council of Community Associations was set up, independent of, but supported by, the Council.

These early experiments were not always a success. Brasnett concludes that the movement was 'frustrated by the lack of premises or leadership, or the means of financing them'.[105] A survey carried out in 1938 of 71 community associations found that 32 had their own premises, 17 used schools or temporary accommodation, and 22 were homeless.[106] Leadership in particular was found to be a problem and, in the absence of sufficient skilled local individuals, volunteers were often brought in from outside, which worked against local accountability.[107] Recent historical writing has been intensely critical of the Council's work in this area, accusing it of being top down, controlling, and reinforcing negative stereotypes of the working class.[108] Patricia Garside has called it 'a lamentable failure' and argues that it compares unfavourably with other, more bottom-up approaches to community development pioneered at the time by organisations such as the Sutton Trust.[109] Such conclusions seem overly harsh. Despite more than a whiff of the paternalistic in its approach, many community associations succeeded in becoming locally managed and in attracting the active participation of local residents. The 1938 survey found that associations were involved in over 150 different physical activities, including fitness training, table tennis, football, folk-dancing, and boxing; and over 200 educational and cultural pursuits, such as music, drama, gardening, cinema, debates, thrift clubs, and trade union branches.[110] One notable success was Downham Estate in South East London built in 1924, which within a few years was boasting a community centre with a nursery, a weekly local parliament, whist drives, concerts, a free library, and young people's clubs.[111]

POLICY WORK

With the Council's focus very much on support for local initiatives in the villages, towns, and new estates, it is no surprise that its national work took a back seat for much of the period. 'The National Council's work is to be judged mainly', it wrote in 1931, 'by the extent to which these local movements grow in vigour and usefulness and a community spirit is revealed in co-operative activity.'[112] But national work was by no means absent. In its first few years, the Council responded to government reports on widows' pensions and the registration of charities and contributed to a BBC committee on the broadcasting of charity appeals.[113] In what can be seen as a clear commitment to the *insider* approach to influencing public policy, which would be its favoured stance throughout its history, the annual report for 1923 noted that a detailed record of government consultations 'would be unsuitable', but that 'such friendly negotiations undertaken during the year have been fruitful in removing misunderstandings, and in leading to concerted action along agreed lines'.[114] Such an approach in the future laid the Council open to criticism that it wasn't forceful enough in its dealings with government, a danger acknowledged at this time. Reviewing its progress at the end of the period, it admitted that sometimes it had been accused of 'not taking a definite stand on major issues'.[115] The Council was set up to build stronger relations between the state and the voluntary movement and it is therefore understandable that its chosen approach to policy influence was the diplomatic route. But this shouldn't be confused with compliance. Voluntary action was deemed too important to be left to the whim of government. Democracy, it argued in 1938, will only be safeguarded 'by the free criticism and constructive public effort of the community expressing itself outside, as well as through, the formal machinery of government'.[116] Such a position would be sorely tested in the years to come.

A key element in strengthening the position of the voluntary movement was improving the working conditions of staff. A report from Political and Economic Planning in 1937 noted the 'growth of a salaried bureaucracy' in voluntary groups between the wars, and the 1931 Census put the figure of people working in voluntary agencies at 10,000.[117] The movement, the Council acknowledged, required people of 'first-rate abilities', but it recognised that salaries could not compete with business or the public sector. Work for voluntary groups, it suggested, must 'involve some measure of self-denial', but in order to attract and retain staff, conditions should be as favourable as possible.[118] In 1927, discussions were held about the feasibility of establishing a pension scheme for those working in the movement, and this focus on improving working conditions for staff was a recurring preoccupation of the Council.[119] Alongside such support, early notice was given that the Council would also see its role as challenging the voluntary movement to improve its performance. There was, it wrote in 1938, a danger of 'too much elaboration, of overlapping, of the creation of vested interest' and it acknowledged that a legitimate criticism could be levelled that 'its organisation today is better than its results'.[120] A similar criticism was made by Political and Economic Planning in its 1937 report which, while acknowledging the 'good will' and 'self-sacrifice' of much of the voluntary movement, pointed to the 'untidiness', 'hypocrisy', and 'humbug' which existed in some agencies.[121] Supporting, and in some instances challenging, the voluntary movement to improve its performance emerged in future as a key focus of the Council's work.

Another area given priority during this period was young people. In 1925 the Council helped set up the National Association of Boys' Clubs, providing secretarial support and accommodation and helping it move to full independence the following year.[122] In 1928 it was instrumental in the establishment of a National Federation of Young Farmers' Clubs, which became independent in 1931.[123] This focus was replicated at a local level, and many rural community councils and councils of social service set up young people's committees to promote greater youth participation. Emphasis was placed on building citizenship, but also on 'strengthening of character'.[124] The work was not without its challenges. 'One of the chief difficulties in the way of opening new branches of organisations such as the Boy Scouts or Girl Guides, or of starting clubs', the Council reported in 1926, 'is the finding of men and women who will and can act as leaders', identifying a challenge that remains today.[125] In 1936 the Council brought together the main youth organisations to form the Standing Conference of National Juvenile Organisations to advise on youth matters. Representing a combined membership of over one million young people, the Conference greatly expanded the Council's reach, but it also created a governance challenge that exercised it for much of its first 50 years.[126] The Conference was nominally independent and free to set its own policy direction, with the Council providing administrative support. It was the first of a series of *associated groups* that followed a similar decentralised structure, allowing the Council to support a wide range of interests, while retaining a relatively small central core. But the Council had little control over the work of these groups, despite having ultimate responsibility, and it was this tension that led eventually to the abandonment of the model in favour of greater central control.

Perhaps the key national development of the period was the establishment of a new charitable covenant scheme. Some relief for charitable activities had been available since the introduction of income tax in 1799. From 1842, individuals could get tax relief on their donations by establishing a deed of covenant with a charity.[127] This was taken a stage further following the Income Tax Finance Act of 1922, which led to the development of the 'discretionary deed of covenant' in which a charitable organisation agreed on a covenant for a seven-year period with a donor to secure tax advantages, but allowed them to make an onward donation to other charities of their choosing. The idea was first advanced by the Liverpool Council of Social Service and adopted by the Council in 1924 with the establishment of a Charitable Annuities Department.[128] By 1925 it was distributing over £40,000 to charities and recovering an additional £6000 of tax on their behalf.[129] The scheme appears to have been an accidental by-product of a provision in the 1922 Act and critics accused the Council of manipulating the system.[130] The historian, Owen, felt there was some truth in these accusations and concluded that there was 'some disposition to regard the seven-year covenant as hardly more than legalized tax evasion'.[131] In 1927 the Conservative chancellor of the exchequer, Winston Churchill, put forward proposals to amend the Act to deal with the anomaly. The Council acted swiftly. In what amounted to its first major political campaign, letters were sent to all members of Parliament outlining the damage such change would cause. An amendment to the proposed changes was moved in the House of Commons and supported by members of all parties. The government backed down. It was seen as a major victory.[132] 'A grave danger to charities has thus been avoided by carefully organised joint action', the Council wrote in its annual report the following year.[133] The success of this campaign safeguarded a crucial income stream for charities. It also secured an important source of income for the Council, as it was able to charge 'commission' on each transaction. By 1938 it had over 2000 subscribers on its books and had distributed over £2 million to charities at a charge of 3 per cent on the sums distributed.[134] The Charitable Annuities Department (renamed the Charities Department) evolved into the National Council of Social Service Benevolent Fund in 1939 and in 1959 became the Charities Aid Fund. In 1974 a new independent organisation, the Charities Aid Foundation (CAF), was established to run the scheme and develop further tax-efficient methods of giving. An agreement reached at the time of transfer provided an ongoing source of revenue for the Council from the new organisation, which would prove hugely valuable for its future sustainability.[135]

INTERNAL MATTERS

On 8 June 1928, with its offices at Stapley House earmarked for demolition, the Council moved into new premises at numbers 26 and 27 Bedford Square. At the formal opening, a letter of support was read out from the Prince of Wales, who had recently become patron.[136] In his launch address, the Council's president, the Speaker of the House of Commons, J.H. Whitley, expressed hope that the new offices would become the 'headquarters of a sort of University of Social Service' so that 'when people wanted to find out where to apply their enthusiasm or financial help … they would only have to come there to find the avenue they sought'.[137] In its early years Bedford Square functioned as a charitable hub, with other groups such as the Rural Industries Bureau, the National Association of Boys' Clubs, the Library Association, and the London office of the Carnegie UK Trust sharing the space. This vision of the Council as a headquarters for voluntary action would resurface on several occasions in the future.[138] In 1931 a memorial plaque in memory of Birchall was installed in the building.[139] For its first 15 years the Council operated purely out of its London office, but by 1933, as its unemployment work expanded, it had more spacious accommodation in the capital and regional bases in Leeds, Birmingham, and Cardiff.

In 1936 Ellis resigned to take up the position of director of the new National Advisory Council for Physical Training and Recreation (later the National Fitness Council). Set up to improve the physical health of the population, it established a close relationship with the Council, making significant grants to support its work in rural areas and on the new estates. However, it closed after just three years with the outbreak of war.[140] Ellis had been general secretary at the Council for its first 17 years and steered the organisation through its difficult early development and controversial work on unemployment when criticism was at its height. After leaving the national advisory council, he had a distinguished career as a military historian and in the 1950s served as associate warden at Toynbee Hall.[141] In a letter to *The Times*, following his death in 1970, the director of the Council, J.K. Owens, paid tribute to his 'vision and energy' and his 'great administrative skill', which had been essential 'to activate so new and complex an association of national bodies, voluntary and statutory'.[142] Richard Clements, a former deputy secretary of the Council, described

him as 'a remarkable man' with opinions 'that were conservative and orthodox', although 'none could doubt his courage, resource and vision'.[143] Ellis'
successor was the Rev. Leonard Shoeten Sack, who joined the Council in 1936
as assistant secretary in charge of the rural department. His credentials were
good, having worked at the Ministry of Health and as secretary of the Kent
Council of Social Service from 1925 to 1936.[144] His appointment was approved
by the Executive Committee without a formal recruitment process, although
Adams admitted some might hold that 'an appointment of this nature should
have been advertised'.[145] He was director for only four years, until forced to
resign on grounds of ill health. One tribute, written after his death, described
him as a 'gifted, restless, humble and deeply religious man'.[146]

Financially, the Council ended the period solvent but by no means flush.
Despite the huge sums of state funds it had administered for its unemployment
work, its decision not to accept a management fee until 1936 had stretched it
to the limit. For the 1937–38 financial year, core costs were reported as
£31,678 against income of £31,985, two-thirds of which came from voluntary
and non-statutory funds. The Council, it reported, 'has steadily maintained the
principle that the major part of the cost of its own direct services must be met
from private voluntary funds'.[147] It could rely on generous support from key
charitable trusts, but its capacity to significantly increase its voluntary income
was limited by the decision not to launch public appeals to avoid diverting
funds away from its members. Neither of these principles—the refusal of statutory funding to contribute towards core costs and the ban on public appeals—
would prove sustainable in the long run.

The Council had long harboured an ambition to function as an engine room
of new thinking on voluntary action, and in 1930 the Executive Committee
agreed to the establishment of a new 'intelligence department' as 'a matter of
first importance'.[148] In the event, the pressure of its unemployment work meant
the plan was put on hold, but the period saw the launch of a new journal, the
Social Service Bulletin, and its later replacement with the more expansive
monthly journal, *Social Service Review*. The need to influence public opinion
took on an added urgency in the wake of the negativity that surrounded the
Council's work on unemployment. In 1936 the Executive Committee established an advisory committee on public relations to advise on improving public
awareness of its work and securing 'the general goodwill of the Press'.[149] The
outcome was two documentary films commissioned in 1936 with the support
of a grant from the Carnegie UK Trust. *Today We Live: A Film of Life in Britain*
focused on the building and use of a village hall and occupational club, while
Today and Tomorrow explored the social conditions in the countryside and on
new housing estates. The films were produced by the Strand Film Company
and premiered in November 1937 at the Regal Cinema in London, attended
by the Duke and Duchess of Kent.[150] They provide a fascinating insight into
the work of the Council and life in depression-hit Britain. Both films were
directed by the highly acclaimed filmmaker, Ruby Grierson, sister of the
founder of the British Documentary Movement and noted Idealist, John

Grierson.[151] Her co-director on *Today We Live* was the communist, Ralph Bond, also noted as one of the movement's 'most talented workers'.[152] Reception at the time was favourable and the films were applauded for such ground-breaking devices as allowing the miners featured in *Today We Live* to improvise with only a skeleton script. Today, however, critics find the films 'both immature and clumsy'.[153] Some 40 years later they were rediscovered for a new generation dealing with the bitter effects of mass unemployment and rebroadcast in the UK and overseas. The public relations committee also recommended that the Council should consider changing its name 'if a short and really expressive name could be found'. This was not felt possible and the idea was dropped.[154] It was another 45 years before the idea was seriously discussed again and the complexity of reaching agreement became only too apparent. But for now, the Council carried on with its founding name.[155]

The rapid expansion of the Council's work put pressure on its governance structure, and in October 1932 Ellis submitted a paper to the Executive Committee proposing changes. The weakness in the current model was seen as twofold. First, there was too great a distance between ordinary members (who met just once a year in full Council) and the Executive Committee, which oversaw the running of the organisation, the impact of which was seen as disempowering. 'Membership of the Council', he wrote, 'does not therefore give the ordinary member any direct voice in the work that is carried out in the Council's name.' Second, there was an expectation on the Executive Committee to deal with both administration and policy with the result, he argued, 'that both suffer'. Ellis' recommendation was to increase the size of the Executive Committee to provide more 'adequate representation' for members in running the organisation, and to establish a series of sub-committees to share the load and separate more clearly the administrative functions from policy making. He proposed increasing the number of elected members on the Executive Committee from 10 to 24 and establishing a new finance and general purposes sub-committee and other specialist committees to oversee specific areas of work.[156] The proposals were accepted and put in place the following year.

CONCLUSION

In 1929, as its work on unemployment was about to take off, the Council looked back on its performance over its first ten years. It was a frank assessment, which dealt honestly with its successes and failures. On the credit side, it noted the establishment of several new organisations, including the National Association of Boys' Clubs, the National Federation of Young Farmers' Clubs, and the Youth Hostels Association. But progress against its core aims of promoting voluntary action in villages and towns was seen as disappointing. It hinted that its long-term future was by no means guaranteed: 'If the Council's work is to be made permanently secure', it concluded, 'there must be a large body of men and women bound together by common membership of the movement and ready in their own circles to help it forward.'[157] Macadam writing in 1934 said that the early work of the Council showed encouraging signs, but that the future was unclear and that the 'real test' will be the 'strength of its endurance'.[158] Looking back, Brian Harrison suggested that the Council between the wars 'skirmished resourcefully along the advancing frontiers of the state, discovering new needs and inventing new organisations to meet them'.[159] It would take the unemployment crisis of the 1930s to fully transform its fortunes.

NOTES

1. Brasnett, 1969, p. 56.
2. Taylor, 1965, p. 175.
3. Finlayson, 1994, pp. 231–2; Owen, 1964, p. 527.
4. Braithwaite, 1938, pp. 110 and 131.
5. McCarthy and Thane, 2011, pp. 217–29. See also, Thane and Evans, 2012.
6. McCarthy, 2011, p. 48. See also McCarthy, 2008.
7. See, for example, McCarthy, 2011, p. 54, and Kent, 1992.
8. On democratic engagement in tenants groups, see Shapely, 2011.
9. On the dominance of the rural community councils by the rural aristocracy, see Burchardt, 2012, p. 91.
10. McKibbin, 1988.
11. McCarthy, 2011, p. 49.
12. For a discussion of these issues, see McCarthy, 2011, p. 55.
13. NCSS Annual Report 1937–38, p. 16.
14. McCarthy and Thane, 2011, pp. 228–9. See also McCarthy, 2007.
15. Macadam, 1934.
16. For a contrary view that the degree of collaboration between the state and the voluntary movement at this time has been overstated, see Prochaska, 1988, p. 80.
17. McCarthy, 2007, p. 908.
18. Marwick, 1964, pp. 285–98.
19. Prochaska, 1988, p. 80; Finlayson, 1994, pp. 250–1.
20. NCSS Annual Report 1919–20, p. 7.
21. The role of voluntary action during times of austerity is explored further in Chap. 10.
22. NCSS, March 1919a.
23. NCSS, December 1919b, p. 3.
24. Ibid., p. 3. Social capital became the buzz phrase during the 1990s and early years of the twenty-first century, popularised by the writings of Robert Putnam, 1993 and 2000, and adopted by politicians of the Left and Right as providing an 'intellectual' underpinning to the call for an expansion of voluntary action.
25. First Annual Report from the British Institute and National Council of Social Service 1919–20, p. 4.
26. A memorandum from the Council, dated April 1920, gives the address as 8A New Cavendish Street, London; Uncatalogued papers; London Metropolitan Archives (LMA).
27. Brasnett, 1969, p. 27.

28. Sir Richard Stapley was a businessman, philanthropist, and Liberal politician, who unsuccessfully contested the general elections of 1892 and 1910. He died in 1920, leaving his fortune to the Educational Trust, also based at 33 Bloomsbury Square, London. See *The Times*, 21 May 1920, p. 18.
29. A tradition had been established from its founding that the Speaker of the House of Commons would occupy the position of president of the Council. This continued until 1932 when the then Speaker Captain FitzRoy resigned his position on the grounds that his impartiality as Speaker could be compromised with the government grants being paid to the Council for its unemployment work.
30. Brasnett, 1969, p. 28.
31. NCSS Annual Report 1919–20.
32. Members of the Executive Committee were 'relieved' of this responsibility in April 1925. Minutes of Executive Committee, 2 April 1925; LMA/4016/IS/A/01/028.
33. NCSS Annual Report 1919–20, p. 7.
34. NCSS Annual Report 1923, p. 8. The appeal was launched by the Council's president, the Speaker of the House of Commons, the Rt. Hon. James Lowther, in a letter to *The Times*, 23 November 1920, p. 8.
35. NCSS Annual Report, 1923. The Council had been told in 1925 that it was not regarded as a charity and therefore could not claim relief against income tax. It appealed against the ruling but was unsuccessful. Minutes of Executive Committee, 8 May 1925 and 14 January 1926; LMA/4016/IS/A/01/028.
36. NCSS Annual Report 1919–20, p. 4.
37. On Ellis, see Brasnett, 1969, p. 17, and Clements, 1971.
38. See Snape, 2015a, p. 62.
39. NCSS, 1920.
40. For a good discussion of this conference, see Adderley, 2015, pp. 67–68.
41. Ibid., p. 79.
42. Ibid., pp. 10–11.
43. On the development of Idealism in Britain, see Offer, 1999 and 2003.
44. On Green and other British Idealists, see Den Otter, 1996; Vincent and Plant, 1984; and Harris, 1992. On the importance of active citizenship to Idealist thought, see Beaven and Griffiths, 2008.
45. The contribution of Barker and Lindsay to the Council and wider movement is discussed in this and the following chapter. J.L Stocks played a smaller, but still important, role in the Council's development, chairing its housing committee between the wars. Like Lindsay, he drew his civic inspiration from Greek philosophy and Labour politics. He was professor of philosophy at the University of Manchester and vice-chancellor of the University of Liverpool. He was active in the settlement movement and WEA and fought Oxford for Labour unsuccessfully at the 1935 general election. *The Times* said 'he combined the precepts of a teacher of philosophy with the active practice of civic virtue'. He died in 1937. See *The Times*, 14 June 1937, p. 9.
46. Den Otter, 1996, p. 208.
47. On the influence of Green and other Idealists on Adams, especially in relation to rural policy, see Burchardt, 2011.
48. Campbell, 1970, pp. 2–3.
49. On the influence of Plunkett on Adams, see Burchardt, 2011.

50. On Adams, see Brasnett, 1969, pp. 33–35 and his obituary in *The Times*, 1 February 1966, p. 12.
51. On Adams' time heading up Lloyd George's secretariat, see Turner, 1980.
52. NCSS Annual Report 1930–31.
53. See Snape, 2015a, pp. 51–83.
54. Snape, 2015b.
55. Coles, 1993, p. 6.
56. Snape, 2015a, p. 65.
57. Quoted in Jones, 1986, p. 167.
58. NCSS Annual Report 1929–30, p. 14.
59. Snape, 2015a, p. 62.
60. Harris, 1992, p. 126.
61. In July 1923 the Council published a memorandum setting out the objects and structure of a local council of social service and throughout this period it sought ways to strengthen the movement NCSS, 1923.
62. Minutes of Executive Committee, 24 June 1926; LMA/4016/IS/A/1/028.
63. NCSS Annual Report 1922; Finlayson, 1994, p. 265.
64. NCSS had given evidence to the inter-departmental committee of inquiry on Public Assistance. The recommendation to establish councils of social service to help with the coordination was supported by the Association of Municipal Corporations, Brasnett, 1969, p. 38.
65. Deedes had a distinguished career in the army, fighting in the Gallipoli campaign and serving as chief secretary of the Palestine government. In addition to his work with the Council, he was active locally in Bethnal Green in London and chaired the London Council of Social Service for ten years from 1936. See Mitchell, 1957, pp. 127–128.
66. Brasnett, 1969, p. 62.
67. Laybourn, 1994, p. 31.
68. A Central Churches group was established in May 1938. See Chap. 5 for a fuller discussion.
69. NCSS Annual Report 1926, p. 7.
70. NCSS Annual Report 1926, p. 7.
71. It is not entirely the case that the Council had no tradition of rural engagement to draw on. A rural department had been established before the First World War by Horace Plunkett and W.G.S. Adams and was instrumental in the setting up of the Development Commission by Lloyd George in 1909 to support rural affairs. In 1919 the rural department transferred its assets to the new Council to continue its work. Interview with David Clark, 15 August 2017.
72. Stevenson, 2003; Burchardt, 1999, p. 197.
73. NCSS Annual Report 1930–31, p. 10.
74. NCSS Annual Report 1936–37, p. 33.
75. Burchardt, 2012.
76. On the life and work of Grace Hadow, see Deneke, 1946, and Smith, 2004.
77. The Women's Institute was established in 1915 by suffragists as part of an international movement to improve the status of rural women. See, for example, Andrews, 1997.
78. On the history of the Oxfordshire Rural Community Council, see Campbell, 1970.
79. Burchardt, 2012, p. 90.

80. On the history of the Development Commission, see Rogers, 1999. See also Cripps, 1985.
81. Burchardt, 2012, p. 83.
82. Sir Henry Rew was a civil servant and agricultural economist and statistician, assistant secretary to the Board of Agriculture and secretary to the Ministry of Food. In addition to chairing the Village Clubs Association, he was chair of the farmers' club and president of the Royal Statistical Society. He unsuccessfully contested South Oxfordshire as a Liberal at the general elections of 1922 and 1923. He died in 1929. See *The Times*, 9 April 1929, p. 18.
83. See Morgan, 1947, p. 90.
84. Burchardt, 2012, p. 100.
85. Ibid., p. 94.
86. Burchardt, 1999, p. 208.
87. Brasnett, 1969, p. 51.
88. NCSS Annual Report 1936–37, p. 35.
89. NCSS Annual Report 1938–39, p. 33.
90. NCSS Annual Report 1922.
91. Burchardt, 2012, p. 98.
92. NCSS Annual Report 1938–39.
93. Coles, 1993, pp. 3–4.
94. Burchardt, 2012, p. 96. See also Jeans, 1990, p. 250.
95. Brasnett, 1969, p. 65.
96. Snape, 2015a, p. 66.
97. Mess and King, 1947, p. 70.
98. Snape, 2015a, p. 67.
99. See Stapleton, 1994.
100. Barker, 1953, p. 176.
101. On Becontree and Dagenham, see Young, 1934.
102. Mess and King, 1947, p. 71.
103. NCSS Annual Report 1936–37, pp. 20–21.
104. NCSS Annual Report 1936–37, p. 22.
105. Brasnett, 1969, p. 64.
106. NCSS Annual Report 1938–39, p. 47.
107. Snape, 2015a, p. 68.
108. See, for example, Olechnowicz, 1997.
109. Garside, 2004, p. 262. See also Garside, 2000.
110. NCSS Annual Report 1938–39, p. 47.
111. Snape, 2015a, p. 68.
112. NCSS Annual Report 1930–31, p. 14.
113. Brasnett, 1969, p. 26; NCSS Annual Report 1927–28.
114. NCSS Annual Report 1923, p. 7.
115. NCSS Annual Report 1937–38, p. 19.
116. NCSS Annual Report 1937–38, p. 16.
117. Political and Economic Planning, 1937, p. 174; NCSS Annual Report 1937–38.
118. NCSS Annual Report 1927–28, p. 32.
119. NCSS Annual Report 1927–28, p. 32.
120. NCSS Annual Report 1937–38, p. 21.
121. Political and Economic Planning, 1937, p. 174.

122. Minutes of Executive Committee, 14 January 1926; LMA/4016/IS/A/01/028.
123. Minutes of Executive Committee, 10 December 1931; LMA/4016/IS/A/01/029.
124. NCSS Annual Report 1927–28, p. 8. In 2013 a new charity, Step Up to Serve, was established with the support of the three main political parties in the UK to promote youth social action. It too had a focus on action and 'character'. See www.iwill.org.uk
125. NCSS Annual Report 1926, p. 32.
126. NCSS Annual Report 1936–37.
127. Davies, 2015, p. 109.
128. Finlayson, 1994, p. 236.
129. Brasnett, 1969, p. 55.
130. See, for example, Benn, 1925, p. 227.
131. Owen, 1964, p. 337.
132. Minutes of Executive Committee, 16 June 1927; LMA/4016/IS/A/01/028.
133. NCSS Annual Report 1926, p. 50.
134. NCSS Annual Report 1937–38, p. 78. See also Mess and Braithwaite, 1947, p. 189.
135. The establishment of CAF is discussed further in Chap. 7.
136. The Prince of Wales became patron in 1927. He continued in this role during his short-lived tenure as King and was replaced as patron by his successor George VI, with the Duke of Kent becoming vice-patron.
137. *The Times,* 9 June 1928, p. 11.
138. NCSS Annual Report 1927–28.
139. Minutes of Executive Committee, 23 April 1931, LMA/4016/IS/A/01/029.
140. Brasnett, 1969, p. 84.
141. Ellis wrote well-received military histories of the Welsh Guards, 1946 and the war in France and Flanders, 1953.
142. Owens, J. 1970, 'Major L. Ellis', *The Times,* 26 October 1970, p. 10.
143. Clements, 1971.
144. NCSS Annual Report 1936–37.
145. Minutes of Executive Committee, 25 February 1937, LMA/4016/IS/A/01/030(2).
146. Smeal, 1969, p. 10.
147. NCSS Annual Report 1937–38, p. 81.
148. Minutes of Executive Committee, 10 April 1930; LMA/4016/IS/A/01/029.
149. Minutes of Executive Committee, 16 July 1936; LMA/4016/IS/A/01/030(1).
150. NCSS Annual Report 1937–38; Minutes of Executive Committee, 29 April 1937; LMA/4016/IS/A/01/030(2).
151. On the link between Idealism and the documentary movement, see Aitken, 1989.
152. Ffrancon, 2004, p. 107.
153. Ibid., p. 115.
154. Minutes of Public Relations Committee, 21 December 1937; LMA/4016/IS/A/01/030(4).
155. The Council finally changed its name to the National Council for Voluntary Organisations in April 1980. See Chap. 8 for a fuller discussion.

156. *Memorandum on NCSS constitution* from L. Ellis, 12 October 1932; LMA/4016/IS/A/01/029.
157. NCSS Annual Report 1928–29, p. 18.
158. Macadam, 1934, p. 71.
159. Harrison, 1988, p. 7.

References

Adderley, S. (2015). *Bureaucratic conceptions of citizenship in the voluntary sector (1919–1939): The case of the National Council of Social Service*. Unpublished PhD thesis, Bangor University.

Aitken, I. (1989). John Grierson, Idealism and the inter-war period. *Historical Journal of Film, Radio and Television, 9*(3), 247–258.

Andrews, M. (1997). *The acceptable face of feminism: The Women's Institute as a social movement*. London: Lawrence & Wishart.

Barker, E. (1953). *Age and youth*. Oxford: Oxford University Press.

Beaven, B., & Griffiths, J. (2008). Creating the exemplary citizen: The changing notion of citizenship in Britain, 1870–1939. *Contemporary British History, 22*(2), 203–225.

Benn, E. (1925). *The confessions of a capitalist*. London: Hutchinson.

Braithwaite, C. (1938). *The voluntary citizen: An enquiry into the place of philanthropy in the community*. London: Methuen.

Brasnett, M. (1969). *Voluntary social action*. London: NCSS.

Burchardt, J. (1999). Reconstructing the rural community: Village halls and the National Council of Social Service, 1919 to 1939. *Rural History, 10*(2), 193–216.

Burchardt, J. (2011). Rethinking the rural idyll: The English rural community movement, 1913–26. *Cultural and Social History, 8*(1), 73–94.

Burchardt, J. (2012). State and society in the English countryside: The rural community movement, 1918–39. *Rural History, 23*(1), 81–106.

Campbell, M. (1970). *The Oxfordshire Rural Community Council: A history of the first fifty years, 1920–1970*. Oxford: Hadow House.

Clements, R. (1971). Lionel Ellis. *Social Service Quarterly, 44*(3), 100–102.

Coles, K. (1993). *National Council for Voluntary Organisations from 1919 to 1993: A selective summary of NCVO's work and origins*. London: NCVO.

Cripps, J. (1985). *Christmas coals to community care: The countryside – Past, present and future. The Sir John Haynes memorial lecture 1984*. London: NCVO.

Davies, R. (2015). *Public good by private means: How philanthropy shapes Britain*. London: Alliance Publishing Trust.

Den Otter, S. (1996). *British idealism and social explanation: A study in late Victorian thought*. Oxford: Clarendon.

Deneke, H. (1946). *Grace Hadow*. London: Oxford University Press.

Ellis, L. (1946). *Welsh Guards at war*. Aldershot: Gale and Polden.

Ellis, L. (1953). *The war in France and Flanders, 1939–40*. London: Imperial War Museum.

Ffrancon, G. (2004). Documenting the depression in South Wales: Today we live and Eastern Valley. *Welsh History Review, 22*(1), 103–125.

Finlayson, G. (1994). *Citizen, state, and social welfare in Britain 1830–1990*. Oxford: Clarendon Press.

Garside, P. (2000). *The conduct of philanthropy: William Sutton Trust, 1900–2000*. London: The Athlone Press.

Garside, P. (2004). Citizenship, civil society and quality of life: Sutton model dwellings estates, 1919–39. In R. Colls & R. Rodger (Eds.), *Cities of ideas: Civil society and urban governance in Britain, 1800–2000* (pp. 258–282). Aldershot: Ashgate.

Harris, J. (1992). Political thought and the welfare state, 1870–1940: An intellectual framework for British social policy. *Past and Present, 135*, 116–141.

Harrison, B. (1988). Historical perspectives. In B. Harrison & N. Deakin (Eds.), *Voluntary organisations and democracy: Sir George Haynes lecture, 1987*. London: NCVO.

Jeans, D. (1990). Planning and the myth of the English countryside in the interwar period. *Rural History, 1*(2), 249–264.

Jones, S. (1986). *Workers at play: A social and economic history of leisure, 1918–1939*. London: Routledge & Kegan Paul.

Kent, J. (1992). *William Temple: Church, state and society in Britain, 1880–1950*. Cambridge: Cambridge University Press.

Laybourn, K. (1994). *The Guild of Help and the changing face of Edwardian philanthropy: The Guild of Help, voluntary work and the state, 1904–1919*. Lampeter: The Edwin Mellen Press.

Macadam, E. (1934). *The new philanthropy: A study of the relations between the statutory and voluntary social services*. London: Allen and Unwin.

Marwick, A. (1964). Middle opinion in the thirties: Planning, progress and political "agreement". *English Historical Review, 79*, 285–298.

McCarthy, H. (2007). Parties, voluntary associations, and democratic politics in interwar Britain. *The Historical Journal, 50*(4), 891–912.

McCarthy, H. (2008). Service clubs, citizenship and equality: Gender relations and middle-class associations in Britain between the wars. *Historical Research, 81*(213), 531–552.

McCarthy, H. (2011). Associational voluntarism in interwar Britain. In M. Hilton & J. McKay (Eds.), *The ages of voluntarism: How we got to the big society* (pp. 47–68). Oxford: Oxford University Press for British Academy.

McCarthy, H., & Thane, P. (2011). The politics of association in industrial society. *Twentieth Century British History, 22*(2), 217–229.

McKibbin, R. (1988). *Classes and cultures: England, 1918–1951*. Oxford: Oxford University Press.

Mess, H., & Braithwaite, C. (1947). The finance of voluntary social services. In H. Mess (Ed.), *Voluntary social services since 1918* (pp. 188–203). London: Kegan Paul.

Mess, H., & King, H. (1947). Community centres and community associations. In H. Mess (Ed.), *Voluntary social services since 1918* (pp. 69–79). London: Kegan Paul.

Mitchell, G. (1957). Sir Wyndham Deedes – A tribute. *Social Service Quarterly, 30*(3), 127–128.

Morgan, J. (1947). The National Council of Social Service. In H. Mess (Ed.), *Voluntary social services since 1918* (pp. 80–105). London: Kegan Paul.

NCSS (1919a, March). *Memorandum*. London: NCSS.

NCSS (1919b, December). *Memorandum on the relation of voluntary social service to the work of the public authorities: With special reference to the proposed reconstitution of the public assistance authority*. London: NCSS.

NCSS. (1920). *Reconstruction and social service: Being the report of a conference called by the National Council of Social Service.* London: NCSS.

NCSS. (1923). *Social service in towns: A programme.* London: NCSS.

Offer, J. (1999). Idealist thought, social policy and the rediscovery of informal care. *British Journal of Sociology, 50*(3), 467–488.

Offer, J. (2003). Idealism versus non-idealism: New light on social policy and voluntary action in Britain since 1880. *Voluntas: International Journal of Voluntary and Nonprofit Organizations, 14*(2), 227–240.

Olechnowicz, A. (1997). *Working-class housing in England between the wars. The Becontree Estate.* Oxford: Clarendon Press.

Owen, D. (1964). *English philanthropy, 1660–1960.* London: Oxford University Press.

Political and Economic Planning. (1937). *Report on the British social services: A survey of the existing public social services in Great Britain with proposals for future development.* London: PEP.

Prochaska, F. (1988). *The voluntary impulse: Philanthropy in modern Britain.* London: Faber and Faber.

Putnam, R. (1993). *Making democracy work: Civic traditions in modern Italy.* Princeton: Princeton University Press.

Putnam, R. (2000). *Bowling alone: The collapse and revival of American community.* New York: Simon & Schuster.

Rogers, A. (1999). *The most revolutionary measure: A history of the Rural Development Commission, 1909–1999.* Salisbury: Rural Development Commission.

Shapely, P. (2011). Civil society, class and locality: Tenant groups in post-war Britain. In M. Hilton & J. McKay (Eds.), *The ages of voluntarism: How we got to the big society* (pp. 94–113). Oxford: Oxford University Press for British Academy.

Smeal, J. (1969). Leonard Shoeten Sack. *Social Service Quarterly, 43*(1), 7–10.

Smith, T. (2004). Grace Eleanor Hadow. In *Oxford dictionary of national biography.* Oxford: Oxford University Press.

Snape, R. (2015a). The new leisure, voluntarism and social reconstruction in inter-war Britain. *Contemporary British History, 29*(1), 51–83.

Snape, R. (2015b). Voluntary action and leisure: An historical perspective, 1830–1939. *Voluntary Sector Review, 6*(1), 153–171.

Stapleton, J. (1994). *Englishness and the study of politics: The social and political thought of Ernest Barker.* Cambridge: Cambridge University Press.

Stevenson, J. (2003). The countryside, planning and civil society in Britain, 1926–1947. In J. Harris (Ed.), *Civil society in British history: Ideas, identities, institutions* (pp. 191–211). Oxford: Oxford University Press.

Taylor, A. J. P. (1965). *English history, 1914–1945.* Oxford: Oxford University Press.

Thane, P., & Evans, T. (2012). *Sinners? Scroungers? Saints? Unmarried motherhood in twentieth-century England.* Oxford: Oxford University Press.

Turner, J. (1980). *Lloyd George's secretariat.* Cambridge: Cambridge University Press.

Vincent, A., & Plant, R. (1984). *Philosophy, politics and citizenship: The life and thought of the British idealists.* Oxford: Blackwell.

Young, T. (1934). *Becontree and Dagenham: A report made for the pilgrim trust.* London: Pilgrim Trust.

CHAPTER 4

Out of Adversity

INTRODUCTION

Historians are divided on the significance of the depression of the inter-war period. For many it was the defining feature, impacting not only on the lives of the individuals most affected but shaping the spirit of the age.[1] Others have suggested that too much has been made of it and that, although it cast a shadow over the worst-hit areas, the reality for the majority of the population was very different.[2] They point to the fact that the economy grew overall and the economic downturn in Britain was less pronounced than in many other countries. Moreover, outside of the Special Areas, much of the population experienced rising living standards and a reduction in working hours which, when combined with a growth in commercial leisure opportunities, meant the experience for many people was less grinding poverty and more one of opportunity after the privations of the war. The truth is probably somewhere in between and points to a vast split within UK society, largely along geographic lines. For every 'murdered' town like Jarrow, there were communities that in the resonant phrase of Martin Pugh 'danced all night'.[3]

This dichotomy was reflected in the work of the Council. Although from 1928 to the outbreak of the Second World War its main preoccupation was the *unemployment question*, it didn't abandon its other activities. Work continued to build up the network of rural community councils and village halls and also, though less successfully, a network of councils of social service in towns and cities. Much attention was also paid to the provision of social and community facilities for families uprooted from the inner cities after the war to new towns and housing estates. Here the focus was on building and strengthening locally controlled residents and community associations and the construction of community centres, which it was hoped would serve as the engine house of community regeneration. And at the heart of all this activity was a belief, imbued by the Idealist philosophy of the Council's founding fathers, in the power of voluntary action to change lives. In a sense it mattered not what the conditions

© The Author(s) 2019
J. Davis Smith, *100 Years of NCVO and Voluntary Action*,
https://doi.org/10.1007/978-3-030-02774-2_4

of the individual were. For those blighted by the scourge of long-term unemployment and those enjoying the fruits of economic success, voluntary action was deemed essential for individual and collective fulfilment. 'Human personality', whatever the individual circumstances, the Council wrote, 'can be fully developed only by the voluntary exercise of individual ability, and the riches of the common wealth can only be realised fully if all will make their personal contribution of experience, skill and self-sacrifice to the common effort'.[4]

The Council's unemployment work was hugely controversial, with critics accusing it of providing a cover for the failed employment policies of the National Government. But it was also its making. For ten years it had made solid, if rather slow, progress towards its founding goals. It had achieved one or two notable successes, but its influence and visibility outside a small band of devotees was limited and its funds extremely tight. While there was never any serious question about its ongoing sustainability, the annual report produced on its tenth anniversary was honest in its appraisal about its limitations and what was required for it to forge ahead in its second decade.[5] By the outbreak of the Second World War, the picture looked very different. The Council, if not a household name, was increasingly well known throughout the country. It had the King as its patron, was the subject of numerous interventions in Parliament, had commissioned two documentary films by leading film-makers, received more than £1 million of public money to distribute to the voluntary movement, and could draw upon the support of some of the most senior academics, public servants, and industrialists of the age.

The Unemployment Question

After a brief bounce following the end of the First World War, the British economy took a sharp downturn in the early 1920s, resulting in severe contraction in the old industrial heartlands of Scotland, South Wales, and the north of England. From 1920 to the outbreak of war, the number of registered unemployed never fell below one million and reached almost three million in 1932.[6] There was a long history of support for unemployed people within the voluntary movement, embracing philanthropy and mutual aid. The guilds of help were active in providing relief in the years leading up to the First World War and such support intensified following the general strike of 1926.[7] Many councils of social service got involved in relief activities, with the Society of Friends and the Workers' Educational Association (WEA) also prominent.[8] In 1928 the Lord Mayor of London's Mansion House Fund was reopened to collect and distribute money and clothing for the relief of distress in the coalfields. Concerned about the lack of organisation, the Council set up a network of local committees to coordinate the relief, overseen by a national committee of voluntary organisations and local mayors from the affected areas.[9] In total, over £1.7 million was collected and distributed to communities in need over a two-year period.[10] In 1929, with the economic situation worsening, the Council embarked on two new initiatives aimed at finding, according to Margaret

Brasnett, 'a cautious middle course' between 'soup kitchen and revolution'.[11] First, it set up a small scheme to relocate miners and their families to villages where work was available, offering low-cost prefabricated accommodation to ease the process. Second, it launched a pilot educational programme for unemployed workers in South Wales and the north east of England, with support from the Carnegie UK Trust.[12]

From the outset the Council was clear its contribution was not primarily about helping those out of work to find employment, but deal with the social impact of worklessness or, as its annual report for 1928–29 put it, 'to provide mental stimulus and to re-awaken interests'.[13] The period saw the publication of a number of reports on the psychological impact of 'enforced idleness', one of the most influential being the Pilgrim Trust's *Men Without Work*, commissioned by the future Archbishop of Canterbury, William Temple, on which the Council collaborated.[14] 'Those who cannot get work', the Council would later argue, 'need more than the means to keep body and soul together – they need also food for their minds and some purpose to fill empty days.'[15] Educational classes were set up in the pilot areas on topics as diverse as literature, biology, and the lives of great composers (1000 records were donated by HMV and wireless sets loaned by the BBC) and men were encouraged to put on plays, concerts, and sporting events, under the instruction of trained leaders.[16] Take up was deemed good, although it was acknowledged that the numbers reached merely scratched the surface. What was required was a national programme to deal with a national crisis.

THE OCCUPATIONAL CLUB MOVEMENT

In 1932 an event occurred that transformed the fortunes of the Council. On 27 January the Prince of Wales, patron since 1927, delivered a speech at the Royal Albert Hall calling for the nation to unite in service to communities most affected by the depression. 'My appeal here', he said, 'is not to statesmen, nor even to philanthropists, but to all those who are in work, to play the part of neighbour and friend to the man out of work.' Personal service, he added, is 'the open road of duty and a short cut to happiness all round'.[17] The speech was broadcast across the nation, with the *Manchester Guardian* noting it had been listened to at over 200 schools and on board HMS Courageous and the Royal Marine Depot at Deal.[18] Within a few months, the Council was in touch with over 700 local projects set up to offer assistance. Messages of support were received from the Archbishops of Canterbury and Westminster and the Chief Rabbi.[19] It was the first of a series of interventions by the Prince who, over the next few years, made numerous visits to the depressed areas. Frank Prochaska locates such work within the tradition of a *Welfare Monarchy* and it marked the beginning of a long association between the royal family and the Council.[20] Such patronage could bring benefits in terms of increased profile. George Haynes remembers the Prince having 'a charisma in those days which was unique'.[21] However, it could also bring problems. In November 1936 the

Council organised a visit for the now King Edward VIII to projects in South Wales. In October it wrote to the Palace expressing concern over the timing of the visit and asking if it could be changed. New controversial unemployment policies were being introduced, and it suggested that 'the agitators will say that his visit is intended to distract attention from the regulations, and to mark by royal approval what is being done by the Ministry of Labour and other bodies'.[22] The Palace turned down the request and the visit went ahead without any problems, although the minister of labour, Ernest Brown, decided to stay away.[23] The King's official biographer, Philip Ziegler, suggests that his reception in South Wales was par for the course and that during the visits, while 'occasionally, though, rarely, he was angrily rebuffed, more often he was met by sullen apathy'.[24]

In the aftermath of the speech, the Council set up new structures to deal with the increased demand. A special unemployment committee was established in November 1932 and regional offices opened in Leeds, Birmingham, and Cardiff. The chair of the unemployment committee was A.D. Lindsay, master of Balliol College, Oxford, who was involved in several pilot educational projects in the depressed areas in the late 1920s and served on the Pilgrim Trust's *Men Without Work* inquiry.[25] An Idealist, Christian socialist, and keen supporter of the WEA, Lindsay shared the Council's belief in the value of *meaningful* leisure and the importance of voluntary action as a route to citizenship.[26] Like the Council, he believed that the main scourge of unemployment was not material need but psychological deprivation. The unemployed, he wrote in 1933, 'felt like ghosts – they had no function or status in the community'.[27] The state, he argued, had a role to play in alleviating distress, but so too did the voluntary movement.[28] Lindsay led the Council's unemployment work for over a decade and later stood, unsuccessfully, as an Independent Progressive candidate against the government in the Oxford City by-election in 1938.[29]

GOVERNMENT FUNDING

The early 1930s saw increased levels of protest and civil unrest in towns and cities throughout the UK in the face of rising levels of unemployment, which had reached three million by 1932. It was a time of hunger marches and street battles and, according to Richard Flanagan, represented 'the bloodiest era of the politics of the unemployed in Britain'.[30] On 19 December 1932 the prime minister, Ramsay MacDonald, addressed the nation on the BBC from his constituency in Lossiemouth and announced that the new National Government had asked the Council to coordinate the work of the unemployment clubs. Later that same evening in the House of Commons, it was confirmed that the Council would be given a grant of £10,000 to support this work.[31] The original intention had been to channel the grants through local authorities, but the Cabinet Committee on Unemployment had expressed a clear preference to work through the voluntary movement.[32] The Council, which had been in discussion with the government for several months, agreed to the request only after securing a commitment that the scheme would be voluntary and it would be free to influence the shape of the programme.[33] It turned down a contribution towards running costs, a decision that helped combat the fierce criticism that came its way for associating so closely with the government but placed great strain on its finances. The first grant of £10,000 was made to the Council in 1933 and the amount grew rapidly over the next few years. By the outbreak of war, it had reached over £1.5 million.[34]

The initial grant came from the Ministry of Labour and carried with it certain conditions. It had to be matched pound for pound from voluntary sources and could only be used for capital costs and direct work with the unemployed, although a separate strand was available to support the activities of national and regional organisations. The main use of the funds was to support the development of the occupational centre movement, a network of clubs set up to provide social, occupational, and educational support to unemployed men and women. Although support for this movement was to dominate the Council's work for the next decade, it cannot lay claim to having founded it. It was modelled on two separate but related developments in 1927, one in the Rhondda Valley in South Wales and another one in Lincoln.[35] The Maes-yr-Haf Educational Settlement in Trealaw, in the Rhondda, was set up by the Quaker, Emma Noble, while the Lincoln People's Service Club was established by Alice Cameron of the WEA, both with involvement from Lindsay. Over the next few years, the Council supported hundreds of similar projects across Britain. Much of this work was bottom up and drew upon a 'working-class civilisation of the older type', based on notions of mutual aid and solidarity.[36] The Council steered away from imposing a national template for action, although a series of regional committees were established to oversee the work that served as a useful model for coordination when war broke out in 1939.

The focus of the occupational clubs changed over time. To start with, they were seen as a place for unemployed people to meet and carry out such practical tasks as boot repairing and mending clothes. But over the next few years, they broadened their scope to encompass a range of educational and leisure activities, especially drama and music, as it 'was soon felt that the men should be offered activities which would enable them to use their imagination as well as their hands'.[37] Two drama advisers were appointed to lead the work, one in the north of England, one in the Midlands and interest was high with over 40 drama groups being established in Durham alone. Feedback from members was generally positive, although concern was expressed in some areas that volunteers were pushing their own tastes. The 'most serious' problem, it was noted by one adviser, is that 'voluntary workers often have a wrong approach' and are 'inclined to foist the kind of drama to which they are accustomed on individuals to whom it is alien'.[38] Alongside drama and music, there was support for the development of allotments and, in association with the Society of Friends and the Ministry of Agriculture, a Land Settlement Association was established to help people relocate to cooperative smallholdings.[39]

Some clubs were self-governed by members, but in many of the larger areas a paid manager was employed, funded from government grants. Leadership was seen as crucial to success. Ellis told the unemployment committee in April 1933 that the quality of the clubs was variable and 'where a Centre is poorly equipped and lacks good leadership, interest tends to flag and membership to fall away'.[40] A central training centre was established at King's Standing near Burton-on-Trent in a building provided rent-free by the King. The Council also financed several centres run by other organisations, including Hardwick Hall in County Durham, Wincham Hall in Lancashire, and the Beeches in Birmingham, which catered for women only.[41] Here leaders were trained in a variety of craft skills to take back to their clubs. The quality of instruction appears to have been reasonably high, although a *courtesy* inspection on King's Standing by the Board of Education in January 1937 noted deficiencies in the quality of the equipment and accommodation on offer.[42] Accommodation for the local clubs was also a problem. Many were forced to rely on existing space, such as in Tyneside where a disused police station, Methodist chapel, and derelict paper mill were taken over, although in some areas clubs built their own centres using volunteer labour and donated materials.[43]

Although the main focus of the clubs was to support unemployed men and women, much was made of the fact that members took part in voluntary action. A leaflet produced by the Council, *Unemployment and Community Service*, emphasised the extent of this reciprocity, with members organising parties for young people and making children's toys and *comforts* for the elderly.[44] There were also larger public work projects, including reclaiming derelict sites for children's playgrounds and building community centres and clubhouses. One of the most celebrated examples was at Brynmawr in South Wales, where club members transformed a mining tip into a park with an open-air swimming pool.[45] Funding for the clubs came from a mix of sources. The stipulation that government grants had to be matched locally gave a boost to fundraising and by March 1937 over £600,000 had been raised from voluntary sources.[46] In addition, a number of local businesses donated materials, equipment, and even premises. Members were required to make a contribution to the running of the clubs through a subscription, usually a penny a week.[47] Support also came from parts of the country unaffected by the depression. At the end of the war a number of British towns *adopted* communities in France and Belgium to help with reconstruction, and the same spirit of solidarity was now extended to depression-hit towns. Surrey adopted Jarrow, Bath adopted Redruth, Oxford twinned with Risca in South Wales, and Ruislip adopted South Hylton, with over 100 adoptions in total, most supported by grants administered by the Council.[48] In addition to town-to-town adoptions, there was support of individual clubs by groups of staff, such as that given in Gateshead by employees of the BBC and by Bristol tobacco workers to clubs in Somerset and South Wales. Public sector employees were especially active, supporting over 150 clubs and setting up their own civil service national committee to coordinate relief activity. Examples included adoption by the Government Actuary's Department of a town in the Potteries and by the Patent Office of towns in Lancashire and Durham.[49]

THE SPECIAL AREAS

From 1935 a second wave of funding came from the Special Areas Commission. The new funding was to support activity taking place in the Special Areas, designated communities worst hit by the depression, such as Northumberland, Cumberland, Durham, South Wales, and Scotland, and it carried fewer restrictions than the Ministry of Labour grant.[50] The women's clubs in particular benefited from the removal of the earlier restrictions and expanded rapidly after 1935. They were mainly set up to cater for the wives of unemployed men and were often offshoots of the men's clubs. Close links were made with existing bodies such as Women's Institutes and Townswomen's Guilds and with local education authorities, which provided teachers to run the educational sessions. As with the men's clubs, the focus of the women's clubs was on crafts and education and the range of interests catered for was wide. For example, in West Cumberland a small group of clubs offered instruction in such diverse fields as dressmaking, handicrafts, weaving, cookery, keep fit, joinery, drama, choral singing, geography, European history, biology, literature, and foreign affairs.[51] The women's clubs were usually separate from men's, although often shared the same premises. Relations were not always cordial, with Henry Mess noting that 'in the early days there was considerable ungraciousness on the part of the men in some areas, and a good deal of friction'.[52]

Grants were also used for holiday camps for women and children in the Special Areas, with 150,000 children attending by 1939.[53] Feedback was generally positive, with one attendee in South Wales telling the camp organiser that 'this is the first holiday I have had since I was married fourteen years ago'.[54] There were claims of health benefits for young people attending, with one report suggesting an average weight increase per young person of £3.[55] Some of the camps were organised by students under the banner of the Universities Council for Unemployed Camps, again with funding from the Council.[56] Camps were also provided for unemployed men, but the Council was keen to emphasise their voluntary nature and draw a distinction with the compulsory work camps set up by the Labour and National governments.[57] These were hugely controversial, with the Communist-controlled National Unemployed Workers' Movement (NUWM) accusing the governments of creating 'slave camps'.[58] For the Council, voluntary action was incompatible with compulsion. In November 1933 Ellis wrote to the minister of labour, Sir Henry Betterton, arguing for the removal of the provision within the Unemployment Bill requiring anyone claiming benefit to attend a training camp if required. 'In the long run', he wrote, 'the welfare of those who cannot get work will best be secured by measures which foster their self-respect, rather than by those which hurt their pride, and there is always danger that compulsion may destroy the moral value of effort and lead to resentment rather than self-respect.'[59] Betterton replied offering minor concessions but refused to rule out compulsion.[60] He later resigned as minister of labour and took up a new role as chair of the Unemployment Assistance Board, which took over responsibility for funding the Council's unemployment work. During the war, now Lord Rushcliffe, he chaired the committee set up by the government to oversee relations with the voluntary movement.[61] With its work expanding, the Executive Committee was forced to reconsider its refusal to accept a management fee. 'It had been thought desirable', it noted, 'that the whole of the Council's Headquarters work should be financed from voluntary sources.'[62] This was no longer deemed possible. A small contribution of £2000 was negotiated for 1935–36, which increased slightly over the next few years, but never rose above six per cent of total costs, according to Brasnett.[63] Adherence to the principle of full-cost recovery was still many years away.

OPPOSITION

The Council's work on unemployment was hugely controversial. It faced criticism within Parliament and outside, and its reputation in some quarters was severely damaged. It attempted to build bridges with its critics, but stood by its principles, arguing that it was its duty to mobilise the voluntary movement to relieve the suffering it observed. A similar debate took place 50 years later, when the Council again played a significant role in mobilising the voluntary sector, with government funds, to support communities affected by high levels of unemployment. As with the experience in the 1930s, it again faced accusations that it was letting the government off the hook for not doing more to get people back into work.[64] Both episodes raised fundamental questions about the Council's relationship with government and whether, by taking significant sums of money, it was in danger of being co-opted. Bernard Harris has argued that the payments taken by the Council in the 1930s 'transformed the nature of the relationship between the state and the voluntary sector' and resulted in it, and other organisations in receipt of statutory funding, being seen 'increasingly as the agents and instruments of government policy'.[65] The Council would spend much of the next 70 years attempting to shift this perception.

Within Parliament the loudest voices of condemnation came from Labour members representing the depression-hit areas, reflecting a long-held antipathy within parts of the Labour movement towards charity.[66] In December 1932 George Buchanan, MP for Gorbals, told the House of Commons that the unemployed 'do not need charity from anyone', but 'decent social justice' and 'the conditions and the income that other people possess'.[67] Pushing the criticism further, Joseph Batey, MP for Spennymoor in Durham, told the House that the government 'are simply using the National Council of Social Services and the Personal Service League in order to justify doing nothing themselves', and he demanded that any money available should be given 'to the unemployed to feed and clothe them' rather than to the Council 'in order that unemployed young men may attend dramatic classes or physical culture classes'.[68] Ellen Wilkinson, MP for Jarrow, later accused the voluntary movement of not being 'concerned with a frontal attack on the problem'.[69] The criticism was echoed outside Parliament. In *The Road to Wigan Pier*, George Orwell wrote that the occupational centres were 'simply a device to keep the unemployed quiet and give them the illusion that something is being done for them', although he admitted that the 'rubbish' being provided was better than nothing.[70] J.B. Priestley was similarly critical when visiting clubs and settlements during his *English Journey*, suggesting that as a nation we ought to be 'ashamed of ourselves' for the lack of action, although he praised the Tyneside Council of Social Service for the 'determined efforts' it was making.[71] The Communist Party was particularly scathing. Wal Hannington, leader of the NUWM, described by the *Guardian* in 1923 as 'The Napoleon of the unemployed' suggested that the work of the Council demonstrated 'how craftily the ruling class, by evoking the sentiment of charity, have sought to cover up their sins and omissions in the treatment of the unemployed'.[72] The government was aware of the criticisms. In December 1932 the prime minister wrote to the Council expressing concern about the negative reaction to the work, which, he said, was being spread 'by a number of persons who wish to make political capital out of our present distress or to use it for the purpose of stirring up evil temper'.[73] In January 1933 the prime minister's private secretary, Thomas Jones, wrote to a friend that 'there has been a feeling since the P.M.'s Lossiemouth speech that the Government were trying to fob off the unemployed with a miserable grant of a few thousand pounds to Ellis's show'.[74]

The Council could afford to ignore the criticism from the NUWM, but it was aware of the dangers of alienating the mainstream Labour movement, whose support was required to recruit men to the clubs. Attempts were made to get the Trades Union Congress (TUC) to join the unemployment committee, without success, although relations were better at a local level, with trade union branches cooperating with clubs in a number of areas.[75] Union opposition was focused on occupational activities and public works, which it was feared would take work from members and undercut rates of pay.[76] Some local traders also complained of unfair competition, although the Council tried to allay these fears by insisting that no items made in the clubs should be available for sale.[77] In 1939 the Council admitted that cooperation with the trade unions had been 'rather incomplete' and that many 'have suspected the movement of political bias and of using the clubs and workshops to undercut local tradesmen'.[78] There was also criticism from other voluntary groups. Some thought they should have been given the central coordinating role. Others expressed concern about competition, with Lady Denman telling the unemployment committee in January 1938 that the work of the women's clubs 'will overlap that of the Townswomen's Guilds'.[79] One anonymous correspondent wrote to the chair of the Council in 1938 complaining that it had 'placed itself in the position of exclusive receiver of grants from HM's Government and the national Trusts' and was not 'universally popular'.[80]

Opposition, however, was not universal. The Labour movement itself was by no means united in its condemnation. The Labour Party leader, George Lansbury, expressed his support, both in Parliament and in a foreword he wrote to a Council booklet, *Unemployment and Opportunity*, in which he praised 'the human effort being made by men and women of all parties, creeds and churches on behalf of the victims of the cruel, pitiless unemployment which curses our land'.[81] The Party's spokesman on unemployment, John Lawson, also gave his backing, describing the Council's work as 'estimable'.[82] Support, perhaps less surprisingly, was also forthcoming from the other main political parties. Sir Geoffrey Mander, Liberal MP for Wolverhampton East, told the Commons in March 1933 that through the Council 'most admirable work can be and is being done', while Godfrey Nicholson, Conservative member for Morpeth, said his criticism of the government is not that it 'spends too much in grants to the Council, and to kindred associations' but that it has 'spent far too little', adding that in his experience 'the vast majority of unemployed men approach these centres most willingly and are most anxious that they should flourish'.[83]

A REASSESSMENT

Historians have generally been harsh on the Council. John Stevenson and Chris Cook have argued that the numbers of people involved in the clubs 'were too small to have a really significant impact' and that the government saw the voluntary response 'as a cheap palliative for a minority of those out of work rather than a mass programme'.[84] Flanagan is even more critical. He suggests the Council was 'a creature of the government' and its job 'was to politically emasculate the unemployed'.[85] The quality of the clubs and accommodation provided, he argues, was poor and they were never controlled by members.[86] He also criticises the content of the courses taught, suggesting there was little attempt to engage with the rich heritage of working-class culture and that they 'strived to impress upon the unemployed the great virtue of bourgeois literature'.[87] Robert Snape agrees and suggests that the clubs failed to draw on alternative traditions of working-class leisure, exemplified by the Miners' Institutes or the Clarion movement, with its mix of socialism and communal activities based around cycling, rambling, choirs, and sport.[88]

Before concurring with these conclusions, it is worth looking at the evidence of impact. First, the numbers involved. By 1939 it was estimated that there were about 900 occupational clubs for men and about 600 for women, with a total membership of about 150,000.[89] Critics can rightly argue that this represented less than one in ten of the eligible people out of work who could have joined, but the numbers are significant. In Crook, Durham, it was estimated that almost half the unemployed were members of one club or another.[90] Second, members had to pay to join and many continued in the clubs after they found work, which suggests they saw a value in membership. Clearly not all experiences were positive. A report published by the Council in 1939, *Out of*

Adversity, based on a survey of 250 men's and women's clubs, gave an even-handed assessment. Overall the report was upbeat. The most significant finding was felt to be 'the confidence, expressed by the majority of those who responded, that their club has found its place in its community'.[91] However, take up was not uniform, with most clubs catering mainly for unskilled workers and greater success reported in small towns than large cities. There was acknowledgement of the limitations of the clubs in dealing with people who had been out of work for more than a year and for whom, it was admitted, 'no kind of provision can be adequate for them, except work or training which will lead to work'.[92] One critic has argued that the evidence points 'to a lack of interest, disillusionment and suspicion' among the unemployed.[93] Such a judgement is difficult to uphold. While it might have been true for some people, it was not true for others. Take, for example, this letter from a participant at the King's Standing Residential Centre:

> I am sure you will be pleased to hear I have found work. My three weeks at King's Standing put new life and vim in me. I went back determined not to stay out of work. So I packed up on Wednesday and came to Birmingham, got a job on the Thursday morning, started on the Friday and had my wife and bairns with me in a fortnight. I owe it all to you and the staff at King's Standing. My outlook on life changed and the aimless, hopeless existence on the dole I saw in a new light. Please remember me to all the staff and tell them one Yorkshire man blesses the day he went to King's Standing.[94]

Or this note from the wife of an unemployed miner who attended a residential training course at the Beeches:

> How quickly the time has passed since I left the Beeches and yet each day, I seem to live every day, of that fortnight over again, it will be a memory to me, for a long time to come. I enjoyed every moment of it. I am trying to carry out the things that I learnt there. I had a big reception, at the club last Thursday evening, I gave a lengthy account of the work, we had to do, I have never spoken at a meeting before ... I realise it is difficult to get people to make new paths in their brain, but they will do it, if someone will show them how, that is our duty.[95]

The occupational clubs were clearly insufficient to deal with the magnitude of the crisis affecting the nation. As a voluntary response, however, especially in comparison to the paucity of official provision, they can be judged to have made a significant contribution to alleviating distress. It is worth reflecting on what other options were available to the Council. It could have refused the government's request and not taken the money. But there would have been little justification. The pilot projects in 1929 had convinced it of the value of such interventions and it had been looking for ways to extend them. The Council was clearly well placed to coordinate the work and the nature of the activity aligned closely with its aims. There is no suggestion that by taking the money it was guilty of mission drift, an accusation that would be levelled against it later in the century. With an establishment dominated by Treasury orthodoxy, it is inconceivable that by refusing the grant it could have forced the government to adopt a more expansive, interventionist policy. The Council was doing what it was set up to do, mobilising voluntary action for the benefit of society, and it achieved all that could reasonably have been expected.

There was a second option open to the Council, which was to take the money, use it for good purposes, but make a firmer public statement about its limitations. A stronger case can be made for this course of action. The Council was under no illusion that the voluntary response was only a partial solution to the crisis: 'Its importance would be over-rated and indeed the movement would be wholly misunderstood', it wrote, 'if it were regarded as in any way a substitute for whatever can be done by other means to increase employment or to better the lot of those who cannot get work.'[96] Lindsay, as chair of the Council's unemployment committee, wrote to Ellis in February 1933 acknowledging that 'our trouble at present is that people think the Government is trying to cover what they regard as an unsatisfactory policy on unemployment and the Means Test by encouraging voluntary organisations'. He concluded by suggesting that the Council needed to be better at articulating a case that 'whatever the State may do, there are certain things that can only be done by voluntary service'.[97] Even the Prince of Wales was minded to point out the limitations. In his speech to the nation on the second anniversary of his Albert Hall address, in January 1934, again broadcast live on the BBC, he emphasised that occupational clubs were 'only a stop-gap' and that 'no one wants to go on indefinitely mending boots or making book-shelves'.[98] The Council should have been more strident in making this point. The timing of the government's approach, at the conclusion of the largest of the hunger marches and with significant cuts being made to unemployment benefit, meant it was imperative that it distance itself from official employment policies. Some within the Council welcomed the cuts of 1931 as giving a boost to voluntary action, but this viewpoint was not widespread.[99] Its failure to draw a clear distinction between the voluntary response and government policy meant criticism was inevitable.

It might have helped if the Council had done more to ally itself with some of the more radical forms of social action prevalent at the time. The inter-war years saw an outpouring of informal, spontaneous action, from the mass trespass by the Ramblers' Association at Kinder Scout in the Peak District in 1932, to the anti-fascist confrontations at Cable Street in London in 1936, to the hunger marches themselves, all of which passed the Council by. There was no suggestion that these protests were seen as a legitimate form of voluntary action with which it might engage, or at least acknowledge. There is no evidence to support the accusation that the Council 'saw the unemployed clubs as an alternative to the politics of the street'.[100] But, by failing to engage with the more radical social movements of the time, it played into the hands of critics who argued that it was privileging a particular type of voluntary action used to reinforce the status quo, rather than bring about fundamental change.

The Council would find itself in a similar place in the 1960s when a new wave of social movements threatened to pass it by, and it once more faced accusations of being out of touch, too closely aligned with the establishment and the champion of a narrow conceptualisation of voluntary action.[101] For some on the Left who saw voluntary action in more radical terms, the Council's work would always fall short. Snape has argued that 'the dominant historical narrative' of the Council's work with the unemployed 'is one of resentment'.[102] But this is far from the whole story and the Council's work is surely due for reassessment. The clubs were far from perfect. Many suffered from poor accommodation and a lack of leadership, and the Idealist-inspired vision of a community of locally controlled, democratically run institutions remained largely unrealised. Despite these failings, however, they were generally popular among members and provided a level of support not available elsewhere. Overall, the Council can be proud of its record. Ralph Hayburn concludes that, although much more was needed, the clubs were a success.[103] And one would probably concur with Harris, who writes that, although the work of the Council and the wider movement was 'certainly less "heroic" than many of its supporters maintained', it was also 'more flexible and more democratic than many of its critics have alleged'.[104]

By the end of the period, the Council had distributed over £1.5 million of grants from government. In 1939, funding was transferred from the Ministry of Labour to the Unemployment Assistance Board, and in 1941 all grants to the Council to support its work with the unemployed were wrapped up into a consolidated grant from the board.[105] Funding continued throughout the war, although at a much-reduced level and the Council scaled back its work. By 1939 the centres had largely transitioned from occupational clubs into community service clubs and the hope was that they would become a permanent fixture in local communities. This vision was not realised. Central government funding was brought to an end in 1947 with unemployment at a very low level and responsibility for the clubs transferred to the new local education authorities.[106] The minister responsible for this transfer in the new post-war Labour government was Wilkinson, who had been such a critic of the occupational club movement as MP for Jarrow. The Council's unemployment committee was wound up and the men's clubs largely ceased to exist, although the clubs for women continued to flourish throughout the post-war period.

CONCLUSION

In 1936 Peter Birchall, Edward's nephew, joined the Council. His father, John, Conservative MP for North East Leeds, broke the news to his wife, Adela, in a letter written from the terrace of the House of Commons.[107] Given the opposition to its unemployment work from parts of the Labour movement, John had sought to reassure himself that a future Labour government would be supportive. He spoke to a Labour MP, who said he 'thought any opposition there might have been had died out', a situation John described as 'very encouraging'.

How pleased Edward would be, he wrote, 'to know that the work which he practically funded with his legacy of £1000 was going to be carried on by his nephew'. He was confident 'Peter has done the right thing' and 'will be most useful'.

The Council had come a long way since concerns expressed about its future on its tenth anniversary. Its work on unemployment, hugely controversial though it was, transformed its profile and brought it enormous publicity. Its annual report, published on 10 August 1938, was covered in over 200 newspapers, with most opinion extremely positive.[108] For the *Daily Telegraph* and *Morning Post* the report gave 'a splendid record of achievement in work of diverse kinds all over the country', while *Country Life* proclaimed the Council as the 'G.H.Q. which co-ordinates all the efforts of our social militia, preventing overlapping and distributing the forces to the best advantage'. The *Guardian* said the Council had demonstrated 'a record of striking achievements and of great contributions towards the solution of many social problems' and drew attention to its success in developing 'close co-operation with the State services'. And, in a nod to what was happening in Europe, it concluded that the lesson to be drawn from its work is 'that there should be some share taken by everyone in voluntary enterprise if the social order is to be changed without recourse to the disastrous experiments of totalitarianism'. The next chapter in the Council's history would show the importance of voluntary action in the fight to preserve the nation's freedom.

NOTES

1. For a pessimistic view of the period, see Overy, 2009.
2. For the revisionist view, see Stevenson and Cook, 1977; Pugh, 2008.
3. Wilkinson, 1939; Pugh, 2008.
4. NCSS Annual Report 1932–33, p. 11.
5. NCSS Annual Report 1928–29.
6. Harris, 1995, p. 530.
7. Mess, 1947, p. 42.
8. On the myriad of support during the inter-war period from a range of voluntary traditions, see Harris, 1995, pp. 545–7.
9. NCSS Annual Report 1928–29.
10. Harris, 1995, p. 549.
11. Brasnett, 1969, p. 68.
12. NCSS Annual Report 1928–29.
13. Ibid., p. 10.
14. Pilgrim Trust, 1938. See also Bakke, 1940.
15. NCSS Annual Report 1935–36, p. 17.
16. NCSS Annual Report 1928–29.
17. NCSS, 1932a, p. 8.
18. The *Manchester Guardian*, 28 January 1932, p. 3.
19. *The Times* 29 January 1932, p. 12.
20. Prochaska, 1995.

21. Quoted in Ziegler, 1990, p. 216.
22. Letter from Ellis to Sir Godfrey Bart, Buckingham Palace, 12 October 1936. Uncatalogued papers of NCSS held at London Metropolitan Archives (LMA); Acc 2720/A01/17/01-05.
23. Ward, 2013, p. 223.
24. Ziegler, 1990, p. 216.
25. Grimley, 2004, p. 6.
26. Scott, 1971, p. 150.
27. Lindsay, 1933, p. 82.
28. Grimley, 2004, p. 175.
29. Scott, 1971. For a tribute to Lindsay from George Haynes, see Haynes, 1952.
30. Flanagan, 1991, p. 185.
31. House of Commons Debates, Series 5, Vol. 273, cols. 776–8, 19 December 1932.
32. See The National Archives (TNA) Cab 27/490 Memorandum by the Minister of Health (UC [32] 2), 29 September 1932; also TNA Cab 24/233 CP 307 *Unemployment Committee Interim Report* 24, October 1932.
33. Minutes of Executive Committee, 20 October 1932; LMA/4016/ IS/A/01/029.
34. Memorandum entitled *Grant-aid for the social service club movement: Bid to government for further central funding*, 26 June 1946; uncatalogued papers of NCSS held at LMA; Acc 2720/A01/03/07.
35. On the Maes-yr-Haf Educational Settlement, see Stead, 1979, pp. 100–101. On the Lincoln People's Service Club, see Jones, 1986, p. 125.
36. Olechnowicz, 2005, p. 32.
37. NCSS *Unemployed drama notes*, 2 March 1938; uncatalogued papers of NCSS held at LMA; Acc 2720/A01/02/01-04.
38. Ibid.
39. NCSS Annual Report 1934–35.
40. Paper on *progress on unemployment work* from Ellis, 24 April 1933. Uncatalogued papers of NCSS held at LMA; Acc 2720/A08/01/33.
41. Mess, 1947, p. 49.
42. Note on *King's Standing demonstration centre, 1933–39*. Uncatalogued papers of NCSS held at LMA; Acc 2720/A01/04/01–04.
43. Mess, 1947, pp. 43–44. See also Hayburn, 1971, p. 162.
44. NCSS Annual Report 1935–36.
45. Mess, 1947, p. 45.
46. Memorandum on *The work of the National Council of Social Service in relation to unemployed people and their dependants,* undated. Uncatalogued papers of NCSS held at LMA; Acc 2720/A08/01/32.
47. Mess, 1947, p. 50.
48. Ibid., p. 51.
49. Ibid., p. 50.
50. The Special Areas were designated by the Special Areas (Development and Improvement) Act, 1934.
51. NCSS Annual Report 1937–38.
52. Mess, 1947, p. 51.
53. *The Times* 27 June 1939, p. 25.
54. NCSS Annual Report 1937–38, p. 53.

55. NCSS Annual Report 1938–39, p. 53; *The Times*, 27 June 1939, p. 25.
56. Field, 2013, p. 197.
57. On compulsory training schemes in the 1930s, see Field, 2013, pp. 128–142.
58. Croucher, 1997, p. 163.
59. Letter from Ellis to Sir Henry Betterton, 22 November 1933. Uncatalogued papers of NCSS held at LMA; Acc 2720/A01/05/02.
60. Letter from Betterton to Ellis, 24 November 1933. Uncatalogued papers of NCSS held at LMA; Acc 2720/A01/05/02.
61. Rushcliffe's role during the war is discussed in Chap. 5.
62. Minutes of Executive Committee, 24 January 1935; LMA/4016/IS/A/030/01.
63. Brasnett, 1969, p. 79.
64. The Council's role in coordinating the voluntary movement's response to unemployment in the 1980s, and the criticism it received, is discussed in Chap. 8.
65. Harris, 1995, p. 538.
66. For a discussion of this issue, see Deakin and Davis Smith, 2011.
67. House of Commons Debates, Series 5, Vol. 273, col. 834, 19 December 1932.
68. House of Commons Debates, Series 5, Vol. 292, col. 1842, 25 July 1934. Also, 1 March 1935, col. 1490, and 23 March 1936, col. 870.
69. Wilkinson, 1939, p. 232.
70. Orwell, 1937, pp. 76–77.
71. Priestley, 1934, p. 287 and p. 385.
72. *Guardian*, 5 February 1923; Hannington, 1937, pp. 194–5.
73. Letter from Ramsay MacDonald to NCSS, 24 December 1932. Uncatalogued papers of NCSS held at LMA; Acc 2720/A01/05/02.
74. Quoted in Olechnowicz, 2005, p. 37.
75. Jones, 1986, p. 125.
76. Ibid., p. 125.
77. NCSS, 1932b.
78. NCSS, 1939, p. 32.
79. Uncatalogued papers of NCSS held at LMA; Acc 2720/A08/01/32. Lady Denman was chair of the National Federation of Women's Institutes from its inception in 1917 until 1946, leading its work during the Second World War. Other voluntary roles included chair of the Family Planning Association and trustee of the Carnegie UK Trust. She died in 1954. See *The Times*, 3 June 1954, p. 8.
80. Quoted in Jenkins, 2001, p. 165.
81. NCSS, 1932b.
82. House of Commons Debates, Series 5, Vol. 273, Col. 781, 19 December 1932.
83. House of Commons Debates, Series 5, Vol. 275, Cols. 629–30, 2 March 1933; Vol. 278, Col. 640, 18 May 1933.
84. Stevenson and Cook, 1977, p. 83.
85. Flanagan, 1991, pp. 205–6.
86. Ibid., p. 211 and p. 217.
87. Ibid., p. 220.
88. Snape, 2015b.
89. NCSS Annual Report 1937–38.

90. Burnett, 1994, p. 241.
91. NCSS, 1939, p. 5.
92. NCSS Annual Report 1938–39, p. 53.
93. Olechnowicz, 2005, p. 41.
94. NCSS Annual Report 1936–37, p. 52.
95. Uncatalogued papers of NCSS held at LMA; Acc 2720/A08/01/31.
96. NCSS Annual Report 1932–33, p. 17.
97. Letter from Lindsay to Ellis, 21 February 1933. Uncatalogued papers of NCSS held at LMA; Acc 2720/A01/05/02.
98. NCSS, 1934.
99. See, for example, Grundy, 1931.
100. Flanagan, 1991, p. 206.
101. On criticism of the Council for being out of touch with new developments in the voluntary movement in the 1960s, see Chap. 7.
102. Snape, 2015a, p. 66.
103. Hayburn, 1971, p. 171.
104. Harris, 1995, p. 549.
105. Papers of the unemployment committee, 1937–47; uncatalogued papers of NCSS held at LMA; Acc 2720/A01/20/01-02.
106. Minutes of Executive Committee, 27 February 1947; LMA/4016/IS/A/01/032/01. See also NCSS Annual Report 1946-47.
107. Correspondence between John Birchall and Adela, April 1936; private papers, Birchall Family Archive.
108. Memorandum entitled *Press coverage for annual report, 1937–38,* 19 September 1938. Discussed at Meeting of NCSS Finance and General Purposes Committee; LMA/4016/IS/A/01/045/03.

References

Bakke, E. (1940). *Citizens without work: A study of the effects of unemployment upon the workers' social relations and practices.* New Haven: Yale University Press.

Brasnett, M. (1969). *Voluntary social action.* London: NCSS.

Burnett, J. (1994). *Idle hands: The experience of unemployment, 1790–1990.* London: Routledge.

Croucher, R. (1997). *We refuse to starve in silence: A history of the National Unemployed Workers' movement, 1920–46.* London: Lawrence and Wishart.

Deakin, N., & Davis Smith, J. (2011). Labour, charity and voluntary action: The myth of hostility. In M. Hilton & J. McKay (Eds.), *The ages of voluntarism: How we got to the big society* (pp. 69–93). Oxford: Oxford University Press for British Academy.

Field, J. (2013). *Working-men's bodies: Work camps in Britain, 1880–1940.* Manchester: Manchester University Press.

Flanagan, R. (1991). *Parish-fed bastards': A history of the politics of the unemployed in Britain, 1884–1939.* Westport: Greenwood Press.

Grimley, M. (2004). *Citizenship, community and the Church of England: Liberal Anglican theories of the state between the wars.* Oxford: Oxford University Press.

Grundy, S. P. (1931). Social service and deflation. *Social Service Review, 12,* 183–184.

Hannington, W. (1937). *The problem of the distressed areas.* London: Victor Gollancz.

Harris, B. (1995). Responding to adversity: Government-charity relations and the relief of unemployment in inter-war Britain. *Contemporary Record, 9*(3), 529–561.

Hayburn, R. (1971). The voluntary occupational centre movement, 1932–9. *Journal of Contemporary History, 6*(3), 156–171.

Haynes, G. (1952). Lord Lindsay of Birker. *Social Service Quarterly, 26*(1), 18–19.

Jenkins, J. (2001). The organization man: George Haynes at the National Council of Social Service. In L. Black et al. (Eds.), *Consensus or coercion? The state, the people and social cohesion in post-war Britain* (pp. 151–168). Cheltenham: New Clarion Press.

Jones, S. (1986). *Workers at play: A social and economic history of leisure, 1918–1939.* London: Routledge & Kegan Paul.

Lindsay, A. (1933). *Christianity and economics: The 1933 Scott Holland lectures.* London: Macmillan & Co.

Mess, H. (1947). Social service with the unemployed. In H. Mess (Ed.), *Voluntary social services since 1918* (pp. 40–54). London: Keegan Paul.

NCSS. (1932a). *The national opportunity: A fresh call for service.* London: NCSS.

NCSS. (1932b). *Unemployment and opportunity: Some practical suggestions.* London: NCSS.

NCSS. (1934). *Unemployment and voluntary service, Prince of Wales broadcast, 27 January 1934.* London: NCSS.

NCSS. (1939). *Out of adversity: A survey of the clubs for men and women which have grown out of the needs of unemployment.* London: NCSS.

Olechnowicz, A. (2005). Unemployed workers, "enforced leisure" and education for "the right use of leisure" in Britain in the 1930s. *Labour History Review, 70*(1), 27–52.

Orwell, G. (1937). *The road to Wigan Pier.* London: Victor Gollancz.

Overy, R. (2009). *The morbid age: Britain between the wars.* London: Allen Lane.

Pilgrim Trust. (1938). *Men without work: A report made to the pilgrim trust.* Cambridge: Cambridge University Press.

Priestley, J. (1934). *English journey.* London: William Heinemann.

Prochaska, F. (1995). *Royal bounty: The making of a welfare monarchy.* New Haven: Yale University Press.

Pugh, M. (2008). *We danced all night: A social history of Britain between the wars.* London: Bodley Head.

Scott, D. (1971). *A.D. Lindsay: A biography.* Oxford: Blackwell.

Snape, R. (2015a). The new leisure, voluntarism and social reconstruction in inter-war Britain. *Contemporary British History, 29*(1), 51–83.

Snape, R. (2015b). Voluntary action and leisure: An historical perspective, 1830–1939. *Voluntary Sector Review, 6*(1), 153–171.

Stead, P. (1979). The voluntary response to mass unemployment in South Wales. In W. Minchinton (Ed.), *Reactions to social and economic change, 1750–1939, Exeter papers in economic history, 12* (pp. 97–117). Exeter: University of Exeter.

Stevenson, J., & Cook, C. (1977). *The slump: Britain in the great depression.* London: Routledge.

Ward, S. (2013). *Unemployment and the state in Britain.* Manchester: Manchester University Press.

Wilkinson, E. (1939). *The town that was murdered: The life story of Jarrow.* London: Victor Gollancz.

Ziegler, P. (1990). *King Edward VIII: The official biography.* London: Collins.

CHAPTER 5

Warfare and Welfare

INTRODUCTION

Despite the challenges faced by charities, the Second World War, as with the First, gave a significant boost to voluntary action.[1] While claims of greater national unity, arising out of what Angus Calder famously termed the 'Myth of the Blitz',[2] may be contested, there was an upsurge in voluntary activity to deal with the new national emergency.[3] According to Sonya Rose, the war 'reactivated and gave renewed emphasis to the idea of good citizenship as involving voluntary fulfilment of obligations and willingness to contribute to the welfare of the community'.[4] Whether this resulted in a fundamental shift in attitudes, however, is debatable, and, as Fielding et al. conclude, it is unlikely that people were transformed overnight 'from private individuals uninterested in wider events into active citizens seeking to influence public affairs'.[5]

As in 1914–18, much of the voluntary action unleashed by the war was informal. But a significant amount was organised, with new groups such as the Women's Voluntary Service (WVS) established expressly to mobilise community effort. During the First World War, voluntary effort was largely focused on the needs of service men and women fighting overseas. In the Second, although the making of *comforts* took place, it was less important than support to local communities. Geoffrey Finlayson has suggested that the Second World War gave 'greater scope for service among the civilian population at home than had been the case in World War 1', and hundreds of thousands of volunteers were recruited to support evacuees and their families, assist in bomb-hit areas, and provide advice and information to local citizens.[6] Fundraising remained a key focus of activity and was boosted by the involvement of the BBC, which between 1939 and 1944 broadcast over 250 appeals on its 'Week's Good Cause', generating hundreds of thousands of pounds in donations.[7] Concern over the misuse of charity funds led to the passing of a new War Charities Act in 1940, although, as before, there is little evidence to suggest fraud was widespread.[8] A new director general of voluntary organisations was appointed to

J. Davis Smith, *100 Years of NCVO and Voluntary Action*,
https://doi.org/10.1007/978-3-030-02774-2_5

coordinate charitable appeals, but the role proved less influential than during the earlier conflict.[9]

The Council had no doubt that voluntary action was needed to deal with the national emergency. In its annual report for 1939–40 it acknowledged that some people argued it was time for government 'to take over all authority', but it rejected this view out of hand. On the contrary, it suggested that voluntary groups, 'rightly conceived and planned', could 'harness to the nation's effort a tremendous volume of individual and constructive effort which would otherwise be lost'.[10] It issued a rallying cry to the movement:

> There is, then, a tremendous challenge in the present situation to every society to play its part. It calls for the strenuous exercise of all those imaginative qualities which have created the great tradition of voluntary service, and which enabled it so often to pioneer in new ways of social progress. There is no group, however, humble, but can find some useful sphere of service at the present time. There is no member of any society who ought to be left at a loss to know where he can help. A job to do at a time of crisis is the most effective remedy for despondency or doubt.[11]

The Council, for its part, threw itself into the challenge with great energy. Although much of its existing activity was put on hold due to wartime restrictions, it launched a number of new initiatives that had a significant impact during the war and left a lasting legacy. It established new structures to coordinate the work of voluntary organisations and link with statutory agencies, nationally and locally. It expanded its international work and set up a new information and research department. It also found time to revise its internal structures and refresh its mission. The war gave the voluntary movement a new sense of purpose. But it also exposed weaknesses and, in its planning for the future, the Council identified a number of challenges that needed addressing if the movement was to retain its influence once peace was secured.

CHANGE IN LEADERSHIP

Not long after the outbreak of hostilities, the Council faced a crisis at the top. In August 1940 its director, Leonard Shoeten Sack, who had been in post just four years after replacing Lionel Ellis, stood down due to ill health.[12] This was not a good time for a change in leadership, but the Council was fortunate in being able to turn to George Haynes, Sack's deputy, who had forged an impressive career in the voluntary movement as warden of Liverpool University Settlement and, later, as regional organiser for the Council in the north west. He had joined the Council's headquarters in 1936 and played an important part in the occupational club movement. He was put in charge on a temporary basis for the duration of the war, but the appointment was made permanent in 1946, and he led the organisation with great skill for over a quarter of a century.[13]

Although only 38 when appointed director, Haynes was steeped in the traditions and values of the Council. Coming from Liverpool, like so many leading social workers of the day, he was influenced by the work of Frederic D'Aeth and shared the Idealist notions of the Council's founders. He also had formidable organisational skills, which proved invaluable in leading the Council at a time when it was massively extending its reach. Haynes did a superb job during the war and continued to excel into the era of post-war reconstruction, contributing to the establishment of the National Association for Mental Health in 1946 and the transformation of the Charity Organisation Society into the Family Welfare Association.[14] He also significantly extended the international reach of the Council, particularly through his work in reconstituting the International Conference on Social Work. John Jenkins has characterised him as 'the Organisation Man'.[15] But he was more than a mere bureaucrat. He was a passionate advocate for voluntary action and had a clear vision for the Council as a federation of semi-autonomous organisations providing arms-length support for a range of specialist groups. However, he stayed too long. When he left in 1967, after 27 years of service, the organisation was badly out of touch with new developments in the voluntary movement and in danger of being left behind. It would take another dynamic young director, Nicholas Hinton, to put the Council back on track after a decade of stagnation following his departure.[16]

COORDINATING THE WAR EFFORT

In September 1938 the Council brought together a group of national voluntary organisations to consider the growing international crisis. A follow-up conference was held in December and a decision taken to establish a Standing Conference of Voluntary Organisations in Time of War.[17] This was despite the view of some members that 'all war and all preparation for war was in itself wrong'.[18] The standing conference, involving 100 leading charities, met throughout the war to coordinate activity and provide a channel of communication with government. Although independent, the Council seconded staff and provided the secretariat. The Council's vice-chair, Sir Wyndham Deedes, took the chair.[19] In April 1940 the Council's Executive Committee expressed concern that there was a 'danger of creating parallel bodies' and a decision was taken to set up a Special Emergency Committee, chaired by the Council's chair, W.G.S. Adams, to represent the Council and the conference.[20] This Emergency Committee acted as the de facto decision-making arm of the Council for the duration of the war and, as a result, the Executive Committee took a back seat, meeting just a couple of times a year to receive reports from the Emergency Committee and discharge a few constitutional responsibilities such as organising the Council's annual meeting.

The setting up of the standing conference can be seen as an example of strong leadership, or a sign of weakness. Finlayson has suggested that the new structure was 'an indication that the National Council could not be taken to speak for the whole voluntary service movement'.[21] There is no doubt truth in this, but there is also a sense in which the Council, by sharing the leadership of the voluntary movement, was sending out a powerful signal of its willingness to collaborate. It was aware of criticism that, in its work before the war, it had done too much at the expense of other organisations and was increasingly convinced that its future lay less in the direct delivery of services and more in leadership and coordination. A consistent thread emerged during the war of the Council initiating and supporting new initiatives and moving as quickly as possible to put them on an independent footing. It was an approach that became even more clearly defined in the post-war years, driven by an acceptance that its resources would always be constrained and a desire to avoid duplication. Such a process of incubation had its challenges, and tensions between the *associated groups* and the Council surfaced on a number of occasions over the subsequent decades.[22] But this federated model was among the Council's most successful innovations, resulting in an outpouring of creativity that revolutionised its work and left a lasting legacy of social advance.

In addition to establishing a forum for voluntary groups to collaborate nationally, the Council strengthened its representation in the regions. In summer 1939 the government, concerned that a sustained bombing campaign would seriously disrupt the machinery of state in London, established a system of regional commissioners. The Council immediately followed suit and appointed, with the approval of the Lord Privy Seal's office, a regional officer in each of the 12 civil defence regions.[23] A Social Service Emergency Committee was established in each county to connect voluntary and statutory agencies and a series of leaflets published outlining ways the community could assist with the emergency.[24] In 1944 the Council reported positively on the initiative, noting that the regional officers 'have enriched its experience, widened its knowledge, and informed its national discussions with a sympathetic understanding of local problems'.[25] Not everyone was convinced. Some groups expressed concern that the Council was competing for increasingly scarce resources, and it acknowledged there was 'considerable danger of overlapping between the activities of the regional officers and the existing voluntary organisations'.[26] This tension was a recurring theme in the future and pointed to the inherent difficulties faced by membership organisations.

RELATIONS WITH GOVERNMENT

Relations between the Council and government, which had always been strong, were strengthened further during the war. New coordinating structures were established and regular engagement took place over a range of issues of concern to voluntary groups. Looking back in December 1944 the Council concluded that, of all the work carried out over the previous five years, 'many, valuable, enduring things have emerged, and not least of these has been the deepening understanding between the great agencies of State and the voluntary organisations'.[27]

Key areas of concern for voluntary organisations were personnel, premises, and finance and, in all three, the Council achieved a measure of success. Conscription raised concerns that the voluntary movement would be deprived of key staff at a time when it was being asked to take on more work. In 1939 an agreement was reached with the Ministry of Labour and National Service over the inclusion of certain full-time voluntary staff, 'whose training and experience renders them indispensable', in the list of reserved occupations exempt from national service.[28] The Council was informed that its own work was seen as immensely valuable in an emergency and that its staff shouldn't 'be dispersed on other duties'.[29] In the event most remained, although some enlisted or were redirected to other wartime work, which caused some disruption, although the Council fared better in this regard than many other charities. Premises were also a major problem for voluntary groups due to the commandeering of buildings for war purposes. Many village halls and community centres were taken over, but, in a number of cases, the Council secured concessions to keep them open or persuade the government to offer up alternative accommodation.[30]

Finance was perhaps the major issue. In October 1939 a deputation from the Standing Conference of Voluntary Organisations met with the Treasury requesting additional support for organisations involved in war service.[31] The conference was adamant it would not accept government control as a condition of additional money made available and proposed that an independent, arms-length body be set up to administer the funds. The government accepted the case for additional funding but rejected the proposal for a new central body, insisting that funding continue to be channelled through individual Whitehall departments. Instead, it proposed an inter-departmental committee to consider funding requests falling outside the remit of any one department 'to ensure coordinated action and to prevent, as far as possible, the overlap of grants for similar purposes'.[32] This committee, although not heavily utilised during the war, was symbolically important in that it was the first cross-departmental body for supporting voluntary organisations. It was a model that emerged fully developed some 30 years later with the creation of the Voluntary Services Unit in 1972.[33] To further strengthen links with voluntary organisations the government established a voluntary service advisory committee, chaired by Lord Rushcliffe, to act as the main point of contact with the standing conference.[34]

In April 1940 Rushcliffe addressed a meeting of the standing conference, setting out the government's view on the importance of the voluntary movement. He dismissed the notion that as the state assumed more responsibility there would be less need for voluntary action, as 'profoundly mistaken'. Drawing attention to what he called the 'pioneering spirit' of the movement, he stressed that 'as long as Democracy retains its vitality there can never be an end to social improvement, nor a cessation of voluntary effort in pointing the way to better things'. He paid tribute to the Council for bringing voluntary organisations together, describing it as 'a significant move forward in the direction of concentration of effort in a vast and complicated field'.[35] In 1942 the paymaster-general, Sir William Jowitt, addressed the Council's annual meeting and gave a similar message. He observed that his presence, as chair of the ministerial committee dealing with reconstruction, 'symbolised and would, he hoped, strengthen the connection there must be between the Government's efforts for reconstruction and the efforts of voluntary societies such as the National Council'.[36]

Despite its closeness to government, the Council guarded its independence and on occasions pushed back against what it saw as undue state interference. In 1940, for example, it was approached by the Ministry of Information with a request to allow the ministry access to its membership, as part of an exercise being carried out with the public 'to allay undue fears and strengthen morale'. Staff within member groups would be asked to call a select number of people each day to ask about their confidence and provide details on 'any rumours being circulated' and what could be done to dispel them. After consulting its members, the Council responded that, although they would be 'perfectly willing' to receive 'straightforward information', they were a 'little apprehensive lest they should be used for purposes of propaganda'. In the end a compromise was reached whereby it agreed to ask individual groups if they were willing to circulate ministry publications to their members.[37]

NEW INITIATIVES

Much of the Council's most valuable work during the war was carried out through new groups and networks established to deal with the emergency. Perhaps the most important was the citizens' advice bureaux (CAB) movement, described at the time as 'the outstanding addition to voluntary service in war-time'.[38] The first bureaux were piloted in 1938 under the auspices of the standing conference of voluntary organisations, but it was the Council that provided support locally and oversaw the distribution of funding from central government.[39] The premise behind the movement was simple and compelling. The war was set to unleash on the public a barrage of new rules and regulations and what was needed was 'some place to which bewildered citizens could turn with confidence for help and advice'.[40] The idea was not entirely new. Frederic D'Aeth had proposed something similar during the First World War and citizens' friend services were established by a number of councils of social service in the 1920s and 1930s. Indeed such was the success of these early initiatives, Margaret Brasnett has suggested a national citizens' advice service would probably have developed even without the impetus provided by war.[41]

The movement grew rapidly after 1938 and by the end of 1940 there were over 900 bureaux in existence.[42] Many were located within existing organisations and good coverage was achieved across the country, with the exception of some rural areas. In the beginning most bureaux were staffed by paid workers, but volunteers increasingly took over and it is estimated that, of the 10,000 people active in the movement during the war, over 90 per cent were volunteers.[43] Funding from the Ministry of Health was secured to support local development and contribute to the costs of running a dedicated advice service within the Council's London office. A series of 'Citizens' Advice Notes' was produced to advise local groups on new regulations and a slot was secured on the BBC to broadcast a regular programme dealing with the most commonly asked questions, under the title 'Can I Help You?'.[44] The Citizens' Advice Notes survived the war and became one of the Council's most widely read and valued publications. By 1942 over 1000 local groups were in existence, handling over two million enquiries a year.[45] In addition to dealing with domestic inquiries, many local groups operated a postal message scheme in cooperation with the British Red Cross to help people stay in touch with relatives in enemy-occupied territories. By 1941 the scheme was handling 360,000 outgoing and incoming messages.[46] The biggest demand for the bureaux came in 1944 during the flying bomb period, when in July alone inquiries totalled a quarter of a million. Mobile teams of volunteers travelled across the country to the most badly affected areas, mainly in the south east of England.[47]

One person who deserves particular mention for her part in the success of the movement is Dorothy Keeling, who joined the Council from the Liverpool Personal Service Society in 1940 to lead the work. Keeling had long been associated with the Council and was one of the individuals who can be credited with playing a central part in its formation.[48] She was one of the last remaining survivors of this select group. The Rev. John Pringle and Thomas Hancock Nunn died before the war started and D'Aeth and Grundy before it was over.[49] Keeling was steeped in the voluntary movement, having worked at the Bradford Guild of Help and as general secretary of the National Association of Guilds of Help, before moving to Liverpool to set up and run the Liverpool Personal Service Society.[50] She remained with the Council for the duration of the war and played a pivotal role in the CAB movement and in the development of another key wartime initiative, aimed at the support of older people.[51] Alongside Grace Hadow, who was instrumental in the development of the rural community council movement, Keeling was perhaps the most influential women in the first 50 years of the Council's history.[52] She was by reputation something of a left-wing firebrand and represented a strand of socialist thought committed to the voluntary cause. Along with other key figures from the Left in the Council's early history, such as A.D. Lindsay, Keeling provides a useful corrective to the view that the Labour movement at the time was implacably hostile to the philanthropic tradition.[53] At her death in 1967 Haynes paid tribute to 'her courage and skill, which won the unbounded admiration of all who worked with her'.[54]

Two issues dominated discussions in the Council in relation to the bureaux. How to secure funding once war was over and when to put the movement on an independent footing? A measure of independence was secured in 1941 when a Central Citizens' Advice Bureaux Committee was established to advise on policy and in 1945 a National Standing Conference of Volunteer Bureaux was established to plan for the future.[55] The Council had no doubt the movement would be needed after the war and gave full support to a resolution, passed unanimously at the first national bureaux conference in May 1945, asserting that 'to meet the problems of peace there will be an increasing need for the Citizens' Advice Bureaux service as an independent and voluntary movement'.[56]

The future, however, was by no means guaranteed. The Council reacted strongly to a suggestion by William Beveridge, in his 1942 report on social insurance, that advice centres should be located within the proposed new social security offices of local government. 'The Council's experience', it argued, 'leads quite clearly to the view that the Bureaux should remain in character and management voluntary enterprises, co-operating with the authorities, drawing on their goodwill and support.'[57] Much of course would depend on funding. In November 1945 the Ministry of Health, which had announced that grants to bureaux would end the following year, issued a circular to local authorities drawing attention to the importance of local advice services and to the work of bureaux as potential suppliers. The Council, while 'warmly welcoming' this move, noted that not all authorities were enthusiastic about using bureaux with many preferring to set up in-house services and reflected that, unless other sources of funding were forthcoming, many would be forced to close.[58] The post-war period, despite inevitable bumps along the way, would prove relatively kind to the CAB movement and it would go on to flourish as an indispensable community service, first under the Council's auspices, and, later, after a difficult separation, as an independent charity.[59]

One of the Council's most enduring legacies has been the support given to organisations that have gone on to become independent, household name charities. The war years were a particularly fertile period for such innovation, with the CAB perhaps the best example. In 1940 the Council was involved in another initiative that can claim to match it for impact. The issue was older people and the widespread concern that as an age group they were particularly at risk during the war. In 1940 the Council, at the request of the National Assistance Board, brought together a number of organisations in the basement of its offices in Bedford Square to discuss what could be done.[60] Keeling, who had pioneered work with older people at the Liverpool Personal Service Society, was again heavily involved. The result was the establishment of an Old People's Welfare Committee, under the chair of Eleanor Rathbone, another influential social entrepreneur from Liverpool, and Independent MP for the Combined Universities.[61]

As was becoming the norm with such initiatives, the Council agreed to provide the secretariat to get the committee up and running, but the Executive Committee expressed the desire that it should, as soon as possible, be given an 'independent existence'.[62] This goal was achieved to some extent within four years when the National Old People's Welfare Committee (NOPWC) was established as a semi-autonomous central group within the Council. By the end of the war there were over 100 local old people's welfare committees in existence, providing a wide range of services from home visiting and lunch and social clubs to residential homes for older people.[63] Although the main focus of the committee was on meeting the challenges of ageing, it also developed a more positive vision for older life, looking forward to an era when medical advancement had relieved the 'ills of old age' and people were no longer 'content to withdraw from active life at sixty'.[64] In 1970 the NOPWC achieved full independence from the Council and was reconstituted as Age Concern.

Another group set up at the outbreak of the war, which would leave a lasting legacy, was the Women's Group on Public Welfare (WGPW). The group, originally called the Women's Group on Problems Arising from Evacuation, arose out of a meeting convened by the Council in September 1939 at the instigation of the National Federation of Women's Institutes and the National Union of Townswomen's Guilds, concerned about the problems for families arising from civilian evacuation.[65] Chaired by the Labour MP, Margaret Bondfield, who had been Britain's first female cabinet minister in Ramsay MacDonald's second inter-war minority Labour government, its aim was to share information and coordinate action between statutory and voluntary agencies in public welfare.

The group was comprised of national organisations concerned with welfare issues, with the Council again providing administrative support. As with the Old People's Welfare Committee, the group delivered much of its work through a network of local committees, made up of a mix of local voluntary agencies. Membership of the local committees, or Standing Conferences of Women's Organisations as they were called, was reasonably broad based, although James Hinton has suggested that they revealed 'tensions between professional women and organised housewives, and … the continuing hostility of Labour women to the middle-class organisations in general'.[66] He concludes that there is little evidence to suggest that the work of the WGPW, or similar voluntary bodies, significantly transformed the position of women during the war.[67] Caitriona Beaumont disagrees. She sees the WGPW as part of a movement of women's organisations after the First World War that served an important function in facilitating the involvement of women in civic life. 'Focusing on citizenship rights instead of feminism', she writes, 'these groups encouraged members to participate in local and national politics and campaigned to ensure that women benefited from the rights of equal citizenship bestowed upon them in 1928.'[68]

The first priority of the WGPW was evacuation. By January 1940 almost one million children had been evacuated from London and other major cities and volunteers, coordinated by the local committees, were providing reception centres, day nurseries, and other services to alleviate distress and encourage integration.[69] Later the focus of the work would change and volunteers would be involved in a wider range of activities including running classes on food production, clothes rationing, and first aid, and even helping with the transfer of children from concentration camps in Germany.[70] In 1941 the group launched a national *Make Do and Mend* campaign and by the end of the year over 20,000 classes had been established.[71]

As with the Old People's Welfare Committee, the WGPW was not concerned entirely with practical relief but also with questions of longer-term planning and public policy. To inform thinking it commissioned a series of large-scale studies, the most important of which was an investigation into the health of evacuated children. *Our Towns: A Close Up* was published in 1943 and provided a devastating critique of the poor health of many evacuees.[72] It generated a national debate on conditions in the inner cities and called for universal nursery school provision for all children over two so they could develop 'initiative, self-respect and a sense of citizenship'.[73] It has been credited with influencing wartime and post-war social policy and John Morgan, writing in 1947, called it 'a significant milestone in the Council's history'.[74] However, it was not universally welcomed. In pointing the finger at what it saw as poor standards of parenting, or 'mother-craft', demonstrated by some evacuated mothers, it has been accused of providing a very middle-class perspective on family life and of denigrating the role of working-class mothers.[75]

The WGPW, as a federation of different organisations, ensured the Council enjoyed generally good relations with most leading voluntary welfare agencies. The exception was with arguably the most influential of all such agencies, the newly formed WVS. This was established by the government in 1938, under the leadership of Lady Reading, with the aim of recruiting and training women for air-raid precaution work, although it soon expanded its activities to focus on evacuation and other areas.[76] The decision by government to set up a new organisation suggested a lack of confidence in the Council and inevitably led to a measure of tension between the two bodies. The WVS was very different to the Council. It was not an independent voluntary agency, getting the vast majority of funding from the state and being reliant on government for the appointment of key staff. Relations between the two organisations were strained for much of the war, although effective joint work took place at a local level. Lady Reading liked to characterise the WVS as an organisation of doers, compared to the 'impractical theorists' of the WGPW.[77] After the war these tensions were brought into sharp relief when an attempt by the Labour government to bring about a merger between the Council and the WVS foundered on the inability of the two organisations even to agree on terms of reference for discussions. In one respect, however, the setting up of the WVS did the Council a favour. By introducing the principle of central government funding to support voluntary action, it paved the way for the Council to eventually persuade the government to contribute towards its own running costs. The Council broached the subject during the war and a small one-off payment was made in 1940 to cover some additional administrative costs incurred. But no further progress was made and in January 1944 the finance and general purposes sub-committee was forced to concede that, although it might be possible in the future to get the government to agree to wrap up its various departmental grants into a block payment, it was 'doubtful whether it would be possible to secure grant for the work of the Council as a whole'.[78] It would be another 15 years before the Council was able to convince the government otherwise.[79]

There had always been a strong religious underpinning to the Council's work. From its inception, key figures such as Ernest Barker, Wyndham Deedes, and Lindsay had drawn much of their inspiration from their Christian beliefs.[80] Such views chimed well with emerging thinking within the Church of England in the inter-war period, which was beginning to conceive of its role at the heart of a new welfare society where the voluntary movement had an essential role to play alongside the state. Frank Prochaska has accused the established church at this time of abandoning its commitment to the voluntary movement and of colluding in its demise in the face of the growing statutory advance.[81] Putting to one side for the moment the issue of whether or not the development of the state squeezed out the voluntary movement, such criticism is a misrepresentation of the church's position. It was not anti-voluntary action and, as Matthew Grimley has argued, went out of its way to defend the voluntary principle.[82] Rather it accepted the widely held view of the importance of a partnership between the voluntary movement and the state, a view which went to the heart of the Council's philosophy.

In May 1938 the Council set up a new body, the Central Churches Group, aimed at harnessing the spirit of philanthropy within faith communities.[83] From the outset, the group was ecumenical, bringing together the various Protestant denominations and representatives of the Roman Catholic and Jewish faiths. Its first chair was Dr. Geoffrey Fisher, Bishop of London 1939–45 and Archbishop of Canterbury 1945–61. The Council once more provided the secretariat. Local committees were established throughout the country and a *Bulletin* was distributed to church leaders aimed at encouraging faith groups and their members to get involved in voluntary action.[84] The group took on a strategic role and produced reports on a wide range of social issues, such as the future of town planning and the organisation of air-raid services. The group continued after the war and played a part in the development of the post-war voluntary movement, taking a particular interest in setting up good neighbour schemes in the 1960s. Renamed the Churches and Religious Bodies Group, it was closed down in 1974 as part of the Council's economy drive and policy of centralisation.[85]

One other associated group worthy of note for its wartime work was the Standing Conference of National Juvenile Organisations (which changed its name during the war to the Standing Conference of National Voluntary Youth Organisations). This group had been established in 1936 to bring together national organisations interested in youth work and during the war it did much to keep the issue at the forefront of policy. It carried out detailed inquiries into a range of topics, including the problems of young people in industry, juvenile delinquency, and international youth work.[86] In 1939 the government gave a boost to the youth movement with the publication of a circular, *The Service of Youth,* which advocated setting up youth committees in all local authorities and called for a new spirit of youth voluntary national service.[87] Grants were made available to voluntary groups to take the work forward and in 1940 the standing conference launched a campaign for more adult volunteers to provide leadership for youth work.[88] As with the other associated groups, it continued to play an important role in the work of the Council and wider voluntary movement after the war, eventually setting up as an independent organisation in 1980.[89]

The governance of these associated groups was complicated. Although ultimately accountable to the Council's Executive Committee, which was responsible under charity law for their actions, each in practice was free to develop its own policy. The Council provided administrative support and received regular reports on their activities. But these were for information only, and little attempt was made to influence their work. This was both a strength and weakness. The strength was that it allowed the Council to extend its influence over a much wider range of issues than it would ever have been able to do through its own efforts. The drawback was that it had minimal influence over the policies being pursued and for which it was accountable. For the time being the advantages were held to outweigh the drawbacks. The Council's new director, Haynes, was a firm believer in this federated model and would write a lengthy paper towards the end of the war arguing that it should form the basis of the Council's post-war development. Ultimately, the tensions inherent in such a structure proved too great to manage and the Council embarked on a radically different course. Over time, all the associated groups and networks moved to independence and the Council revised its governance structure to exercise greater central control. What the Council gained with authority it lost with reach and influence.

EXISTING ACTIVITIES

Although the Council enjoyed much success through the work of the new groups it helped establish, it was forced to suspend many of its existing activities. The community centre movement, which had been championed by the Council since 1925 to provide a focal point for neighbourhood activity on the new housing estates, was badly impacted by the restrictions on new building and commandeering of community premises. According to Bourdillon, the number of active community associations dropped from 220 in 1939 to 62 by 1944.[90] Much important work, however, continued and existing centres became the focus for a range of new services, from support for evacuees and the care of older people to the organisation of firewatchers' groups and day nurseries.[91] A boost was given in 1944 when the Education Act imposed a requirement on local authorities to provide facilities for 'further education' and the ministry published a leaflet on community centres suggesting they could be used for this purpose.[92] As if to reflect its new-found sense of purpose, the consultative council was replaced by the semi-autonomous National Federation of Community Associations, with the Council again providing the secretariat.[93]

The same frustrations were experienced with village halls. The development of village halls before the war was one of the Council's biggest success stories.

Over 1200 halls were built by 1939, funded by a mix of loans and grants from the Development Commission and the Carnegie UK Trust.[94] However, as with the community centres, village halls faced an uncertain time during the war. Funding was curtailed, premises requisitioned for war purposes, and new building stopped. Despite these difficulties, many halls played an important role in the war effort, offering themselves for a wide range of activities, from lectures on pig keeping and herb collection to campaigns on recycling, food production and allotments.[95] As the war came to an end, there was a renewed focus on the need to build new halls. The Council was adamant that the movement should be locally led. 'There is all the difference in the world', it stressed, 'between a centre which has been in some measure created by the activities of the people themselves and a building which has been dumped in their midst, no matter how excellently planned or well-equipped.'[96] The village halls movement remained a central element of the Council's post-war programme, and this focus on local accountability connected in later years with a growing emphasis within social policy discourse on participation and community development.[97]

Another mainstay of the Council's work before the war was the occupational club movement, which provided a range of social support to individuals affected by the depression. Not surprisingly, with unemployment less of an issue during the war, the men's clubs declined in most areas, although they remained in demand in parts of South Wales and Scotland where levels of unemployment remained high.[98] In other areas, there was a shift in focus away from support for unemployed people towards adult education and educational provision for troops and evacuees.[99] Women's clubs did better and expanded during the war. By 1941 there were over 670 women's clubs, with a membership of 31,000, compared to 530 clubs for men and a membership of 34,000.[100] The women's clubs were involved in a wide range of activities, such as making comforts for soldiers and providing social activities for evacuated children.[101] However, their main success was judged to lie in the impact they had on the lives of the women. Following a meeting in London of the Standing Conference of Women's Clubs in June 1945, reference was made in the Executive Committee to 'the striking development since the work started in 1933 in the capacity of many of the women club members to speak and take part in meetings'. This, in itself, it was felt, 'made the work worthwhile and was a most encouraging feature'.[102]

Despite wartime pressures, the Council continued its pre-war focus on the promotion of cultural activities. This was classic Idealist thinking, which informed the work of the Council from its inception. Voluntary action wasn't just about the relief of poverty but had a higher purpose of enriching lives and building communities. Music and drama were not luxuries to be disposed of during the war; rather they were integral to the development of strong and resilient communities and the maintenance of civilian morale. The *Black Out* and the requisitioning of premises had an inevitable impact on what could be done locally, but with support from the Carnegie UK Trust a way could often be found around the restrictions. In 1940, for example, the Council helped organise a travelling school for variety entertainment, which held 40 schools in 9 weeks across the country, attended by over 4000 students.[103] In the same year the Essex Rural Community Council ran a travelling cinema for local residents.[104] According to Brasnett, the music and drama activities sponsored by the Council did not merely survive the war but grew 'in size and strength'.[105]

LOCAL NETWORKS

No new rural community councils or councils of social service were set up during the war, but much important activity was carried out under their auspices. Both helped in coordinating voluntary action on the ground and connecting local groups with statutory authorities. The rural councils made a significant contribution to the nation's food production through the administration of the new Rural Industries Equipment Fund, which provided interest-free loans to blacksmiths to update their equipment.[106] The development of councils of social service before the war had been slower than hoped. By 1939 it was estimated that there were about 120 councils across the UK, but only a quarter provided the full range of services. Many had become little more than specialist social work agencies and had moved away from their main function as focal points for local voluntary action and bridges between voluntary groups and local government.[107] In October 1941 a national conference was convened by the Council to examine what more could be done to expand the movement and a Councils of Social Service Committee was set up to advise on the way forward.[108]

At a second national conference in December 1943, a memorandum for the future was unveiled.[109] It suggested a two-tier approach to development might be necessary, with a simpler service being provided in smaller towns where funding was scarcer. The memorandum called for the establishment of a Standing Conference of Councils of Social Service, with a representative central committee for guiding policy and development. A provisional committee was set up charged with bringing the standing conference into being and, in November 1945, following considerable discussion with local bodies over the constitution, the standing conference met for the first time.[110] The development of local councils was seen as a key post-war priority: 'The problems of peace are proving in many ways no less difficult than those of wartime', the Council noted in its annual report for 1944–45. 'The local authorities day by day are finding their burdens of responsibility mounting; they are looking for the assistance of voluntary organisations'. It is difficult to see, it argued, 'how all this help can be effectively mobilised unless there is at work in each town and area a body which seeks to fulfil the ideals of a Council of Social Service'.[111] Building a strong network of local resource agencies remained a priority for the Council for much of the next 50 years.

One significant development at this time was the establishment of an independent, Scottish Council of Social Service. Plans had been prepared before the war but put on hold when hostilities began and, instead, a Scottish advisory committee was set up to support the Council's regional officer in Scotland. In 1942 a new independent organisation was launched in Edinburgh, with Lord Elgin as president and the Council's regional officer for Scotland, A.M. Struthers, as secretary.[112] The Council provided financial support for the new organisation. By the following year it was able to report excellent progress: 'During the past year this Council has thoroughly established itself as the recognised co-ordinating agency in social and community work in Scotland and the closest contacts are maintained with the National Council on questions of general policy.'[113] Scotland joined Northern Ireland, which established its own council in 1938, and an independent agency in Wales followed soon after the war. This was an important moment in the history of the Council. When it was formed in 1919 it had seen its remit as being UK-wide, although in reality most of its work focused on England and Wales. With the setting up of independent councils in Scotland and Northern Ireland, soon to be followed in Wales, its sphere of influence was significantly reduced.[114] The positive relations between the Council and the Scottish council remained and extended to the other councils. New structures were put in place to ensure cooperation over policy and for much of the post-war period the other councils were content to cede responsibility for matters affecting the UK as a whole to the National Council. Tensions arose on occasions, usually over matters of funding or policy, but, in the main, independence was handled with sensitivity and skill by all sides.

FINANCE

Despite the importance of the work the Council was engaged in, and the government's acceptance in principle of the need to provide additional support for voluntary organisations to cover increased wartime costs, funding remained as tight as ever. Budget deficits were an annual reality and the question of financial sustainability was never far from the minds of the Executive Committee. In 1941 the Council noted that 'increased taxation and the prior claims of specific war charities have made it more difficult than ever to raise money for the advisory and co-ordinating work of the Council' and it was estimated that at least £10,000 was required to maintain current activities.[115] A number of familiar strategies were examined to address the financial shortfall. There was an annual round of cost-cutting to bring the projected budget deficit within acceptable levels. The Council reduced staff numbers in the first six months of 1939–40, but in June 1941 the finance and general purposes sub-committee was advised that any further reduction would seriously impact on its work.[116] The option of reducing salaries was explored, but was felt to be the wrong step at the current time.[117] With little scope for further cuts to expenditure, the Council turned its attention to fundraising. In March 1940 the finance and general purposes sub-committee agreed to a target of at least £5000 a year from voluntary income.[118] In its annual report for 1941–42, the Council made 'an urgent appeal for more subscriptions and donations, whether large or small, so that, as a pioneer body in social service, its capacity to live and move with the times can be adequately safeguarded'.[119] The fundraising drive was not confined to the UK, and it was suggested that support might be forthcoming from the US and from British communities overseas.[120] There was some success. In October 1941 it was reported that £10,000 had been raised by the British community in Argentina, and in December a further £900 was reported having been raised in South Africa for the specific purpose of the relief of distress in South Wales. Money came from some unexpected sources, with an annual donation of £50 being received from the King, the Council's patron.[121] From July 1942 a concerted effort was made to generate business support. Over the next couple of years big-name backers were secured, including Imperial Chemicals Industries, Unilever Brothers, British Oxygen Company, Rolls Royce, Shell-Mex, and BP. Most were secured with seven-year covenants, channelled through the charities department, enabling the Council to take advantage of the available tax concessions.[122]

INTERNAL DEVELOPMENTS

To support its wartime activities the Council took steps to strengthen its internal services, particularly those relating to information, advice, and research. These developments laid the foundations for the new shape the Council would take in the post-war years, with a greater emphasis on generic support for the voluntary movement as a whole. An information department was established to support the work of the CAB and the production of the 'Citizens' Notes', but gradually it began to take on a wider remit to provide information and intelligence to underpin the rest of the Council's work.[123] Funding was also secured for a new library and a lending scheme was established for members.[124] In 1941 a central planning group was set up to oversee a comprehensive research agenda to consider 'the part which is being played by voluntary associations, and how best they can prepare themselves to meet the social problems which will arise after the war'.[125] A new studies and research department was established and the Council seconded Dr. Henry Mess from Bedford College in London to become its new director of studies. Mess joined Bedford College from the Council of Social Service in Tyneside, which he had directed between the wars and where he had pioneered a number of innovatory programmes in the field of unemployment. At the Council, he produced a series of thoughtful papers on the future of voluntary action, some published posthumously, but his premature death in 1944 and ongoing financial difficulties cut short the work of the new department.[126] Mess' work, although incomplete, put down a marker for a more systematic approach to the study of the voluntary movement and the post-war years would see the Council, with a growing number of universities, begin to carry out more documentation and research.

With the Council expanding its operations, attention turned to the question of accommodation. In addition to its headquarters in Bedford Square, it was renting several other premises in London, as well as office space in Leeds and Birmingham. In 1944 it gave consideration to an ambitious plan for a new headquarters that would provide more space for the Council and could be shared with other groups: 'There is a great need for a national focus for voluntary work', it noted in its annual report, 'which could serve as a general information centre, providing a library and common room, canteen, committee rooms and certain other facilities, which, while beyond the resources of a single organisation, might well be within the range of a well-planned co-operative venture.'[127] Lack of funds prevented the Council from moving forward with the plan immediately and it was another 70 years before the dream was fully realised with the opening of the Council's newly purchased King's Cross headquarters in London.

Another development with a long-term impact was the growth of its international work. An overseas and international committee was set up early in 1943 to oversee activities.[128] An international common room for social workers was opened at 32 Gordon Square in London, where the Council's library was housed, offering a meeting space and lecture room for overseas visitors. Guests during the war included the American social anthropologist, Margaret Mead, and Princess (later Queen) Juliana of the Netherlands.[129] Visits and tours were arranged to share ideas, although they were deemed of only limited value as 'the impressions they leave are often fleeting'. 'Something more', the Council felt, was 'required if true understanding between nations is to grow'.[130] The British Committee for the International Exchange of Social Workers and Administrators was established in 1944 to encourage dialogue.[131] Voluntary action, it was argued, could bring nations together just as much as local communities. After the horrors of the war, such internationalism would come to be seen as an increasingly urgent priority.

FUTURE DIRECTION

In 1941 the Nuffield College Social Reconstruction Survey was established to assist with post-war planning. A sub-committee was formed on the role to be played by the statutory and voluntary social services, and the Council was asked to contribute to its work. W.G.S. Adams joined the sub-committee, along with Lindsay, master of Balliol, who was influential in the work of the occupational club movement before the war. A report on the work of the sub-committee was published in 1945 in a volume of essays, *Voluntary Social Services: Their Place in the Modern State*.[132] It provides a revealing insight into the state of thinking on the voluntary movement at the end of the war and of the opportunities and challenges ahead. It suggested that there were three very different directions the voluntary movement could take. It could disappear, with its functions taken over altogether by the state. It could continue in a limited capacity, focusing mainly on pioneering new models of social care, which would then be subsumed within the statutory services. Or it could continue to grow and develop alongside the statutory services, filling gaps where needed, pioneering new responses to social need, and advocating and campaigning for change. The report's sympathy clearly lay with this third, more expansive vision. G.D.H. Cole, who chaired the main committee, suggested that the history of the voluntary movement meant that it would be 'a great mistake' to assume 'that as the scope of State action expands, the scope of voluntary social service necessarily contracts'.[133] For Lindsay, it was clear that voluntary movement had 'a part to play in a 'positive' as much as in a laissez-faire state'.[134]

As well as mapping a future direction for the voluntary movement, the report raised challenges it felt would need to be addressed after the war. It pointed to a major shift that had taken place within the voluntary movement since the beginning of the century, away from a largely volunteer-run movement to one increasingly reliant on paid professionals, and to the tensions that this would likely cause in the future. The push for greater effectiveness and efficiency, it argued, would continue, and there would be an increased need for training for the voluntary leaders of the future. The challenge would be to achieve this without compromising values. 'Voluntary work', Lindsay wrote, 'ought to be efficient and yet efficiency is sometimes its undoing.' Somewhat prophetically, given the fundraising scandal the movement was to face 70 years later, he noted that, although voluntary groups needed money, it was impossible to 'regard with complacency the methods of some of their financial drives'. He concluded that voluntary organisations 'will continue to be bothered by the problems of reconciling variety and spontaneity with efficiency and co-ordination'.[135] In its post-war work the Council was increasingly confronted with the challenge of reconciling this tension. It focused much of its efforts on providing voluntary groups with advice and training to support their professionalisation, but it also became more assertive in challenging poor practice, especially in fundraising, where it threatened to damage the reputation and standing of the movement. In doing so it laid itself open to charges that it was taking the movement in the wrong direction, by blurring the boundaries with the commercial and public sectors and undermining the values and methods that made it distinctive.[136]

As well as contributing to thinking about the future shape of the voluntary movement, the Council began to plan for its own post-war existence. In February 1944 the Emergency Committee gave approval to a statement prepared by Haynes. It was far-reaching in scope, covering both governance and mission, and provided the 'guiding document' for the Council's post-war development.[137] That the Council's governance was in need of an overhaul was not open to question. The current structure was unwieldy in the extreme. It consisted of a Council of 173 representatives drawn from its membership and other stakeholders, including 10 central government departments, which met annually; an Executive Committee of 61, including representatives from 6 government departments in an advisory capacity, which met quarterly; a finance and general purposes sub-committee; and a series of policy committees to lead on particular areas of activity.

The question of reform had first been considered in 1940, but wartime pressures and the establishment of the Emergency Committee meant that long-term decisions were delayed.[138] When the Council returned to the matter at the end of the war, the most pressing issue was felt to be the need to slim down the Executive Committee to more manageable proportions. The first suggestion for a committee of 50 was seen not to go far enough and a figure of 36 was finally settled upon, although with flexibility for co-options. As before, members would be largely chosen to represent different interests on the Council. The changes were formally ratified at the annual meeting in December 1945, although it was noted that a letter had been received from the Tyneside Council of Social Service suggesting that the representation of area councils of social service was inadequate.[139] This issue of representation, and who the Council could legitimately be held to be speaking on behalf of, grew in importance after the war, particularly as its membership expanded and it took a more active role in advocacy and campaigning.

Haynes also set out his vision for the future of the Council.[140] His starting point was his 'belief in the value of individual personality' and his assertion that 'the individual can only find himself (sic) and the outlet for his powers in association with others'. While informal community action was important, the Council's main concern should be with 'organised group life', which, he argued, was a 'vital part of our society' and 'a measure of our freedom'. He outlined the main ways the Council should seek to support these groups. On the one hand, it should continue to offer 'special services' to the associated groups and committees within a federated structure that would recognise their 'freedom and autonomy', but it should also seek to develop a range of 'basic services' to support the needs of all voluntary groups. This dual strategy formed the basis of the Council's work for the next 20 years. Associated groups were given almost complete autonomy to pursue their goals, unencumbered by any restrictions from the Council, while a range of core services, such as policy, information and research, were developed to support the needs of the wider movement.

As for future relations with government, Haynes restated his belief that the Council should continue to play a coordination role between voluntary groups and statutory bodies. While he reflected on 'twenty-five years of a fruitful partnership', he warned against any attempt by government to interfere with the movement's independence. The state, he argued, 'should not seek to incorporate into itself all those self-directing group activities which help to make the rich texture of social life', but instead 'should rather help and foster them'. This notion of the state as an enabler of independent voluntary action came to define the Council's view about the terms of the partnership to be struck between the government and the voluntary movement. But it was laden with controversy. Critics accused the Council of leading the voluntary movement into an unholy alliance with the state and for being willing to trade independence for influence, an accusation it would fiercely reject. It argued that partnership did not inevitably lead to co-option and pointed to numerous advances it secured as a result of its closeness to government and to many examples where it had opposed policies held to be against the interests of the movement.[141]

Conclusion

The Council can be judged to have had a *Good War*. It played a crucial role in coordinating the work of voluntary organisations and strengthening relations with government. It helped establish a number of influential groups that carried out important wartime work and went on to have further success after the war. It strengthened its regional structure and invested in an enhanced role for information and research. Despite wartime restrictions, it managed to sustain those programmes in the countryside, towns, and new estates that had been such a feature of its work in the inter-war period. It contributed to debates about reconstruction and the future of the voluntary movement and found time to strengthen its governance and reformulate its mission. *The Times* in March 1945, looking back on its first 25 years of 'fruitful work', believed the war 'was a turning-point in the Council's work' that had resulted in 'a strengthening of relations with the Government' and with 'independent voluntary associations'. It suggested that, 'strengthened and refreshed by its war-time experiences', it could aim 'with confidence at reconstituting itself as the national centres of common counsel for all forms of voluntary social service'.[142]

But the war had also taken its toll. Alongside other voluntary organisations, and indeed the nation itself, its people were exhausted and resources depleted and it entered the post-war era with a measure of uncertainty and trepidation. The war had greatly expanded the role of the state across large areas of public life. The voluntary movement had not been pushed to the margins, as some commentators feared, but its future was unclear. Whichever political party was given the mandate to rebuild the nation, one thing was certain: the state would take a far greater role in the lives of citizens than ever before. Voluntary action would need to adapt to this changing world and find a new and compelling articulation of its purpose to retain its relevance. Helping with this task was the Council's next chapter in its history.

Notes

1. Prochaska, 2011, p. 37.
2. Calder, 1992.
3. See, for example, Ferguson and Fitzgerald, 1954.
4. Rose, 2003, p. 20.
5. Fielding et al., 1995, p. 213. See also Smith, 1986.
6. Finlayson, 1994, p. 226.
7. Finlayson, 1994, pp. 227–28. See also Colpus, 2011.
8. Mess and Braithwaite, 1947.
9. Grant, 2014, p. 126.
10. NCSS Annual Report 1939–40, p. 14.
11. NCSS Annual Report 1939–40, p. 15.
12. Meeting of Executive Committee, 20 August 1940; Special Minute Book; London Metropolitan Archives (LMA): LMA/4016/IS/055/01. Sack was

ordained the following year and appointed rector of Elstead in Surrey. He died in 1953. For a tribute, see Smeal, 1969.

13. For a critical examination of Haynes' work, see Jenkins, 2001. For a more positive review, see Pimlott Baker, 2004.

14. For an excellent history of the COS and Family Welfare Association, see Lewis, 1995.

15. Jenkins, 2001.

16. Hinton's time at the Council is dealt with in Chaps. 7 and 8.

17. Minutes of Executive Committee, 26 October 1939; LMA/4016/IS/A01/031(1).

18. Minutes of Executive Committee, 27 October 1939; LMA/4016/IS/A/01/030(5).

19. NCSS Annual Report 1939–40, p. 5. Deedes is discussed more fully in Chap. 3.

20. Minutes of Executive Committee, 25 April 1940; LMA/4016/IS/A/0/031(2); Minutes of Executive Committee, 24 October 1940; LMA/4016/IS/A/0/031(2).

21. Finlayson, 1994, p. 241.

22. For a fuller discussion of these tensions, which led to the abandonment of the federated model, see Chap. 7.

23. NCSS Annual Report 1939–40.

24. Leaflets issued by the Council included *Voluntary social service organisations and the national service campaign* and *Voluntary social service organisations in time of war*, quoted in Haynes, 1939.

25. NCSS Annual Report 1943–44, p. 4.

26. Minutes of Executive Committee, 26 October 1939; LMA/4016/IS/A01/031(1).

27. NCSS Annual Report 1943–44, p. 4.

28. Minutes of Executive Committee, 27 April 1939; LMA/4016/IS/A01/030(7).

29. Minutes of Executive Committee, 27 April 1939; LMA/4016/IS/A01/030(7).

30. NCSS Annual Report 1939–40.

31. Minutes of Executive Committee, 25 January 1940; LMA/4016/IS/A01/031(1).

32. Letter from J.A. Barlow from the Treasury to William Deedes, 9 November 1939; LMA/4016/IS/A01/031(1).

33. The establishment of the Voluntary Services Unit is discussed in Chap. 7.

34. Letter from J.A. Barlow from the Treasury to William Deedes, 9 November 1939; LMA/4016/IS/A01/031(1). Rushcliffe, as Sir Henry Betterton, was a Conservative politician and Minister of Labour, 1931–34, in Ramsay MacDonald's National Government. See Chap. 4.

35. Minutes of Executive Committee, 25 April 1940; LMA/4016/IS/A/0/031(2).

36. NCSS Annual Report 1941–42, p. 4.

37. Letter from Sandford Carter to F. Sharpley at the Ministry of Information, 1 March 1940; NCSS uncatalogued archives, LMA.

38. Bourdillon, 1945a, p. 194.

39. For a good discussion on the establishment and early years of the CAB movement, see Blaiklock, 2012.
40. NCSS Annual Report 1939–40, p. 8.
41. Brasnett, 1969, p. 99.
42. NCSS Annual Report 1939–40.
43. Brasnett, 1969, p. 100.
44. Ibid., p. 103.
45. NCSS Annual Report 1941–42.
46. NCSS Annual Report 1941–42.
47. Minutes of Joint Meeting of Executive and Emergency Committees, 14 December 1944; LMA/4016/IS/A/01/031(2).
48. For a discussion of Keeling's role in the establishment of the Council, see Chap. 2.
49. Brasnett, 1969, p. 97.
50. See Keeling, 1961, for a personal account of her life and work, and Pederson, 2004, for a summary of her achievements.
51. Keeling's role in the foundation of the National Old People's Welfare Committee is discussed below.
52. Hadow's contribution to the Council and the rural community council movement is discussed in Chap. 3.
53. Bingham, 2005, p. 117. For a discussion on the 'myth' of Labour's hostility to voluntarism, see Deakin and Davis Smith, 2011.
54. Jowett, 1967.
55. NCSS Annual Reports 1941–42 and 1944–45.
56. NCSS Annual Report 1944–45, p. 17.
57. NCSS Annual Report 1942–43, p. 5.
58. NCSS Annual Report 1944–45, p. 17.
59. On the post-war work of the CAB movement, see Blaiklock, 2012. The tensions between the movement and the Council, which led to a difficult divorce in 1975, are discussed in Chap. 7.
60. Brasnett, 1969, p. 105.
61. Ramsey, 1949.
62. Minutes of Executive Committee, 25 April 1940; LMA/4016/IS/A/0/031(2).
63. NCSS Annual Report 1944–45.
64. NCSS Annual Report 1943–44, p. 8.
65. Beaumont, 2013, p. 138.
66. Hinton, 2002, p. 179.
67. Ibid., p. viii.
68. Beaumont, 2013, p. 3.
69. Ibid., p. 138.
70. NCSS Annual Report 1944–45.
71. Beaumont, 2013, p. 142.
72. Women's Group on Public Welfare, 1943.
73. Ibid., p. 106.
74. Morgan, 1947, p. 94.
75. Beaumont, 2013, p. 141. See also Rose, 2003, pp. 58–59.
76. Hinton, 1998, pp. 277–78.
77. Ibid., p. 283.

78. Minutes of the Finance and General Purposes Sub-Committee, 4 January 1944; LMA/4016/IS/A/01/047(2).

79. The government finally agreed to a grant to support the core work of the Council in 1961. See Chap. 7.

80. On Barker and Lindsay, see Grimley, 2004.

81. Prochaska, 2008. See also Prochaska, 2011, p. 45.

82. Grimley, 2004.

83. NCSS Annual Report 1939–40.

84. See, for example, NCSS, 1941.

85. Minutes of Churches Consultative Group, 8 January 1974; Uncatalogued NCSS Archives, LMA.

86. Brasnett, 1969, p. 97.

87. Beard, 1945.

88. NCSS Annual Report 1939–40.

89. See Chap. 7 for further details.

90. Bourdillon, 1945b, p. 186.

91. NCSS Annual Report 1940–41.

92. Mess and King, 1947.

93. NCSS Annual Report 1944–45.

94. NCSS Annual Report 1944–45.

95. NCSS Annual Report 1939–40.

96. NCSS Annual Report 1943–44, p. 15.

97. The concept of 'participation' took root in the 1960s and covered many aspects of social policy. See, for example, Richardson, 1983.

98. NCSS Annual Report 1940–41.

99. Minutes of Special Meeting of Executive Committee, 8 July 1941; LMA/4016/IS/A/01/031(2).

100. NCSS Annual Report 1940–41.

101. Minutes of Executive Committee, 25 January 1940; LMA/4016/IS/A01/031(1).

102. Minutes of Joint Meeting of Executive and Emergency Committee, 28 March 1945; LMA/4016/IS/A/01/031(3).

103. NCSS Annual Report 1940–41, p. 11.

104. Minutes of Executive Committee, 25 January 1940; LMA/4016/IS/A01/031(1).

105. Brasnett, 1969, p. 110.

106. Morgan, 1947.

107. NCSS Annual Report 1942–43.

108. NCSS Annual Report 1941–42.

109. NCSS Annual Report 1943–44.

110. NCSS Annual Report 1944–45.

111. NCSS Annual Report 1944–45, p. 14.

112. Brasnett, 1969, p. 94.

113. NCSS Annual Report 1943–44, p. 12.

114. The Council had opened a Welsh office in Cardiff in 1933 at the height of the unemployment crisis. In 1934 an independent South Wales and Monmouthshire Council of Social Service was set up. This grew rapidly, resulting in the Council closing its Welsh department in 1938 to avoid confusion.

115. NCSS Annual Report 1940–41, p. 17.

116. NCSS Annual Report 1939–40.
117. Minutes of the Finance and General Purposes Sub-Committee, 5 June 1941; LMA/4016/IS/A/01/0/46(4).
118. Minutes of the Finance and General Purposes Sub-Committee, 10 September 1941; LMA/4016/IS/A/01/047(1).
119. NCSS Annual Report 1941–42, p. 15.
120. Minutes of the Finance and General Purposes Sub-Committee, 10 September 1941; LMA/4016/IS/A/01/047(1).
121. Minutes of the Finance and General Purposes Sub-Committee, 23 October and 16 December 1941; LMA/4016/IS/A/01/047(1).
122. Minutes of the Finance and General Purposes Sub-Committee, April to October 1944; LMA/4016/IS/A/01/047(3).
123. NCSS Annual Report 1941–42.
124. NCSS Annual Report 1943–44.
125. NCSS Annual Report 1940–41, p. 17.
126. Brasnett, 1969, pp. 120–129. Some of Mess' articles appeared in an edited book of essays under his name published as Mess, 1947.
127. NCSS Annual Report 1943–44, p. 23.
128. Brasnett, 1969, p. 117.
129. Ibid., p. 118.
130. NCSS Annual Report 1943–44, p. 12.
131. NCSS Annual Report 1943–44.
132. Bourdillon, 1945c.
133. Cole, 1945, p. 29.
134. Lindsay, 1945, p. 299.
135. Ibid., p. 306.
136. See Chaps. 8 and 9 for a fuller discussion of these issues.
137. Haynes, G. (1944) *The future purpose and organisation of the National Council of Social Service*, paper presented to Joint Meeting of the Executive Committee and Emergency Committee, 8 February 1944; LMA/4016/IS/A/01/027(2).
138. NCSS Annual Report 1940–41.
139. Minutes of Joint Meeting of the Executive and Emergency Committees, 5 June 1946; LMA/4016/IS/A/01/031(3).
140. Haynes, 1944, *Op. Cit.*
141. This issue is discussed in detail in Chaps. 8, 9 and 11.
142. *The Times*, 31 March 1945, p. 5.

REFERENCES

Beard, F. (1945). Voluntary youth organisations. In A. Bourdillon (Ed.), *Voluntary social services: Their place in the modern state* (pp. 135–149). London: Methuen & Co.

Beaumont, C. (2013). *Housewives and citizens: Domesticity and the women's movement in England, 1928–64*. Manchester: Manchester University Press.

Bingham, D. (Ed.). (2005). *Margaret Simey: From rhetoric to reality: A study of the work of F.G. D'Aeth, social administrator*. Liverpool: Liverpool University Press.

Blaiklock, O. (2012). *Advising the citizen: Citizens Advice Bureaux, voluntarism and the welfare state in Britain, 1938–1964*. Unpublished PhD thesis, King's College, London.

Bourdillon, A. (1945a). Voluntary organisations in war-time—Citizens' Advice Bureaux. In A. Bourdillon (Ed.), *Voluntary social services: Their place in the modern state* (pp. 194–205). London: Methuen & Co.

Bourdillon, A. (1945b). Voluntary organisations to facilitate co-operation and co-ordination. In A. Bourdillon (Ed.), *Voluntary social services: Their place in the modern state* (pp. 164–193). London: Methuen & Co.

Bourdillon, A. (Ed.). (1945c). *Voluntary social services: Their place in the modern state.* London: Methuen & Co.

Brasnett, M. (1969). *Voluntary social action.* London: NCSS.

Calder, A. (1992). *The people's war: Britain 1939–1945.* London: Pimlico.

Cole, G. D. H. (1945). A retrospect of the history of voluntary social service. In A. Bourdillon (Ed.), *Voluntary social services: Their place in the modern state* (pp. 11–30). London: Methuen & Co.

Colpus, E. (2011). The week's good cause: Mass culture and cultures of philanthropy at the inter-war BBC. *Twentieth Century British History, 22*(3), 305–329.

Deakin, N., & Davis Smith, J. (2011). Labour, charity and voluntary action: The myth of hostility. In M. Hilton & J. McKay (Eds.), *The ages of voluntarism: How we got to the big society* (pp. 69–93). Oxford: Oxford University Press for British Academy.

Ferguson, S., & Fitzgerald, H. (1954). *History of the Second World War: Studies in the social services.* London: Longmans, Green & Co.

Fielding, S., Thompson, P., & Tiratsoo, N. (Eds.). (1995). *'England arise!': The Labour Party and popular politics in 1940s Britain.* Manchester: Manchester University Press.

Finlayson, G. (1994). *Citizen, state and social welfare in Britain, 1830–1990.* Oxford: Clarendon Press.

Grant, P. (2014). *Philanthropy and voluntary action in the First World War: Mobilising charity.* London: Routledge/Taylor & Francis Group.

Grimley, M. (2004). *Citizenship, community and the Church of England: Liberal Anglican theories of the state between the wars.* Oxford: Oxford University Press.

Haynes, G. (1939). Voluntary service in time of war. *Social Service Review, 20*(5), 171–175.

Hinton, J. (1998). Volunteerism and the welfare state: Women's Voluntary Service in the 1940s. *Twentieth Century British History, 9*, 274–305.

Hinton, J. (2002). *Women, social leadership, and the Second World War.* Oxford: Oxford University Press.

Jenkins, J. (2001). The organisation man: George Haynes at the National Council of Social Service. In L. Black et al. (Eds.), *Consensus or coercion?: The state, the people and social cohesion in post-war Britain* (pp. 151–168). Cheltenham: New Clarion Press.

Jowett, A. (1967). Dorothy Keeling. *Social Service Quarterly, 41*(2), 55–57.

Keeling, D. (1961). *The crowded stairs: Recollections of social work in Liverpool.* London: NCSS.

Lewis, J. (1995). *The voluntary sector, the state and social work in Britain: The Charity Organisation Society/Family Welfare Association since 1869.* Aldershot: Edward Elgar.

Lindsay, A. (1945). Conclusion. In A. Bourdillon (Ed.), *Voluntary social services: Their place in the modern state* (pp. 298–306). London: Methuen & Co.

Mess, H. (Ed.). (1947). *Voluntary social services since 1918.* London: Kegan Paul.

Mess, H., & Braithwaite, C. (1947). The finance of voluntary social service. In H. Mess (Ed.), *Voluntary social services since 1918* (pp. 188–203). London: Kegan Paul.

Mess, H., & King, H. (1947). Community centres and community associations. In H. Mess (Ed.), *Voluntary social services since 1918* (pp. 69–79). London: Kegan Paul.

Morgan, J. (1947). The National Council of Social Service. In H. Mess (Ed.), *Voluntary social services since 1918* (pp. 80–105). London: Kegan Paul.

NCSS. (1941). *In the service of the community: The bulletin of the Churches Group, No. 1.* London: NCSS.

Pederson, S. (2004). Dorothy Clarissa Keeling. In *Oxford dictionary of national biography*. Oxford: Oxford University Press.

Pimlott Baker, A. (2004). Sir George Ernest Haynes. In *Oxford dictionary of national biography*. Oxford: Oxford University Press.

Prochaska, F. (2008). *Christianity and social service in modern Britain: The disinherited spirit.* Oxford: Oxford University Press.

Prochaska, F. (2011). The war and charity. In M. Oppenheimer & N. Deakin (Eds.), *Beveridge and voluntary action in Britain and the wider British world* (pp. 36–50). Manchester: Manchester University Press.

Ramsey, D. (1949). The National Old People's Welfare Committee. *Social Service Quarterly, 25,* 26–28.

Richardson, A. (1983). *Participation.* London: Routledge and Kegan Paul.

Rose, S. (2003). *Which people's war?: National identity and citizenship in wartime Britain, 1939–1945.* Oxford: Oxford University Press.

Smeal, J. (1969). Leonard Shoeten Sack. *Social Service Quarterly, 43*(1), 7–10.

Smith, H. (Ed.). (1986). *War and social change: British society in the Second World War.* Manchester: Manchester University Press.

Women's Group on Public Welfare. (1943). *Our towns: A close up.* London: Oxford University Press.

CHAPTER 6

Marking Time

INTRODUCTION

The immediate post-war period was a difficult time for the voluntary movement. Continuing austerity and wartime restrictions, combined with rising prices and higher rates of taxation, led to concerns about a reduction in individual giving and a shortage of volunteers.[1] More fundamentally, the movement was faced with something of a crisis of identity. There was a feeling that voluntary organisations and volunteers that had equipped themselves so well during the war were out of step with the times. The election of the first majority Labour government in 1945 under Clement Attlee saw a significant increase in the role of the state across all aspects of the lives of citizens and the question was asked whether the voluntary movement had a future. By the end of the period, however, it had recovered its poise. The Labour administration turned out more supportive than expected, the up-turn in the economy helped its financial position, and it confounded sceptics by continuing to grow. New national organisations such as the National Association for Mental Health (now MIND), the Association of Parents of Backward Children (now MENCAP), and the Spastics Society (now SCOPE) were established and a new breed of voluntary agencies emerged that transformed the face of voluntary action in the following decades.[2]

The Council's fortunes mirrored those of the wider movement. At the end of the war its finances were in a perilous state, resulting in a series of cost-cutting measures and a new fundraising drive. Although it had largely recovered by the mid-1950s, there were few developments of note. Most of its work continued to be delivered through its associated groups and its involvement was primarily limited to an administrative role. There was growth in some of its generic work, especially policy and information, but long-planned developments in research and publications were held back by financial difficulties. Perhaps the major area of expansion was in the international arena, where it

© The Author(s) 2019
J. Davis Smith, *100 Years of NCVO and Voluntary Action*,
https://doi.org/10.1007/978-3-030-02774-2_6

101

worked closely with the welfare agencies of the United Nations and helped revive the International Conference on Social Work as a forum for global debate. In 1978 the Wolfenden report on the future of voluntary organisations described this period as one of steady but unspectacular advance for the voluntary movement, a period when it 'marked time' after the heroics of the war and before the seismic changes that occurred in the 1960s and 1970s.[3] *Marking time* serves as a good descriptor of the Council's own performance.

FINDING ITS PLACE

The question of what role the voluntary movement should play in the post-war welfare state was never far from the Council's mind. In its first annual report after the war, it reported on the 'revolution' that was taking place in social welfare and the 'ferment of discussion among the voluntary societies as to how these vast changes will affect them'. It observed that the big issue facing the movement was 'whether the great extension of state action threatens to narrow the field for voluntary effort that it may cease to have any significant influence on the social life of the country'.[4] In 1949 it returned to the theme, commenting on the 'widespread apprehension' that had existed within the movement since the war 'lest in the vast changes of recent years voluntary societies may find themselves denied any effective role in community life'.[5] There was a concern that public opinion might be flowing away from the voluntary movement. Responses to a Mass Observation directive suggested a hardening of attitudes towards voluntary action, although antipathy was largely to the notion of *charity* rather than the work of voluntary organisations, which the study suggested retained a good deal of support.[6] The Council rejected the view that there was no role for voluntary action in the new welfare state, but it also dismissed the idea that it was only voluntary action that 'can bring real human understanding to human problems'. It was formed out of a belief in the benefit of partnership and argued that it was a profound mistake to 'see voluntary and statutory agencies in conflict, the one struggling to resist the encroachment of the other'.[7]

The voluntary movement, it suggested, had four roles to play in the new post-war partnership: first, to 'supplement' state services 'and so extend their range beyond what would otherwise be possible'; second, to pioneer new services 'to break new ground which the State is reluctant to till'; third, to develop areas of activity which in the future will 'be generally accepted as more suitable for voluntary action than for public control', such as advice work; and fourth, to carry on with the 'the vast and all-important field of leisure', where the state had little locus and where 'much must be left to the spontaneous activities of citizens themselves'.[8] In an article in *Social Service Review* in 1949, Major Eyre Carter, assistant secretary at the Council, summed up these four functions as experimentation, supplementation, interpretation, and stimulus.[9] But it wasn't just about complementing state services and trying out new solutions to meet the challenges of the time. For the Council, the involvement of the voluntary movement alongside the state was essential for the health and vitality of public services: 'Somehow the people must develop the sense of personal pride and ownership in these new services', it argued, as 'it is through the living sense of direct possession, of personal, individual responsibility, of a share in a common task and a pride in a common achievement that the new services will become an integral part of the shared life of the community'.[10] This role of voluntary action in humanising public services, what the Council called 'a compensating influence', was a crucial element in the movement's search for a new identity in the post-war years. In 1954 the Council concluded that not only had the movement's fears been misplaced and the expansion of the state not led to 'a decline in the exercise of initiative or in the willingness to help oneself', but the new role being carved out had advantages. For too long, it suggested, the movement had to focus 'disproportionate resources' on 'ambulance work'. Freed from these constraints, it could now concentrate on the longer-term aims of developing 'constructive voluntary action'.[11]

The post-war Labour government has been wrongly characterised as implacably opposed to voluntary action. There had always been a strand of thought within the Labour movement hostile to charity, and there were certainly those who saw the disappearance of charity as something to be desired in the forward march of Labour. But there was an equally strong, alternative tradition that saw voluntary action as an essential element of democratic advance, rooted in the friendly societies and mutual aid movements of the nineteenth century, and this tradition was well represented within the new government.[12] Attlee had spent some time after university volunteering within the settlement movement in London and was a committed supporter of voluntary action.[13] He had spoken at the Council's first conference in Oxford in 1920 as mayor of Stepney and written a book on social work supportive of the new spirit of partnership.[14] Other senior ministers such as Herbert Morrison held similar views and even Nye Bevan, architect of the National Health Service, who railed against voluntary hospitals during the passage of the enabling legislation, was committed to ensuring a role for volunteers and voluntary groups within the new system.[15] In 1946 Attlee found an early opportunity to extol the value of voluntary action when opening the Canons Park Community Centre in London: 'This work is absolutely vital', he said, 'if we are to create a real living democracy where people do things for themselves and do not wait to have things done for them.'[16]

The Labour government, perhaps surprisingly, showed itself less than sympathetic to friendly societies, which were removed from their role in the administration of national insurance in 1946.[17] But in other areas, voluntary organisations were explicitly written into new legislation. In 1946 a report from the Ministry of Education recommended an expansion of community centres to augment the provision of further education, and in 1948 provisions were made in the National Assistance Act, which finally repealed the hated Poor Laws, to enable local government to make grants to voluntary organisations to provide care, especially for old and disabled people.[18] During the passage of the Bill, Bevan spoke of the intention of the government 'to make full use of voluntary organisations'.[19] In January 1949 the Ministry of Health issued a circular to local authorities, urging them to encourage voluntary organisations to carry out 'services of the more personal kind which are not covered by existing statutory provision and which indeed can probably best be provided by voluntary workers actuated by a spirit of good neighbourliness'.[20] The difficulty for the voluntary movement was that such support was often dependent on the enthusiasm of individual authorities and many Labour-controlled councils remained hostile. 'It was already clear', the Council noted in 1949, 'that authorities were interpreting their powers in different ways.'[21] Antipathy from some Labour-controlled administrations remained a problem for the voluntary movement, although, ironically, as the century wore on, it would be high-profile Labour-run metropolitan councils like the Greater London Council (GLC) that were in the vanguard of a new wave of municipal support.[22]

On 22 June 1949 a debate, described by the Council as one 'of great significance for voluntary organisations', took place in the House of Lords.[23] It was initiated by the Liberal peer, Lord Samuel, to discuss the Beveridge report, *Voluntary Action,* which had been published the previous year, and offered the Labour government the perfect platform to clarify its position.[24] Summing up for the government, Lord Pakenham couldn't have been clearer: 'We consider that the voluntary spirit is the very lifeblood of democracy', he said, and we are 'convinced that voluntary associations have rendered, are rendering, and must be encouraged to continue to render, great and indispensable service to the community'.[25] The Council applauded Lord Pakenham for having 'made a striking statement which will have come as a welcome reassurance to leaders and workers in the voluntary movement'.[26]

VOLUNTARY ACTION

Beveridge's report, although widely regarded at the time within the voluntary movement, did not make much impact. According to Oppenheimer and Deakin, it 'provoked very little interest and rapidly disappeared from view'.[27] It was the third of his major reports, following his landmark report of 1942 on social insurance and a 1944 report on tackling unemployment.[28] It was the report he felt compelled to write as a corrective to the view that, as the father of the welfare state, he was against voluntary action. Nothing was further from the truth. He had been a volunteer resident at Toynbee Hall and during the war, even while promoting his work on social insurance, made a plea for voluntary action not to be forgotten: 'The essence of Britain', he argued in a speech in Oxford in 1942, consisted of people finding 'a single common purpose' of doing something which is not for 'personal gain', but 'as a member of a community'.[29] He always disliked the label *welfare state,* preferring the term *social service state,* which he believed gave more credence to the need for a balance of statutory and voluntary provision.[30] *Voluntary Action* gave him the perfect opportunity to restate his commitment to the voluntary movement.

The report was commissioned by the National Deposit Friendly Society and much of it was taken up with a plea for the societies to be accorded a greater role in social provision; Beveridge was to remain hugely disappointed that they weren't given a place in the national insurance system introduced in 1946.[31] It was rather disjointed. It called for a Minister-Guardian of Voluntary Action to oversee relations with the voluntary movement, the establishment of an inquiry to examine the use of the tax system to stimulate giving and for a greater focus on the training of staff of voluntary groups. It suggested there was a need for more state funding of voluntary groups, but ruled out the creation of a new cross-governmental body to administer such funds, proposing that the existing separate departmental arrangements should remain in place. It did, however, suggest establishing a new independent corporation, endowed by the state for 'social advance by Voluntary Action', to fund organisations like the Council that found it difficult to attract sufficient private funds.[32]

Reaction was mixed. *The Times* gave a fairly positive verdict, but G.D.H. Cole found it 'interesting but scrappy'.[33] Jose Harris, Beveridge's biographer, suggests that the report, even at the time, seemed 'curiously quixotic and out of date'.[34] It was imbued with Idealist thinking that had long gone out of fashion.[35] In public the Council was supportive, claiming it provided 'a striking vindication of the National Council's purposes and work in contemporary society' and demonstrated 'how illimitable is the field which still remains for voluntary service'.[36] In private, however, it had reservations. It felt the scope of the inquiry was rather narrow, that it failed to address key issues such as funding for local councils of social service, adult education, and staffing shortages and focused too much on the role of the voluntary organisations 'as agents for getting work done', rather than as vehicles for the expression 'of freedom of thought and opinion'.[37]

ORGANISING THE MOVEMENT

The joining up of the voluntary movement was one of the founding aims of the Council, and through its support for specialist groupings at national and local level, it could claim a measure of success. But before the war, it was less successful as a representative for national organisations on matters of common interest. As it searched for its new role after the war, this notion of the Council as a voice for the voluntary movement took on a new sense of urgency. 'The special call to voluntary organisations at the present time', the Council argued in 1947, 'is for more and better co-operation.'[38]

An opportunity to test the post-war appetite of national organisations to come together, and their willingness to see the Council take on the leadership role, came in the aftermath of the Lords debate. During the debate, Lord Samuel proposed the government should consider the establishment of 'Common Good Funds' to support voluntary organisations, financed by the proceeds of 'dormant accounts' held in banks and charitable trusts.[39] A conference of national voluntary organisations, organised by the Council in October

1949, gave strong support to the proposal. The Council was requested 'to inform the Government of the views expressed at this meeting and to keep the national voluntary organisations closely informed of any steps which may be proposed'.[40] It was a clear endorsement of its role in representing the movement to government on matters of national importance and this approach, of convening organisations to discuss issues prior to a submission being put to government, became the *modus operandi* of its advocacy work over the following years. It was an approach that would not go unchallenged, and the extent to which the Council could be held to represent the views of the wider voluntary movement was a question raised on many occasions.[41] The Council was aware of the significance of this episode. It noted in its annual report that it was 'deeply conscious of the responsibilities which have devolved upon it in the discussion of these important matters' and suggested that it provided 'perhaps the most striking example in recent years of the way in which the Council can serve as a forum of discussion for the voluntary movement and of the will to work together which has been such a happy feature of the relationships of voluntary organisations during and since the war'.[42]

Following the conference, a delegation from the Council, led by Lord Samuel, met the lord president of the council, Herbert Morrison, who announced the intention to establish a committee, chaired by the Labour peer, Lord Nathan, to examine the law relating to charitable trusts in England and Wales.[43] The issue of dormant funds was held to raise 'some special problems' and was examined separately. It was estimated that a figure of £13 million might be involved, but in the event nothing came of the idea and it was quietly shelved.[44] The Nathan committee was formally established in 1950 and reported in 1952.[45] It was wide-ranging in scope, covering charity law, tighter regulation of charities, and an extended role for the Charity Commission. Nathan concluded that the voluntary movement was in good health. There had, he said, been 'growing pains' at the start of the welfare state, but these had largely disappeared and been replaced by a positive 'statutory-voluntary partnership'.[46] He called for a new register to be established covering all charities and for a widening of the scope and membership of the Charity Commission, with a minister responsible in Parliament for its work; his committee had heard criticism of the Commission for its 'unimaginative departmentalism' and 'coercion difficult to distinguish from tyranny'.[47] He also called for the updating of the definition of charity and the replacement of the famous preamble to the Statute of 1601, which had governed charity law for the past 350 years.

The Council was broadly supportive of the recommendations, although concerns were expressed that a new register might pose a threat to the independence of charities by bringing them 'under greater supervision and control'. An important freedom, it was suggested, was 'for the voluntary movement to be a minority movement on occasion' and that 'some degree of untidiness might be an inevitable accompaniment of this freedom'. On charity law, it expressed the hope that the definition of community benefit would 'be interpreted in practice in a liberal and up-to-date manner' and would include recreation as a charitable purpose; while on plans to reform and expand the Charity Commission, it noted 'that even with the larger staff, the machine might be cumbrous'.[48]

The government's response was lukewarm. The committee was established under a Labour government, but by the time it reported, the Conservative Party was in power. A white paper was produced two years after the report that accepted some, but not all, the recommendations and there was a further lengthy delay before a new Charities Act was finally introduced in 1960.[49] When the Bill received its royal assent, the Council noted that it 'marked the culmination of the most important piece of work of this kind' and 'a new era of equal partnership and voluntary co-operation between statutory authorities and charities at all levels'.[50] According to David Owen, despite the government's decision not to go for a new definition of public benefit, it represented possibly the most important change to charity law since 1601.[51]

RESOURCING THE MOVEMENT

Financial difficulties continued to plague the Council. It received grants from several government departments, but they were earmarked for specific areas of work and did little to help with administrative costs. Attempts to persuade the government to support core costs had come to nothing, apart from a small contribution during the war. The Council was fortunate to have the long-term support of several trusts and foundations, such as the Carnegie UK Trust and the Nuffield Foundation, and the Development Commission had been supporting the rural work of the Council almost from its inception. The Benevolent Fund, which had been set up by the Council in 1924 as a tax-efficient mechanism for distributing money to charities, also continued to bring in a useful overhead contribution. But with costs rising and its reserves greatly depleted, it was in a difficult financial situation. In 1945–46 it returned a deficit of £5000 that had risen to over £13,000 by the following year.[52] With little hope of attracting more government funding, it was forced to concentrate on fundraising and reducing costs. In May 1946 a notice was placed in the personal columns of *The Times* asking would-be benefactors to 'please remember the National Council of Social Service in your will and assist the Council to promote a fuller community life'.[53] In February 1948 the Executive Committee considered holding a large public meeting 'to restate the underlying principles of the voluntary movement' and 'revitalise the spirit of voluntary service by individuals which had been so strong during war-time', but the idea was shelved as it was felt not practicable to mix a fundraising drive with a public awareness-raising event.[54] In 1949 the Council warned that the combination of rising costs, the need to improve the conditions of service of its permanent staff and the effects on giving of continuing high taxation, meant that 'many urgent problems are at present not being dealt with simply because of lack of the necessary finance'.[55]

In 1950 the Council introduced a freeze on all new appointments and the following year it agreed to significant cuts to balance the books.[56] There was a lively discussion within the Executive Committee about where the axe should fall. There was general support for safeguarding investment on policy and research, but views on international work were divided. Some members called for it to be cut, others felt that it was highly regarded, the 'moral results were far greater than the small amount of expenditure involved' and that the Council must continue to play its part 'in Great Britain's contribution to leadership in the world'.[57] In 1952 plans were put in place to reduce costs in Bedford Square and the regions by £15,000. It was suggested that a public education campaign be launched 'to educate those sections of the community who are now more wealthy than before and have not acquired a tradition of charitable giving'.[58] In 1955 a special appeals committee of industrialists was set up under the chairmanship of Lord Heyworth, later to become the Council's president, to target corporate support, drawing on the successful model adopted during the war. Results were again encouraging and corporate subscriptions tripled within two years.[59] In 1958 the Council reported that the ground that had been lost following the significant reductions at the beginning of the decade 'has now been substantially recovered, although not all the cuts have been restored'.[60] The improved financial position enabled it to implement long-planned improvements to staff salaries and pensions and to rebuild its reserves. But money remained tight and financial concerns continued to plague the Council for many years to come.

Internal Developments

Haynes' strategy of 1944 not only called for an expansion of the associated group model but also for the development of services for the voluntary movement as a whole. As a result, the immediate post-war period saw a greater focus on key support functions such as policy, information and research, although developments were held back by financial difficulties. In addition to reform of charity law, the Council lobbied successfully on a number of other issues of concern to the movement, including rate relief for voluntary groups and copyright charges on the playing of recorded music in community centres and village halls.[61] It also gave evidence to a wide range of government committees and inquiries, covering child adoption, homelessness, legal aid, marriage, divorce, general medical practice, youth work, training for social workers, and the laws relating to homosexual offences and prostitution.[62]

The Council's plans for an ambitious research function were put on hold during the war due to a shortage of funds and continuing financial pressures meant that they were not revisited. However, one important study was carried out, in association with the King's Fund for London, on the role of voluntary action in hospitals. The report, *Voluntary Service and the State: A Study of the Needs of the Hospital Service,* was published in 1952 and suggested that the movement was in good shape within the new National Health Service.[63] The journal of the Medical Women's Federation wrote that 'the amount of kindliness, effort, generosity and sacrifice entailed in these multitudinous services staggers the imagination and warms the heart' and suggested that the report was 'the complete and conclusive reply to those who bewail the selfishness of to-day and the disappearance of the spirit of service'.[64]

The increased focus during the war on publications and information also continued into peacetime. By 1946 the library had grown to encompass over 8000 books, although the lending facility for members was stopped when the landlord ruled that it constituted an infringement of the lease.[65] In 1947 a new periodical, *Social Service: A Quarterly Survey*, was launched to replace *The Social Service Review*, which had been published before the war.[66] It represented the realisation of a long-held dream by the Council to produce a quality periodical to showcase the best writing on voluntary action and over the next 30 years was to attract writers of the highest calibre, along with renowned illustrators such as W.E.C. Morgan and Conroy Maddox, a key figure in the Birmingham surrealist movement. At its height it had subscriptions in over 60 countries.[67] It joined *The Village* magazine, which focused on the rural work of the Council. In April 1948 a publications board was established, charged with expanding the range and quality of publications in ways 'that would not unduly burden the National Council's finances'.[68] By 1949, despite continuing paper shortages, there were over 100 publications in circulation, including another new periodical, *The Good Neighbour*, launched in February 1949. Print runs for individual titles were fairly small, although the Council noted, perhaps optimistically, that their 'influence may be very important'.[69] By 1951, however, with another financial crisis looming, the decision was taken to scale back its publishing ambitions and focus only on those works deemed 'essential' to support core activities. The Council's ambition to be a publishing house 'for a wider and more effective range of books and pamphlets on the social services and social problems' was shelved, for the time being at least.[70] The number of new titles commissioned was substantially reduced and *The Good Neighbour* ceased publication after just one year.

The information service, however, continued to expand. The range of inquiries dealt with, largely by a group of dedicated volunteers, was vast and mirrored the multiplicity of issues the Council was involved with. In 1950 it was reported that in one day the information department 'had to deal with inquiries from a New Town Corporation, the British Council, a Government Commission, the Library of the House of Commons, an export firm, [and] a service benevolent institution'.[71] In 1957 a new legal department was established, primarily to provide advice to members considering building village halls.[72]

Space continued to be an issue. Although the Council remained wedded to the ambition of consolidating all London staff into one new building, preferably with space for other charities, the financial difficulties meant little progress could be made towards this goal. As a temporary solution, it took on additional rented space. In 1959 a lease was secured on a property at 99 Great Russell Street, described as 'a fine William and Mary' building, which was a stone's throw from Bedford Square and had the advantage of providing much-needed conference facilities. It was also considerably cheaper.[73] The Council continued to operate a number of regional offices to support its local networks. In 1948 it had bases in Leeds, Birmingham, Cambridge (with a branch office at Norwich), Bristol (with a branch at Reading), and Penrith, although this regional presence was scaled back as the decade wore on.[74] A small team of staff was based at each, in some cases employed directly by the Council and in others working through regional organisations.[75] Of the 156 staff employed by the Council in 1948, 110 were based in London and 46 in the regions.[76] Relations with the newly established Scottish council remained cordial, and in 1947 the Council agreed to a request to underwrite a small deficit it had incurred for the year.[77] In the same year, the independent Council of Social Service for Wales and Monmouthshire came into being and took over all activities previously carried out in Wales by the Council. On 1 April 1948 the South Wales Council of Social Service was incorporated into the new body.[78]

In December 1949 Dr Adams stood down as chair of the Council. He had been in post, barring a couple of months at the beginning of 1919, for its entire history. It is impossible to overstate his influence. He took on the role at a time when the responsibility for running a voluntary organisation resided not with paid staff but with the senior members of the Executive Committee. He was undoubtedly fortunate to have administrators of the calibre of Lionel Ellis and George Haynes to support him and, by the end of his time at the Council, the power had begun to shift away from the Executive Committee towards the senior staff. But for most of his 30 years at the helm, he was the driving force behind the Council and its public face. He combined prodigious intellectual gifts and administrative ability, with a passionate commitment to voluntary action. His greatest interests were the countryside and the arts, and he played a pivotal role in the development of the rural community council movement and the Council's work on music and drama. But his influence spanned all areas and, as chair of the Emergency Committee throughout the Second World War, he can be credited with having a major impact on the voluntary movement's war effort.

For Adams, steeped in the Idealist philosophy of the Council's founders, the value of voluntary action resided not so much in what it did for others, as what it did for those who took part. It was the contribution the voluntary movement made to local communities, and ultimately to democracy itself, that he deemed most important. 'A Good society', he wrote, 'recognises not only able direction from above but initiative and development from below – a free exercise of the abilities of the individual conditioned by the general interest of the community.'[79] When he died in 1966 at the age of 91, George Haynes, by now Sir George Haynes, wrote a personal tribute, recalling 'the noble head on robust shoulders, the deep melodious voice ringing across the conference hall, the firm friendly handshake for friends and strangers alike, the strong, kindly gaze

both compelling and reassuring'. And he remembered his 'boundless generos-
ity of spirit' and 'over-flowing enthusiasm, which he retained to the end'.[80]
Adams' successor was Dr Keith Murray, rector of Lincoln College, Oxford, a
previous vice-chair of the Council and chair of the rural committee.[81] Murray
stood down in December 1953 to take up the position of chair of the University
Grants Committee and was replaced by John Wolfenden, headmaster of
Uppingham and Shrewsbury Schools and vice-chancellor of the University of
Reading, who went on to make an even more significant contribution to the
voluntary movement 25 years later when he chaired a major inquiry into its
future.[82] He was succeeded in 1960 by Leslie Farrer-Brown, another former
vice-chair of the Council and chair of the National Citizens' Advice Bureaux
Committee, who held the post for 13 years. He is best known for his role in
helping establish the Nuffield Foundation in 1944 and serving as its first secretary until his retirement in 1964. He also chaired the University of London and
the Institute of Race Relations. His major contribution to the Council was
chairing the review committee, which met from 1968 to 1969 and led to a
fundamental shift in strategy, away from the federalism of Haynes to a centralised, integrated structure.[83] Sara Morrison, a future chair of the Council,
remembers him as a 'big man' and 'impressive'.[84] Ian Bruce, who joined the
National Old People's Welfare Council on its first day in December 1970,
recalls him as 'a rather imperious sort of character'.[85] Farrer-Brown described
his philanthropic work as 'dispensing bounty, its nature as a craft', and his role
as that of 'a benefactotum'.[86]

BUSINESS AS USUAL

For much of the immediate post-war period it was business as usual for the
Council, which continued to support a bewildering array of work through its
semi-autonomous networks and groups. Its reach was vast. In 1951, although
it only had 200 *direct* members, it was accountable for the work of many thousands of organisations. Through the Standing Conference of councils of Social
Service, it supported the work of 9 area councils of social service and 155 local
councils. Through its rural committee, it was involved with 45 rural community councils, plus a number of other voluntary and statutory bodies interested
in rural affairs. It supported the National Federation of Community
Associations, which represented over 300 community associations, which in
turn supported over 1600 local neighbourhood organisations. Through the
National Citizens' Advice Bureaux Committee, it represented over 440 local
bureaux, while the National Association of Women's Clubs represented 564
women's clubs, catering for 19,000 individual members. Then there was the
National Old People's Welfare Committee (NOPWC), which acted as an
umbrella for 50 national agencies linked to over 700 local committees; the
Standing Conference of National Voluntary Youth Organisations, made up of
39 national agencies and linked to hundreds of local groups; the Women's
Group on Public Welfare (WGPW), which represented 45 national organisations

and linked with over 70 local Standing Conferences of Women's Organisations; the Central Churches Group, with its network of local groups; and the British National Conference on Social Work, which met in conference every three years and included representatives from voluntary organisations, central and local government, universities, and social work practice.[87]

The scale of the work being managed inevitably raised questions about whether the Council was trying to do too much. It was estimated that the support work it provided was the equivalent of running ten national voluntary organisations.[88] In 1947 it acknowledged that it was 'deeply conscious of its inevitable shortcomings in undertaking a task of this magnitude' and admitted that 'there is the constant danger that it may try too much for its resources'.[89] In 1958, looking back on its work over 40 years, it reflected that the Council 'has proved to be in practice a more formidable enterprise than the founders could have foreseen' and that it had sometimes ended up 'touching on too many things too lightly' or 'over-concentrating on a few interests where progress was easiest'.[90] These concerns led the Council in the future to focus on providing a much smaller number of core services to the voluntary movement as a whole. But in the immediate post-war years, it was to its networks and groups that it turned for the delivery of the majority of its most important work.

There was much in this work to celebrate. The citizens' advice bureaux (CAB) movement continued to flourish, albeit inevitably at a lower level than during the war. In 1948 the movement dealt with over 1.5 million inquiries a year, of which more than a quarter of a million were related to new legislation.[91] In 1950 the government signalled its intention to withdraw its support for the central services work of the bureaux and the Council was forced to scale back its activities. Calls were made in the House of Commons to reinstate the funding, without success.[92] The Council was told that policy 'was not to subsidise central services'.[93] Support for individual bureaux varied from one local authority to another, but overall the movement did fairly well out of public funds. In 1950 a new National Citizens' Advice Bureaux Committee was established to replace the existing Central Committee, giving more control to members. Growth continued during the 1950s. Individual CAB offered advice to communities hit by severe flooding in the West Country in 1952, and the national association worked with the Law Society on the development of poor man's lawyer schemes and the establishment of legal aid services.[94] By the middle of the century, the movement's stock had risen to a level where *The Economist*, no particular friend of the voluntary movement, gave it a ringing endorsement, with a passing nod to the work of the Council in providing support.[95]

Two of the other associated groups that had been established by the Council to contribute to the war effort, the NOPWC and WGPW, also flourished in the immediate post-war years. Both coalesced around the issue of loneliness, which was beginning to be identified as a major concern, and which continues to this day to occupy the minds of policy makers.[96] In February 1949 the minister of national insurance, James Griffiths, launched an appeal for volunteers 'with time on their hands who perhaps are seeking ways in which they can be of service' to visit an older person in their home.[97] Visiting schemes were developed to coordinate the work of volunteers. In 1957 the WGPW published a report, *Loneliness: An Enquiry into Causes and Possible Remedies,* calling for the extension of these good neighbour schemes, especially in the new towns where the problem of isolation was felt to be particularly acute.[98] Volunteers responded to the challenge in large numbers and new schemes were set up throughout the country. Such was the growth in interest that the Council felt able to report the following year that 'few other spheres of voluntary service can show the same remarkable growth since the war'.[99]

Although volunteer visiting was a priority for these groups, it was one of many and it is possible to give only a flavour of the variety of activities carried out under their auspices at this time. Both groups saw their main contribution as being practical support delivered through their burgeoning local networks. But both were also involved in higher-level policy development. Issues addressed by the WGPW in the early post-war years included problems of child emigration, accommodation for women in London, and the impact of prefabricated bungalows on domestic life; while in the 1950s the group turned its attention to such matters as student grants, food quality, and advertising standards.[100] In 1948 it published a report, *The Neglected Child and His Family,* which, as with its earlier wartime report, *Our Towns: A Close Up,* had a significant influence on public policy.[101] For the NOPWC, which by the end of the period had over 1400 local affiliated committees, policy issues of concern included the provision of housing for older people, the training of wardens and matrons, fuel shortages, and the cost of tobacco.[102] 'No subject concerned with the welfare of old people', Brasnett writes, 'was too complex or too small' for the Committee to consider.[103] In 1954 the committee was given a boost with a grant from the King George VI Foundation to support the work of local clubs. In 1955 it set up a study group to look at preparation for retirement, which in 1964 became the Pre-Retirement Association of Great Britain and Northern Ireland.[104] In 1956 the national committee, as a mark of its growing influence, was reconstituted as the National Old People's Welfare Council.[105]

Another associated group that developed rapidly after the war was the Standing Conference of National Voluntary Youth Organisations (SCNVYO). As with the other groups, it conducted much of its work through member committees at a local level, but it also contributed to policy development at a national level on a range of issues, including young people in industry, the influence of the cinema, sex education, and the leisure activities of schoolchildren.[106] In 1951, as part of the Festival of Britain, it organised a Festival Centre of Youth on a site near the main festival grounds on the South Bank.[107] With over 12,000 visitors from all over the world, it was judged a success. In 1958 the SCNVYO gave evidence to the Albemarle inquiry into the future of the youth service and, with support from the King George VI Foundation, developed training courses in youth leadership.[108] By 1960 the Conference was in good shape and could boast an increase in the number of its local committees.[109]

Two of the most important pre-war strands of the Council's work were also taken forward, but results were more mixed. The community association and village hall movements struggled during the war, due to a shortage of resources and a ban on the building of new premises. Restrictions continued after the war and development in both areas was slow. The new National Federation of Community Associations (NFCA), which had been established at the end of the war to give greater independence to the membership, organised a *Living Communities* exhibition that toured the country to drum up support.[110] But the withdrawal of government grants for the building of new community centres, which weren't restored until the mid-1950s, hit the movement hard.[111] The Council's support for community centres continued to be based on a mix of radical and conservative ideology. Self-ownership and management was a key indicator of success, but there remained an undercurrent of less enlightened sentiment. 'What interest can we find for those middle-aged women who may become frustrated, narrow, and perhaps mischievous?' asked Frank Milligan of the Council at a 'Family at Work and Play' conference in 1947. 'I have seen what the community centre can do for them and what magnificent things they can do in a community centre.'[112] In 1957 the NFCA established a National Advisory Committee for Television Group Viewing to provide a forum for discussion on the role of television in community life.[113] In 1960 it organised the first National Community Week (the forerunner to today's Volunteers' Week), which ran from 7 to 15 May.[114] Over 100 community associations across England, Scotland, and Wales took part in the celebrations and the event was judged to have been a 'qualified success', having brought 'a good deal of publicity to the Associations, co-operation between some areas on large-scale projects, and an unexpectedly substantial addition to funds'.[115] A second week was planned for the following year, with a focus on the training of volunteers and paid staff. Similar challenges confronted the village hall movement, although continuing funding from the Carnegie UK Trust eased the pressure to some extent. As a temporary solution to the shortage of materials, the Council set up a new programme to support the construction of prefabricated buildings and by the early 1950s over 150 such halls had opened, many of them constructed by local volunteers using donated goods from the local community.[116]

The Council's two most important networks, representing the rural community councils and the councils of social service, also struggled during this period. Progress towards achieving nationwide coverage was painfully slow. The rural councils fared slightly better due to the long-term support from the Development Commission and the Carnegie UK Trust, but even here the Council managed only two-thirds coverage in England and Wales by 1950, although development picked up in the 1950s.[117] For the councils of social service, almost entirely dependent on local authorities for their funding, the situation was more challenging still and many groups were forced to scale back on their activities.[118] In 1947 the Council reported the closure of Northumberland and Tyneside 'at a time when it is accepted on all sides that more and better coordinated voluntary service is urgently needed'.[119]

Despite these challenges, work in the countryside and towns continued. The Council's annual Rural Life conference provided a focus for debate on a wide range of rural issues and the rural department continued to provide support to parish councils through the National Association of Parish councils and for rural industries through the Rural Industries Loan Fund.[120] In the late 1950s councils of social service got involved in schemes to support new immigrants coming to Britain. Race riots had broken out in a number of British towns. In Notting Hill Gate in London, it was 'generally felt' by the London Council of Social Service 'that 95% of the problem comes from the Teddy Boys'.[121] Several local councils of social service set up schemes to promote welfare for 'coloured workers' and a special meeting was convened in London in 1958 to discuss what further action could be taken.[122] By 1960, 18 coordinating committees were in place looking into welfare schemes mainly for people of West Indian descent, but also focusing on minority communities of Pakistanis, Indians, Arabs, and Somalis.[123]

Support for amateur music and drama also continued, and in 1947 the Council reconstituted the Central Local History Committee, which had fallen into abeyance during the war. Local history, the Council noted, in true Idealist spirit, was important 'not only as an educational activity, but because an informed interest in the history of a village is a valuable means of building a true community'.[124] In 1948 the Central Local History Committee became the Standing Conference for Local History. In contrast, in 1947 the Council closed its unemployment committee, which had been set up in 1932 to oversee the running of the occupational club movement. The annual report for 1946–47 noted that this marked 'the end of a chapter and a very important chapter in the story of the National Council's work for the community'.[125] The clubs had become less relevant in conditions of fuller employment after the war and had been transformed into broader-based community service clubs. By the end of the period the men's clubs had largely disappeared, but the women's clubs continued to thrive, supported by a new National Association of Women's Clubs established in 1950.[126] In 1958 the Council reported on the 'deep tradition of voluntary service' within the women's clubs and highlighted the support given by members in their communities to activities as varied as visiting older people, providing clinics for mothers and babies, and organising holidays for handicapped children.[127] Even more impressive was felt to be the involvement of large numbers of club members on the committees of voluntary and statutory bodies which, it suggested, 'considering that they are nearly all housewives with families to look after and other responsibilities is no mean contribution to society'.[128] The women's clubs can be seen as part of the tradition of women's groups, identified by Caitriona Beaumont that made a significant impact on the development of the women's movement in the first half of the twentieth century. Such groups might not have been overtly feminist, nor have challenged gender roles, but, through their local networks, they offered an opportunity for women of all classes to exercise their citizenship and assume a leadership role in the community that might not otherwise have been available.[129] The Council as the originator and supporter of these groups can take pride in their achievements.

STIRRINGS OF INDEPENDENCE

The model adopted by the Council of working through semi-autonomous groups was complicated in governance terms and confusing to the outside world. Much good work was carried out, but it was not clear what role the Council was playing. 'The visitor from overseas, and perhaps the home enquirer too', it noted in 1954, 'often finds it difficult to understand what the National Council is and does.'[130] This could prove problematic for fundraising purposes and clearly offered a major administrative challenge, but, despite these draw-backs, it remained committed to the model. It was convinced that such a feder-ated structure was essential for the successful realisation of its mission. For Haynes, it was an article of faith. It was not only a question of being able to get more done with limited resources, but was fundamental to his view of how an umbrella organisation should work. There was a strong feeling that the effec-tiveness of the Council was intimately linked to the presence of a network of local infrastructure agencies in the towns and countryside. In 1954 it admitted that 'it is not easy for national organisations charged with policy and adminis-trative problems to remain sensitive to the needs and interests of those "on the ground"'. And it suggested that, without its local groups and networks, 'it would be impossible to maintain a live, well-informed organisation with a pol-icy firmly based on practical experience'.[131] The advantages, however, were seen to flow both ways and the federated model was seen as good for the local groups, who were given the 'greatest possible freedom of action to develop their own policy', while ensuring that their action 'converges on matters of wide, general concern'.[132]

Not all associated groups were regarded in the same way, however. Specialist groups such as the CAB, and those representing women, young people, and older people, had been destined for independence from the moment they were established; it was a question of getting the timing right. For the councils of social service and rural community councils, it was a different matter. These networks had formed the basis of the Council from its inception and, indeed, in the case of the councils of social service predated the Council by some years and were part of the movement that brought it into being. For the Council, in the immediate post-war period, it was thought inconceivable that it could exist as a standalone national body divorced from its local roots. But because the Council saw things this way, there was no guarantee it would be viewed the same on the ground, and during this period rumblings of discontent began to emerge from within the networks that would ultimately lead to independence. Of course such discontent was not new. Between the wars the rural councils flirted with the idea of independence, and there had been periodic complaints over the years from both local networks that they were receiving inadequate support from the Council.

In 1950 the Standing Conference of councils of Social Service asked the Council for additional resources to support the movement, suggesting that with the growth of specialist groups the councils had 'receded into the background'.[133] The Council refuted this notion, but felt that financial pressures did not allow for any increase in funding. There was a suggestion within the Executive Committee that, rather than continuing to establish new organisations, it might choose to focus resources on the councils of social service, but so entrenched was support for the associated group model that the idea was not pursued.[134] Instead, it agreed to reconsider its vision of universal coverage, suggesting that the policy of 'a Council for Social Service for every town' might no longer be 'realistic'.[135] Such was its commitment to hold on to its two core networks, the Council was keen to control the timing of any independent moves from specialist groups, lest it should act as a spur to action. Thus the Executive Committee firmly rejected a proposal from the National Federation of Community Associations to enter discussions over full independence on the grounds that it would set a dangerous precedent. 'Serious harm would be done to the movement as a whole', it noted, 'if the principle were abandoned in the important question of relationships with the National Federation.'[136] In future the timing of such moves was not always in the Council's hands.

In addition to the calls for independence from some groups, there were counter-veiling pressures in the opposite direction. In April 1947 the home secretary, Chuter Ede, announced in the House of Commons that he had asked the Council and the Women's Voluntary Service (WVS) to explore options for closer working.[137] Given the uneasy relationship that had existed between the two bodies since the WVS was set up in 1938, this was always going to be problematic. The push from government was partly financial, but also reflected concern over aspects of the Council's performance, with one Treasury official suggesting it was in need of 'rejuvenescence'.[138] Meetings took place throughout 1947 and 1948, but stalled on the key issue of whether an option to merge was to be included within the terms of reference of the discussions. The Council felt strongly that all options should be on the table while the WVS was adamant that merger was out of scope. The two organisations wrote to the home secretary for clarification and on 8 July 1948 received a response that, while he wasn't in a position to clarify further, he hoped 'the discussions might result in the formation of some provisional plan for the creation of a new national organisation serving purposes similar to those at present served both by the National Council and WVS'. This was sufficient for the Council, which said it was ready 'to consider any plans affecting the development or modification of its own services which would be in the best interests of community service generally'.[139] But the WVS would not shift on its position that merger was out of the question and, after what James Hinton describes as 'twelve months of tortuous, bad-tempered, and ultimately futile discussions', the matter was dropped.[140]

In 1954 the Council received a request from the London Council of Social Service for additional support.[141] The London Council predated the National Council by almost a decade, having been formed in 1910, but in recent years had been experiencing severe financial difficulties. After lengthy negotiations, it was announced in 1957 that the two organisations had agreed to 'enter into more intimate partnership' and that the London Council would become an associated group of the Council on a par with other groups.[142] The London Council would remain responsible for policies and activities in London, but there would be 'closer integration' of services both nationally and London-wide.[143] The following year the Council reported that the 'increased security' for the London Council had resulted 'in an extension of its influence and activities'.[144] In 2017 the Council, now called the London Voluntary Service Council, closed for lack of funds. It had been in operation for 107 years.

Seeds of Professionalisation

The Council had long been involved in the training of staff and volunteers within its groups and networks. Wardens of community associations and settlements, staff in the occupational clubs and CAB, carers in old people's homes had all received support and instruction in their work for many years.[145] The provision of this specialist training continued throughout the post-war period, but the Council also began to take a more strategic interest in the training and support of staff in the movement as a whole. Even in these early days, there were hints of the concerns that were raised later in the century about the dangers of professionalisation. In 1949 the Council entered discussions with the new Family Welfare Association over the provision of training for CAB volunteers, who were being called upon to deal with increasingly complex issues. But they were advised to be careful over the word 'training', as the volunteers were 'anxious to maintain their "amateur status"'.[146]

Immediately after the war, the Council took on a member of staff to advise on career openings within the voluntary movement and short courses were developed to support individuals thinking of moving into the field.[147] The challenge of attracting new recruits, however, was seen to be only partially one of inadequate training. Low levels of pay and poor conditions of service were also seen to be holding people back from entering the movement. In 1946 the Council sponsored jointly with the British Federation of Social Workers an inquiry into the salaries and conditions of employment of voluntary social workers, under the chair of Professor T.S. Simey.[148] The inquiry reported in 1947 with the unanimous view that 'unless steps are taken drastically to improve the salary scales of whole-time social workers in many fields of effort, the voluntary movement cannot hope to attract in sufficient numbers well-trained and able younger people'.[149]

The Council was becoming convinced that the failure to invest in staff was holding back the movement's development. Paid staff, it argued in 1955, 'are in many instances the hub of the wheel of voluntary action' and yet 'it is not yet sufficiently realised that many agencies could not perform their services ... without a *cadre* of paid staff, trained and experienced in the work'. Many individuals, it acknowledged, 'are often prepared to accept considerably less than their abilities would command in industry or public service'. The problem was that 'the "less" is frequently too little even for an austere standard of living'.

The result was felt to be 'inevitable', with 'more and more individuals qualified and willing to seek a career in the voluntary movement looking elsewhere – to industry and the public services'.[150]

One initiative during this period that was to have long-term benefits for staff in voluntary organisations was the establishment of a new Social Workers' Pension Fund in 1946. Although independent, the Council took on the trusteeship and administration of the scheme. It was contributory and transportable, enabling staff moving jobs to remain in the scheme. It proved a big success and by 1960 had over 2700 members, drawn from over 500 organisations.[151] The Council's Executive Committee had no doubt of its value and felt 'that nothing more important had been done in the movement for many years' and that the scheme would 'become of outstanding importance to the whole status of social workers'.[152] When it became fully independent at the beginning of the next decade, the fund had assets of over £1.5 million.[153]

The concern of the Council about the failure of the voluntary movement to invest sufficiently in its paid staff was a recurring theme in the future. Inevitably, it was linked to the issue of funding and the parlous state many voluntary organisations found themselves in the early post-war period. But it also raised wider issues about the nature of the movement, its ethics and values, the relative balance between volunteers and paid staff and, ultimately, the question of mission and purpose. Few at the time would have argued against the approach taken by the Council in seeking to raise employment standards within voluntary organisations and equip the movement better for the larger role it was seeking to carve out for itself in the new mixed economy of welfare. As the century wore on, however, critics argued that the focus on professional development and standards being championed by the Council was leading the movement in the wrong direction.[154]

REACHING OUT

Much of the Council's international work in this period, as with its domestic activity, was conducted through its associated groups. Immediately after the war, the WGPW and the SCNVYO visited Germany to advise the British and American zones on the development of democratic voluntary associations.[155] In 1948 the SCNVYO was asked by the Foreign Office to convene a conference in London of international youth agencies to examine the establishment of a more permanent body to foster international cooperation.[156] In 1949 the World Assembly of Youth was set up, with the Council providing administrative support until it could function as an independent body.[157] The Council had long harboured international ambitions. Its first annual report listed international cooperation as one of four key objectives, and during the war it set up an international common room to host visitors from overseas.[158] After the war, it expanded its bi-lateral exchange programmes, both with the US through the British Committee for the International Exchange of Social Workers and Administrators, and with Europe in collaboration with the United Nations in Geneva. It also took up a place on the General Council of the United Nations Association.[159] In 1946 it took part in a conference in Brussels aimed at relaunching the International Conference on Social Work (later the International Council on Social Welfare). This body had been established in the 1920s by René Sand, the secretary general of the League of Red Cross, but had fallen into abeyance during the war.[160] Two years later at a conference in the US, the decision was taken to relaunch the organisation with a new constitution. Haynes was appointed president, reflecting both his and the Council's growing reputation on the world stage. The main activity of the International Conference was a biennial world conference, which met during the 1950s in cities as far-flung as Madras, Toronto, Munich, and Tokyo, attracting delegates from over 70 countries, with the Council well represented at each.[161] To feed into the international conference, a decision was taken in 1948 to set up a separate, permanent British National Conference on Social Work (later the British National Conference on Social Welfare). It held its first meeting in Harrogate in 1950, attended by 450 representatives, on the theme of 'Social Services in 1950: The Respective Roles of Statutory Authorities and Voluntary Bodies'.[162] The Council provided the secretariat for the new body, which met every three years for the next quarter of a century, providing a key forum for the exchange of ideas and practice on issues of wider social policy. Local groups were set up in advance of the conferences, often in conjunction with councils of social service, to feed a local perspective into the national debates.[163]

Another manifestation of the Council's growing internationalism during this period was the work undertaken with refugees. In 1950 it worked with the government and the International Refugee Organisation in Geneva on the establishment of the British Council for Aid to Refugees to support displaced people in Germany, Austria, and Italy.[164] In 1956 it provided support for refugees from the revolution in Hungary. A CAB was established at the British Council for Aid to Refugees and at reception centres across the country.[165] The CAB movement was also involved in supporting British nationals expelled from Egypt following the Suez crisis, providing a trained worker at each reception hostel to advise on resettlement.[166] In 1960 the Council agreed to take on the secretariat for the Standing Conference of British Organisations for Aid to Refugees and played a key role in supporting the World Refugee Year.[167]

CONCLUSION

Despite widespread fears expressed by many commentators at the end of the war, the immediate post-war period did not see the demise of voluntary action. Far from disappearing, the voluntary movement adapted well to the changed circumstances brought about by the development of the welfare state. 'So far from voluntary action being dried up by the expansion of the social services', Nathan concluded, 'greater and greater demands are being made upon it.'[168] Owen concurs, suggesting that by the 1950s 'the intervention of the State extended rather than reversed the long tradition of voluntary effort'.[169] New national organisations were established and new forms of mutual aid and self-help groups emerged, which would come to greater prominence in the next decade, and the vast mass of voluntary action continued, as it had always done, untouched by the machinations of the state. The Council continued to deliver impressive work through its associated bodies and strengthened its international and policy work. But there were no new developments of note to match the innovations that had taken place before and during the war and one is left with the conclusion that it was finding its way, somewhat tentatively, in the new world. Increasingly, it came to see its purpose as being less about providing support to a network of quasi-autonomous groups and more about offering a range of generic services to the wider movement. Such a shift would leave it vulnerable to accusations that it was out of touch with the grassroots and ill-equipped to respond to the seismic changes about to take place in the voluntary movement.

NOTES

1. For a contemporary account of the challenges facing voluntary organisations, see Carter, 1949, and Marshall, 1949.
2. Thane, 2012. See also Harris, 2010, p. 35.
3. Committee on Voluntary Organisations, 1978. See also Brenton, 1985, and Taylor and Kendall, 1996, pp. 51–52.
4. NCSS Annual Report 1945–46, p. 5.
5. NCSS Annual Report 1948–49, p. 8.
6. Beveridge and Wells, 1949, p. 39.
7. NCSS Annual Report 1945–46, p. 5.
8. NCSS Annual Report 1945–46, p. 6.
9. Carter, 1949.
10. NCSS Annual Report 1946–47, p. 6.
11. NCSS Annual Report 1953–54, p. 9.
12. For a discussion of these themes, see Deakin and Davis Smith, 2011.
13. See, for example, Bew, 2016, pp. 50–53.
14. Burchardt, 2012. Attlee, 1920, pp. 75–8.
15. At a speech to the London Council of Social Service in August 1948, Morrison spoke about how 'we sometimes fail to realise how fundamental to the health of a democratic society is the volunteer'. Quoted in Carter, 1949, p. 175.
16. NCSS Annual Report 1945–46, p. 16.
17. See Thane, 2011, and Weinbren, 2011.
18. Olechnowicz, 2005; Thane, 2012, p. 424.
19. House of Commons Debates, Series 5, Vol. 450, col. 2136, 12 May 1948.
20. NCSS Annual Report 1949–50, p. 16.
21. Minutes of Executive Committee, 20 January 1949; London Metropolitan Archives (LMA): LMA/4016/IS/A/01/032(2).
22. On tensions between voluntary organisations and local authorities in the 1950s, see Younghusband, 1978, pp. 256–7. For later support for voluntary organisations from metropolitan councils, such as the GLC, see Chap. 8.
23. NCSS Annual Report 1948–49, p. 8.
24. Beveridge, 1948. Hebert, First Viscount Samuel, was leader of the parliamentary Liberal Party, 1931–35, and of the Liberal Party in the House of Lords, 1944–55. He died in 1963. See *The Times*, 6 February 1963, p. 15.

25. House of Lords Debates, Series 5, Vol. 163, col. 119, 22 June 1949. Frank Pakenham, Seventh Earl of Longford, was appointed first lord of the admiralty by Attlee in 1951. He worked with Beveridge on the preparation of his two famous wartime reports, *Social Insurance and Allied Services*, 1942, and the 1944 *Full Employment in a Free Society*. He died in 2001.
26. NCSS Annual Report 1948–49, p. 8.
27. Oppenheimer and Deakin, 2011, p. 1.
28. Beveridge, 1942a and 1944.
29. Speech on 'New Britain', given in Oxford on 6 December 1942 in Beveridge, 1942b, p. 93.
30. Harris, 1997, p. 452.
31. Thane, 2012, p. 424. See also Oppenheimer and Deakin, 2011.
32. Beveridge, 1948, pp. 316–317.
33. Oppenheimer and Deakin, 2011, p. 3.
34. Harris, 2011, p. 11.
35. Harris, 1997, p. 460.
36. NCSS Annual Report 1947–48.
37. Minutes of Executive Committee, 20 January 1949; LMA/4016/IS/A/01/032(2).
38. NCSS Annual Report 1946–47, p. 7.
39. House of Lords Debates, Series 5, Vol. 163, cols. 80–81, 22 June 1949.
40. Minutes of Executive Committee, 13 October 1949; LMA/4016/IS/A/01/032(2).
41. See Chaps. 7 and 8 for a fuller discussion of this issue.
42. NCSS Annual Report 1948–49, p. 10.
43. Nathan was a Liberal MP from 1929 to 1933 but crossed the floor in 1933 and served as a Labour MP from 1937 to 1940, before being made a peer. He was minister for civil aviation, 1946–48, in the post-war Labour government. He died in 1963. See *The Times*, 25 October 1963, p. 15.
44. NCSS Annual Report 1948–49, p. 4.
45. Nathan Committee, 1952.
46. Quoted in Davies, 2015, p. 68.
47. Quoted in Owen, 1964, p. 585.
48. Minutes of Executive Committee 8 January 1953; LMA/4016/IS/A/01/032(5).
49. Finlayson, 1994, p. 290.
50. NCSS Annual Report 1959–60, pp. 5–6.
51. Quoted in Owen, 1964, p. 526.
52. NCSS Annual Reports 1945–46 and 1946–47.
53. Minutes of the Finance and General Purposes Sub-Committee, 28 May 1946; LMA/4016/IS/A/01/048(2).
54. Minutes of Executive Committee, 19 February 1949; LMA/4016/IS/A/01/032(1).
55. NCSS Annual Report 1948–49, p. 42.
56. Minutes of Executive Committee, 12 October 1950; LMA/4016/IS/A/01/032(3).
57. Minutes of Executive Committee, 11 October 1951; LMA/4016/IS/A/01/032(4).

58. Minutes of Executive Committee, 16 April 1952; LMA/4016/IS/A/01/032(4).
59. NCSS Annual Report 1956–57.
60. NCSS Annual Report 1957–58, p. 24.
61. NCSS Annual Reports 1950–51, 1954–55, and 1956–57.
62. Various annual reports from 1945 to 1960.
63. Trevelyan, 1952. For a discussion of the report, see Prochaska, 1992, pp. 170–171.
64. NCSS Annual Report 1951–52, p. 13.
65. Minutes of Executive Committee, 3 October 1946; LMA/4016/IS/A/01/032(1).
66. NCSS Annual Report 1946–47.
67. King, 1979.
68. NCSS Annual Report 1948–49, p. 39.
69. NCSS Annual Report 1948–49, p. 40.
70. NCSS Annual Report 1950–51, p. 34.
71. NCSS Annual Report 1949–50, p. 31.
72. Brasnett, 1969, p. 180.
73. NCSS Annual Report 1958–59.
74. NCSS Annual Report 1947–48.
75. NCSS Annual Report 1945–46.
76. Minutes of Executive Committee, 26 July 1948; LMA/4016/IS/A/01/032(2).
77. Minutes of Finance and General Purposes Sub-Committee, 24 June 1947; LMA/4016/IS/A/01/048(3).
78. NCSS Annual Report 1946–47.
79. Adams, 1928, p. 6.
80. Haynes, 1966. For a tribute to Adams, see also Harrison, 2004.
81. NCSS Annual Report 1948–49. Murray chaired the University Grants Council for ten years. He was director of the Leverhulme Trust, 1964–72, and chair of an inquiry into the governance of the University of London, which led to the merger of several colleges. He was created a life peer in 1964 as Baron Murray of Newhaven, and died in 1993. See, *The Times*, 12 October 1993, p. 21.
82. Wolfenden, like Murray, chaired the University Grants Council, from 1963 to 1968, but is best known for chairing the committee that recommended the decriminalisation of homosexuality in 1957. His 1978 report, *The Future of Voluntary Organisations*, is discussed in Chap. 7. He was knighted in 1956 and made a life peer in 1974. He died in 1985. See *The Times*, 19 January 1985, p. 8.
83. The work of the review committee is discussed below. Farrer-Brown died in 1994. See *Independent*, 3 May 1994.
84. Interview with Sara Morrison, 2 August 2017.
85. Interview with Ian Bruce, 13 September 2017.
86. *The Times*, 6 May 1994, p. 21.
87. NCSS Annual Report 1950–51, pp. 7–9.
88. NCSS Annual Report 1946–47.
89. NCSS Annual Report 1947–48, p. 17.
90. NCSS Annual Report 1957–58, p. 6.

91. NCSS Annual Report 1948–49. For a good discussion of the post-war work of the CAB movement, see Blaiklock, 2012.
92. NCSS Annual Report 1950–51.
93. Minutes of Executive Committee, 13 July 1950; LMA/4016/IS/A/01/032(3).
94. Brasnett, 1969, p. 193.
95. *The Economist*, 30 August 1952.
96. In January 2018 the government announced the appointment of the first minister for loneliness.
97. NCSS Annual Report 1948–49, p. 17.
98. Women's Group on Public Welfare, 1957.
99. NCSS Annual Report 1957–58, pp. 18–19.
100. Various NCSS annual reports through the 1950s.
101. Brasnett, 1969, pp. 145 and 194.
102. Various NCSS annual reports through the 1950s.
103. Brasnett, 1969, p. 146.
104. Coles, 1993, p. 16.
105. Brasnett, 1969, p. 200.
106. Ibid., p. 158.
107. NCSS Annual Report 1949–50.
108. NCSS Annual Report 1957–58.
109. Brasnett, 1969, p. 211.
110. NCSS Annual Report 1947–48.
111. Brasnett, 1969, p. 181.
112. Quoted in The *Guardian*, 'From the Archive, 18 January 1947: Call for country holidays growing in Britain', The *Guardian*, 18 January 2014.
113. NCSS Annual Report 1956–57.
114. NCSS Annual Report 1959–60.
115. NCSS Annual Report 1960–61, p. 20.
116. NCSS Annual Report 1950–51.
117. NCSS Annual Report 1949–50.
118. Brasnett, 1969, pp. 142–43.
119. NCSS Annual Report 1946–47, p. 8.
120. NCSS Annual Report 1949–50.
121. Minutes of Executive Committee, 9 October 1958; LMA/4016/IS/A/01/034(1).
122. NCSS Annual Report 1957–58.
123. NCSS Annual Report 1958–59.
124. NCSS Annual Report 1948–49, p. 34.
125. NCSS Annual Report 1946–47, p. 15.
126. NCSS Annual Report 1949–50.
127. NCSS Annual Report 1957–58, p. 18.
128. NCSS Annual Report 1958–59, p. 16.
129. Beaumont, 2013.
130. NCSS Annual Report 1953–54.
131. NCSS Annual Report 1953–54.
132. NCSS Annual Report 1945–46, p. 26.
133. Minutes of Executive Committee, 12 January 1950; LMA/4016/IS/A/01/032(3).

134. Minutes of Executive Committee, 12 January 1950; LMA/4016/IS/A/01/032(3).
135. Minutes of Executive Committee, 13 April 1950; LMA/4016/IS/A/01/032(3).
136. Minutes of Executive Committee, 19 February 1948; LMA/4016/IS/A/01/032(1).
137. House of Commons Debates, Series 5, Vol. 436, Cols. 133–134, 24 April 1947.
138. Quoted in Hinton, 2002, p. 218.
139. Minutes of Special Executive Committee, 8 July 1948; LMA/4016/IS/A/01/032(1).
140. Hinton, 1998, p. 301.
141. Minutes of Finance and General Purposes Sub-Committee, 27 July 1954; LMA/4016/IS/A/01/050(2).
142. Minutes of Executive Committee, 12 January 1956; LMA/4016/IS/A/01/033(2).
143. NCSS Annual Report 1956–57, p. 12.
144. NCSS Annual Report 1957–58, p. 27.
145. Williams, 1947.
146. Minutes of Executive Committee, 14 July 1949; LMA/4016/IS/A/01/032(2).
147. NCSS Annual Report 1945–46.
148. Simey, an academic and public servant, worked for the Ministry of Labour during the Second World War and sat on numerous official inquiries, including the Fulton Committee on the Civil Service. He was Charles Booth professor of social science at the University of Liverpool for over 30 years and wrote widely on social welfare and social policy. He was made a life peer in 1965 and took the Labour Whip. He died in 1969. See *The Times*, 30 December 1969, p. 8.
149. NCSS Annual Report 1946–47, p. 7.
150. NCSS Annual Report 1954–55, pp. 7–8.
151. NCSS Annual Report 1959–60.
152. Minutes of Executive Committee, 3 October 1946; LMA/4016/IS/A/01/032(1).
153. Brasnett, 1969, p. 224. The fund later changed its name to the Pensions Trust for Charities and Voluntary Organisations and in 2016 to TPT Retirement Solutions. In 2018 it was managing assets of £9 billion.
154. These issues are discussed fully in Chap. 11.
155. NCSS Annual Reports 1945–46 and 1946–47.
156. NCSS Annual Report 1948–49.
157. NCSS Annual Report 1948–49.
158. See Chaps. 3 and 5 for a discussion of the Council's early international ambitions.
159. NCSS Annual Report 1946–47. On early links with the United Nations, see Seary, 1995.
160. On the early history of the international conference, see Haynes, 1948.
161. Brasnett, 1969, p. 215.
162. Ibid., p. 163.
163. Ibid., p. 215.
164. NCSS Annual Report 1949–50.

165. NCSS Annual Report 1956–57.
166. NCSS Annual Report 1956–57.
167. NCSS Annual Report 1960–61.
168. Nathan committee, 1952, paragraph 54.
169. Owen, 1964, p. 597.

REFERENCES

Adams, W. G. S. (1928). Voluntary social service in the twentieth century. In NCSS (Ed.), *Voluntary social service: A handbook of information and directory of organisations*. London: NCSS.

Attlee, C. (1920). *The social worker*. London: G Bell & Sons.

Beaumont, C. (2013). *Housewives and citizens: Domesticity and the women's movement in England, 1928–64*. Manchester: Manchester University Press.

Beveridge, W. (1942a). *Social insurance and allied services: Scheme for the utilisation of approved society administration*. Manchester: National Conference of Friendly Societies.

Beveridge, W. (1942b). *Pillars of security*. London: Allen & Unwin.

Beveridge, W. (1944). *Full employment in a free society: A report*. London: Allen & Unwin.

Beveridge, W. (1948). *Voluntary action: A report on methods of social advance*. London: George Allen & Unwin.

Beveridge, W., & Wells, A. (Eds.). (1949). *The evidence for voluntary action: Being memoranda by organisations and individuals and other material relevant to voluntary action*. London: George Allen & Unwin.

Bew, J. (2016). *Citizen Clem: A biography of Attlee*. London: Riverrun.

Blaiklock, O. (2012). *Advising the citizen: Citizens Advice Bureaux, voluntarism and the welfare state in Britain, 1938–1964*. Unpublished PhD thesis, King's College, London.

Brasnett, M. (1969). *Voluntary social action: A history of the National Council of Social Service*. London: NCSS.

Brenton, M. (1985). *The voluntary sector in British social services*. London: Longman.

Burchardt, J. (2012). State and society in the English countryside: The rural community movement, 1918–39. *Rural History, 23*(1), 81–106.

Carter, E. (1949). The partnership between the statutory and the voluntary social services in post-war Britain. *Social Service Review, 23*(2), 172–175.

Coles, K. (1993). *National Council for Voluntary Organisations from 1919 to 1993: A selective summary of NCVO's work and origins*. London: NCVO.

Committee on Voluntary Organisations. (1978). *The future of voluntary organisations: Report of the Wolfenden Committee*. London: Croom Helm.

Davies, R. (2015). *Public good by private means: How philanthropy shapes Britain*. London: Alliance Publishing Trust.

Deakin, N., & Davis Smith, J. (2011). Labour, charity and voluntary action: The myth of hostility. In M. Hilton & J. McKay (Eds.), *The ages of voluntarism: How we got to the big society* (pp. 69–93). Oxford: Oxford University Press for British Academy.

Finlayson, G. (1994). *Citizen, state, and social welfare in Britain, 1830–1990*. Oxford: Clarendon Press.

Harris, J. (1997). *William Beveridge: A biography*. Oxford: Clarendon Press.

Harris, B. (2010). Voluntary action and the state in historical perspective. *Voluntary Sector Review, 1*(1), 25–40.

Harris, J. (2011). Voluntarism, the state and public-private partnerships in Beveridge's social thought. In M. Oppenheimer & N. Deakin (Eds.), *Beveridge and voluntary action in Britain and the wider British world* (pp. 9–20). Manchester: Manchester University Press.

Harrison, B. (2004). William George Stewart Adams. In *Oxford dictionary of national biography*. Oxford: Oxford University Press.

Haynes, G. (1948). The international conference of social work. *Social Service Quarterly*, 22(2), 55–59.

Haynes, G. (1966). Dr W.G.S. Adams, CH, a tribute. *Social Service Quarterly*, 39(4), 134–136.

Hinton, J. (1998). Volunteerism and the welfare state: Women's Voluntary Service in the 1940s. *Twentieth Century British History*, 9, 274–305.

Hinton, J. (2002). *Women, social leadership, and the Second World War*. Oxford: Oxford University Press.

King, G. (1979). Thirty years in print. *Social Service Quarterly*, 52(4), 121–123.

Marshall, T. (1949). Voluntary action. *The Political Quarterly*, 20(1), 32–34.

Nathan Committee. (1952). *Report of the committee on the law and practice relating to charitable trusts*. London: HMSO.

Olechnowicz, A. (2005). Unemployed workers, "enforced leisure" and education for "the right use of leisure" in Britain in the 1930s. *Labour History Review*, 70(1), 27–52.

Oppenheimer, M., & Deakin, N. (2011). Beveridge and voluntary Action. In M. Oppenheimer & N. Deakin (Eds.), *Beveridge and voluntary action in Britain and the wider British world* (pp. 1–8). Manchester: Manchester University Press.

Owen, D. (1964). *English philanthropy, 1660–1960*. London: Oxford University Press.

Prochaska, F. (1992). *Philanthropy and the hospitals of London: The King's Fund, 1897–1990*. Oxford: Clarendon Press.

Seary, B. (1995). The early history: From the Congress of Vienna to the San Francisco Conference. In P. Willetts (Ed.), *The conscience of the world: The influence of non-governmental organisations in the UN system* (pp. 15–30). London: Hurst & Company.

Taylor, M., & Kendall, J. (1996). History of the voluntary sector. In J. Kendall & M. Knapp (Eds.), *The voluntary sector in the United Kingdom* (pp. 28–60). Manchester: Manchester University Press.

Thane, P. (2011). Voluntary action in Britain since Beveridge. In M. Oppenheimer & N. Deakin (Eds.), *Beveridge and voluntary action in Britain and the wider British world* (pp. 124–125). Manchester: Manchester University Press.

Thane, P. (2012). The "big society" and the "big state": Creative tension or crowding out? *Twentieth Century British History*, 23(3), 408–429.

Trevelyan, J. (1952). *Voluntary service and the state: A study of the needs of the hospital service*. London: Barber.

Weinbren, D. (2011). "Organisations for brotherly aid in misfortune": Beveridge and the friendly societies. In M. Oppenheimer & N. Deakin (Eds.), *Beveridge and voluntary action in Britain and the wider British world* (pp. 51–65). Manchester: Manchester University Press.

Williams, G. (1947). The training and recruitment of social workers. In H. Mess (Ed.), *Voluntary social services since 1918* (pp. 214–246). London: Kegan Paul.

Women's Group on Public Welfare. (1957). *Loneliness: An enquiry into causes and possible remedies*. London: NCSS.

Younghusband, E. (1978). *Social work in Britain, 1950–1975: A follow-up study*. London: Allen & Unwin.

Captain Edward Vivian Dearman Birchall. (Courtesy of the Birchall Family Estate)

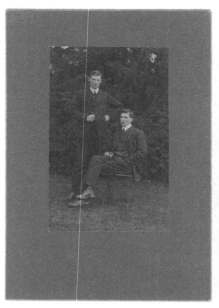

Edward (seated) and Arthur Birchall. (Courtesy of the Birchall Family Estate)

Grace Hadow. (Courtesy of the National Federation of Women's Institutes and Women's Library Collection at the LSE Library)

Left to right, Arthur, Clara, Violet, and Edward Birchall. (Courtesy of the Birchall Family Estate)

Young Farmers in the 1920s. (Courtesy of the National Federation of Young Farmers' Clubs)

Young Farmers' Clubs at the Lord Mayor's Show, 1935. (Courtesy of the National Federation of Young Farmers' Clubs)

Welwyn Garden City Community Centre, 1938. (Courtesy of Community Matters Archive, Bishopsgate Institute)

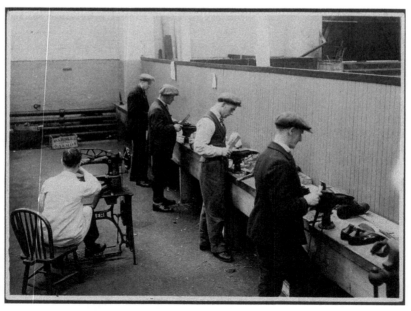

Saltley and Washwood Heath Service Club in the 1930s—'The Cobbling Shop'. (Courtesy of NCVO)

New Malden CAB circa 1964. 'A larger interviewing room for non-confidential advice' (Copyright Citizens Advice. Courtesy of Citizens Advice)

'Visiting'—Old People's Welfare Committee after the Second World War. (Courtesy of NCVO)

Mobile CAB horse box during the Second World War. (Copyright Citizens Advice. Courtesy of Citizens Advice)

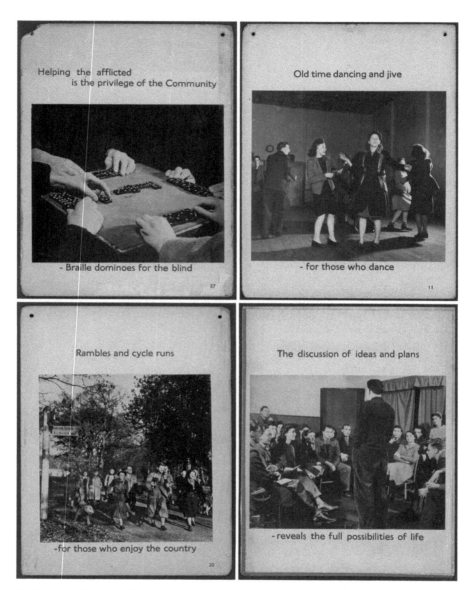

Helping the afflicted
is the privilege of the Community

- Braille dominoes for the blind

27

Old time dancing and jive

- for those who dance

11

Rambles and cycle runs

-for those who enjoy the country

20

The discussion of ideas and plans

- reveals the full possibilities of life

A Community association in action after the Second World War. (Courtesy of NCVO)

CHAPTER 7

Losing Ground

INTRODUCTION

The 1960s, or what Arthur Marwick has called the 'long sixties', stretching from about 1958 to the oil-crisis-induced economic downturn of 1973, was marked by an explosion of voluntary action.[1] Many of the new groups that emerged during this period were imbued with a spirit of self-help and had a radical, campaigning edge that set them apart from those that had gone before.[2] Organisations like the Child Poverty Action Group and the Disablement Income Group set up in 1965 and Shelter, set up in 1966, did not look to the Council for help with their establishment, which found itself in danger of being left behind.[3] The approach to political influence adopted by these groups was also in marked contrast to how the Council operated. Gone was the reliance on quiet diplomacy, replaced by a more confident campaigning style. For the Council, keen to present itself as the voice of the movement, there was a serious risk that large parts of it were beginning to view it as outdated and irrelevant. Peter Shapely has argued that 'the late 1960s and early 1970s gave rise to a new form of civil society which did not necessarily replace but certainly sidelined traditional movements'.[4] The Council, as the central coordinating agency for the traditional voluntary movement, was one of those organisations most at risk.

In contrast to the 'long sixties', the 'short seventies' was a difficult time for the voluntary movement, as rising inflation and higher taxation severely impacted on the economic viability of many organisations. Funding from central government increased, but local authority support continued to fluctuate and public spending cuts from 1979 onwards hit groups hard. 'The whole universe of welfare', Nicholas Deakin suggests, 'became dominated from the late 1970s onwards by "the cuts".'[5] The period also saw the return of significant levels of unemployment following the *oil shock*, after the exceptional period of post-war full employment, and the voluntary movement was once again invited to assist in a variety of special employment initiatives. Just as during the

© The Author(s) 2019
J. Davis Smith, *100 Years of NCVO and Voluntary Action*,
https://doi.org/10.1007/978-3-030-02774-2_7

inter-war period, the Council was an enthusiastic partner in these programmes and, as before, it would be heavily criticised in some quarters for its involvement.[6]

Any political consensus on the welfare state that might have existed in the immediate post-war period had begun to unravel by the late 1950s.[7] From the Right came a hardening of attitudes towards perceived inefficiencies within the welfare system and the dampening effect statutory services were claimed to have on voluntary action, influenced by intellectuals such as Keith Joseph, who served for a short time on the Council's Executive Committee before his election to Parliament.[8] But there was also criticism from sections of the Left, which informed by the 'Rediscovery of Poverty' by Brian Abel-Smith and Peter Townsend, began to call for changes in the system.[9] With the welfare state coming under increasing pressure, governments of all persuasions began to argue for a larger role for the voluntary movement.[10] In 1964 the Housing Corporation was established to direct funds to housing associations, and by the late 1960s voluntary action was identified as an important component in significant areas of economic and social policy, from planning, health, and community care to poverty reduction and inner-city regeneration.[11] The reorganisation of local government following the Seebohm committee report of 1968 also boosted voluntary action, in particular, local infrastructure organisations, such as councils of social service, who were seen as key partners for the new social services departments.[12]

Although the Council was in danger of being left behind by the radical developments in the voluntary movement, it would be wrong to conclude that its work was without value. Much important activity continued through its associated groups, and the period saw the expansion of its central services, aimed at developing the effectiveness of voluntary organisations. Matthew Hilton and colleagues have drawn attention to the 'inexorable' rise of expertise and professionalisation after the war, a process they trace back to the inter-war period and to the work of organisations such as Political and Economic Planning.[13] Such organisations, they argue, drew their authority from their expertise rather than from mass membership and this would become increasingly true for the Council.[14] While its direct membership had always been small, through its networks it could justifiably claim to reach into thousands of local groups, representing hundreds of thousands of volunteers. By the end of the 1960s, however, it had embarked upon a radically different strategy of centralisation, which would lead to independence of all its groups. In future, the Council's claim to legitimacy would rest not on its reach into local communities but on its professional expertise. It was a claim that was challenged by sections of the voluntary movement, who argued that the separation of the national from the local left the Council increasingly out of touch with grassroots opinion.[15]

Not only the Council was changing, but the period witnessed the growing professionalisation of large parts of the voluntary movement, driven in part by new funding relationships with the state that demanded greater accountability and efficiency. More professional approaches to fundraising, marketing, public relations, and campaigning were introduced, and many organisations began to look to inspiration from the business sector.[16] New structures of governance and management appeared and the language of business, of strategy and corporate planning, entered the lexicon of the voluntary movement for the first time.[17] In these developments, the Council was responding to wider forces and leading the change. It too restructured its governance along corporate lines, but it also refocused its work on strengthening and professionalising the movement. It also became more willing to challenge organisations over what it perceived as practices liable to undermine public trust and bring the movement into disrepute, especially in the area of fundraising. Many supported this change of direction, but others were critical and felt the Council was taking a wrong turn, for itself and the wider movement.

In 1968 George Haynes retired from the Council after 27 years as director. His replacement, J.K. Owens, occupied the role for ten years, but did not make a big impression. By the end of his time, the Council's reputation was low. Bypassed by the new wave of self-help and radical campaigning organisations, and shorn of many of its most vibrant and creative networks, it presented a rather outdated and tired image. As the 1970s drew to a close, there was a feeling that it had lost ground and was increasingly out of touch with the spirit of the age. It took the appointment of a new, radical director, Nicholas Hinton, and a dynamic new chair, Sara Morrison, to breathe fresh life into the organisation and begin the slow process of rejuvenation and reform.[18]

Supporting the Movement

Although much of the Council's most important work continued to be delivered through its associated groups, the period also saw the strengthening of its core services. Publishing was again viewed as a priority. In 1968 the Council set up a publishing imprint, Bedford Square Press, and its list grew steadily, with over 19 titles in print in 1972, although profitability was hard to secure.[19] In April 1978 a new specialist bookshop, Campaign Books, was launched in London as a joint venture with Inter-Action Trust, Friends of the Earth, and the National Council for Civil Liberties.[20] In the summer of 1979 the Council ended production of its long-running magazine, *Social Service Quarterly*, replacing it with a new magazine, *Voluntary Action*.[21] Press and public relations were given more prominence, and in 1972 the Council reported on over 1000 column inches of coverage in the press, which if 'circulation figures are to be taken seriously' means 'every household in the country has at one time or another during the year been able to read about the NCSS'.[22] Training was also boosted. Most of the Council's associated groups had provided training for some time. But it was the establishment of a new training department in April 1970, following a major organisational review, which led to a significant expansion in this area.[23] In April 1974 it set up the Voluntary Organisations Register of Training Exercises to provide an index of training programmes offered to voluntary groups, with funding from government.[24] In May 1974 it set up a working group on management advice for voluntary organisations and in 1979 negotiated a deal with the Industrial Society for the delivery of a three-year training programme on leadership, management, and the training of charity trustees.[25] In 1980 a working party was established, chaired by the management guru, Charles Handy, to develop a long-term strategy to improve the effectiveness of voluntary groups, which would herald a further drive towards professionalisation in the years to come.[26]

FUNDRAISING

The post-war years saw many large charities adopt scientific approaches to fundraising and marketing, utilising techniques pioneered in the US, most of which passed unnoticed.[27] But, as with the outcry against the fundraising exploits of a small number of charities in the early years of the twenty-first century, some of these activities attracted criticism from the media.[28] Concerns over aggressive fundraising were nothing new. David Owen has pointed to dubious practice as far back as the mid-nineteenth century, where 'collectors, paid and voluntary, were crossing and recrossing each other's trails ... frequently calling on the same individuals on behalf of identical varieties of charitable endeavour'.[29] Frank Prochaska has described charity fundraising as a Victorian 'obsession' that 'put the public under unrelenting pressure'.[30] During the First World War the government introduced legislation to curb fraudulent activity following the growth of new charities to support the war effort and an abortive attempt was made after the war to regulate fundraising as a whole.[31]

In 1967 the Charity Commission raised fresh concerns with the Council, prompted by complaints it had received from the public following a BBC programme, *Scrutiny*, on 27 January 1967.[32] 'Public disquiet of this kind', it said, 'could be damaging for charities as a whole' and it was 'desirable that some of the more controversial methods of fund-raising should be reviewed'. It identified two main concerns. First, that an insufficient amount from public donations was spent directly on charitable work and, second, that fundraising methods were felt to be 'distasteful or objectionable' and likely 'to tarnish the image of charity'. On the first of these the Commission noted that it was impossible to lay down 'any hard and fast rules' about the proportion of a charity's income that could 'properly' be used on administration, but it warned that the public might be discouraged from giving if they felt that 'too little of what they give actually reaches those whom they intend to benefit'. On the second, the Commission drew attention to the negative impact of professional fundraisers and commercial fundraising firms: 'The employment of professional fundraisers is liable to alienate the public', it argued, 'not only because they object to a part (which may be large) of what they contribute going to the collectors rather than to the charity, but also because the charity sometimes seems to have little control over the collectors and so becomes remote from the donors.' The Commission asked the Council to consider setting up a working party to see if a voluntary code could be developed to address the concerns, offering the hope that it should be done with a 'minimum of publicity in the first instance'.[33]

On 24 August 1967, Haynes met a group of national charities to discuss the proposal. There was broad support, although the meeting suggested preparing 'a code of principles' rather than 'a list of prohibitions'.[34] A working party was established, chaired by Robert Egerton, a solicitor, legal aid champion, and former vice-chair of the National Citizens' Advice Bureau Council, and composed of representatives of large fundraising charities, and it held its first meeting in January 1968.[35] It concluded that the evidence of abuses put forward by the Charity Commission 'was very slight indeed' and that despite 'intensive efforts' to find more evidence, none had been forthcoming.[36] The Egerton report was published in July 1969. It called for a voluntary code of conduct laying down minimum standards for fundraising, supplemented by a guide for charities on the form and content of accounts and the employment of outside consultants, and a guide for the general public to explain 'the philosophy, attitude and problems of charities in connection with fund-raising'. It also called for the Council to set up a standing committee of fundraising experts with a full-time secretary to advise charities on best practice.[37] The idea of a separate association of fundraising charities was dismissed on the grounds that 'this was a function which could be carried out by the NCSS'.[38] The new advisory committee on charitable fund raising met for the first time in April 1971.[39] After more than a year of deliberation, a guide for charities on fundraising was published. It concluded that there 'appears to be little cause for concern', although it acknowledged grumblings about administrative costs and some of the new fundraising methods being employed.[40] It also urged caution in employing fundraising consultants, a recommendation with some prescience given the furore that was to occur in the sector 40 years later.[41] The idea of a code of conduct for charities and a separate guide for the general public was dropped.

RELATIONS WITH GOVERNMENT

In 1961 a breakthrough came in negotiations with government over a block grant to support core work. The Council had been pushing for this for many years, but had failed to make any headway. In November 1960 its president, Lord Heyworth, wrote to the chancellor of the exchequer, Selwyn Lloyd, asking once more for 'a general grant to support the Council in its work as the central co-ordinating body for the voluntary social services'.[42] In his response, the chancellor said that the government shared 'the high regard' that Heyworth had for the work of the Council and that it was willing to 'examine the position' again.[43] In October 1961 the Executive Committee heard that a new three-year consolidated grant had been approved to replace the separate departmental grants.[44] The grant would be channelled through the Ministry of Housing and Local Government and would, for the first time, include an amount for 'general work'.[45] This was an important development that provided a measure of financial security for the Council and, in time, other umbrella bodies. Core funding underpinned its work for the next 50 years until removed, somewhat ironically, by the 2010 Coalition government as part of the *Big Society*.[46]

A second development that had a significant impact on future relations with the government was the decision of Edward Heath's Conservative administration to set up a central unit within Whitehall to manage relations with the sector. In 1972 a small coordinating unit was established in the Home Office.[47] The following year its resources were increased and the now-named Voluntary Services Unit was moved to the Civil Service Department. Such a unit had been under consideration for some time and Heath had been due to announce its launch in a speech at the Council's annual meeting in December 1971.[48] However, failure within Whitehall to agree where it should be housed delayed the announcement. According to Lord Windlesham, who took up the post of responsible minister, first within the Home Office and a year later within the Civil Service Department when he returned from a short stint in the new Northern Ireland Office, the problem was that no one within Whitehall wanted it.[49] Such would be its fate for much of its time, poorly resourced and passed back and forth between government departments, it was soon moved back to the Home Office until significant investment under New Labour in the late 1990s increased its reach and influence.[50] Notwithstanding its limited influence, its establishment was of symbolic importance in that, discounting the wartime experiment under Lord Rushcliffe, it was the first strategic body within government to focus exclusively on the voluntary movement.[51] Morrison describes its establishment as 'pivotal' in the 'context of the healthy, evolving relationship between the voluntary movement and government'.[52]

Relations between the Council and government remained close throughout the 1960s and 1970s, aided by the presence of no fewer than seven representatives from Whitehall departments on its Executive Committee in an advisory capacity, although this was reduced to a single representative in 1975. In 1973 Sir Philip Allen replaced Leslie Farrer-Brown as chair.[53] Allen was permanent under-secretary of state at the Home Office at the time of the establishment of the Voluntary Services Unit, emphasising once more the strong links between the Council and government. Morrison, who replaced Allen, remembers him as 'a marvellous man', a 'big character', and a 'ruthlessly efficient' chair.[54] Foster Murphy recalls him as 'a very nice man, a very gentle man', and a 'brilliant chair of meetings'. He remembers Allen leading a delegation to see James Callaghan, the prime minister:

> Callaghan looked at Allen and Allen looked at Callaghan and they smiled at each other. The prime minister said you're usually on this side of the table I'm not sure how this meeting is going to go. It went that Allen was able to get what the Council wanted, rather than what government wanted, because he was very well prepared, very well able to argue the case.[55]

Such closeness, however, did not prevent the Council from putting pressure on the government when it felt the interests of the movement were being ignored. It continued to be invited to give evidence to numerous official enquiries and working groups. But it also sharpened its campaigning, the tone of which became more confident as the period wore on. 'Whether the partnership is national or local', the Council asserted in 1972, 'it must allow for mutual co-operation and mutual criticism. Mutual co-operation is essential but without criticism, partnership is weakened.'[56] There is a legitimate question as to whether the Council should have taken a more oppositional stance to government at various times in its history. What is not in question is that through a mix of high-level contacts and external pressure it managed to achieve a number of changes of lasting benefit to the voluntary movement.

TAXATION AND CHARITY LAW

In 1965 the Council became concerned about the possible impact of draft proposals for a corporation tax, following Labour's electoral victory in October the previous year. The main concern was with the future position of the seven-year deeds of covenant, which had proved such an effective funding stream for the Council and the wider movement. Lord Heyworth wrote to the chancellor, James Callaghan, asking him to reconsider.[57] The intervention was successful and, in his budget speech of that year, Callaghan announced that the income derived from deeds of covenant would be safeguarded.[58] The Council had another success in 1966 when it persuaded the government to amend its plans for a selective employment tax, which the Council estimated would cost the movement £2.5 million per year.[59] In 1970 the Council set up an advisory group on charities and taxation, again under Lord Heyworth, to explore what changes might be made to tax law to encourage more individual and corporate giving.[60] The committee reported in February 1972, calling for changes to estate duty, capital gains tax and for the zero rating for charities for the new value-added tax (VAT), due to start on 1 April 1973. The Conservative chancellor, Anthony Barber, in his budget of 1972 made concessions on capital gains tax relief and estate duty but was immoveable on the bigger issue of VAT.[61]

One of the biggest campaigns launched by the Council, and one which was to have perhaps the greatest impact, though not in the direction envisaged, concerned the sale of Christmas cards. For many years large charities had been selling cards to raise funds. In 1965 charities were informed that in future they would be liable to pay tax on profits arising from such sales under the terms of the Income Tax Act of 1952, unless the trading was carried out either mainly for its beneficiaries or as part of its primary purpose. As neither exemption was likely to apply, the potential impact on the income of charities was severe. In March 1966 Heyworth led a deputation to the chair of the Board of Inland Revenue. The proposed solution was novel, with Callaghan, the chancellor, agreeing to an amendment to the law to enable charities to establish and control a company to sell Christmas cards and covenant the profits back to the charity without having to pay corporation tax.[62] The change was to have far-reaching consequences. A request to deal with a specific trading issue resulted

in the opening up of a mechanism for charities to trade tax-free in areas uncon-
nected with their primary purpose. The ruling cleared the way for the rapid
expansion of trading activity in the latter years of the century and presaged the
debate, which was to become increasingly strident as the century came to a
close, as to whether some larger charities were in danger of drifting away from
their mission. The Executive Committee was nervous about the potential
implications and at a meeting in July 1966, while welcoming the decision, felt
that this 'very wide concession should be used with care by charities'.[63] In
October it agreed to keep the issue under review: 'Proliferation of this kind of
activity on a large scale', it argued, 'might well cause reactions unfavourable to
the work and the public image of charities in general.'[64]

In October 1974 the Council set up another high-level inquiry, this time to
look into the question of charity law.[65] Chaired by Lord Goodman, its report
was published in December 1976.[66] The Committee was unable to come up
with an acceptable legal definition of charity and instead recommended liberalisation of the prohibitions governing political activity by charities and the establishment of a charities board to advise the charity commissioners on policy. In
February 1977 the Executive Committee discussed progress and noted that
some of the press coverage of the Goodman Committee and its work had been
negative.[67] The Council was accused of timidity, with some critics suggesting
charities were being muzzled.[68] Although there was little appetite to push more
strongly on implementation of the recommendations, the issue of the reform
of charity law was one that the Council returned to on a number of occasions
in the future.

THE AGE OF VOLUNTEERING

The 1960s has been characterised as the age of volunteering and, in particular,
youth volunteering.[69] Several new initiatives were set up, some independent of
government, some with explicit official support, including Voluntary Service
Overseas in 1958, Community Service Volunteers in 1962, Task Force in
1964, and the Young Volunteer Force Foundation in 1968.[70] Claims of a *volunteer boom*, however, may have been overstated. Georgina Brewis argues that
such a narrative ignores the strength of the volunteering movement before the
1960s and the threat posed to it by the forces of professionalisation during the
decade.[71] The Council was closely involved in several of the new initiatives,
particularly those with an international focus. In 1962 the Voluntary Societies
Committee for Service Overseas was set up by the Department of Technical
Cooperation to place predominantly young volunteers from Britain on short-
term placements in developing countries.[72] The first chair of the committee
was Sir John Lockwood, master of Birkbeck College, and the Council was
asked to provide the secretariat and act as the central clearing house for volunteers.[73] Two years later a second committee was established, the Council for
Volunteers Overseas, under the presidency of the Duke of Edinburgh (a future
president of the Council) to provide strategic guidance to the Lockwood

committee and other international volunteering initiatives, with the Council again taking on the secretariat function.[74] The Lockwood committee (which later changed its name to the British Volunteer Programme) grew rapidly and by 1965 was sending almost 900 volunteers to over 70 countries, with the Ministry of Overseas Development contributing 75 per cent of costs.[75] The following year, numbers had risen to almost 1200 volunteers and plans were made to double the length of placements from one year to two.[76] The programme was not without difficulties and in 1968 all volunteers had to be withdrawn from Nigeria due to the civil war.[77] There were also criticisms of inadequate training and support for volunteers and of the narrow age-range from which volunteers were drawn.[78] The Council for Volunteers Overseas was discontinued in the early 1970s following reorganisation of the British Volunteer Programme.[79]

Interest in youth volunteering was not confined to the international stage. The Albemarle report in 1960 marked a watershed in the development of the youth service and provided the impetus for better training and support for paid staff and volunteers.[80] The Standing Conference of National Voluntary Youth Organisations, which celebrated its silver jubilee in 1961, played a key role in these developments. In summer 1964 the Council ran a feature on youth volunteering in *Social Service Quarterly* and gave over its annual meeting later that year to a discussion on the issue, with the debate being chaired by young people.[81] As the decade wore on the question of the appropriate role for volunteers in the new welfare mix took on a new urgency. In 1962 the Ministry of Health issued two circulars to local welfare authorities and hospital boards asking what more could be done to increase the contribution of volunteers in key public services.[82] In its annual report for that year the Council threw its weight behind the call, commenting that 'the expanding needs of a welfare society continue to make increasing demands upon its members' and that effective community care 'depends upon enlightened statutory action in combination with skilled voluntary service'.[83] But doubts were beginning to creep in about the misuse of volunteers. By the end of the decade it was arguing that, although the growth of interest in volunteering was to be welcomed, there was a danger of 'volunteers being used for the wrong reasons – as second best – when no professionals are available, or even as cheap labour when funds are short'.[84] These concerns would intensify significantly in the 1980s.[85]

LOSING THE CROWN JEWELS

In 1966 the Council launched an inquiry into volunteering, in partnership with the National Institute for Social Work Training, to examine the role of volunteers within the personal social services in England and Wales. It was chaired by Geraldine Aves, a former chief welfare officer to the Ministry of Health, well known to the Council, having served on its Executive Committee.[86] The inquiry's report, *The Voluntary Worker in the Social Services*, was published in November 1969.[87] It called for an expansion of volunteering within the social services, a greater role for schools in inculcating a spirit of volunteering, the establishment of a comprehensive network of volunteer bureaux, and, most controversially, setting up a national volunteer foundation to provide the strategic lead for volunteering which, it recommended should be funded at least initially from public funds on the basis that the value of the volunteering unleashed would far outweigh the investment required. The Council noted in its annual report, with more than a degree of understatement, that this final recommendation 'has provoked considerable discussion and no little argument nationally and locally'.[88]

A conference, chaired by Baroness Serota, Labour minister of state at the Department of Health and Social Security, was held in London in March 1970 to discuss the report. Views were generally positive, although 'some doubts were expressed whether the approach through a network of local volunteer bureau would appeal to the increasing number of consumer organisations and radical, unstructured groups'. It was agreed the Institute of Social Work Training would host a separate discussion on the desirability of setting up a separate volunteer foundation.[89] This meeting took place on 18 March with the Council's new director, Owens, in attendance. A few days before the meeting Aves circulated a paper dismissing the claims of the Council to take on the foundation, suggesting it was 'too preoccupied with its own affairs' and still needed 'to prove itself in the eyes of the local authorities and professional bodies'. Her preference was for it to be based at the Social Work Advisory Service. At the meeting, according to a later note prepared by Owens, there 'was a rambling discussion after the dinner in which Miss Aves received very little support for the ideas in her paper'. Owens refuted the suggestion that the Council wasn't ready to take on the role and pointed to the fact that 26 councils of social service were currently running volunteer bureaux. His note to the Executive Committee said there was some support for an independent foundation, but that most people favoured it being based with the Council.[90] Following the meeting a small ad-hoc group was set up, chaired by Sir William Hart, to explore the issue further.[91] The Council was not included in the group, but was invited to give evidence. At its meeting in July 1970 the Executive Committee reiterated its strong opposition to a new foundation and suggested it 'was itself well equipped to undertake' all the proposed new work.[92] The Hart group reported on 22 September. Its recommendation was something of a fudge. Rather than a new foundation, it recommended setting up 'a very small centre' focused on information, research, and facilitation. It should be independent and not tied to any particular organisation and should complement the work of others, including the Council. Its aim would be 'to fructify the social services and develop the quantity and quality of volunteers' and expectation was that it might need to exist only for five years to kick-start the work.[93] On 24 October Aves wrote to Owens reiterating her view of the need for a new organisation and asking for the Council's support.[94] This was reluctantly given and, when the new Volunteer Centre was set up in September 1973, Morrison, the Council's vice-chair, joined the board. Tensions, however, remained. According to Murphy, a future director of the new organisation, 'there was no love lost between the Council and the new centre'.[95] Baroness Pitkeathley agrees, suggesting there was a level of 'discomfort in those early relationships'.[96]

The establishment of the Volunteer Centre did not immediately curtail the Council's work on volunteering. When the Aves report was published there were 33 volunteer bureaux, most based within councils of social service.[97] By the end of 1972, the number had grown to 52.[98] In November that year the Council had an application for three years funding from the Home Office approved for a development officer to help expand coverage further.[99] By 1974 there were 105 bureaux and, although the Council was still leading the work, closer links were being made with the Volunteer Centre.[100] In 1976 an agreement was reached to hand over support for the network (of the now 141 bureaux) to the new organisation.[101] This was a turning point in the work of the Council. Volunteering had always been at the heart of its mission and a central tenet of its philosophy. With the establishment of the Volunteer Centre, it ceded authority on the issue to another national organisation. The split was not absolute. It continued to take an interest in volunteering, especially in matters of public policy, and in future focused its attention increasingly on the work of trustees. But the establishment of the Volunteer Centre marked the end of the Council's day-to-day focus on the issue. In retrospect it can be argued this loss left a hole that was difficult to fill.[102] The severing of ties with volunteering, when combined with the parting of ways with the council of social service movement and the rural community councils some years later, created a disconnection between the national and the local, between high policy and voluntary action on the ground. For the first 50 years of its history the Council had emphasised the importance of this linkage. In future it had to find a new focus for its work and a new legitimacy for its existence.

A NEW DIRECTION

The federated model laid out by Haynes in 1944 had survived, and indeed thrived, for much of the early post-war period.[103] By the mid-1960s, however, concerns were being raised about its sustainability. There were several issues. First, that it placed too great an administrative burden on the central operation in Bedford Square—by the mid-1960s there were 17 separate associated groups. Second, that the time and resources devoted to servicing the groups held back the development of core services such as research, information, policy, and campaigning, which Haynes had also identified as a priority. And third, despite being legally responsible for the groups, the Council had little control over their work. In January 1967 a review committee was established under the chair, Farrer-Brown, to examine the future direction of the organisation, although it did not meet until early the following year to allow for the planned departure of Haynes and the arrival of his replacement, Owens.[104] Over the next 18 months the committee would meet more than 20 times. It led to a fundamental shift in strategy, away from Haynes' federal model towards greater centralisation, resulting in independence being granted to all associated groups and a refocusing on core issues of importance to the movement as a whole. The Council was established in 1919 to act as coordinator of voluntary action at national and local level. It had long believed that the two strands were indivisible and each was required for success. The 1968 review led to the abandonment of this vision.

The review committee reported in October 1969 and its recommendations were accepted at the annual meeting later that month.[105] In its introduction the report explored the changing nature of voluntary action and what it identified as a 'swing from paternalism to self-help' and a desire to work *with* not *for* communities. It reaffirmed the central importance of volunteering to the Council's work, ironically given the deliberations in progress with the Aves review: 'All that concerns volunteers – their recruitment, their training, their opportunities for service, both in voluntary organisations and in association with the statutory authorities, concerns the Council.'[106] It restated the belief that voluntary action served a number of purposes: pioneering, gap filling, paternalism, self-help, and campaigning, but felt the biggest change affecting the movement was the shifting relationship with the state. It called for 'real partnership' and 'high standards, flexibility and adaptability in the voluntary movement' and ended with a passionate plea for recognition that voluntary agencies were about more than doing the work of government. Voluntary groups, it asserted, 'are indispensable instruments of a free society and equal partners in the effort to improve the quality of life of all human beings'.[107]

Its recommendations could not have differed more from those of the 1944 review. Instead of calling for more power to be placed with the associated groups, it proposed greater control at the centre. The Council, it argued, 'should be seen as one living, vigorous entity and not a federation of varied autonomous, associated bodies'.[108] Local groups should be encouraged to 'contribute powerfully to policy-making at national level', but ultimately 'the specialist parts must see that they advance their own work best by being part of the wider assembly'.[109] The report noted that the growth of the associated group model 'has placed a great strain on the organisational structure of the Council' and concluded 'that the present organisation' is not 'adequate for the tasks it has to face today'.[110] Such a shift in direction was not inevitable. During the course of the review, dissenting voices were raised in favour of retaining a federated model. Some Executive Committee members called for 'grassroots' community work to remain a priority, while others argued for greater diversity and innovation and less centralisation. One member bemoaned the fact that the Council had not been centre stage in the setting up of such radical new organisations as Shelter and the Child Poverty Action Group.[111] But the arguments for greater central control won the day, with significant implications for the Council's future.

The review led to a major internal reorganisation. The numerous departments within the Council were grouped into four new blocks: a community work division to support the networks; a national organisations division to support national groups; an administration and central services division, with two new departments for training and intelligence; and a new international department, formed through the merger of the international and overseas development departments, charged with developing the Council's work overseas.[112] To oversee the new structure the Executive Committee was remodelled. A new committee of 40 members (down from 51) was established, including representatives from the national councils of the other home countries, central and local government, business, trade unions, and national and local voluntary organisations. It was to meet three times a year, supported by two sub-committees, a policy and general purposes committee and a finance and staffing committee.[113] Three years later it was revised again. A new Executive Committee was formed of half the size to meet nine times a year without sub-groups.[114] There was concern that the relatively infrequent meetings of the previous Executive Committee had caused delays in decision-making, but the new structure, which required almost monthly board meetings, proved unsustainable and further changes soon ensued.

The most significant implication of the 1969 review was the clear message it sent to the associated groups that the council saw its future not as coordinator of a federation of autonomous groups but as a tighter, more cohesive corporate entity. The path was set for a parting of the ways. The trouble with this strategy was that the Council was determined to hold onto some of its groups. There was still a strong sense that its power lay in its linking of the national and local through the networks of rural community councils and councils of social service. But with the direction of travel towards greater centralisation so clearly set, it proved impossible in the longer term to hold back the tide. Many of the groups moved to independence over the next few years with the active encouragement of the Council. In most cases separation was consensual and the divorce painless, but not always, and disputes with some groups threatened the Council's reputation and left a damaging legacy.

Parting of the Ways

Pressure for independence had been growing for a number of years and the 1969 review in some respects merely speeded up the process. Haynes' strategy had always been to move most of the groups to independence at the right time. The issue was when, and how to keep hold of the groups it wanted to retain. The Council soon found that events were largely outside its control. One of the first of the big groups to go was the National Old People's Welfare Council (NOPWC), which celebrated its silver jubilee in 1965 with a series of events and activities, including a national essay competition on the theme *I remember* adjudicated by J.B. Priestley.[115] In October 1968 the NOPWC gave notice of its intention to set up an independent body as soon as funding became available. The move was greeted with dismay. A letter to its chair stated that 'although it was contrary to its traditions to stand against the wishes of an associated group for independence', the Council felt 'keen regret and misgiving' about the proposal.[116] But there was no turning back and the Council was forced reluctantly to agree to the separation. On 1 April 1970 a new, independent charity for older people, Age Concern, came into being.[117]

The citizens' advice bureaux (CAB) was another of the large associated groups destined for independence. Again the issue was timing, but in this case separation was more difficult. The movement prospered in the 1960s with the return of funding from government after the fallow post-war years and was at the forefront of several new developments, including the new Consumer Council set up as a result of the Molony committee report on Consumer Protection in 1963.[118] The movement began to push for independence, but the Council was reluctant to see it go. Relations became increasingly strained in the early 1970s, resulting in the resignation of the CAB national chair, Sir Harold Banwell and the Council's sacking of the secretary to the movement's national committee who, in supporting independence, was felt to be acting against its interests.[119] *The Times* wrote about 'a year of struggle' that has 'split the bureaux and damaged their relationship with their founders and sponsors, the National Council of Social Service'.[120] A joint letter appeared in the paper on 13 July 1971 from the chair of the Council and the new chair of the national CAB Council, expressing sadness 'about the problems which have arisen' and hope that the two organisations could reach a mutually satisfactory agreement.[121] Questions were raised in Parliament critical of the position taken by the Council and asking for a review of its statutory funding.[122] In May 1973 the National Standing Conference of Citizens' Advice Bureaux adopted a new constitution and created a new body, the National Association of Citizens' Advice Bureaux (NACAB), to run the service, still at this stage under the ownership of the Council.[123] In 1975, agreement was finally reached that NACAB should become independent, although formal separation did not come about until 1977.[124] It was an unfortunate end to a relationship that had delivered so much.

The separation of some other groups went more smoothly. The Standing Conference of National Voluntary Youth Organisations set up a working party to review its future direction. It reported in January 1972 and led to the establishment of the National Council for Voluntary Youth Services the same year, which became independent on 1 April 1980.[125] The National Association of Women's Clubs, which had been integral to the work of the Council since the 1930s when it organised clubs for wives of unemployed men, became independent in April 1976.[126] The Standing Conference of Women's Organisations followed suit in 1980.[127] In 1978 the London Council of Social Service finally returned to independence and the British Volunteer Programme also became independent.[128] In 1974 the Executive Committee agreed on a proposal for the Charities Aid Fund to move to independence, largely to free it to develop new sources of giving. It had existed for 50 years and distributed some £40 million of tax-efficient funding to voluntary groups, with a healthy £1 million returning to the Council in management fees.[129] It moved into new offices in

Tonbridge Kent in the autumn of 1969 and launched as an independent organisation, the Charities Aid Foundation (CAF), in October 1974.[130]

CORE NETWORKS

Part of the Council's reluctance to sanction the independence of its leading associated groups was concern that it would prove a catalyst for the separation of its two core networks. Development of both networks, which had been slow in the immediate post-war years, picked up considerably in the more favourable economic climate of the 1960s. By 1969 there were 194 councils of social service covering most of England and Wales.[131] Many were operating specialist bureaux to recruit and place volunteers and in Oxford and Wakefield junior councils had been formed to respond to the rise of interest in voluntary action among young people.[132] The establishment of local authority social service departments, following the Seebohm review of 1968, gave a boost to the councils in acting as a link between statutory and voluntary services, although the reorganisation of local government in 1974 raised the issue of the alignment of the councils with local authority boundaries.[133] To adjust to the new environment some adjusted their boundaries and new metropolitan councils were formed to cover Merseyside and Greater Manchester.[134] The economic crisis of the 1970s hit the councils of social service hard and many were forced to cut back their activities. The rural community councils also prospered in the 1960s, overseeing further developments of village halls, continuing to offer support to rural industry and organising the successful annual Rural Life conference to showcase developments in the countryside. In 1970 the Bretherton report called for the Development Commission to continue to fund the movement.[135] For the time being both urban and rural networks were content to stay with the Council. The 1968 review committee had received a passionate plea from one council of social service for the network to remain part of the whole: 'Any attempt to turn the NCSS into a purely research/advice set-up without an executive arm in the field', it argued, 'should be resisted', 'the National Council and councils of Social Service stand or fall together. Apart neither has a future.'[136] Such a position would prove increasingly difficult to maintain.

FUNDING AND RESOURCES

In 1969 the Council celebrated its 50th anniversary. It is worth reflecting how its income had grown and diversified over that time. In 1919 its expenditure was £2417, drawn solely from voluntary sources. By 1933 total expenditure stood at £19,953, again made up entirely from voluntary sources, plus a separate grant of £19,000 from the Ministry of Labour to fund projects on unemployment. By 1955 expenditure had grown to almost £95,000, of which £40,000 was from statutory sources. In 1962, the first year of the government's new consolidated grant, total expenditure stood at £230,000, £103,000 of which was from voluntary sources and £92,000 from government grants. In its golden anniversary year of 1969, the Council was spending a total of £369,924 and employed over 266 staff.[137] Despite the cushion provided by the core grant, there was still a need for voluntary funds, particularly from the early 1970s when high inflation led the Council to fall into deficit once more.[138] Making the most of the opportunities afforded by the seven-year covenant, it embarked on a series of fundraising drives with business that raised over £160,000 between 1968 and 1972 and £620,000 between 1974 and 1975.[139] It was not averse to using its high-profile supporters to try to secure additional funding. In October 1972 Owens wrote to Buckingham Palace to ask Prince Philip as president to intervene with the government to secure an increase in its grant. The Council was told that the Prince had no intention of doing so.[140] In 1978–79 the government grant was reduced and it ran a budget deficit of £100,000, which was met from the appeal fund. Income from CAF, it was noted, was 'the mainstay of the Council's voluntary income'.[141] One possible cost-saving measure explored was moving the headquarters out of London, but it was concluded that any financial benefits would be heavily outweighed by the political damage and the matter was shelved.[142]

The Council was not alone in its economic difficulties in the 1970s and several initiatives were explored to help the movement. A Give as You Earn scheme was explored with the Confederation of British Industry (CBI) and TUC and consideration given to setting up a new management advice bureau to advise organisations on 'examining cost effectiveness, possible mergers, sharing of premises and other streamlining measures'.[143] One of the most creative ideas was a new charity stamp, which was launched by the Post Office in association with the Council in January 1975. Carrying a one-and-a-half-pence donation in addition to the first-class rate, it was available for the first half of the year and sold seven million, raising over £60,000 for distribution to a range of health charities.[144] It was a one-off experiment, however, which the Post Office declined to repeat, much to the disappointment of the Council.[145] In April 1968 the Executive Committee discussed plans by the government to set up a national lottery. The general view was that it seemed unlikely charities would benefit to any great extent.[146]

THE RETURN OF UNEMPLOYMENT

In 1975 the prime minister, Harold Wilson, addressed the Council's annual meeting. He gave a stark warning of the economic pressures ahead and the inevitable constraints on public spending. Voluntary organisations, he said, were fundamental and irreplaceable, but should not be seen as 'just a useful adjunct to government services'. Rather they had a 'distinct, indispensable and socially invaluable role' to play 'in tackling social problems and creating a better society'.[147] Over the next few years this role played itself out most clearly in the arena of unemployment, where a range of special programmes was set up with voluntary sector involvement. The Council played a key role in facilitating this engagement, just as it had in the 1930s, and, as before, its involvement proved controversial.[148] Under the Job Creation Programme, voluntary organisations were estimated to have been involved in about a third of all projects, and there was heavy sector engagement in the Youth Opportunities Programme and the Special Temporary Employment Programme.[149] The Council set up an unemployment unit in July 1978, funded by the Manpower Services Commission, to advise voluntary groups on engagement with these schemes.[150] Despite high take up, it was critical of much of the sector's response, arguing that 'despite their reputation for flexibility many voluntary agencies have found it very difficult to adapt to new circumstances'.[151] The Council was criticised for colluding with a programme which, it was claimed, did little more than paper over the cracks of the problem. It was a criticism that increased in intensity in the following decade.[152]

INTERNATIONALISM AND INTEGRATION

Throughout the 1960s and 1970s the Council continued to prioritise its involvement in international affairs, offering active support to both the British National Conference on Social Welfare and the British Committee for the International Exchange of Social Workers and Administrators. Many of its associated groups also continued to get involved in work overseas. The WGPW, for example, organised a series of exchange visits with representatives of women's groups in Eastern Europe, a multi-racial council of social service was set up in Southern Rhodesia, and CAB were established in several countries, including South Africa, India, Israel, Australia, and the US.[153] In 1960 the Council took over the secretariat for the Standing Conference of British Organisations for Aid to Refugees, a coordinating body bringing together 24 British agencies concerned with refugee issues.[154] The Council was active in the European Campaign for World Refugees held in 1966, taking part in an awareness-raising event at the Royal Festival Hall attended by over 2000 school children, which resulted in a number of schools setting up fundraising activities to support vocational training bursaries for young refugees.[155] Through the standing conference, the Council was involved in providing aid to refugees from various conflicts, including the Arab-Israeli war in June 1967, Vietnam, and the civil war in Nigeria.[156]

The Council responded enthusiastically to Britain's decision to enter the European Community.[157] In 1972 it ran a series of conferences on the theme of *social policy in the European Economic Community* (EEC) and in September 1974 appointed a part-time liaison officer in Brussels.[158] In 1975, with EEC support, it opened a European desk, providing regular information and support to its members on European matters and launched a new dedicated monthly publication, *Look Europe* (later changed to *Inside Europe*).[159] In 1979 a proposed EEC Directive to harmonise the legislation of member states concerning the treatment of illegal immigrants from third world countries raised concerns about the possible negative impact on race relations in the UK. The procedures, it was argued, 'could well exacerbate race relations and deter employers from employing members of ethnic minority groups for fear of sanctions if they proved to be illegal immigrants'.[160] The Council hosted a conference in March 1979 on *Migrants and the EEC* and engaged in work with other groups to try 'to bring about the replacement of the draft directive by more positive policies'.[161]

INTERNAL DEVELOPMENTS

At the beginning of the 1960s the Council took a lease on several new buildings in Bedford Square, as well as office space in nearby Great Russell Street and Rathbone Street.[162] Although numbers fluctuated year on year, for most of the decade the Council was employing in excess of 250 members of staff, many of them involved in supporting the associated groups and networks. A staff association was set up with its own regular magazine, *Comment*, which featured news, articles, and poems by staff.[163] It would be another ten years, however, before the Council finally agreed to recognise the bargaining role of the staff union.[164] Staff numbers contracted sharply in the 1970s, as the impact of the recession began to bite, and by the middle of the decade it had closed all its regional offices and replaced them with a team of regional officers.[165]

In March 1967 Haynes retired after 27 years as director. He had joined the organisation in 1933 as regional officer in the north of England and moved to the headquarters in London in 1937. He was succeeded by J.K. Owens, previously acting director for education in Derbyshire.[166] Haynes' contribution to the Council and the wider movement was immense. He was appointed director in 1940, when Leonard Shoeten Sack retired suddenly on health grounds, and steered the Council through the war with huge energy and skill. John Wolfenden, a former chair of the Council, paid tribute to him as 'indomitably patient', 'inflexibly determined', and 'dedicated to the practical and day-to-day realisation of an ideal'.[167] He remained involved with the voluntary movement after retirement, serving as chair of the Standing Conference on Legal Aid and president of the National Association of Citizens' Advice Bureaux. He was knighted in 1962 and died in 1983, aged 81.[168] An annual lecture was later set up by the Council in his memory, with the inaugural presentation given by the Aga Khan on the contribution of voluntary groups to the resettlement of refugees.[169]

Owens remained in post for ten years, but did not have the best of times. He was unfortunate in his timing and his lack of success was not solely down to him. The Council, and indeed Haynes, must share the blame for not having modernised earlier, but Owens was not the leader to revitalise the organisation. Colleagues who worked with him are lukewarm in their assessment. Murphy remembers him as 'a nice man', 'a supportive person to me in my first senior job', but 'sort of straight, not very good at thinking beyond barriers'.[170] Bill Seary agrees, recalling that 'he was a pleasant person, but not particularly effective'.[171] For Ian Bruce, Owens was a 'quiet man who was not highly regarded in the sector', but 'very welcoming' and 'always smiling'.[172] Even Owens himself, reflecting on his ten years in charge, admitted it had been a difficult time for the Council and that it had experienced 'some feelings of anxiety and heart-searching'.[173]

He did not leave the organisation in a strong position. David Clarke, who joined the organisation in 1977, says his first impression of the Council was that it 'looked pretty confused'. There was, he says, 'a real problem about simply a lack of understanding of what the organisation was'. It was all 'pretty vague', 'a sleeping giant really'.[174] A review of the Council carried out by the Civil Service Department in 1975 was critical of its 'highly compartmentalised' structure, which impeded efficiency and effectiveness. It called for a more 'integrated structure' and recommended the Council move towards 'a model of a slimmed-down, more vigorous and purposeful organisation' that was 'better equipped to overcome the difficult problems that lie ahead'.[175] Morrison, who took over as chair from Allen in 1977, recalls a 'highly competent, well intentioned organisation, with enormous deep-seated roots in the voluntary sector', but 'in need of massive rethinking to meet the needs of the emerging, much more active and far more complex plural society into which we were drifting at this time'.[176] One of Morrison's first tasks as chair was to replace Owens with Hinton, who joined the Council in 1977 from the National Association for the Care and Resettlement of Offenders (NACRO) where he was seen as one 'of the new breed of young and radical directors' of the voluntary movement.[177] Hinton went to Marlborough public school, studied law at Selwyn College, Cambridge, then took a course in psychiatric social work. His first job was in Leeds at an intermediate treatment scheme for children and families, and he joined NACRO in 1968 as a training and hostel services organiser, before becoming director in 1973. He was 35 when he joined the Council and brought a reputation of being 'quick and sharp and radical' and a 'breath of fresh air'.[178] The task was immense. He said subsequently he was only 'dimly aware' of the Council when he took over and that it had a reputation for being too passive and 'taking few initiatives of its own'.[179] Hinton formed a hugely successful partnership with Morrison, which did much to transform the fortunes of the organisation. Morrison had a successful career in business and local government, was vice-chair of the Conservative Party from 1971 to 1975 and a close confidant of the prime minister, Heath. The Council wanted her to take over as chair in 1973 when Farrer-Brown retired, but the Conservative Party put pressure on her to stay until the next election and it was generally agreed that she couldn't do both jobs at once.[180] She had a reputation for plain speaking and getting things done and, according to Murphy, 'was a brilliant person to lead the organisation'.[181] Clarke concurs, describing her as 'dynamic' and having 'very good political antennae'.[182] Murphy describes her relationship with Hinton as the 'epitome of the relationship between a chair and a chief executive'.[183]

A MISSED OPPORTUNITY

In 1978 a new report was published on the *Future of Voluntary Organisations.*
It was the product of the Wolfenden committee, which had been co-sponsored
by the Joseph Rowntree Memorial Trust and the Carnegie UK Trust and represented the first major inquiry into the state of voluntary action since the
Beveridge committee 30 years previously.[184] Like its predecessor, it was strong
on rhetoric and made a compelling case for the value of voluntary action in
modern society. But like Beveridge it was weak on recommendations and dis-
appointingly light on practical suggestions as to how the movement should
develop. Wolfenden was a close friend of the Council, having been chair and
president, and a great deal of the report was in line with Council thinking.
Much of the last 30 years, it said, had been 'dominated by the problems of
adaptation by voluntary organisations to the altered role of government', but
in recent years there had been a number of new and welcome developments.
New pressure groups had arisen; there had been a resurgence of interest in self-
help and mutual aid, and a growth in coordinating groups at national and local
level. Government funding to voluntary groups had risen significantly, but had
done so 'without in the main upsetting the perception or status of independent
social agencies in the public mind'. The report concluded that there was no
doubt the voluntary movement would continue to expand and that there
would be a powerful role in the future for local and national 'intermediary
bodies' as part of a new era of voluntary sector/state partnership.[185] The report
was generally positive about the work of the Council, but said it had 'too wide
a field to cover' and should focus primarily on representation rather than service delivery or the support of its networks.[186]

Wolfenden has been credited with the *invention* of the voluntary sector,
which according to Harris, Rochester, and Halfpenny, 'was to be a powerful
influence on the development of policy, practice and academic endeavor over
the following two decades'.[187] Perri 6 and Diana Leat have argued that similar
developments took place at the same time in the US with the creation of the
non-profit sector, following the Filer Commission report of 1977.[188] They
argue that the creation of the voluntary sector in the UK owed much to the
work of the Council and was a deliberate strategy to regain some of the ground
it had lost over the previous two decades. 'Invention', they suggest, 'served to
weld together the very disparate groups of the more radical 1960s pressure
groups and community groups on the one hand, and more established social
services agencies on the other, who would previously hardly have thought of
themselves as part of the same organizational universe, and in many cases, saw
themselves as opponents.'[189] For Harris et al. this was a pivotal moment in the
history of the Council, which they suggest began from this point to shift its
priorities away from concerns with sectional interests to become 'increasingly
concentrated on relations between the voluntary sector and government …
and on ways of improving the effectiveness and capacity of voluntary organisations'.[190] However, notes of caution needed to be sounded. First, Wolfenden

was not the first to use the term the voluntary sector, which had been used in at least one Council document a couple of years earlier.[191] Second, the report was cautious about claiming a cohesive movement, arguing that 'it is not help-ful to imply that there is anything like a unified voluntary movement with a common philosophy guiding its work'.[192] And third, although this shift would indeed come to define the Council's work in the next stage of its development, the timing predated Wolfenden and had been largely settled upon following the major internal review in 1969. Whatever the precise timing, however, the impact would be the same. For the future, the Council was less concerned with its networks and groups and more committed to servicing the needs of the wider voluntary sector.

In February 1978 the Council organised a national conference to discuss the report, attended by 400 representatives from charities, government, and academia.[193] The home secretary, Merlyn Rees, set up an inter-departmental committee and in June the Council submitted its response. Perhaps, surpris-ingly, it felt unable to give the report 'blanket approval', but it welcomed it as 'overdue recognition' of the value of voluntary organisations and expressed hope that it would lead 'to a far more positive attitude by central govern-ment'.[194] Hinton, who had joined the Council just months before the report's publication, was lukewarm, saying it offered no 'direct, clear recommenda-tions' and had little to say about the role of the sector in campaigning and advocacy.[195] *The Times* felt it was insufficiently radical.[196] F.J.C. Amos, from the Institute of Local Government Studies at the University of Birmingham, thought it was an 'opportunity missed'; it was stuck in a post-war world, paying little heed to the rise of the self-help movement and the trend for voluntary groups not simply to pioneer services later taken over by the state, but to meet needs 'independently and sometimes in defiance of the statutory services'.[197] Jeremy Kendall and Martin Knapp suggest that the report was a reflection of a 'welfare consensus' that no longer existed and was thus doomed to failure.[198] The Labour government produced a delayed response but lost power before it could act.[199] The new Conservative government, under Margaret Thatcher, had a very different view on the role of the sector and Wolfenden had no impact on future policy.[200] In 1979 the Council produced a major report of its own setting out a far more expansive role for the voluntary movement as part of a new *welfare pluralism*. And it was this report, rather than Wolfenden, that provided the intellectual underpinning to its work over the following decade.[201]

CONCLUSION

In 1969 the Council marked its 50th anniversary. A reception was held in the Guildhall on 17 July, hosted by the Lord Mayor of London and attended by over 900 guests, including the Queen and Prince Philip. The following day a special service of thanksgiving was held in Westminster Abbey, conducted by the Dean of Westminster, with fanfares played by trumpeters from the Royal Military School of Music in the presence of representatives of 800 local groups.

On 30 November the BBC allocated a special radio appeal for the Council as the Week's Good Cause. A specially bound copy of Margaret Brasnett's anniversary history was presented to the Queen and placed in the library at Windsor Castle.[202]

The celebrations, justified as they were for the impressive work of the Council over 50 years, masked a serious concern about its current standing. The 1960s and 1970s had seen some success, especially in the international arena, and, despite the abandonment of the federated model, it was setting up new organisations well into the 1970s. For example, it helped with the establishment of the Association for Research into Restricted Growth in 1970 and the Festival Welfare Services organisation in 1973.[203] However, there was a growing sense as the 1970s ended that it had lost its way and was out of touch with the needs and aspirations of large parts of the voluntary sector. Writing on Hinton's appointment in 1977 Des Wilson, editor of *Social Work Today* and former director of Shelter, was scathing in his judgement. Many large charities, he wrote, saw the Council as 'irrelevant, even suffocating, and virtually ignore it all together', while local groups question whether it is 'entitled to represent voluntary opinion to Government at all'. His less than flattering conclusion was that 'to put it bluntly the NCSS is seen by many as a stuffy, committee-spawning, sherry-drinking, patronising anachronism'.[204] Wilson's proposed remedy was at odds with the new direction the Council had embarked upon. Rather than getting rid of local groups and networks, it needed to 'go back to the grassroots from where volunteers come and where they work', 'decentralise more' and 'build on its strength – its local councils – and create more-democratic and thus more-informed lines of communication to Government'.[205] Such was the scale of the challenge facing the Council and its new leadership as it embarked on its second 50 years.

NOTES

1. Marwick, 1998.
2. See, for example, Brenton, 1985, p. 36, and Taylor and Kendall, 1996, pp. 55–56.
3. The Child Poverty Action Group applied for membership of the Council in 1967, and it was approved by the Executive Committee subject to consideration of 'the possible political implications of this particular organisation'. Minutes of Executive Committee, 12 January 1967; London Metropolitan Archives (LMA)/4016/IS/A/01/36(1). On the rise of these new groups, see, for example, Thane, 2011, pp. 126–27. On CPAG, see Thane and Davidson, 2016.
4. Shapely, 2011. See also Lent, 2001, and Berridge and Mold, 2011.
5. Deakin, 1995, p. 54.
6. Ibid., pp. 54–55.
7. Many academics dismiss the idea of a post-war consensus on the welfare state. See, for example, Glennerster, 1990.
8. Finlayson, 1994, p. 356.

9. For example, Abel-Smith and Townsend, 1965. See also Evans, 2009.

10. See, for example, Kendall and Knapp, 1996, especially Chap. 5.

11. On growing statutory support for voluntary action at this time, see Taylor and Kendall, 1996, pp. 56–57, and Deakin, 1995, pp. 50–51.

12. Deakin, 1995, p. 52.

13. Hilton et al., 2013, p. 65.

14. Hilton, 2011.

15. See Chap. 8 for a discussion of these issues.

16. See, for example, Hilton et al., 2013.

17. On the adoption by charities of the language of business, see Kramer, 1990, p. 48.

18. Hinton and Morrison are discussed further below.

19. NCSS Annual Reports 1967–68 and 1972–73.

20. NCSS Annual Report 1977–78.

21. NCSS Annual Report 1978–79.

22. NCSS Annual Report 1971–72, p. 23.

23. This is discussed further below.

24. NCSS Annual Report 1974–75.

25. NCSS Annual Reports 1974–75 and 1978–79.

26. The Handy working party is discussed further in Chap. 8.

27. Finlayson, 1994, p. 380.

28. Hilton et al., 2013, pp. 88–89.

29. Owen, 1964, p. 480.

30. Prochaska, 1988, p. 59.

31. Finlayson, 1994, p. 266.

32. Memorandum prepared by the Charity Commission on *Fund-raising by Charities*, tabled at the meeting of the Executive Committee, 13 July 1967; LMA/4016/IS/01/36(2).

33. Ibid.

34. Minutes of Executive Committee, 12 October 1967; LMA/4016/IS/A/01/36(2).

35. NCSS Annual Report 1967–68. Egerton had been a 'poor man's lawyer' and was a passionate advocate for legal aid, writing a book of the same name. See Egerton, 1945.

36. Minutes of Executive Committee, 10 April 1969; LMA/4016/IS/A/01/37(1).

37. NCSS Annual Report 1968–69.

38. Minutes of Executive Committee, 10 April 1969; LMA/4016/IS/A/01/37(1).

39. NCSS Annual Report 1970–71.

40. National Council of Social Service, 1973.

41. Johnson, 1981, p. 130.

42. Minutes of Finance and General Purposes Sub-Committee, 22 February 1961; LMA/4016/IS/A/01/052(2). Lord Heyworth was president of the Council from 1957 to 1970. He was chair of Unilever and lead author of *The Heyworth Report* in 1965, which led to the establishment of the Social Science Research Council. He sat on numerous public bodies and according to *The Times*, after the war was 'increasingly drawn into Government and academic circles as advi-

sor and friend', just what the Council needed in their president. He was made a Baron in 1955 and died in 1974. See *The Times*, 17 June 1974, p. 14.

43. Minutes of Finance and General Purposes Sub-Committee, 22 February 1961; LMA/4016/IS/A/01/052(2).

44. Minutes of Executive Committee, 12 October 1961; LMA/4016/IS/A/01/34(3).

45. Minutes of Executive Committee, 12 April 1962; LMA/4016/IS/A/01/35(1).

46. See Chap. 10 for a discussion of the *Big Society*.

47. On the setting up of the Voluntary Services Unit, see Windlesham, 1975, pp. 59–70.

48. Ibid. In his speech, the prime minister said his objective was to create the conditions 'under which voluntary effort can thrive', and he announced additional funding of £3.5 million over four years to support the movement. Following the event the Council wrote to the government asking for funding for 20 new posts to support this work. Lord Windlesham replied, politely declining the offer. Minutes of Executive Committee, 10 February 1972; LMA/4016/IS/A/01/38(3).

49. Ibid.

50. On criticisms of the VSU, see Kendall and Knapp, 1996, pp. 147–48. On its strengthening under New Labour, see Chap. 9.

51. It wasn't quite the first committee. The previous Labour prime minister, Harold Wilson, had set up a small coordinating unit on voluntary social services in the Cabinet Office as early as 1964. See 6 and Leat, 1997. On the Rushcliffe Committee, see Chap. 5.

52. Interview with Sara Morrison, 2 August 2017.

53. Allen had a glittering career within Whitehall serving as permanent secretary to four home secretaries. He was made a life peer by James Callaghan in 1976 and joined the cross-benches. In addition to his role at the Council he was chair of the Occupational Pensions Board and Mencap and member of the Royal Commission on Standards of Conduct in Public Life. He died in 2007. See *The Times*, 4 December 2007, p. 53, and Cubbon, 2013.

54. Interview with Sara Morrison, 2 August 2017.

55. Interview with Foster Murphy, 24 May 2017.

56. Minutes of Executive Committee, 10 February 1972; LMA/4016/IS/A/01/38(3).

57. Minutes of Executive Committee, 8 April 1965; LMA/4016/IS/A/01/35(3).

58. NCSS Annual Report 1964–65.

59. Brasnett, 1969, pp. 233–34.

60. NCSS Annual Report 1970–71.

61. NCSS Annual Report 1971–72.

62. NCSS Annual Report 1965–66.

63. Minutes of Executive Committee, 14 July 1966; LMA/4016/IS/A/01/36(1).

64. Minutes of Executive Committee, 13 October 1966; LMA/4016/IS/A/01/36(1).

65. NCSS Annual Report 1973–74.

66. Arnold Goodman, who led many Council committees, was described in an obituary in the *Independent* as 'the greatest negotiator of the age' and for many years 'possibly Britain's most distinguished citizen outside government'. A renowned lawyer and adviser to the prime minister, Harold Wilson, it is said

that when appointed master of University College, Oxford, in 1976 he was chair of 19 significant public bodies and numerous private ones. He was made a life peer in 1965 and died in 1995. See The *Independent*, 15 May 1995. The Charities Aid Foundation established a lecture series in his honour.

67. Minutes Executive Committee, 22 February 1977; LMA/4016/IS/A/01/41(1).
68. Finlayson, 1994, p. 350.
69. See, for example, Sheard, 1992 and 1995.
70. Brenton, 1985, p. 38, and Dartington, 1971.
71. Brewis, 2013, p. 17.
72. NCSS Annual Report 1961–62.
73. On the contribution of Lockwood to the work of the committee, see the letter following his death in 1965 in *The Times*, 16 July 1965, p. 18.
74. NCSS Annual Report 1963–64. The Duke of Edinburgh succeeded Lord Heyworth as president of the Council in April 1970 and held the post for three years. At the annual meeting in November 1970 he gave the keynote address on The Human Environment. NCSS Annual Report 1970–71.
75. NCSS Annual Report 1965–66.
76. NCSS Annual Report 1966–67.
77. NCSS Annual Report 1967–68.
78. Brewis, 2011, pp. 102–104.
79. NCSS Annual Report 1973–74.
80. The committee chaired by Countess Albemarle was established in 1958 and reported to Parliament in 1960, leading to a significant expansion in funding for youth work in England and Wales. Ministry of Education, 1960.
81. NCSS Annual Report 1963–64.
82. Ministry of Health, 1962a, b.
83. NCSS Annual Report 1961–62.
84. Minutes of Executive Committee, 10 October 1968; LMA/4016/IS/A/01/37(1).
85. For a discussion of these issues, see Chap. 8.
86. Geraldine Aves was chief welfare officer and head of the welfare division at the Ministry of Health from 1941 to 1963; governor of the National Institute for Social Work; and chair of the National Corporation for the Care of Old People. She was vice-president of the new Volunteer Centre she helped establish from 1977. She died in 1986. For a good account of her life and work, see Willmott, 1992.
87. Aves, 1969.
88. NCSS Annual Report 1969–70.
89. Note from J.K. Owens on *Aves Report* dated 25 March 1970, included in Minutes of Executive Committee, 9 April 1970; LMA/4016/IS/A/01/37(4).
90. Ibid.
91. Sir William Hart was a local government administrator and legal writer.
92. Minutes of Executive Committee, 9 July 1970; LMA/4016/IS/A/01/38(3).
93. Minutes of Executive Committee, 8 October 1970; LMA/4016/IS/A/01/38(1).
94. Minutes of Executive Committee, 11 February 1971; LMA/4016/IS/A/01/38(1).
95. Interview with Foster Murphy, 24 May 2017.

96. Interview with Baroness Pitkeathley, 24 April 2018.
97. NCSS Annual Report 1969–70.
98. NCSS Annual Report 1972–73.
99. NCSS Annual Report 1972–73.
100. NCSS Annual Report 1973–74.
101. NCSS Annual Report 1975–76.
102. On the significance of the loss of volunteering to the Council, see 6 and Leat, 1997.
103. For a discussion of Haynes' model, see Chap. 5.
104. NCSS Annual Report 1967–68.
105. NCSS Annual Report 1969–70.
106. Report of the review committee discussed at Meeting of Executive Committee, 17 October 1969; LMA/4016/IS/A/01/37(1).
107. Ibid.
108. NCSS Annual Report 1969–70.
109. Report of the review committee discussed at Meeting of Executive Committee, 17 October 1969; LMA/4016/IS/A/01/37(1).
110. Ibid.
111. Minutes of 13th Meeting of the review committee, 25 April 1969; LMA/4016/IS/A/01/092(4).
112. NCSS Annual Report 1969–70.
113. NCSS Annual Report 1969–70.
114. NCSS Annual Report 1973–74.
115. NCSS Annual Report 1965–66.
116. Minutes of Executive Committee, 10 October 1968; LMA/4016/IS/A/01/37(1).
117. NCSS Annual Report 1968–69.
118. NCSS Annual Report 1962–63. The Molony committee on consumer protection reported in 1962.
119. Sir Harold Banwell was the first full-time secretary of the Association of Municipal Corporations and chair of the National Council of Citizens' Advice Bureaux from 1961 until his resignation in 1971. He died in 1982. See, *The Times*, 17 April 1982, p. 12.
120. *The Times*, 28 June 1971, p. 3.
121. *The Times*, 13 July 1971, p. 13.
122. See, for example, House of Lords Debates, Series 5, Vol. 322, cols. 349–50, 14 July 1971 and Vol. 322, cols. 613–22, 15 July 1971.
123. NCSS Annual Report 1972–73.
124. NCSS Annual Report 1976–77.
125. NCSS Annual Reports 1971–72 and 1979–80.
126. NCSS Annual Report 1975–76.
127. NCSS Annual Report 1979–80.
128. NCSS Annual Report 1977–78.
129. NCSS Annual Report 1973–74.
130. NCSS Annual Reports 1968–69 and 1973–74.
131. NCSS Annual Report 1968–69.
132. NCSS Annual Report 1961–62.
133. The Seebohm committee was established in 1965 and reported in 1968. The Council discussed the report in January 1969 and, while welcoming its 'basic

philosophy', expressed concern over the dangers of creating 'monolithic structures' and the report's 'ambivalence' towards voluntary organisations. Minutes of Executive Committee, 9 January 1969; LMA/4016/IS/A/01/37(1).

134. NCSS Annual Report 1972–73 and 1973–74.
135. The Bretherton report on *The present state and future prospects of rural community councils* was published in 1970.
136. Correspondence from the organising secretary of the Northumberland and Tyneside CSS to the review committee, LMA/4016/IS/A/01/092(2).
137. NCSS Annual Report 1968–69.
138. There were small deficits in 1972–73 and 1973–74, rising to £93,000 in 1978–79. NCSS Annual Reports 1972–73, 1973–74, and 1978–79.
139. NCSS Annual Reports 1971–72 and 1976–77.
140. Letters from J.K. Owens to William Willett at Buckingham Palace, 31 October and 18 December 1972; LMA/4016/IS/A/04/052.
141. NCSS Annual Report 1978–79.
142. The possibility of a move out of London had also been considered and dismissed in 1967. Minutes of Executive Committee, 13 July 1967; LMA/4016/IS/A/01/036(2).
143. Minutes of Executive Committee, 17 October 1974; LMA/4016/IS/A/01/40(1).
144. NCSS Annual Report 1975–76.
145. Interview with Foster Murphy, 24 May 2017.
146. Minutes of Executive Committee, 4 April 1968; LMA/4016/IS/A/01/036(3).
147. NCSS Annual Report 1975–76, pp. 5–6.
148. For a discussion of the criticism faced by the Council in the 1930s, see Chap. 4.
149. NCSS Annual Report 1978–79.
150. NCSS Annual Report 1977–78.
151. NCSS Annual Report 1978–79, p. 8.
152. This is discussed further in Chap. 8.
153. Brasnett, 1969, pp. 264–5.
154. Ibid., p. 266. The role of secretariat to the standing conference ended in 1971; NCSS Annual Report 1971–72.
155. NCSS Annual Report 1966–67.
156. NCSS Annual Report 1967–68.
157. Britain joined the European Community on 1 January 1973.
158. NCSS Annual Reports 1971–72 and 1973–74.
159. NCSS Annual Report 1974–75.
160. NCSS Annual Report 1978–79, p. 9.
161. NCSS Annual Report 1978–79, p. 9.
162. NCSS Annual Report 1963–64.
163. NCSS Annual Report 1969–70.
164. NCSS Annual Report 1978–79.
165. NCSS Annual Report 1973–74.
166. NCSS Annual Report 1966–67.
167. Wolfenden, 1967, pp. 139–40.
168. Pimlott Baker, 2004. See also, *The Times*, 9 March 1983, p. 14.

169. Minutes of Executive Committee, 6 September 1983; LMA/4016/IS/A/01/042(3).
170. Interview with Foster Murphy, 24 May 2017.
171. Interview with Bill Seary, 6 July 2017.
172. Interview with Ian Bruce, 13 September 2017.
173. Owens, 1977, pp. 46–48. Owens died in 1987.
174. Interview with David Clarke, 15 August 2017.
175. Management Services Civil Service Department (1975) *Management Review of the National Council of Social Service*; LMA/4016/IS/A/05/027.
176. Interview with Sara Morrison, 2 August 2017.
177. Article on Nicholas Hinton by Des Wilson, 12 March 1977, source unknown; unpublished archives of NCVO.
178. *Social Work Today*, 1977, p. 1.
179. Hinton, 1984, pp. 10–11.
180. Letter from J.K. Owens to William Willett at Buckingham Palace 31 October 1972; LMA/4016/IS/A/04/052.
181. Interview with Foster Murphy, 24 May 2017.
182. Interview with David Clarke, 15 August 2017.
183. Interview with Foster Murphy, 24 May 2017.
184. Wolfenden Committee, 1978.
185. NCSS Annual Report 1977–78, pp. 5–6. The term 'intermediary body' coined by Wolfenden didn't find favour and was later replaced in common parlance, first by 'local development agency' and then 'infrastructure body'. See Rochester, 2012, p. 104.
186. Wolfenden Committee, 1978.
187. Harris et al., 2001, p. 2.
188. 6 and Leat, 1997. See also Hall, 1992.
189. 6 and Leat, 1997, p. 42.
190. Harris et al., 2001, p. 2.
191. It was used by the authors of the government review of the Council in 1975. Management Services Civil Service Department (1975) *Management Review of the National Council of Social Service*; LMA/4016/IS/A/05/027.
192. Wolfenden Committee, 1978, p. 15.
193. NCSS Annual Report 1977–78.
194. NCSS Annual Report 1977–78, p. 6.
195. Hinton, 1978.
196. 'Reforming the corner shops of the social services', *The Times*, 17 April 1978, p. 10.
197. Amos, 1978, pp. 129–30.
198. Kendall and Knapp, 1996, pp. 136–7.
199. The Home Office, 1978.
200. The Conservative government produced a response to Wolfenden but its priorities for the voluntary movement lay elsewhere, Home Office, 1981.
201. Gladstone, 1979. The significance of this report for the Council's work is discussed in Chap. 8.
202. Minutes of Executive Committee, 4 April 1968; LMA/4016/IS/A/01/036(3); Minutes of Executive Committee, 11 July 1968; LMA/4016/IS/01/037(1). NCSS Annual Report 1968–69.
203. Coles, 1993, pp. 24–27.

204. Article on Nicholas Hinton by Des Wilson, 12 March 1977, source unknown; unpublished archives of NCVO.
205. Ibid.

References

6, P., & Leat, D. (1997). Inventing the British voluntary sector by committee: From Wolfenden to Deakin. *Non-Profit Studies, 1*(2), 33–47.

Abel-Smith, B., & Townsend, P. (1965). *The poor and the poorest*. London: Bell.

Amos, F. (1978). An opportunity missed. *Social Services Quarterly, 51*(4), 129–130.

Aves, G. (1969). *The voluntary worker in the social services: Report of a Committee jointly set up by the National Council of Social Service and the National Institute for Social Work Training under the chairmanship of Geraldine M. Aves*. London: Allen & Unwin.

Berridge, V., & Mold, A. (2011). Professionalisation, new social movements and voluntary action in the 1960s and 1970s. In M. Hilton & J. McKay (Eds.), *The ages of voluntarism: How we got to the big society* (pp. 114–134). Oxford: Oxford University Press for British Academy.

Brasnett, M. (1969). *Voluntary social action*. London: NCSS.

Brenton, M. (1985). *The voluntary sector in British social services*. London: Longman.

Brewis, G. (2011). Youth in action? British young people and voluntary service, 1958–70. In M. Oppenheimer & N. Deakin (Eds.), *Beveridge and voluntary action in Britain and the wider British world* (pp. 94–108). Manchester: Manchester University Press.

Brewis, G. (2013). *Towards a new understanding of volunteering in England before 1960?* Institute for Volunteering Research 'Back to Basics' Working Paper Series: Paper Two. London: IVR.

Coles, K. (1993). *National Council for Voluntary Organisations from 1919 to 1993: A selective summary of NCVO's work and origins*. London: NCVO.

Cubbon, B. (2013). Philip Allen, Baron Allen of Abbeydale. In *Oxford dictionary of national biography*. Oxford: Oxford University Press.

Dartington, T. (1971). *Task force*. London: Mitchell Beazley.

Deakin, N. (1995). The perils of partnership: The voluntary sector and the state, 1945–1992. In J. Davis Smith, C. Rochester, & R. Hedley (Eds.), *An introduction to the voluntary sector* (pp. 40–65). London: Routledge.

Egerton, R. (1945). *Legal aid*. London: Kegan Paul.

Evans, T. (2009). Stopping the poor getting poorer: The establishment and professionalisation of poverty NGOs, 1945–95. In N. Crowson, M. Hilton, & J. McKay (Eds.), *NGOs in contemporary Britain: Non-state actors in society and politics since 1945* (pp. 147–163). Basingstoke: Palgrave Macmillan.

Finlayson, G. (1994). *Citizen, state and social welfare in Britain* (pp. 1830–1990). Oxford: Clarendon Press.

Gladstone, F. (1979). *Voluntary action in a changing world*. London: Bedford Square Press.

Glennerster, H. (1990). Social policy since the Second World War. In J. Hills (Ed.), *The state of welfare: The welfare state in Britain since 1974* (pp. 11–27). Oxford: Clarendon Press.

Hall, P. (1992). Inventing the nonprofit sector. In P. Hall (Ed.), *Inventing the nonprofit sector and other essays on philanthropy, voluntarism, and nonprofit organisations* (pp. 13–84). Baltimore: Johns Hopkins University Press.

Harris, M., Rochester, C., & Halfpenny, P. (2001). Voluntary organisations and social policy: Twenty years of change. In M. Harris & C. Rochester (Eds.), *Voluntary organisations and social policy in Britain* (pp. 1–20). Basingstoke: Palgrave.

Hilton, M. (2011). Politics is ordinary: Non-governmental organisations and political participation in contemporary Britain. *Twentieth Century British History, 22*(2), 230–268.

Hilton, M., McKay, J., Crowson, N., & Mouhot, J. (2013). *The politics of expertise: How NGOs shaped modern Britain.* Oxford: Oxford University Press.

Hinton, N. (1978). The Wolfenden report: Building for the future. *Social Service Quarterly, 51*(4), 125–127.

Hinton, N. (1984, December). *Voluntary Action,* pp. 10–11.

Home Office. (1978). *The government and the voluntary sector: A consultative document.* London: Home Office.

Home Office. (1981). *The government and the voluntary sector: Analysis of the responses to the consultative document.* London: Home Office.

Johnson, N. (1981). *Voluntary social services.* Oxford: Basil Blackwell.

Kendall, J., & Knapp, M. (1996). *The voluntary sector in the UK.* Manchester: Manchester University Press.

Kramer, R. (1990). Change and continuity in British voluntary organisations, 1976 to 1988. *Voluntas: International Journal of Voluntary and Nonprofit Organizations, 1*(2), 33–60.

Lent, A. (2001). *British social movements since 1945: Sex, colour, peace and power.* Basingstoke: Palgrave.

Marwick, A. (1998). *The sixties: Cultural revolution in Britain, France, Italy and the United States, c1958–1974.* Oxford: Oxford University Press.

Ministry of Education. (1960). *The youth service in England and Wales.* London: HMSO.

Ministry of Health. (1962a). *Development of local authority health and welfare services: Co-operation with voluntary organisations, circular 7/62.* London: HMSO.

Ministry of Health. (1962b). *National Health Service: Voluntary help in hospitals, 62/29.* London: HMSO.

National Council of Social Service. (1973). *Fundraising by charities.* London: NCSS.

Owen, D. (1964). *English philanthropy, 1660–1960.* London: Oxford University Press.

Owens, J. (1977). Ten years of social service. *Social Service Quarterly, 51*(2), 46–48.

Pimlott Baker, A. (2004). Sir George Ernest Haynes. In *Oxford dictionary of national biography.* Oxford: Oxford University Press.

Prochaska, F. (1988). *The voluntary impulse: Philanthropy in modern Britain.* London: Faber and Faber.

Rochester, C. (2012). Councils for voluntary service: The end of a long road? *Voluntary Sector Review, 3*(1), 103–110.

Shapely, P. (2011). Civil society, class and locality: Tenant groups in post-war Britain. In M. Hilton & J. McKay (Eds.), *The ages of voluntarism: How we got to the big society* (pp. 94–113). Oxford: Oxford University Press for British Academy.

Sheard, J. (1992). Volunteering and society, 1960–1990. In R. Hedley & J. Davis Smith (Eds.), *Volunteering and society: Principles and practice* (pp. 11–32). London: Bedford Square Press.

Sheard, J. (1995). From lady bountiful to active citizen. In J. Davis Smith, C. Rochester, & R. Hedley (Eds.), *An introduction to the voluntary sector* (pp. 114–127). London: Routledge.

Social Work Today. (1977, March 22). Nicholas Hinton – A good choice for the National Council for Social Service. *Social Work Today, 8*(24), 1.

Taylor, M., & Kendall, J. (1996). History of the voluntary sector. In J. Kendall & M. Knapp (Eds.), *The voluntary sector in the United Kingdom*. Manchester: Manchester University Press.

Thane, P. (2011). Voluntary action in Britain since Beveridge. In M. Oppenheimer & N. Deakin (Eds.), *Beveridge and voluntary action in Britain and the wider British world* (pp. 121–134). Manchester: Manchester University Press.

Thane, P., & Davidson, R. (2016). *The Child Poverty Action Group, 1965–2015*. London: Child Poverty Action Group.

Willmott, P. (1992). *A singular woman: The life of Geraldine Aves* (pp. 1898–1986). London: Whiting & Birch Ltd.

Windlesham, B. (1975). *Politics in practice*. London: Cape.

Wolfenden, J. (1967). George Haynes: A tribute. *Social Service Quarterly, 40*(4), 139–140.

Wolfenden Committee. (1978). *The future of voluntary organisations: Report of the Wolfenden Committee*. London: Croom Helm.

CHAPTER 8

Recovery and Challenge

INTRODUCTION

The Council opened the 1980s with a dynamic new director and a new name. It needed a lift and an injection of fresh thinking. It had lost its way during the 1960s and 1970s, and its reputation was diminished, seen by some commentators as staid, bureaucratic, and out of touch with developments in the sector.[1] The period saw a number of changes at the top of the organisation after the relative stability of the previous half a century, with four directors holding office in just over a decade. Further governance changes were introduced, aimed at strengthening links with the membership and, under the leadership of Nicholas Hinton and Usha Prashar, it began to reconnect with the wider voluntary movement and reclaim some of the ground it had lost. However, the period also saw the speeding up of the move to independence of its associated groups, including the core networks in the towns and shire counties, which threatened to undermine its reach and claim to legitimacy. To mitigate this effect it embarked on a major membership drive, although the full impact of this strategy did not become apparent for another decade.[2]

Relations between the Council and the Conservative government were strained for much of the period. Although it could still utilise the political standing of members of its senior Executive Committee, such as Sara Morrison and Peter Jay, lines of communication were reduced.[3] The government's approach to policy making was top-down and, in the view of one writer, 'unencumbered by the constraints provided by interest groups'.[4] The Thatcher administration, which came to power in 1979, promised a new relationship between the state and the voluntary sector, although the break with the past was not as marked as has often been presented. It is convenient to present the post-war period up to the late 1970s as a golden age of political consensus, in which the voluntary sector was seen as having a crucial role alongside the state in the mixed economy of welfare. But the reality was always more nuanced. Cracks in support for the welfare state had opened up well before Margaret

© The Author(s) 2019
J. Davis Smith, *100 Years of NCVO and Voluntary Action*,
https://doi.org/10.1007/978-3-030-02774-2_8

Thatcher came to power and the New Right, with its radical vision for the voluntary sector (which harked back to the role played by the sector in the past and founded on its deep mistrust of the state), had its roots in the late 1960s and early 1970s.[5] Nor should we take at face value the rhetoric of the Thatcher administration on *rolling back the state*. As many commentators have pointed out, one of the ironies of the period was that the central state grew rather than shrunk during the 1980s.[6] However, if we need to be cautious about some of the more hyperbolic claims for the reshaping of society after 1979, it is clear that there were major transformations in many areas of economic and social policy that had far-reaching implications for the sector, at the time and later.[7]

The period saw the beginning of a shift from public sector grants towards more formal contracts and the introduction of a care market in which voluntary organisations (or at least the larger ones) were identified as having an increasingly important part to play, alongside the private sector, in the delivery of services.[8] Many organisations responded enthusiastically to the new opportunities and the Council, as it had in the 1930s, became a key intermediary, helping to channel significant funds to the sector. It also embarked upon a drive to increase the efficiency and effectiveness of voluntary organisations, deemed essential if the sector was to stake a legitimate claim to take over the running of public services. Not all were convinced. Some accused the sector of selling out and the Council of colluding with government in an attack on public services and taking the sector down the wrong path of professionalisation and state control.[9] The Council began the decade as an enthusiastic champion of *welfare pluralism*. It ended it increasingly disillusioned with the way things had developed.

INTO THE 1980s

On 20 November 1979 a major exhibition was organised to mark the Council's 60th anniversary. Ten years previously, the centrepiece of the celebrations was the publication of the official history by Margaret Brasnett. This time the focus was forward-looking. 'While we have reason to be proud of the many achievements and initiatives of the past sixty years', the annual report stated, 'this is a time for looking to the future.'[10] *Voluntary Organisations into the Eighties* was held at the Royal Horticultural Society Hall, Vincent Square, London. It was formally opened by the Queen and included a keynote speech from the new home secretary, William Whitelaw. It attracted over 3000 visitors. Supported by the NatWest Bank and the Charities Aid Foundation (CAF), it was seen as an opportunity to showcase the work of the Council and 45 national charities were given stands, including Age Concern, Barnado's, Oxfam, Mind, and the Child Poverty Action Group.[11]

The exhibition offered a platform for the new director, Hinton, to communicate his vision for the future. It was radical, drawing heavily on a book written by Francis Gladstone, director of policy at the Council, which was launched at the event. *Voluntary Action in a Changing World* called for a revolution in the way public services were delivered.[12] It was a bold restatement of the *welfare pluralist* thesis, which argued for public services to be opened up to a range of non-statutory providers, including the voluntary sector.[13] For Gladstone, the welfare state had foundered on the weakness of bureaucratic mass production and what was needed was a wholesale shift in delivery to the voluntary sector to take advantage of its flexibility and localism. The state would still determine resource allocation, but delivery of welfare services would be transferred to voluntary groups. Press response to the book was mixed. The *Guardian* was sceptical of the claims made for the sector and suggested that, if it took over the wholesale running of welfare services, it 'would probably bring little except even more problems of equity than we have now', although it did acknowledge there might be an enhanced role for voluntary action.[14] *The Times* concentrated on what it saw as the challenges facing organisations in attracting new funds and volunteers and worried that there was a danger the sector could become a 'political football'.[15] The *Observer* followed a similar line. Voluntary action, it warned, was in danger of becoming increasingly politicised. In many ways, it suggested, the exhibition couldn't have come at a worse time to outline such a radical manifesto. With cuts already announced, the event, it wrote, was 'redolent with unintentional irony'.[16]

Voluntary Action in a Changing World set the direction for the Council's work for its next stage of development, though academics poured scorn on the intellectual basis for *welfare pluralism*.[17] Maria Brenton suggested that 'the lack of precision of the NCVO case for gradualist *welfare pluralism*' gave it 'the quality of a vision and the effect of a stirring exhortation rather than establishing a firm basis for concrete action and systematic development'.[18] The Executive Committee discussed the book in September 1979 and felt it provided 'the philosophical basis for future NCSS work and development'.[19] For Hinton, however, any such expansion of the sector would be predicated on it proving its professionalism, and he gave early notice that he saw one of the Council's main tasks as improving the effectiveness of the movement. Hinton reorganised the Council's structures to place far greater emphasis on support for national organisations, but he made clear that the identification of poor practice was part of his strategy. 'Bad practice, waste, duplication of services will undoubtedly come in for criticism', he warned, 'albeit' that any such criticism would aim to be 'constructive'.[20] These dual ambitions—expanding the role of the sector in welfare delivery and raising its performance to enable it to compete alongside other providers—defined Hinton's tenure as leader and dominated Council policy for the next decade and more. Some would argue that it remains the dominant narrative.

A NEW NAME FOR NEW TIMES

In April 1980, just over 60 years after its formation, the Council changed its name. The annual report for that year commented drily that 'while any change of name is not something to be undertaken lightly, the sense of doing so had been apparent for some time'.[21] It had been under discussion for over a decade and had been the subject of heated debate within the membership.[22] The initial push for a change came not from the Council but from the local councils of social service, who were worried their name sounded like a government welfare agency, a concern given added credence with the setting up of social service departments in 1971 following the Seebohm review.[23] Many local groups took unilateral action and changed their name to councils for voluntary service or community councils to emphasise their voluntary roots. A change had been mooted in 1968, but in June 1972 the Council again considered the matter. Four options were put forward: *National Community Service Council; National Council of Community Organisations; Community Concern;* and *Community Action*, with no agreement reached on a preferred option.[24] The Council took soundings from a number of advertising agencies. One recorded that the present name was unsatisfactory as NCSS 'sounds like a government authority' and is 'not suitable as a dramatic and memorable name for publicity purposes'. They proposed *Community,* with the slogan 'Today's problems are our concern' and also played around with *Charity HQ* or *Link-up*.[25] A second agency suggested *The Community Trust, Neighbours, Humankind,* even *Charity*.[26] In 1973 the policy sub-committee rejected all the recommendations.[27]

Market research commissioned in April 1973 reinforced the case for change, with 60 per cent of the public saying they thought the Council was a government department and only 2 per cent a voluntary organisation. Two new options were put forward: *Voluntary Action* and *Council for Voluntary Service*. In July the membership was asked to approve a change to *Voluntary Action,* but only as a 'trading name', with NCSS being retained for company and Charity Commission purposes to avoid 'unnecessary administrative difficulties'.[28] The proposal was narrowly defeated, with concern expressed that *Voluntary Action* was more of a 'slogan' than a name and 'conveyed the wrong kind of impression regarding the work of the Council and its associated bodies'.[29] In December 1973 the Standing Conference of Council of Social Service proposed that the Council adopt the name *National Council for Voluntary Service*, but this was also defeated. In September 1974 the standing conference upped the stakes by changing its own name to the Standing Conference of councils for Voluntary Service. In September 1976 the Executive Committee backed a proposal for a change to *National Council for Voluntary Service* and a resolution was put to the membership in November.[30] It was rejected, with the councils of voluntary service being particularly vocal in their opposition. The problem was that, since the proposal had first been put forward, relations between the network and the Council had soured and the issue had become tied up with the question of local independence. The Greater Manchester Council for Social Service summed up the mood in a letter in which it suggested that 'it has become clear' that the Council 'as presently constituted and organised' could not represent the local network 'because it's interests and commitments are much more diverse and range over a wider field'.[31] To complicate matters further, the issue became intertwined with tensions at a UK level. The Scottish Council of Social Service complained that it should have been consulted before any proposal was put to the membership and, that with devolution of power to Edinburgh and Cardiff, 'the NCSS should consider changing its name to the English Council for Voluntary Service'.³² There was also opposition from some quarters to the term 'service', with the director of the Northern Ireland Council of Social Service saying it smacked to many people of a 'lady-bountiful' approach and nowadays 'everyone seems to talk about involvement and participation'.³³ In 1979 the Executive Committee put another proposal to members to change the name to the *National Council for Voluntary Organisations*, and this time it was passed with the required 75 per cent majority, although not without a heated debate over whether it should be *for* or *of* voluntary organisations.³⁴ The new name was formally adopted on 1 April 1980. It had taken over ten years, but the Council had a new name to take it forward into the new decade.³⁵

CHANGES AT THE TOP

The period saw a number of changes at the top, with four directors in relatively short succession. Two can be judged to have been successful, one moderately so and one a disaster. The first, Hinton, left the Council at the end of 1984 to join Save the Children Fund as its director general. Hinton had briefly flirted with politics and stood unsuccessfully as a candidate for the new centre-left Social Democratic Party at the 1983 general election, which, according to Nicholas Deakin, caused the Council 'a great deal of difficulty' in 'trying to argue that it was politically impartial when its Chief Executive was almost a successful parliamentary candidate'.³⁶ Hinton can be credited with rejuvenating the Council after many years of stagnation. Under his relatively brief tenure, it took on a more dynamic and professional feel, increasing its visibility and profile especially within government, where he was seen as a consummate operator. In an interview before his departure, he said that he had set out to make the Council feel 'needed' and he believed it now carried 'sufficient clout for its views to be taken seriously'.³⁷ Peter Jay, his chair at the time of his departure, said that under his leadership the Council had become 'a sharper, more effective and respected organisation, with a clearer sense of purpose'.³⁸

His reputation endures. Among the staff he worked with he is remembered with huge admiration. Bill Seary, who joined the Council's national organisation division in the late 1970s before going on to head the international department, recalls Hinton as being 'very dynamic' and 'stimulating', though 'quite challenging as well'.³⁹ David Emerson, who worked in the rural department, remembers him as 'both a visionary leader' and 'a very fine, supportive, generous man'.⁴⁰ Andrew Purkis, who headed the policy analysis unit, remembers him as having 'very good people skills ... very good at talking to ministers and civil servants and all sorts of different people', although he recalls him also as 'restless' with a 'minimal attention span'.⁴¹ He was an excellent judge and nurturer of talent and built a team of exceptional individuals. David Clark, who led the Council's rural work, remembers his 'charisma', 'charm' and 'energy' and his ability at 'drawing in new staff'. There was, he recalls, 'a real gulf between the old guard who were, I guess you could call them gifted amateurs ... and the new team, who were energetic and very, very purposeful'.[42] Ian Bruce credits Hinton with turning the organisation 'into the TUC or CBI of the voluntary sector'.[43] And Sara Morrison, who appointed him as director, pays tribute to his 'potent, energising, influential leadership effect on a lot of the people that were working in the organisation'.[44] He was excellent at courting publicity. His widow, Deborah Hinton, remembers him 'wooing the press without shame' and says he 'achieved his lifelong goal one morning when he had letters in *The Times*, the *Guardian*, and the *Telegraph* simultaneously'.[45] Despite his achievements, Hinton was aware that the job of reforming the Council was only half done when he left. Top of the list for his successor was 'to reach those parts of the voluntary sector that existing mechanisms don't reach'.[46] Hinton had done much in his short stay to rebuild the reputation of the Council. It was left to his successors to continue the rebuilding process.

As is often the case after the departure of a high-profile and charismatic leader, the organisation struggled to find an adequate replacement. Bill Griffiths must suffer the ignominy of being the shortest-lived director in the history of the Council, lasting less than a year. He took up the post on 2 January 1985 and resigned in October. The staff he worked with remember his tenure as being extremely taxing for all concerned and 'a bit of a disaster' and feel 'he should never have been appointed'.[47] He came from a similar background to Hinton, having been a chief probation officer for Northern Ireland for eight years and a probation officer at the Home Office.[48] There the similarity ends. According to David Clark, it was clear that 'he had no pedigree in terms of working with the voluntary sector, particularly on the mainland'. Clark suggests his appointment was a failure of governance and reflects badly both on the chair and on Hinton himself, who 'should have spent more time either briefing Peter Jay or more time involving himself'.[49] Jay had taken over the chair from Morrison in 1981. He was another political big hitter. After a successful career in journalism, he spent two years as British ambassador to the US under the Callaghan government. Colleagues at the time have mixed feelings about his tenure. Purkis remembers him as 'complex, an intellectual heavyweight', with some 'outstanding abilities', but not necessarily 'the perfect mix of skills to be chair'.[50] Deakin recalls a 'very brusque chairing style' that made discussion within the Executive Committee difficult.[51] For Morrison, Jay 'should have been a very great addition to the voluntary sector but he never quite got under its skin'.[52] He was succeeded in 1986 by the Rev. Alan Morgan, who held the post until 1989 upon appointment as suffragan Bishop of Sherwood. He played a key role in the council for voluntary service movement and was widely regarded and much loved, with Jay paying tribute to his 'magic', 'passion' and 'wisdom'.[53]

Griffiths' replacement was Usha Prashar who, like Hinton, quickly set about making her mark on the organisation, albeit with a different set of priorities. Her background was very different from Hinton's, having been a senior fellow at the Policy Studies Institute and former director of the Runneymede Trust.[54] Prashar took up post in April 1986, which meant there was a six-month inter-regnum at the Council. Bharat Mehta, policy officer at the Council in the mid-1980s, recalls the senior management team 'stepping up to the plate' and working 'extremely well together' to fill the vacuum.[55] Purkis agrees, suggest-ing there were a 'core of people who'd been there a long time who kept the momentum and kept the show on the road at quite a difficult time'.[56] Prashar shared Hinton's view that the voluntary sector had the potential to play a larger role in the delivery of public services and she continued the drive to profes-sionalise the sector. But she had more concerns about the political dangers of the sector being used by the state to do its business and the threat this posed to its independence. She was also more interested in reaching out to the new style voluntary movement, which she felt, with some justification, had lost touch with the Council. Prashar continued Hinton's task of rebuilding the organisation. She suggests that when she took over 'it was an organisation in a little bit of turmoil' and she saw her job as being 'not only to reorganise it and to rebuild confidence, but to position it as a membership organisation that was there to serve and in the political context where there were big agendas to be fixed'.[57]

Like Hinton, Prashar was with the Council for only a relatively short period of time. But, like him, she is remembered by colleagues as hugely impressive and having left a definite stamp on the organisation. David Clark says she was 'a milestone in terms of NCVO's image and profile'.[58] For Mehta, she gave the Council just the 'sort of direction and leadership' it needed, while Richard Gutch praises her 'strategic' approach, which enabled the council to 'become more focused in what it did rather than cherry pick lots of projects for which they happened to be able to get funding'.[59] Her chair, Sir Geoffrey Chandler, said she left the organisation 'better shaped for the challenge of the 1990s, with a clarity of purpose and of voice adapted for dealing with strategic issues com-mon to the sector as a whole'.[60]

Prashar's replacement, Judy Weleminsky, did not have the best experience at the Council. She knew the organisation well, having been on the Executive Committee for several years and the director of one of its longest standing and most influential networks, the National Federation of Community Associations.[61] It was Weleminsky who took the Federation out of the Council's offices as its first independent director and changed its name to Community Matters. She remembers a degree of tension linked to the divorce settlement, which she felt had been unfair.[62] She took over as director of the Council in September 1991 from the National Schizophrenia Fellowship. Although her tenure was short-lived, and generally seen by her contemporaries as not a suc-cess, she left the Council a valuable legacy in overseeing the move from Bedford Square to a newly purchased building overlooking the canal near King's Cross in London.[63] Weleminsky could not have predicted the scale of regeneration in this part of London 25 years later that saw the value of the building rocket, helping to cushion the organisation from the financial crisis that engulfed many voluntary groups, but she should be credited with the vision and administrative skill to make the move happen. According to Bruce, it 'was the best strategic move in resource terms that NCVO has ever made, apart from setting up CAF, and it wouldn't have happened without her'.[64]

THE CONTRACT CULTURE

Just two years after the launch of *Voluntary Action in a Changing World*, Hinton expressed reservations about the way things were developing. In the introduction to the annual report for 1981–82 he wrote that, while the Council remained committed to *welfare pluralism*, it was aware of the tensions that 'may arise at the boundaries between services provided by voluntary organisa-tions and statutory agencies; over the adequacy and duration of government funding; and the strings attached to it'.[65] Tensions, however, were not only the fault of government. 'Some voluntary organisations', he argued, 'have been seduced by the cash and have not paused to think whether the goals of a par-ticular programme are compatible with their own aims and objectives.' The result, he wrote, was often a 'considerable muddle', with some organisations finding it 'increasingly uncomfortable trying to reconcile the policy aims of the government with their own objectives'.[66] Prashar was even more outspoken about the risks. Writing before the general election in 1987, she called for a 'positive, clear and coherent policy' from the government towards the volun-tary sector, based on the recognition that 'voluntary action is not a cheap option but an essential component in the development of services in the future'. What was required, she argued, was 'a constructive division between the two sectors, building on the strengths of each', a partnership that acknowl-edged the important role to be played by voluntary organisations in advocacy and campaigning. 'They should not be stifled', she wrote, 'because they are uncomfortable or inconvenient.'[67]

The Council was not an uncritical supporter of the *contract culture*. In its response to the Griffiths review of 1988, which called for the opening up of care provision to the voluntary sector, it expressed concern that 'greater involvement in mainstream service provision' could 'reduce voluntary organ-isations' flexibility and endanger the work of some of the new user groups'.[68] It saw its role not as championing the contract culture but as offering advice to members on whether or not to enter into a contract and what was required to make them a success.[69] A quarterly magazine, *Contracting In or Out?*, was produced and a study tour organised to the US to learn lessons from the Reagan administration where contracting was well entrenched and there was 'a genuine feeling' that voluntary organisations 'were losing their indepen-dence and becoming just other bits of government'.[70] Such an approach drew criticism that it was acting as a sop to government and colluding in the dis-mantling of the public sector. It insisted this was not its position: 'It is no part of NCVO's argument to suggest reduced levels of public expenditure' in social services 'or a reduction in the services offered', it stated in 1981. 'But there is', it argued, 'a need for examination of alternative ways in which that public money might be spent and services delivered, and the part that voluntary organisations might play.'[71]

VOLUNTEERING

One particularly sensitive issue concerned the role of volunteers within these 'alternative' solutions to deal with pressures on the public purse. The Council had long advocated a greater role for volunteers in the delivery of public services, but this was less easy to articulate at a time of high unemployment and cuts to public services, when concerns abounded that volunteers would be marshalled as cheap replacement labour. Union antipathy, which had long bubbled under the surface, flared up during the industrial disputes in the winter of 1978 when public bodies were accused of deploying volunteers to replace striking workers. To calm the situation, the Volunteer Centre issued guidelines arguing that volunteers should only be introduced in such circumstances with the agreement of management and the unions, and the Council gave its backing to this line, warning any unilateral call to action would 'retard severely' plans to develop volunteering in the public services 'in the subsequent normal situation'.[72] For the Council and the Volunteer Centre, the larger prize of more volunteering in the public sector was not to be put at risk by the knee-jerk use of volunteers at times of national crisis.

Thatcher gave early notice that volunteering was to be a key priority of her administration. Thatcher, like many within her party, was always more interested in volunteering than the voluntary sector.[73] Voluntary organisations were seen primarily as a conduit through which volunteers could be mobilised and engaged. In her address to the Women's Royal Voluntary Service in January 1981, she argued that the role of government was to help voluntary organisations 'do the administration and work of mobilising this enormous army of volunteers' without their becoming 'creatures of Government'.[74] As the decade wore on, the Council became increasingly concerned about volunteers being seen as an alternative means of delivering public services. Volunteering, it asserted in 1985, 'is an essential and important part of community life', bringing 'benefits to the recipients as well as self-fulfilment to the volunteers themselves'. But volunteers should not be used to 'replace paid employment' and should occupy a largely complementary role in the public sector to paid staff.[75] At a conference of northern charities in 1989, Prashar expressed this growing unease: 'Who is the real active citizen?' she asked, 'The person who puts a fiver in a charity collection box, or the single mother who gets involved in community action, sets up a childcare scheme, but also demands adequate services from the council or adequate benefits from the state.'[76]

UNEMPLOYMENT

As in the 1930s, unemployment was again a big issue for the Council.[77] This time it was not involved in the direct delivery of programmes, but in the provision of training, advice, and the distribution of funds. But its involvement proved equally controversial. The government set up a range of training and community schemes for the unemployed, directed through the Manpower Services Commission (MSC), and the voluntary sector was invited to get involved. Many within the sector responded enthusiastically and, at the height of its work, the MSC was providing 20 per cent of funding for the voluntary sector, of which over 70 per cent flowed through the Community Programme.[78] The Council worked closely with the MSC, sitting on task forces, offering advice and guiding members on how to secure funds. Much of the work was directed by its new employment unit, which it established in 1979.[79] In 1981 the Council joined the Volunteer Centre in forming a consortium to administer a new scheme, Opportunities for Volunteering, established by government to provide opportunities for volunteering by unemployed people in the health and personal social services.[80]

Supportive though the Council was of these official programmes, it was prepared to take a more critical position. In 1980 it joined a number of other national voluntary organisations in establishing the Unemployment Alliance to raise awareness of the social and economic costs of unemployment and promote constructive measures to combat it. Briefing papers were produced on the impact of unemployment on such issues as poverty, health, and older people.[81] The Alliance argued for a restoration of previous levels of unemployment benefit and set up a social dividend group to push for a basic minimum wage.[82] A report published by the Council, *Social Security After Beveridge*, called for a guaranteed basic income for all, irrespective of work or marital status.[83] In May 1981 it helped launch another new alliance, Youth Choice, to represent the voice of young people in training and employment debates, and the group spoke out strongly against government plans for compulsory community service as an abuse of the values of volunteering.[84] In July 1985 it launched a campaign on the back of the publication of a booklet, *The Long-Term Unemployed—Action for a Forgotten Million*, drawing attention to the needs of the more than one million people who had been unemployed for over a year.[85] A series of community-based pilots were established to explore alternative forms of paid work, including cooperatives and mutuals, with active support from the Council.[86]

Such work did little to appease critics who argued that the training schemes were attempts by the government to massage the unemployment figures, a view given some weight in retrospect by the admissions of the junior minister for employment, Alan Clark, who referred in his diary to the programmes as 'these tacky schemes to get people off the Register'.[87] For critics, the sector, and by implication the Council, had allowed itself to be co-opted by the government to do its dirty business. Susanne MacGregor and Ben Pimlott argued at the time that some organisations were transformed into '*de facto* agencies of the state, which financed them and indirectly determined their policy'.[88] Tony Addy and Duncan Scott compared the impact of the MSC on the sector to the impact of climate change on the Russian mammoths, 'a ferocious flash-flood of energy which scoured, disrupted, re-arranged and was gone again'.[89]

LOCAL GOVERNMENT

While the rhetoric of the Thatcher administration was to cede more responsibility to the voluntary sector, the reality on the ground was often very different. The government's attempt to curb what it saw as irresponsible levels of spending by local authorities by the introduction of rate capping, led to a reduction in funding to voluntary groups. The impact was severe, reflecting the fact that many voluntary organisations had become increasingly reliant on local statutory funding for their existence. A survey by the Personal Social Services Council in 1979 found that 65 per cent of local authorities were making cuts to voluntary organisations and the trend continued throughout the decade.[90] The Council's response can be best described as measured. It argued that it was unrealistic to expect voluntary organisations 'should be immune from cuts', but that any reductions needed 'to reflect a concern for social policy priorities rather than the relative ease or difficulty with which certain functions can be discarded'.[91] A monthly *Rates Mailing* was produced to support lobbying activities against disproportionate cuts to voluntary groups.[92] There were some successes, mainly achieved in the House of Lords, which was targeted as more likely to be supportive than the Commons with its large Conservative majority.[93] During the passage of the Local Government Finance Act in 1988, which introduced the new community charge or poll tax, the Lords supported an NCVO-sponsored amendment to allow charitable rate relief of 80 per cent, a concession that was estimated to be worth £55 million to the sector.[94]

The abolition of the metropolitan county councils and the Greater London Council (GLC) in 1986 was seen as a particular threat to voluntary groups.[95] In 1985 it was estimated that direct funding to the sector from the councils amounted to £60million. The Council established a national abolition group of 70 organisations to run its campaign and a parliamentary task group lobbied MPs and peers, drafted amendments, and secured significant public attention. Some substantial improvements to the Bill were secured as a result.[96] Not all voluntary groups, however, were happy with the Council's approach and believed it should be going further. Purkis, who joined in 1980 as head of the new policy analysis unit, recalls it being 'a very difficult and vicious kind of time'. He remembers a meeting when 'Nicholas Hinton was spat at by activists from London voluntary organisations' and was accused of 'being a traitor' for not speaking out more forcibly against the abolition of the GLC.[97] In the end, he concludes that the Council 'was regarded as having done a good job' by most of its members in securing a number of important concessions.[98] In February 1987 it produced a joint report with the London Voluntary Service Council, *After Abolition*, on the impact of abolition on voluntary organisations.[99]

INDEPENDENCE

If the impact of government policy on the finances of the sector was a major policy priority at this time, so was another issue that re-emerged some years later as a key focus of conflict. Emboldened by its higher-profile campaigning activities, the Council took an uncompromising stand against government attempts to curb the campaigning role of charities, particularly those in receipt of statutory funds. The background was the rise of more radical voluntary organisations such as Shelter, War on Want, and the Child Poverty Action Group that were willing to utilise more active campaign strategies to advance their cause.[100] Such approaches were not entirely new; many of the methods adopted drew on traditions laid down by charities in the Victorian age, but there was a confidence and directness about their advocacy that set them apart.[101] The fact that many were publicly funded, often by Labour-controlled local authorities, raised the ire of many on the Right, both inside and outside Parliament. Just as later attempts by a Conservative-led government to muzzle the sector were fuelled by a report from a right-wing think-tank, much of the tone of the debate at this time was set by a similarly provocative and much-criticised report from a research outfit with close ties to the Conservative Party.[102]

Qualgos Just Grow was published by the Centre for Policy Studies in February 1985. It was written by Teresa Gorman, Barbara Robson, Bernard Sharpe, and Cyril Taylor and carried the sub-title *Political Bodies in Voluntary Clothing*, which flagged clearly its main line of attack. The voluntary sector, it said, was no longer voluntary. Volunteers had been replaced by highly paid, professional staff; voluntary agencies were becoming too political, fuelled by the left-wing sympathies of their staff and the funding received from sympathetic Labour-controlled local authorities; and too much emphasis was placed on lobbying and campaigning at the expense of the sector's core work.[103] The Council hit back with equal force, describing the report as 'a particularly hostile and ill-informed attack on the voluntary sector', expressing its wish to 'lift the debate about the voluntary sector away from a series of hysterical attacks on individual organisations and towards a more balanced discussion about the role of voluntary organisations and their relationships with local authorities'.[104] The Council confronted the accusation that the sector's increased professionalism somehow implied a loss of values: 'Many voluntary organisations', it argued, 'are engaged in sophisticated work and require a high level of managerial, organisational and professional skills like other modern organisations.' Any suggestion that the involvement of paid staff and a commitment to effectiveness undermined the 'true character' of voluntary groups was dismissed as 'anachronistic'.[105]

The attack was not launched in isolation. The previous year the Conservative MP, Michael Forsyth, had brought similar charges in a report for the Conservative Political Centre, and the Council was concerned that, if left unchallenged, such criticisms, however ill-founded, could erode public trust.[106] The attacks, it said, can easily 'be refuted', but they run the risk of creating 'a feeling of suspicion about the voluntary sector, at worst a feeling of hostility based on ill-informed prejudice'.[107] The attacks went to the heart of government. Richard Fries, chief charity commissioner from 1992 to 1999, recalls hostility within government towards campaigning 'was very marked' and that the prime minister was pushing for all government grants to come with a complete ban on campaigning.[108]

But criticism was not only coming from the Right. Although some Labour-controlled local authorities were sympathetic towards the voluntary sector, particularly the more radical groups, which they sought to organise into a 'rainbow coalition' against central government, there were others who dismissed it for being 'the Tories fifth column' and 'co-operating in the Government's privatisation-by-stealth policy in social welfare provision and management'.[109] In Liverpool the Militant-controlled local authority engaged in its own battle with the voluntary sector, choosing to keep funds and services in-house rather than outsource to voluntary agencies.[110] Such a toxic political environment, the Council argued, brought uncertainty to the sector over funding, over whether to expand or contract, about 'where volunteering stops and paid employment starts' and, 'above all', 'about what the respective roles of local authorities, voluntary organisations and the private sector should be in the second half of the 1980s'.[111]

For the Council, the sector's right to campaign was sacrosanct. It submitted a spirited defence to the Widdicombe inquiry into the conduct of local authority business and lobbied vigorously against provisions in the 1985 Local Government Bill aimed at restricting the ability of voluntary organisations in receipt of local government funding to comment on political issues, achieving a few important concessions.[112] Following the passage of the Act in 1986, it launched a guide, *Publish and Not Be Damned,* advising voluntary organisations how to operate within the law without compromising their right to campaign. 'The last thing we wanted', remembers Gutch who authored the report, 'was them to think because of this legislation that they couldn't do any sort of campaigning work'.[113]

Growing disquiet within the Council about the threat to independence led to the publication in March 1984 of a new *Code for Voluntary Organisations in Relations Between the Voluntary Sector and Government.*[114] It had 16 clauses covering funding relations with government, the importance of realistic costing for overheads and the essential requirement that voluntary organisations, even in receipt of public funds, should be able to 'assert and exercise their freedom to advocate changes or continuity in public policy'.[115] It can be seen as a precursor to the Compact negotiated with the New Labour administration over a decade later, although its influence on the ground was limited.[116] Deakin recalls it being 'full of high-sounding sentiment about how government should behave, but was pretty ineffectual in the field'.[117] Following from the Code, the Council negotiated an agreement with the Voluntary Services Unit for its own funding, based on mutual acceptance of the dual principles of 'independence of policy making' and the need for 'full accountability' for expenditure of public funds.[118] It had grown alarmed over attempts to impose tighter control over the use of core funds, a move which it argued carried 'serious implications for NCVO itself and the voluntary sector as a whole'.[119] Government funding was to be warmly welcomed and proper accountability should be exercised for all organisations in receipt of public funds, but the independence of the sector was non-negotiable. This was a challenging time for the Council in its relations with government. According to its chair, Jay, it was forced to spend too much time in the early years of the decade on 'rearguard actions'.[120]

TAX AND CHARITY LAW

The 1980s was a difficult time financially for many voluntary organisations. Concerns over a decline in individual giving, led to renewed attempts by the Council to negotiate more favourable tax treatment for charities. Here the government was more supportive. A fiscal working group was established, which recommended, among other things, a reduction in the minimum period for covenants and doubling of the exemption on capital transfer tax of gifts to charities. In the Budget of 1980, five of the ten recommendations were accepted.[121] Value-added tax remained a bone of contention. The Council made repeated overtures to the government for further relief, without success and in the 1981 Budget the request was turned down as unaffordable.[122] Much of its work on fiscal measures was routed through CAF, which its chief executive at the time, Michael Brophy, has described as 'a bit like Eve – a rib of the NCSS'.[123] Brophy recalls a number of big successes on tax for charities during the 1980s, with most of the new ideas having been 'simply cribbed' from the US.[124] Important changes to the covenant system were followed by the abolition of all limits on tax-exempt giving, which, he has suggested, 'was beyond our wildest dreams'.[125] This was followed by the introduction of a payroll-giving scheme, single gifts for companies, an embryonic gift aid scheme, and much else. Brophy remembers the decade, not as 'the years of crisis' some have depicted, but the 'years of growth'.[126] CAF grew in influence under Brophy and was seen by some as an alternative leader on policy. According to Perri 6, who worked at the Council at this time as a parliamentary officer and then head of policy analysis and research, the increased standing of CAF, and other organisations such as the Directory of Social Change, meant that 'NCVO's leadership was contested'. The Council, he says, 'felt very threatened ... and there was a real sense of defensiveness'.[127]

The Council had long been pushing for a change to charity law. The Goodman Committee report in 1976 called for an extension of the number of activities eligible for charitable status, but had largely been ignored by government.[128] High-profile controversies, such as the charitable status enjoyed by the Unification Church (the 'Moonies') and the refusal of the Methodist Church to end its financial support for race relations as demanded by the Charity Commission, threatened to bring the law into disrepute and impact on public confidence. The Council's chair, Morrison, wrote to the home secretary in 1980 suggesting there was 'a clear demand for a modern restatement of the principles from which the meaning of "charity" and "charitable purposes" is derived'.[129] A second influential book by Francis Gladstone, following his earlier one on *welfare pluralism*, was published in 1982 and examined in detail the legal concept of public benefit and the law's capacity to adapt to social and economic change.[130] The same year the Council set up a charity law working group under Christopher Zealley of the Dartington Hall Trust.[131] In June 1983 it produced a consultation document, *Charity Law: A Case for Change*, setting out ten recommendations for reform. Charity law, it argued, was impeding social change in its failure to recognise the relief of unemployment and improvement of race relations as charitable objectives.[132] In May 1989 the government published a white paper, *Charities: A Framework for the Future,* proposing reform of charity law and increased powers for the Charity Commission.[133] The Council supported the recommendation not to attempt a statutory definition of charity and to strengthen the investigative powers of the Commission.[134] There was a long wait for legislation. When it finally came in the form of the Charities Act, 1992, the Council was enthusiastic, suggesting that it 'represents the most radical overhaul of charity law for over thirty years' and expressing hope that the increased powers to the Commission to encourage good practice and weed out fraud means 'the public should now have greater confidence in the charities' world'.[135] Such confidence would not entirely be borne out by events.

SPREADING THE WORD

The Council retained its international focus during this period, although it was seen as less of a priority as financial difficulties mounted. It continued its active involvement in the International Council on Social Welfare (ICSW) and in 1982 organised the 21st international conference in Brighton on the theme of *Action for Social Progress—the Responsibilities of Governmental and Voluntary Organisations.* The event attracted over 1000 delegates and is remembered by the organiser, Seary, as 'very stressful but very, very rewarding'.[136] Towards the end of the 1980s, Prashar took the decision to disband the international department, a decision she recalls as not being 'very popular', but justified 'given all the things on the agenda and the money constraints'.[137] It was not until 1991 that the Council finally severed links with the ICSW, partly on cost grounds, but also because its international priorities increasingly were seen as tied to Europe. It was the end of over 60 years of involvement with the organisation, which it had helped launch in 1928. The decision was not universally popular, with one trustee arguing that the Council should not retreat into a 'eurocentric' world.[138]

Relations with the four home countries were generally cordial during this period. A new joint international committee, serviced by the Council, but with an independent chair, was established to advise the individual councils on their international work and to act as the UK committee to the ICSW.[139] In 1985 a revised concordat was signed between the councils to strengthen collaboration, giving NCVO 'primary responsibility' for the UK and international dimensions to any joint work.[140] In 1986 it was agreed that the funds coming to the Council from CAF would be split on a population basis among the four councils. In 1988 a new concordat was agreed to strengthen the work of the four national councils on matters of UK interest.[141]

Increasingly, however, the Council's international interests were focused on Europe and, in particular, on helping the sector access money made available through the European Social Fund.[142] It also saw its role as selling the European project to a sceptical public. Writing in 1982 the deputy director, Roy Manley, reflected that polls continue to show how 'unpopular the European Community is with the British people'; the European Community, he said, was out of touch with communities and needed to change, but the sector could help influence public opinion if it could learn to speak with one voice.[143] The Council was especially active in the lead up to the introduction of a Single European Market in 1992. It produced research on the social impact of the single market and brought together a range of groups in the 1992 coordination group to help the sector understand and make the most of the new opportunities.[144] It organised study trips, arranged travel bursaries, and provided advice on funding. Seary, who headed the international department for much of the period, recalls the support given to organisations undertaking international work for the first time: 'We could just make a small grant available and the paperwork wasn't stressful and it was all done very amicably.'[145] As a member of the European Council for Voluntary Organisations (CEDAG), the Council was involved in lobbying the European Commission on a pan-European legal status for voluntary organisations to assist those wanting to carry out cross-border work.[146]

Inside the Organisation

Funding remained a problem. Although the Council was cushioned to some extent from the effects of rising inflation and cuts in government expenditure by its core grant and the funding agreement with CAF, it was not immune from economic pressures. Its core grant was reduced on several occasions during the 1980s and membership income, although buoyant, remained only a small proportion of its overall income. Operating deficits were an annual reality, reaching £100,000 in 1982–83 and almost £300,000 in 1987–88 (some 10 per cent of total turnover).[147] As in previous periods, the Council embarked upon a series of fundraising drives to balance the books. Major appeals were launched in 1982 and 1991, which resulted in several hundreds of thousands of pounds of additional income, although it was acknowledged that the CAF contribution remained 'the mainstay of the Council's voluntary income'.[148] In 1983 it set up with CAF and Business in the Community a pilot project to explore the potential for developing a payroll-giving scheme, drawing on a similar successful initiative in the US. A new organisation, United Funds, was established, which was later handed over to CAF and in time had a significant impact on personal giving in the UK.[149] The Council also joined CAF in the newly established Council for Charitable Support in 1985 to explore other ways of increasing individual and corporate support.[150]

One new initiative, however, did not have the Council's backing. Plans for a national lottery had been debated over many years, but, when in December 1992 the government published its National Lottery Bill, the Council raised a series of concerns. Chief among them was the possible negative impact on charitable giving, with research it had commissioned suggesting that as much as £230 million a year could be lost to the sector in individual donations.[151] It mounted an energetic lobbying campaign and managed to get a number of safeguards introduced into the Bill, which was finally enacted in October 1993. Stephen Lee, director of the Institute of Charity Fundraising Managers, said the campaign 'has seen NCVO at its best – constantly campaigning and achieving real benefits through sheer hard work'.[152] The prime minister, John Major, was less happy, berating the Council in his memoirs for its opposition.[153]

The Council's opposition to the Lottery owed something to a distaste, shared by many within the voluntary sector, at being seen as profiting from gambling and to a wider concern about the ethics of income generation. In June 1987 the Executive Committee considered a paper on *Ethical Investments*.[154] It recognised the potential negative impact on public opinion of doing nothing, but felt there was a limit to what it could do under charity law and, that as an umbrella body, it had a 'wide range of interests and members' wishes to take into account'. It decided to concentrate any action on de-investing in companies that had significant interests in South Africa, a position it felt could be justified by the Council's anti-racist position and would likely carry members with it. This did not prevent it, however, from accepting funding from Shell UK for its new Waste Watch project, despite the request from the anti-apartheid movement to voluntary organisations to sever all ties with companies with an interest in South Africa. The Council justified this apparent contradiction on the basis that Shell UK was a separate legal entity from its Dutch parent company and had no dealings with South Africa, and that not taking money for such projects would have a 'very serious' impact on beneficiaries.[155] An investment panel was established to advise on the ethical considerations of future corporate support.

One impact of the funding challenge was the impetus given to the drive to move more affiliated groups to independence. This was never solely about efficiency savings, but the funding difficulties provided a further push in this direction. Over the next few years a number of long-standing groups were moved to independence, including the National Federation of Community Associations, the Standing Conference for Local History, the National Council for Voluntary Youth Services, the Standing Conference for Amateur Music, the Standing Conference of Women's Organisations, and the London Voluntary Service Council.[156] Most went amicably, most survived and some thrived. But there were casualties and not all the partings were harmonious.

MEMBERSHIP

Although the Council had always been a membership organisation, its federated structure meant that individual organisations were never seen as a priority and for many years membership hovered around 200. The associated group model meant that the Council could claim attachment to many thousands of organisations affiliated to these groups, even though they weren't directly members. It was only once the associated groups began to leave, taking their affiliates with them, that boosting the number of direct members took on more urgency. It was not only a question of numbers. There was a growing aware-ness that the Council needed to attract not only more, but a wider variety of members if it could claim to speak for the movement. It has become 'increas-ingly apparent', it admitted in 1981, 'that national voluntary organisations in membership of NCVO are no longer fully representative of the current range of NCVO activities, nor indeed of the voluntary sector as a whole'.[157]

To address the situation, it embarked on a membership drive that included, controversially, amending the stipulation that had been in place since its estab-lishment of taking on only national organisations.[158] Now organisations active in specific fields, such as employment, self-help, or supporting the black and ethnic minority community, were to be recruited, even if they were not work-ing on a national basis.[159] By 1984 there were over 400 individual organisations in membership, plus almost 200 individual councils of voluntary service and rural community councils.[160] In 1989 the Executive Committee held a special meeting to focus on membership. The debate suggests how difficult it was to get the balance right. One member noted how some members complained that the organisation in recent years had been 'high-jacked by new, emerging vol-untary bodies to the detriment of more conventional organisations', while another felt that, despite progress, the Council was 'still shackled to some extent in historic traditions and expectations'. The option was discussed of abandoning membership in favour of a subscription model, although the con-sensus reached was that it was essential for its legitimacy.[161] Deakin recalls some of the tensions within the Council at this time, with some of the old guard complaining that the sector 'was becoming much more political than it should be' and others pushing for a more radical approach. There was, he remembers, 'a very different constellation of pressures coming to bear on the management of the NCVO in the early 1980s'.[162] Julia Unwin, head of the voluntary sector liaison team at the GLC, agrees. A new voluntary sector was growing at the time, she has noted, organised around identity politics and 'NCVO and others took time to grasp what that meant because ... it was extremely challenging'.[163] Even among larger charities, suspicions ran deep. Perri 6 recalls antipathy from some national organisations who accused the Council of 'upstaging them or boxing them into common programmes which restricted their particular con-cerns'. Many groups, he suggests, 'saw themselves not as part of a sector with a common interest, but as pressure groups for a particular cause'.[164]

But things were changing, albeit slowly. Marilyn Taylor, who worked as head of policy analysis in the late 1980s, recalls the sense of the organisation 'going in a new direction', feeling 'much more relevant' and 'reaching out to smaller organisations and to people on the ground'.[165] A new call went out for mem-bers, although progress was slow and by 1993 numbers were only 650. It took the appointment of Stuart Etherington as chief executive in the early 1990s before the Council could claim anything approaching a mass membership.[166]

By the mid-1980s it was providing members with specialist advice on a wide range of topics, including the law, fundraising, HR, finance, and international matters. Information services remained a priority and the Council again built up its library. In 1984 it was reported it contained over 13,000 books and reports, had made 2000 loans, and hosted over 140 researchers.[167] In November 1979 a new quarterly magazine was launched, *Voluntary Action*, replacing the long-running *Social Service Quarterly* and for a couple of years it was published as a weekly supplement in *New Society* magazine, resulting in a rise in circulation from 2500 to 25,000.[168] In 1988 it was replaced by another monthly magazine, *NCVO News*. In 1986, Bedford Square Press reported its most successful year in commercial terms.[169]

ADAPTING TO THE NEW VOLUNTARY SECTOR

The Council can rightly be accused of having ignored the new voluntary sector for much of the 1960s and 1970s. While it continued to carry out valuable work at a national level, it had fallen asleep while the sector changed.[170] Despite numerous reviews of its purpose and structure, the changes did little more than tinker at the edges, and the Council in many ways still looked and felt like an Edwardian institution, with its labyrinth of committees and groups and air of quiet diplomacy in dealings with the state. It took the vision, energy, and organising genius of Hinton to bring it kicking and screaming into the late twentieth century. But his interests, radical as they were, were still largely focused on the established voluntary sector with the aims of delivering *welfare pluralism* on the back of an ever more efficient and effective sector. Still by the mid-1980s, little in the work of the Council appealed to the mass of single issue, self-help, and community groups that had emerged. It took the arrival of Prashar for it to respond to the needs of the new voluntary sector and key to this response was yet another governance overhaul.

The governance of the Council had last been reviewed in the mid-1970s, but by the mid-1980s decision-making had slipped still further away from the membership. An Executive Committee of 34 met quarterly, but detailed business was carried out in a resources and development sub-committee.[171] Although the Executive Committee included a number of representatives elected by members, there were also several appointees and observers, including from CAF, the national councils of the other three home countries, the Volunteer Centre, the Voluntary Services Unit, the Association of Metropolitan Authorities, the Association of County councils, and the TUC.[172] For Prashar, making the Executive Committee more representative of the membership was essential if the Council was to be seen as relevant to the new, more democratically minded voluntary sector. Adapt or die was her mantra: 'The files of the Charity Commissioners are a testament not to lost causes, but to failure to adapt to change', she wrote in the annual report for 1986–87. 'NCVO, perhaps more than most of its members, has to be aware of this danger and to adjust itself to changes in the political, economic and social climate and the nature of the voluntary sector.'[173] The Council, she acknowledged, like many national voluntary organisations, could be seen as 'a white, male establishment body'.[174]

A constitutional commission was established in 1985, before Prashar's arrival. Chaired by the Council's vice-chair, Kenneth Lamb, it reported to the annual meeting in November 1986.[175] Its recommendations, which were accepted, included opening up the election of honorary officers and establishing an electoral college where members, organised according to different interest groups, could elect representatives to serve on the Executive Committee.[176] It was seen as a small, but important step towards greater accountability. In 1993, further changes were made aimed at increasing the number of members on the Executive Committee. An advisory council was established to draw in a broader range of viewpoints, although membership was largely confined to senior figures from politics and business.

Perhaps even more significant than the governance changes was the new focus on diversity. This had started under Hinton, particularly the emphasis on black and minority ethnic communities in the wake of the inner-city riots in 1981, but it was under Prashar it took on a new sense of urgency.[177] In 1982 the Council appointed a two-year project worker to encourage voluntary organisations to be more aware of the needs of black and minority ethnic communities and strengthen links between these communities and councils of voluntary service.[178] A report published in June 1984, *A Multi-Racial Society—the Role of National Voluntary Organisations,* highlighted the poor representation of black and minority ethnic people on the boards and senior management teams of voluntary organisations.[179] In 1985 an Organisation Development Unit (ODU) was established to provide technical assistance to black and minority ethnic groups.[180] The ODU, which provided advice, consultancy, and training, particularly in the inner cities, became independent of the Council in April 1991.[181] It later changed its name to Sia and became embroiled in a dispute with the Home Office over claims of poor management and the *political* nature of its work, which led to it being defunded.[182] A separate body, the Voluntary Organisations Services to Ethnic Minorities Group, was set up alongside the ODU to support national organisations keen to develop links with black and minority ethnic groups.[183]

Not all such groups, however, were anxious to work with the Council. 'Some Black activists', the Council acknowledged, saw 'state funding as a form of social control, accommodating racial discontent within the state as an alternative to rebellion on the streets'.[184] Gutch, who worked at the Council as a senior director for seven years from the mid-1980s, recalls that 'smaller organisations and black and minority ethnic groups were all quite suspicious of NCVO'.[185] In 1990 the head of the ODU, Michael Jarrett, pointed to advances that had been made over the previous decade in support for the black and minority ethnic voluntary sector, but suggested serious challenges remained, including underfunding, lack of specialist infrastructure, and their being squeezed out in the contract culture. He concluded with the need to be concerned, not with further support from the mainstream sector, but 'with the autonomy and independence of the Black voluntary sector'.[186] Looking back on this period, Prashar suggests that, although the organisation 'tried to engage with the agenda, it's not something we pushed as hard as we could have done'.[187]

Ethnicity was not the only marginalised issue the Council was keen to champion. A women's organisations' interest group was formed, leading to the establishment of the National Alliance of Women's Organisations.[188] There was a major effort on self-help. A National Self-Help Support Centre was established with the Volunteer Centre in January 1986 as a clearing house for ideas and information, with funding from the King's Fund and the Carnegie UK Trust.[189] A Self-Help Alliance was set up in partnership with the Volunteer Centre to help local self-help groups.[190] Slowly the Council was changing. It would never be a radical campaigning organisation; this is not what it was set up to do. But it could at last claim to be speaking, if not for the whole sector, at least with significantly more authority than previously.

Action was also taken internally to improve the Council's standing on diversity. All papers submitted to the Executive Committee had to carry an impact statement to identify the likely implications of any policy changes on equal opportunities. An ethnic minorities working group and a women's issues group were set up, anti-sexism and anti-racism awareness training days were organised for all staff, and a declaration of intent on racism was issued.[191] Attempts were made to make the staff group more diverse, with some success. Overall numbers of staff had dropped significantly by the 1980s, from a high in the 1970s of almost 250, but the group was becoming more reflective of the changing population of the nation. In April 1986 there were 152 staff—47 men and 105 women, and 27 were from black and minority ethnic communities.[192]

MANAGEMENT DEVELOPMENT

The Council had long been interested in issues concerning the effectiveness and efficiency of the voluntary movement, but from the 1980s this became an increasing priority. The focus shifted from support for individual development to an emphasis on management, leadership, and good governance. In the early 1980s it linked with the Industrial Society to run courses on leadership, and in May 1980, it established a working party under Charles Handy to develop a strategy for improving effectiveness in the sector.[193]

Professor Handy, from the London Business School, was one of the first management gurus to take an active interest in the voluntary sector, and his work was hugely significant in influencing the strategic direction of the Council and driving forward a more business-like culture within the sector.[194] Morrison suggests that he was one of the architects in the movement of 'trying to knit together necessary competence and maximum enthusiasm and dedication to the task in hand'.[195] Over time, other business schools in the UK, including Henley and Cass, took up the issue of voluntary sector management and leadership as key areas of academic inquiry and practice. *Improving Effectiveness in Voluntary Organisations* reported in 1981.[196] The report identified two levels of problems: first level, or 'presenting' problems, such as staff and volunteer shortages, or the need for better management information and control, which it felt could be resolved relatively easily; and second level problems, related to goals, values, and relationships, which were deemed much harder to address. 'Muddling-through', it argued, 'cannot be good enough and is increasingly seen to be inadequate.'[197] Organisations needed help with diagnosis and implementing new ideas and methods. It recommended a 'brokerage' unit to provide information to voluntary organisations on resources available, including from business. The Council reacted positively to the recommendations and set up a Management Development Unit (MDU) to play the brokerage role and provide training courses and consultancy to the sector.[198]

In 1989 Lord Nathan was asked to chair a working party to investigate what more was needed.[199] His report, *Effectiveness and the Voluntary Sector*, published in April 1990, contained 68 recommendations aimed at government, the Charity Commission, charitable trusts, and voluntary organisations.[200] Commenting on the report, Prashar said, 'the time has come for voluntary organisations not just to react to outside pressures, but to develop and articulate our own agenda'.[201] Nathan's recommendations included investing in fundraising and administration and 'appropriate management development education', but he paid particular attention to redressing what he saw as the paucity of support and training for trustees who 'hold the ultimate power and authority' in voluntary organisations.[202] Trustees, he said, should be given the support they needed to do their job and be appointed for fixed-term periods as part of good governance. But he rejected calls for payment, arguing that the unpaid nature of trusteeship helped to preserve the unique position of voluntary organisations as not-for-profit agencies.

The trustee issue particularly caught the attention of the Council. A trustee training working party was established in March 1991 with the Charity Commission, chaired by Winifred Tumin.[203] Its report, *On Trust*, published the following year, reinforced Nathan's concerns.[204] Of the one million charitable trustees in England and Wales, 60 per cent were found to be unaware of their financial and legal responsibilities. Only one in five had received induction and one in eight training. Trustees were not diverse, the overwhelming majority being white, male, over 45, and from a professional background. Following the report, a trustee services unit was established in January 1993.[205] Support for trustees became an increasingly important feature of the Council's work over the next 20 years. Tesse Akpeki, the first head of the trustee and governance team, recalls much excellent work, but also frustrations, especially in getting boards to think seriously about training and diversity: 'It was awfully hard work', she remembers, 'to get boards to embrace the need to do these things and take trusteeship seriously.'[206] Twenty-five years later, the Charity Commission and the Centre for Charity Effectiveness at Cass Business School carried out another review of the composition and operation of charity boards.[207] There had been some significant improvements over the years in trustee awareness and training, but in other respects, such as diversity, change had been slow. Akpeki admits a sense of frustration 'that there has not been improvements in a lot of areas'.[208]

Much of the drive for improved management and leadership came from the sector and was enthusiastically led by the Council. 'Caring without efficiency', wrote the chair, Chandler, in 1990, 'betrays the trust of those we seek to serve as much as does efficiency without caring.'[209] Matthew Hilton and colleagues argue that the period after the Second World War, and more specifically from the late 1970s, marked a time of increasing professionalism within the voluntary sector, much of it led from within.[210] But there was also pressure from outside for the sector to improve its performance, particularly following the publication of the government's *Efficiency Scrutiny of the Supervision of Charities* in 1987 and the later *Efficiency Scrutiny of Government Funding of the Voluntary Sector*.[211] New Public Management was reshaping the way the public sector conducted its work and the voluntary sector was not immune from the pressures.[212] According to Hilton and colleagues, 'the new managerialism and corporate culture' at this time 'infected' the voluntary sector.[213]

The adoption of more business-like practice was not without critics.[214] Some later pointed to this as the moment when the sector and the Council took a wrong turn by becoming fixated with professionalism at the expense of their historic mission.[215] Even within the Council, there were early concerns about the long-term implications of the direction being taken. In 1980 Gladstone wrote to Charles Handy expressing the hope that his committee would not focus exclusively on modern business management methods, but that it will 'give some attention to the needs of that minority of voluntary organisations who are seeking help with unconventional forms of management – self-management, co-operative working, etc.'. He had a 'slight worry' that the Council 'may move to establish some kind of organisational effectiveness unit' that had little interest in such matters and 'by trying to be all things to all voluntary organisations we shall end up doing little to promote more unorthodox forms of organisation'.[216] Handy later wrote eloquently about what the sector could teach business, particularly in the art of managing volunteers, and it would be wrong to conclude that the MDU aimed simply to ape business practice.[217] A contemporary recalls the unit promoting 'developmental, participatory' approaches to management and producing some 'significantly newish and original observations'.[218] Purkis agrees. He recalls that the Council at the time 'was not just wanting the sector to be managerial', rather 'the excitement of that period was trying to think through how we could be competent and efficient at doing the things that needed to be done and achieved, while at the same time preserving our distinctive ethos and distinctive nature'.[219]

FUNDRAISING

One of the areas of competency that needed addressing was fundraising. In the late 1960s the Council had responded to pressure from the Charity Commission to set up a working party to look into alleged dubious practice among some fundraising charities, although it had concluded there was little cause for alarm.[220] In 1985 the issue resurfaced. The Charity Commission reported its concerns in its annual review for three successive years and the Council again felt obliged to take action.[221] A new working party was established, chaired by Harry Kidd, director of the Legislation Monitoring Service for Charities, to look into the accusations and advise on action to be taken.[222] Its report, *Malpractice in Fundraising for Charity,* was published in July 1986.[223] It concluded that, although there was no evidence of widespread abuse, there was 'a need for continued vigilance by charities backed by simple but effective measures to safeguard the public'.[224] Charities, it argued, should take responsibility for putting their own house in order, backed by the Council and the newly formed Institute of Charity Fundraising Managers. Prashar welcomed the report as a means of ensuring 'that both donor and receiver are fully protected' and of helping to 'prevent any recurrence of the few examples of malpractice which might otherwise threaten the good name of charities'.[225] Many of the recommendations in the Kidd report later found their way into the 1992 Charities Act.[226]

Rural Services

Throughout the late 1970s and 1980s the Council continued to focus on rural issues. Support for traditional priority areas such as village halls was maintained, but attention was also paid to the decline of rural services and the impact on rural communities. A report, *The Decline of Rural Services,* in 1978 attracted significant press and public interest for highlighting the extent of the problem and suggesting alternative approaches to the delivery of service, including 'more use of joint provision, for example, the shop, post office or garage, part-time travelling services, and volunteers to run bulk-buy co-operatives and to help in village schools'.[227] David Emerson recalls the report 'got the biggest mailbag *The Times* had ever had'.[228] A follow-up report, *Alternative Rural Services,* published in 1981 expanded on the recommendations and called for community-run shops and doctors surgeries in village halls as a means of dealing with the decline in services and reinvigorating local communities.[229] In 1980 a new alliance of organisations interested in rural issues was formed, Rural Voice, with the Council taking on its well-established role of secretariat.[230]

The heart of the Council's rural operation remained the network of rural community councils, and there was cause for celebration in 1984 when the establishment of a council in Norfolk (which brought the total to 38) meant for the first time the network covered all shire counties in England.[231] Such success, however, could not hide the tensions between the network and the Council, which had been simmering for more than a decade, and demands for independence intensified. In 1984, the Development Commission, which was still the main funder of the Council's rural work, commissioned a review of the status of the Standing Conference of Rural Community councils.[232] The

Leavett report, published in June 1985, stopped short of calling for full independence for the network.[233] However, in exploring the range of options available, it made it clear that the standing conference would settle for nothing less. When the Development Commission intimated that it would be happy to fund a new independent national organisation to take over running the network, the writing was on the wall. At its annual meeting in September 1985 the standing conference voted unanimously for independence.[234] A joint working group was established to consider the review and its recommendation in favour of independence was accepted by the Council, despite reservations.[235] Action with Communities in Rural England (ACRE) was launched at the Rural Life conference in Cirencester in April 1987. Responsibility for most of the Council's rural work was taken over by the new organisation, although it committed itself to 'maintaining a vigorous rural dimension to its work in support of voluntary action'.[236]

The separation was difficult for the rural staff involved at the Council, most of whom supported independence and some of whom moved across to work for the new organisation.[237] But despite tensions internally, the process of independence ran fairly smoothly. In addition to financial concerns over losing the Development Commission grant, the move made little strategic sense to the Council. The network had been the bedrock of its work in the countryside for more than 60 years and responsible for some of its most significant successes. The loss cut the Council adrift from its rural constituency and threatened to undermine its legitimacy in dealing with rural issues. It also encouraged criticisms that it was cut-off from the real concerns of voluntary groups on the ground. Alternatives to complete separation had been explored, including giving greater freedom to the network to determine policy and control its own resources under the umbrella of the Council, but for the network, full independence was the only acceptable option.[238] Its chair, Dr. Alan Rogers, who was also on the Council's Executive Committee, told the Council that, like other associated groups, it had 'grown up' and was ready to leave 'the parental fold'.[239]

COUNCILS FOR VOLUNTARY SERVICE

Similar developments were taking place within the Council's other main local network, representing the councils for voluntary service. The 1980s were a tough decade for local infrastructure. Cuts to local authority budgets hit many voluntary groups, but intermediary bodies fared worse than most. In such a climate, it is perhaps not surprising that relations between the network and the Council, which had long been difficult, became even more fraught. For the network and its umbrella body, the semi-autonomous Standing Conference of councils for Voluntary Service, the Council was seen as doing insufficient to deal with the funding pressures and champion the cause of local infrastructure. In April 1982 the standing conference changed its name to the councils for Voluntary Service–National Association (CVS-NA).[240] Deakin, who took over as chair of CVS-NA from Morgan in 1983, recalls taking many a national tour with Hinton to try to smooth relations between the two parties.[241] In 1984 an agreement between the two sides ceded greater responsibility for policy making to the local council movement.[242] In 1985 the Council delivered a coup when, after many years of lobbying, the government finally agreed to the establishment of a fund to provide three-year core funding to local infrastructure agencies.[243] The fund, worth £1 million per year for three years, was administered, in association with the Volunteer Centre and the newly established National Association of Volunteer Bureaux.

For many within the local movement, it was too little, too late. The drive for independence was becoming unstoppable and the movement, according to Gutch, was 'in quite a hurry to disassociate themselves' from the Council.[244] The differences were not simply about funding. The network was generally more radical than the Council and took a different view on many matters of policy. For example, it criticised the decision to take funding from Shell UK for the Waste Watch project and called for the Community Programme to be boycotted on the grounds that it was being used to massage unemployment figures. A joint working party was set up in 1987 to review relations between the two sides.[245] It considered four options: keeping the status quo; more control for the network within existing governance arrangements, which was rejected by the Council on the grounds that they 'would be left with the responsibility without the power to exercise adequate control'; closer integration within the Council, which was unacceptable to the network; and full independence. The group concluded that independence was the only viable option, which was reluctantly accepted by the Council's Executive Committee. A three-year tapering grant was provided by the Council to help the new organisation get started and a place reserved for it on its Executive Committee. It was agreed the Council would not seek to recruit individual local council representatives as members.[246] The National Association of councils for Voluntary Service (NACVS) was formally launched in Sheffield in April 1991.[247] Just four years after the independence of the rural community council network, it marked a watershed in the history of the Council. The Council had been created in 1919 with the explicit aim of providing a national focus for the burgeoning movement of local councils in urban areas, an ambition that within a few years had been extended to rural areas. Now, after over 70 years, the Council had lost its two most significant local networks.

The questions need to be asked whether the split was inevitable and what was the long-term strategic impact. On the question of inevitability, the answer is probably yes. It seems unlikely the Council could have done anything to prevent the separation. The clamour for independence had reached a crescendo from both networks and it would have gained little from trying to retain control. Deakin believes separation was inevitable: 'There were', he recalls, 'pressures pulling apart all the time.' The ability to respond flexibly to local situations demanded separation. 'It could', he suggests, have 'been done from the centre, but it was much better done from the periphery'.[248] Not everyone within the

Council mourned the split. For both Hinton and Prashar, separation chimed with their vision of a Council focused more on strategic issues affecting the sector as a whole. However, the minutes of the Executive Committee at this time convey a recognition that losing these two networks was of a different order of magnitude than giving up, for example, the Citizens' Advice Bureaux or the National Old People's Welfare Council. Important though such single-issue networks were, it made perfect sense to take them to a stage where they could flourish on their own. Resources within the Council would always constrain their ability to grow and thus divert attention away from issues of relevance to the voluntary movement as a whole. The rural community councils and councils of social service were different. They were generic, development agencies and had been the Council's point of entry into the grassroots for 70 years, keeping it furnished with intelligence about the state of voluntary action within towns and villages and adding legitimacy to its campaigning at national level.

Looking back, it is clear that the loss of these networks left the Council more vulnerable to accusations of being out of touch with developments on the ground. Deakin believes the separation 'did make it difficult in some respects for the NCVO to represent the voice of the locality in a systematic way'.[249] Gutch concurs, suggesting that, post-separation, there wasn't 'enough outreach work with the networks done' to build strong national, local partnerships.[250] The fate of the independent networks post-independence is outside the scope of this book. Both went on to do important and creative work, although both found it difficult in the long term to secure the resources needed to deliver fully on their mission.[251] One can only speculate as to whether if they had remained within the umbrella of the Council they would have found survival easier, or whether the inevitable compromises required would have made accommodation impossible, whatever the financial benefits.

Despite the move during this period towards independence for many of its networks, the Council still experimented with new groups and projects. A Neighbourhood Energy Fund was set up in May 1981 to help voluntary organisations tackle unemployment and fuel poverty by developing a programme of local energy conservation projects. It became an independent charity in 1984.[252] In 1987 the Council launched a campaign against waste, following the publication of a report on *Waste Recycling in the Community*, and Waste Watch was later spun off as a separate organisation.[253] Other networks formed by the Council during the 1980s included the National Food Alliance, focused on effective labelling and consumer representation in the food industry; the National Agency on Alcohol Misuse, which provided support and training for local care and rehabilitation services; and Family Forum, focusing on family concerns. In 1993, BOND (British Overseas NGOs for Development) was established. All went on to become successful organisations in their own right, with support from the Council.[254] But this tradition of innovation was coming to an end, as both Hinton and Prashar sought to focus more narrowly on issues of concern to the whole sector. The Council did not stop seeking funding for new projects altogether, but its tradition of piloting new approaches to social need through the nurturing of new networks and groups no longer formed a major part of its work. Several commentators view this as a loss. Purkis, for example, has suggested that 'the long-term consequence has been that NCVO has stopped being a laboratory' and, as a result, one of its 'great creative contributions to civil society' has come to an end.[255]

While many of the most significant innovations during this period were in the voluntary sector, the Council also increased its work with business. It had long looked to the corporate sector for financial support, but now began to take a wider interest in the contribution business could make as part of a growing interest in corporate social responsibility. In the early 1980s, the Council ran a pilot programme, Young Volunteers from Industry, to encourage young people to get involved in community action.[256] It forged strong links with the new business forum, Business in the Community, and in 1989 launched a Corporate Affiliation Scheme, with support from Prince Charles, the CBI, and the Institute of Directors, aimed at enhancing mutual understanding between the two sectors.[257]

A New Home

By the mid-1980s the Council had outgrown its home in Bedford Square. Over the years, it had rented several additional properties from the Bedford Estate, and in 1987 it moved some staff into nearby accommodation in Metropolis House in Tottenham Court Road. When the lease on Bedford Square came up for renewal, it took the opportunity to explore other longer-term options. As an office, Bedford Square had never been ideal. Staff remember it as a Georgian delight, a 'film set', but wholly unsuited to a modern, dynamic office. Emerson describes it as 'a rabbit warren ... a series of houses joined by interconnecting doors that weren't always on the same level, so to go between the houses you were going up and down rickety stairs'.[258] Mehta remembers it as 'a sprawling building', totally unsuited to modern times, but 'of its time, a great location'.[259] Seary agrees, describing it as a 'wonderful place to work', quiet, and with 'exclusive access to the gardens' on the square, but not conducive to 'the most effective way of running a coherent organisation'.[260] For Morrison, it was 'an absolutely hopeless building, in all sorts of ways. I loved it dearly.'[261] Its lack of disability access jarred with the growing demands of the age. Seary remembers that 'the interior of the building was all under various listings of one sort and another and it was very difficult to get things like a lavatory for disabled people fitted'.[262] In March 1990 the Executive Committee set up a working group to explore options. The non-negotiables were that any new premises must be in London, deemed essential for ease of access to government and for retaining staff, have good disability access, and be easy to reach from other parts of the UK.[263]

In June 1991 the Executive Committee considered a shortlist of four options and in October agreed to the purchase of Regents Wharf in King's Cross.[264] The purchase was funded two-thirds by a bank loan, repayable over 20 years, and one-third from reserves, taking advantage of 'the depressed property market'.[265] The new offices were opened in June 1992. Weleminsky reported that 'staff have settled down well to the new environment and are mostly positive about the improved communications and sense of togetherness from being under one roof and in an open plan environment'. The building, she added, 'with its excellent conference facilities and lovely outlook over the canal has been much admired by our visitors'.[266] The Council had long harboured a desire to own its own property to provide a sustainable source of income through the renting out of conference facilities and hub for other national charities to share. Over the next quarter of the century, it saw both these ambitions come to fruition.

CONCLUSION

The Council began the 1980s with high hopes for a new radical *welfare pluralism* in which the voluntary sector would play a larger role in the delivery of public services. It finished disappointed with the way the contract culture had developed and concerned about the long-term implications for the sector's independence and sustainability. The value of government grants in real terms increased significantly over the decade, from £93 million in 1979–80 to £292 million in 1987–88, but this growth masked a wide variety of experiences within the sector.[267] Some organisations did well out of the expansion of public funding, others, particularly local groups and those representing minority interests, found their funding severely reduced.

The Council was increasingly concerned about the lack of equity in the relationship with the state. As Deakin has recalled, 'the terms of trade with government were extremely one sided'.[268] Jane Lewis, writing about the contract revolution a decade later, argued that while the 'process of formalisation' that accompanied contracts may have encouraged 'greater clarity', they also led to more bureaucracy within the sector which worked against 'flexibility and responsiveness, the commonly agreed strengths of the voluntary sector'.[269] The Council shared some of these concerns. It was never a flag-bearer for the contract culture. It could see the benefits and opportunities, but was acutely aware of the drawbacks, of the lack of flexibility, and of the potential for squeezing out smaller groups. Contracts, it argued in 1991, 'can provide clarity, ensure quality, and benefit the user', but they can also 'debase relationships, lead to narrow penny-pinching, and leave the user isolated and devalued'.[270] The marketised model of contracting, which developed during the decade, was very different from the bottom up, co-produced dream of Gladstone and Hinton.[271]

The Council was alarmed by the politicisation of the sector and the coarsening of relations with government and strongly challenged attempts to muzzle voluntary organisations and limit what it held to be their inalienable right to advocate and campaign, even when receiving public funds. The period saw some successes with government, particularly in the tax concessions aimed at promoting individual and corporate giving, and there was some progress with the reform and liberalisation of charity law. But for much of the decade the Council felt it was on the back foot, fighting a rearguard action in defence of the sector. Partnership with the state, which had been its aim from the beginning, had not developed in the direction it had hoped. The next decade saw the election of another radical administration, this time of the Left, led by the new prime minister, Tony Blair, who, as with his Tory successor over ten years later, made closer relations with the voluntary sector part of his personal credo. The period was later described as a 'golden age' for the sector and the Council, after more than a decade of being marginalised from the policy process, saw its influence with government increase markedly. Not everyone, however, saw the period in a positive light, and some argued that the sector and the Council were in danger of being co-opted by the state by trading funds and influence for independence.

NOTES

1. See Chap. 7 for a discussion of this issue.
2. This is discussed further in Chap. 9.
3. Crowson, 2011, p. 496.
4. Rhodes and Marsh, 1992.
5. See, for example, Finlayson, 1994, pp. 353–356 and Clarke, Cochrane, and Smart, 1987.
6. On the growth of welfare spending after 1980, see Le Grand, 1991 and Deakin, 1988.
7. See, for example, Taylor, 1992 and Milligan and Conradson, 2006.
8. The term *independent sector* was increasingly used by government to link together the private and voluntary sectors. See Finlayson, 1994, pp. 364–5; Lewis, 1999a, b.
9. Craig and Taylor, 2002.
10. NCSS Annual Report 1978–79, p. 6.
11. London Metropolitan Archives (LMA)/4016/PA/B/03/(1-5).
12. Gladstone, 1979.
13. On the development of *welfare pluralism* as an *ideology*, see, for example, Brenton, 1985, pp. 154–174. Apart from Gladstone, other key advocates at the time included Stephen Hatch and Roger Hadley. See Hatch, 1980, and Hadley and Hatch, 1981.
14. 'The missing link', The *Guardian*, 21 November 1979, p. 9.
15. 'Voluntary service: The problems of propping up the welfare state', *The Times*, 20 November 1979, p. 14.
16. 'You, you and you', The *Observer*, 18 November 1979, p. 54.
17. See, for example, Knapp, 1984, and Webb and Wistow, 1987.
18. Brenton, 1985, pp. 168–9.
19. Minutes of Executive Committee, 4 September 1979; LMA/4016/IS/A/01/042(5).

20. Press note, 20 November 1979; LMA/4016/PA/B/03/001.
21. NCSS Annual Report 1979–80, p. 5.
22. In fact, a change of name had been discussed as early as 1937. See Chap. 3 for details.
23. The Council's response to Seebohm is discussed in Chap. 7.
24. *Brief for NCSS chair, Sir Philip Allen, for Extraordinary General Meeting 1973*; LMA/4016/IS/A/05/001.
25. Director's Statement to Executive Committee, 15 July 1975; LMA/4016/IS/A/05/001.
26. Ibid.
27. *Brief for Sir Philip Allen, Op.Cit.*
28. *Brief for Sir Philip Allen, Op.Cit.*
29. NCSS Annual Report 1973–74, p. 9.
30. Minutes of Executive Committee, 2 September 1976; LMA/4016/IS/A/01/041(1).
31. Letter dated 16 November 1976; LMA/4016/IS/A/05/001.
32. Letter dated 29 September 1976; LMA/4016/IS/A/05/001.
33. *Briefing paper*, August 1976; LMA/4016/IS/A/05/001.
34. Interviews with Bill Seary, 6 July 2017, and David Clark, 15 August 2017.
35. Minutes of Executive Committee, 4 September 1979; LMA/4016/IS/A/01/042(5).
36. Crowson et al., 2011, p. 516. Hinton contested the seat of Somerton and Frome, securing 35 per cent of the vote in losing to the Conservative, Robert Boscawen.
37. NCVO, 1984d, pp. 10–11.
38. NCVO Annual Report 1983–84, p. 7.
39. Interview with Bill Seary, 6 July 2017.
40. Interview with David Emerson, 3 May 2017.
41. Interview with Andrew Purkis, 23 August 2017.
42. Interview with David Clark, 15 August 2017.
43. Interview with Ian Bruce, 13 September 2017.
44. Interview with Sara Morrison, 2 August 2017.
45. Interview with Deborah Hinton, 26 October 2016.
46. NCVO, 1984d, p. 11.
47. Interviews with Marilyn Taylor, 14 June 2017, and Bill Seary, 6 July 2017.
48. Minutes of Executive Committee, 4 December 1984; LMA/4016/IS/A/01/042(2).
49. Interview with David Clark, 15 August 2017.
50. Interview with Andrew Purkis, 23 August 2017.
51. Interview with Nicholas Deakin, 4 April 2017.
52. Interview with Sara Morrison, 2 August 2017.
53. *NCVO News*, November 1989, p. 1.
54. Prashar took up post on 14 April 1986. Minutes of Executive Committee, 4 March 1986; LMA/4016/IS/A/01/043(10).
55. Interview with Bharat Mehta, 27 July 2017.
56. Interview with Andrew Purkis, 23 August 2017.
57. Interview with Baroness Prashar, 9 October 2017.
58. Interview with David Clark, 15 August 2017.

59. Interviews with Bharat Mehta, 27 July 2017, and Richard Gutch, 23 August 2017.
60. NCVO Annual Report 1990–91, p. 2.
61. The national federation became independent in April 1982.
62. Interview with Judy Weleminsky, 27 September 2017.
63. Various interviews with contemporaries conducted for the book.
64. Interview with Ian Bruce, 13 September 2017.
65. NCVO Annual Report 1981–82, p. 11.
66. NCVO Annual Report 1981–82, p. 11.
67. NCVO Annual Report 1985–86, p. 2.
68. NCVO Annual Report 1987–88, p. 8. The influential Griffiths report, *Community Care: Agenda for Action*, was published in 1988.
69. Interview with Richard Gutch, 23 August 2017.
70. Interview with Richard Gutch, 23 August 2017. See also Gutch, 1992.
71. Annual Report 1980–81, p. 6.
72. Paper submitted to Executive Committee on *Voluntary organisations, volunteers and industrial disputes* on 27 February 1979; LMA/4016/IS/A/01/042(5). The original *Drain* guidelines, named after Geoffrey Drain of the National Association of Local Government Officers, who chaired the working group, was published in 1975. They were revised in 1990. See Davis Smith, 1982.
73. Crowson et al., 2011, p. 501.
74. Quoted in Hilton et al., 2012, p. 347.
75. NCVO, 1985, p. 7.
76. Quoted in Williams, 1989, p. 179.
77. For a discussion of the Council's unemployment work in the 1930s, see Chap. 4.
78. Hilton et al., 2012, p. 356.
79. NCVO Annual Report 1980–81.
80. NCVO Annual Report 1981–82, p. 23.
81. NCVO Annual Reports 1980–81 and 1981–82.
82. NCVO Annual Report 1983–84.
83. NCVO Annual Report 1983–84, p. 11.
84. NCVO Annual Report 1981–82, p. 14. In contrast, in 2014 the Council refused to sign up to the 'Keep Volunteering Voluntary' campaign launched in response to the implementation of the government's 'Help to Work' programme, which included mandatory six-month placements in voluntary groups linked to benefit sanctions for non-compliance. It argued that such activity wasn't volunteering as it was coerced and that to call it such threatened to undermine the value of 'real' volunteering. It urged charities to 'consider carefully whether to be involved'. NCVO Press Release 28 April 2014, *NCVO Comment on Help to Work Launch*. This position was heavily criticised by the National Coalition for Independent Action; NCIA, 2014, pp. 4–5.
85. NCVO Annual Report 1984–85.
86. The Council helped establish a local economic initiatives working party in 1983 alongside the newly formed Business in the Community. Its report, *Joint Action—the Way Forward*, NCVO, 1984c, looked at community-based initiatives for economic regeneration.
87. Clark, 1993, 5 July 1983. Hilton et al., 2012, p. 304.

88. MacGregor and Pimlott, 1990, p. 9.
89. Addy and Scott, 1987, p. 4.
90. NCSS Annual Report 1979–80, p. 5. A further survey published in March 1992 demonstrated the extent of the cuts. NCVO Annual Report 1991–92, p. 9.
91. NCVO Annual Report 1979–80, p. 5.
92. NCVO Annual Report 1984–85.
93. Interviews with Marilyn Taylor, 14 June 2017, and Bharat Mehta, 27 July 2017.
94. NCVO Annual Report 1987–88.
95. The GLC and metropolitan county councils were abolished under the provisions of the Local Government Act, 1985.
96. NCVO Annual Report 1984–85.
97. Interview with Andrew Purkis, 23 August 2017.
98. Interview with Andrew Purkis, 23 August 2017.
99. NCVO Annual Report 1986–87.
100. Hilton et al., 2012, pp. 319–320. On CPAG, see Thane and Davidson, 2016.
101. On campaigning methods in the nineteenth century, see Davies, 2015.
102. For attempts by the Conservative-led Coalition government in 2014 and 2015 to restrict the right of charities to campaign, see Chap. 10.
103. Gorman, Robson, Sharpe, and Taylor, 1985.
104. NCVO, 1985, pp. 1–3.
105. NCVO, 1984b, p. 6.
106. Forsyth, 1984.
107. NCVO, 1985, p. 4.
108. Crowson et al., 2011, pp. 499–519 and pp. 501–502.
109. NCVO, 1985, p. 3. See also Crowson, 2011, p. 496.
110. The Trotskyist Militant, or Militant Tendency, took control of Liverpool City Council for much of the 1980s.
111. NCVO, 1985, p. 5.
112. Minutes of Executive Committee, 3 September 1985; LMA/4016/IS/A/01/042 (1).
113. NCVO Annual Report 1985–86. Interview with Richard Gutch, 23 August 2017.
114. NCVO, 1984a.
115. NCVO Annual Report 1983–84.
116. On the Compact negotiated between the New Labour government and the voluntary sector in 1998, see Chap. 9.
117. Crowson et al., 2011, p. 512.
118. NCVO Annual Report 1984–85, p. 5.
119. Minutes of Executive Committee, 5 March 1985; LMA/4016/IS/A/01/042 (2).
120. NCVO Annual Report 1984–85.
121. NCSS Annual Report 1979–80.
122. NCSS Annual Report 1980–81, p. 7.
123. Crowson et al., 2011, p. 505.
124. Ibid., p. 514.
125. Ibid., p. 505.
126. Ibid., p. 505.
127. Interview with Perri 6, 30 April 2018.

128. Some critics felt that Goodman didn't go far enough in its recommendations and that charities were in danger of being gagged. See Finlayson, 1994, p. 350. See also Morgan, 2012. On Goodman and his contribution to the voluntary sector, see Chap. 7.

129. NCVO Annual Reports 1980–81, p. 6, and 1982–83, p. 21.

130. Gladstone, 1982.

131. The Dartington Hall Trust is a charity focusing on the arts, social justice, and sustainability. Zealley was director/trustee from 1970 to 1987.

132. NCVO Annual Report 1982–83, p. 21.

133. Home Office, 1989.

134. NCVO Annual Report 1989–90, p. 8.

135. NCVO Annual Report 1991–92, p. 6.

136. NCVO Annual Report 1980–81. Interview with Bill Seary, 6 July 2017.

137. Interview with Baroness Prashar, 9 October 2017.

138. Minutes of Executive Committee, 11 June 1991; LMA/4016/IS/A/01/043(3).

139. NCSS Annual Report 1978–79.

140. Minutes of Executive Committee, 10 December 1985; LMA/4016/IS/A/01/042(1).

141. NCVO Annual Report 1987–88.

142. NCSS Annual Report 1980–81. Interview with Bill Seary, 6 July 2017.

143. NCVO Annual Report 1981–82, p. 12.

144. NCVO Annual Report 1989–90, p. 8.

145. Interview with Bill Seary, 6 July 2017.

146. NCVO Annual Report 1990–91.

147. NCVO Annual Reports 1982–83 and 1987–88.

148. NCSS Annual Report 1978–79.

149. Minutes of Executive Committee, 1 March 1983; LMA/4016/IS/A/01/042(3).

150. NCVO Annual Report 1985–86.

151. NCVO Annual Report 1992–93.

152. NCVO Annual Report 1992–93, p. 11.

153. Major, 1999.

154. Paper entitled *Ethical Investments* submitted to Executive Committee on 9 June 1987; LMA/4016/IS/A/01/043(9).

155. Paper entitled *Ethical Investments* submitted to Executive Committee on 9 June 1987; LMA/4016/IS/A/01/043(9).

156. The Standing Conference of Women's Organisations became independent in December 1980; the Standing Conference for Amateur Music in April 1983; the National Council for Voluntary Youth Services in April 1980; the Standing Conference for Local History in April 1982, as the British Association for Local History; and the National Federation of Community Organisations in April 1982.

157. NCSS Annual Report 1980–81, p. 14.

158. The amendment covered only specific areas of activity. A wholesale relaxation on the ban on recruiting local members did not come about until 2000. See Chap. 9 for details.

159. NCVO Annual Report 1983–84.

160. NCVO Annual Report 1983–84.

161. Minutes of Executive Committee, 7 March 1989; LMA/4016/IS/A/01/043(6).
162. Crowson et al., 2011, p. 512.
163. Ibid., p. 513.
164. Interview with Perri 6, 30 April 2018.
165. Interview with Marilyn Taylor, 14 June 2017.
166. See Chap. 9 for further details.
167. NCVO Annual Report 1983–84.
168. NCVO Annual Report 1985–86.
169. NCVO Annual Report 1985–86.
170. This issue is discussed further in Chap. 7.
171. NCVO Annual Report 1985–86.
172. The Association of Metropolitan Authorities was represented on the Executive Committee by Tessa Jowell, later a Labour cabinet member, while the Association of County councils was represented by Gillian Shephard, later a Conservative cabinet member; NCVO Annual Report 1981–82.
173. NCVO Annual Report 1986–87, p. 3.
174. NCVO Annual Report 1985–86, p. 9.
175. The Hon Kenneth Lamb was head of religious broadcasting and director of public affairs at the BBC and secretary to the church commissioners. He died in 1995. See The *Independent*, 24 June 1995.
176. NCVO Annual Report 1985–86; NCVO Annual Report 1986–87.
177. Riots broke out in London, Birmingham, Leeds, and Liverpool in 1981, the result of racial tension and inner-city deprivation, according to the *Scarman report*, commissioned by the government in the aftermath of the disturbances.
178. NCVO Annual Report 1982–83, p. 18.
179. NCVO Annual Report 1983–84, p. 11.
180. NCVO Annual Report 1985–86.
181. NCVO Annual Report 1990–91.
182. Craig, 2011, p. 374.
183. NCVO Annual Report 1985–86.
184. NCVO Annual Report 1985–86, p. 5.
185. Interview with Richard Gutch, 23 August 2017.
186. Jarrett, 1990, pp. 7–8.
187. Interview with Baroness Prashar, 9 October 2017.
188. NCVO Annual Report 1988–89. The alliance, formed in 1989, is an umbrella organisation of 140 organisations advocating for women's human rights.
189. NCVO Annual Report 1985–86.
190. NCVO Annual Report 1986–87.
191. NCVO Annual Reports 1983–84 and 1982–83, p. 24.
192. NCVO Annual Report 1985–86.
193. NCSS Annual Report 1979–80.
194. Charles Handy, one of the most influential management thinkers of the last 50 years, started his career at Shell International before moving to the London Business School. He is the author of numerous best-selling books on management, chaired the Royal Society of Arts from 1987 to 1989, and in 2006 was awarded an honorary Doctor of Laws at Trinity College, Dublin.
195. Interview with Sara Morrison, 2 August 2017.
196. Handy, 1981.

197. Report of the Handy working party discussed in Executive Committee on 24 February 1981; LMA/4016/IS/A/01/042(4).

198. NCVO Annual Report 1981–82.

199. NCVO Annual Report 1988–89. The second Lord Nathan, 1922–2007, solicitor and environmental campaigner, was chair of the Royal Society of Arts from 1975 to 1977 and a cross-bench member of the House of Lords. See *The Times*, 24 August 2007. His father, the first Lord Nathan, chaired the 1950 Committee that led to the 1960 Charities Act. See Chap. 6 for details.

200. Nathan, 1990.

201. NCVO Annual Report 1989–90, p. 3.

202. Nathan, 1990, p. 1.

203. Tumin would later become chair of the Council. See Chap. 9 for details.

204. Tumin, 1992.

205. NCVO Annual Report 1992–93.

206. Interview with Tesse Akpeki, 21 November 2017.

207. Charity Commission and Centre for Charity Effectiveness, 2017.

208. Interview with Tesse Akpeki, 21 November 2017.

209. NCVO Annual Report 1989–90, p. 2.

210. Hilton et al., 2012, p. 349.

211. Woodfield, 1987; Home Office, 1990.

212. See, for example, Lewis, 1999b, and Crowson et al., 2011, p. 499.

213. Hilton et al., 2012, p. 350. On growth of managerialism within the sector, see also Butler and Wilson, 1990, and Hilton, 2011.

214. See Finlayson, 1994, p. 338, and Butler and Wilson, 1990.

215. Rochester, 2013.

216. Letter from Gladstone to Handy, 1 December 1980; LMA/4016/IS/A/03/040(2).

217. See, for example, Handy, 1999.

218. Interview with Marilyn Taylor, 14 June 2017. Crowson et al., 2011, p. 512.

219. Interview with Andrew Purkis, 23 August 2017.

220. This issue is discussed in Chap. 7.

221. The Council was concerned by a series of reports in the national press and on the BBC about alleged dubious fundraising practice. Note to Executive Committee, *Malpractice report: Origins,* 29 April 1986; LMA/4016/IS/A/03/041.

222. NCVO Annual Report 1985–86.

223. NCVO, 1986.

224. NCVO Annual Report 1985–86, p. 23.

225. NCVO Annual Report 1985–86, p. 23.

226. The 1992 Charities Act amended the 1960 Act and tightened regulation on fundraising.

227. NCSS Annual Report 1978–79, p. 9. Standing Conference of Rural Community councils, 1978.

228. Interview with David Emerson, 3 May 2017.

229. NCSS Annual Report 1980–81, p. 18. Woollett, 1981.

230. NCSS Annual Report 1980–81.

231. NCVO Annual Report 1985–86, p. 16.

232. The standing conference had commissioned its own review in 1983 and the two reviews ran concurrently. Minutes of Executive Committee, 3 September 1985; LMA/4016/IS/A/01/042(1).

233. Leavett, 1985. Alan Leavett was a development commissioner.

234. NCVO Annual Report 1985–86.

235. *Report of joint NCVO/SCRCC working party set up in September 1985 to take forward consultation on Leavett Review*, Executive Committee 10 June 1986; LMA/4016/IS/A/01/043(10).

236. NCVO Annual Report 1986–87, p. 18.

237. Letter from Dr. Alan Rogers, chair of the standing conference, to the Executive Committee on 19 August 1985 on *Review of Rural Community councils*. Rogers said that whilst Nicholas Hinton had been broadly supportive of independence, the new chief executive, Bill Griffiths, made a last ditch effort to keep the movement within the Council; LMA/4016/IS/A/01/042(1). Rogers later wrote a history of the Development Commission. See Rogers, 1999.

238. Paper entitled *SCRCC (ACRE)/NCVO Joint Review* submitted to the Executive Committee on 10 June 1986; LMA/4016/IS/A/01/043(10).

239. Letter from Dr. Alan Rogers, *Op. Cit.*

240. NCVO Annual Report 1981–82.

241. Interview with Nicholas Deakin, 4 April 2017.

242. Minutes of Executive Committee, 5 June 1984; LMA/4016/IS/A/01/042(2).

243. NCVO Annual Report 1985–86.

244. Interview with Richard Gutch, 23 August 2017.

245. NCVO Annual Report 1987–88.

246. Paper entitled *NCVO/CVSNA working party*, submitted to Executive Committee, 7 June 1988; LMA/4016/IS/A/01/043(7).

247. NCVO Annual Report 1990–91. NACVS was renamed the National Association for Voluntary and Community Action (NAVCA) in 2006.

248. Interview with Nicholas Deakin, 4 April 2017.

249. Interview with Nicholas Deakin, 4 April 2017.

250. Interview with Richard Gutch, 23 August 2017.

251. On the ongoing struggle of resources for councils for Voluntary Service, see Rochester, 2012.

252. NCVO Annual Report 1983–84.

253. NCVO Annual Report 1986–87.

254. On National Food Alliance, see NCVO Annual Report 1987–88; on National Agency on Alcohol Misuse, see NCVO Annual Report 1982–83; on Family Forum, see NCVO Annual Report 1980–81.

255. Interview with Andrew Purkis, 23 August 2017.

256. NCVO Annual Report 1980–81.

257. NCVO Annual Report 1988–89.

258. Interview with David Emerson, 3 May 2017.

259. Interview with Bharat Mehta, 27 July 2017.

260. Interview with Bill Seary, 6 July 2017.

261. Interview with Sara Morrison, 2 August 2017.

262. Interview with Bill Seary, 6 July 2017.

263. Minutes of Executive Committee, 6 March 1990; LMA/4016/IS/A/01/043(5).

264. Minutes of Executive Committee, 1 October and 11 June 1991; LMA/4016/IS/A/01/043(3).
265. NCVO Annual Report 1991–92, p. 17.
266. Director's Report to Executive Committee on 6 October 1992; LMA/4016/IS/A/01/043(3).
267. Crowson, 2011, p. 496.
268. Crowson et al., 2011, p. 499.
269. Lewis, 1999a, p. 267.
270. NCVO Annual Report 1990–91, p. 9.
271. Lewis, 1999a, p. 266.

REFERENCES

Addy, T., & Scott, D. (1987). *Fatal impacts? The MSC and voluntary action*. Manchester: William Temple Foundation.

Brenton, M. (1985). *The voluntary sector in British social services*. Harlow: Longman.

Butler, R., & Wilson, D. (1990). *Managing voluntary and non-profit organisations: Strategy and structure*. London: Routledge.

Charity Commission and Centre for Charity Effectiveness. (2017). *Taken on trust: The awareness and effectiveness of charity trustees in England and Wales*. London: Charity Commission.

Clark, A. (1993). *Diaries*. London: Weidenfeld & Nicolson.

Clarke, J., Cochrane, A., & Smart, C. (1987). *Ideologies of welfare: From dreams to disillusion*. London: Hutchinson.

Craig, G. (2011). Forward to the past: Can the UK black and minority ethnic third sector survive? *Voluntary Sector Review, 2*(3), 367–389.

Craig, G., & Taylor, M. (2002). Dangerous liaison: Local government and the voluntary and community sectors. In C. Glendinning, M. Powell, & K. Rummery (Eds.), *Partnerships: New Labour and the governance of welfare* (pp. 131–149). Bristol: The Policy Press.

Crowson, N. (2011). Introduction: The voluntary sector in 1980s Britain. *Contemporary British History, 25*(4), 491–498.

Crowson, N., Hilton, M., McKay, J., & Marway, H. (Eds.). (2011). Witness seminar: The voluntary sector in 1980s Britain, abridged. *Contemporary British History, 25*(4), 499–519.

Davies, R. (2015). *Public good by private means: How philanthropy shapes Britain*. London: Alliance Publishing Trust.

Davis Smith, J. (1982). An uneasy alliance: Volunteers and trade unions. In R. Hedley & J. Davis Smith (Eds.), *Volunteering and society: Principles and practice*. London: Bedford Square Press.

Deakin, N. (1988). Shaped to Fit? In NCVO (Ed.), *Sir George Haynes Lecture 1987: Voluntary organisations and democracy* (pp. 13–21). London: NVCO.

Finlayson, G. (1994). *Citizen, state, and social welfare in Britain 1830–1990*. Oxford: Clarendon Press.

Forsyth, M. (1984). *Politics on the rates: How the Left are using public money to finance their activities*. London: Conservative Political Centre.

Gladstone, F. (1979). *Voluntary action in a changing world*. London: Bedford Square Press.

Gladstone, F. (1982). *Charity, law and social justice*. London: Bedford Square Press.

Gorman, T., Robson, B., Sharpe, B., & Taylor, C. (1985). *Qualgos just grow: Political bodies in voluntary clothing, Policy study, no. 69.* London: Centre for Policy Studies.

Gutch, R. (1992). *Contracting lessons from the United States.* London: NCVO.

Hadley, R., & Hatch, S. (1981). *Social welfare and the failure of the state: Centralised social services and participatory alternatives.* London: Allen & Unwin.

Handy, C. (1981). *Improving effectiveness in voluntary organisations.* London: NCVO.

Handy, C. (1999). *Understanding organisations.* London: Penguin.

Hatch, S. (1980). *Outside the state: Voluntary organisations in three towns.* London: Croom Helm.

Hilton, M. (2011). Politics is ordinary: Non-governmental organisations and political participation in contemporary Britain. *Twentieth Century British History, 22*(2), 230–268.

Hilton, M., Crowson, N., Mouhot, J., & McKay, J. (2012). *A historical guide to NGOs in Britain: Charities, civil society and the voluntary sector since 1945.* Basingstoke: Palgrave Macmillan.

Home Office. (1989). *White Paper: Charities, a framework for the future,* Cmd. 694. London: HMSO.

Home Office. (1990). *Efficiency scrutiny of government funding of the voluntary sector: Profiting from partnership.* London: HMSO.

Jarrett, M. (1990, November). The black voluntary sector. *NCVO News.*

Knapp, M. (1984). *The Economics of social care.* Basingstoke: Macmillan.

Le Grand, J. (1991). The state of welfare. In J. Hills (Ed.), *The state of welfare: The welfare state in Britain since 1974.* Oxford: Clarendon Press.

Leavett, A. (1985). *Role and relationships of RCCs: Review on behalf of the Development Commission.* London: Rural Development Commission.

Lewis, J. (1999a). Voluntary and informal welfare. In R. Page & R. Silburn (Eds.), *British social welfare in the twentieth century* (pp. 249–270). Basingstoke: Macmillan.

Lewis, J. (1999b). Reviewing the relationship between the voluntary sector and the state in Britain in the 1990s. *Voluntas, 10*(3), 255–270.

MacGregor, S., & Pimlott, B. (Eds.). (1990). *Tackling the inner cities: The 1980s reviewed, prospects for the 1990s.* Oxford: Clarendon Press.

Major, J. (1999). *John Major: The autobiography.* London: Harper Collins.

Milligan, C., & Conradson, D. (Eds.). (2006). *Landscapes of voluntarism: New spaces of health, welfare and governance.* Bristol: The Policy Press.

Morgan, G. (2012). Public benefit and charitable status: Assessing a 20-year process of reforming the primary legal framework for voluntary activity in the UK. *Voluntary Sector Review, 3*(1), 67–91.

Nathan, L. (1990). *Effectiveness and the voluntary sector: Report of a working party established by NCVO.* London: NCVO.

National Coalition for Independent Action. (2014). *NCIA inquiry into the future of voluntary services: Working paper 1: The position and role of national infrastructure bodies concerning the cuts to and privatisation of public services.* London: NCIA.

NCVO. (1984a). *Relations between the voluntary sector and government: A code for voluntary organisations.* London: NCVO.

NCVO. (1984b). *The management and effectiveness of voluntary organisations.* London: NCVO.

NCVO. (1984c). *Joint action – The way forward: Community involvement in local economic development.* London: Bedford Square Press.

NCVO. (1984d, December). Interview with Nicholas Hinton. *Voluntary Action.*

NCVO. (1985). *The voluntary sector: A response to the Centre for Policy Studies' publication 'Qualgos just grow', subtitled 'political bodies in voluntary clothing.* London: NCVO.

NCVO. (1986). *Malpractice in fundraising for charity: Report to the National Council for Voluntary Organisations of a working party.* London: NCVO.

Rhodes, R., & Marsh, D. (1992). Implementing Thatcherism: Policy change in the 1980s. *Parliamentary Affairs, 45*(1), 33–50.

Rochester, C. (2012). Councils for Voluntary Service: The end of a long road? *Voluntary Sector Review, 3*(1), 103–110.

Rochester, C. (2013). *Rediscovering voluntary action: The beat of a different drum.* Basingstoke: Palgrave Macmillan.

Rogers, A. (1999). *The most revolutionary measure: A history of the Rural Development Commission.* Salisbury: Rural Development Commission.

Standing Conference of Rural Community councils. (1978). *The decline of rural services: A report.* London: NCSS.

Taylor, M. (1992). The changing role of the non-profit sector in Britain: Moving towards the market. In B. Gidron, R. Kramer, & L. Salamon (Eds.), *Government and the third sector: Emerging relationships in welfare states* (pp. 147–175). San Francisco: Jossey-Bass Publishers.

Thane, P., & Davidson, R. (2016). *The Child Poverty Action Group, 1965–2015.* London: Child Poverty Action Group.

Tumin, W. (1992). *On trust report: Increasing the effectiveness of charity trustees and management committees.* London: NCVO.

Webb, A., & Wistow, G. (1987). *Social work, social care and social planning.* Harlow: Longman.

Williams, I. (1989). *The alms trade: Charities, past, present and future.* London: Unwin Hyman.

Woodfield, P. (1987). *Efficiency scrutiny of the supervision of charities: Report to the home secretary and the economic secretary to the treasury.* London: HMSO.

Woollett, S. (1981). *Alternative rural services: A community initiatives manual.* London: Bedford Square Press.

CHAPTER 9

A Golden Age?

INTRODUCTION

Despite the uncertain political climate, the Council emerged from the 1980s in a stronger position. The changes initiated by Nicholas Hinton and Usha Prashar enhanced its reputation, and it entered the new decade as a leaner, more focused organisation. The associated groups and networks had been moved to independence, and it had taken the decision to concentrate on a smaller range of issues relevant to the sector as a whole. The wisdom of this strategy would be questioned in the future, and some argued that severing the local from the national undermined its legitimacy and ability to innovate.[1] But at the time it was seen as a logical response to financial insecurity and the need to develop a more strategic approach. With a stronger membership base, an improved financial position, and newly purchased accommodation in central London, the Council felt confident enough to turn its attention to the longer-term future of the sector.

The Deakin commission set the agenda for the sector and the Council for the next decade and heralded a new era of constructive partnership with the state.[2] Significant institutional changes were introduced by New Labour, following its electoral victory in 1997, many of them arising from the commission's recommendations. Unprecedented public funds were made available to voluntary organisations, with a focus on public service delivery and infrastructure. A new Charities Act was put in place, bringing about the most far-reaching changes to the legal definition of charity for 400 years. New tax regulations were introduced to encourage individual and corporate giving and a Compact was signed between the government and the sector, laying down fundamental principles to govern their relationship. Looking back on this era, it is no surprise to hear Stuart Etherington, who took over as director of the Council in 1994, describe it as 'a golden age'. It is a verdict shared by a number of academics.[3]

© The Author(s) 2019
J. Davis Smith, *100 Years of NCVO and Voluntary Action*,
https://doi.org/10.1007/978-3-030-02774-2_9

Not all commentators, however, were convinced. For some, the growing reach of the state raised fundamental questions about the sector's independence and concerns were raised about a split that was developing between large charities with access to contract funding and smaller groups without.[4] The Council, perhaps surprisingly, shared these concerns. By the end of the period it had begun to distance itself from what it saw as an overemphasis on service delivery and push for a new agenda for the sector, more reminiscent of its early founding values, with an emphasis on civil society and local community action. Prescient, opportunistic, or simply fortuitous with its timing, just as the New Labour government was running out of steam, the Council found that such ideas chimed with a new political project being developed by the youthful leader of the main opposition party. When the *Big Society* was launched by the prime minister, David Cameron, following the general election of 2010, the Council was well placed to lead the sector into what promised to be another era of constructive relations with the state.[5] That events did not turn out as anticipated is the subject of the next chapter.

CHANGES AT THE TOP

Judy Weleminsky's tenure as director came to an end in 1994, after just three years. Her time had not been happy, although she can claim success for the move from Bedford Square to King's Cross and a new focus on membership. She feels she was badly treated by the Council's Executive Committee and suggests it was less than supportive of her desire to combine motherhood with her leadership role. On returning from maternity leave, she says, 'I knew from the minute I got back that my cards were marked and I was not flavour of the month anymore.'[6] Weleminsky had cut her teeth within the community movement in Brixton and at the National Federation of Community Organisations, where she was well respected. By the time she arrived at the Council it had shed its local networks and was focusing almost exclusively on policy and research, which did not play to her strengths. She has acknowledged that she was always 'a bit more of an action person'.[7] She left with unfinished business. There was more she wanted to do on membership and to change the style of the organisation to be 'a little less superior and keen on itself'.[8] One thing is clear. Future leaders all had reason to be grateful for her leadership in steering through the move to King's Cross, which proved fundamental in ensuring the Council's sustainability.

Weleminsky's replacement was better suited to the organisation's new focus. Stuart Etherington, appointed director in November 1994, came from a large national charity, the National Institute for Deaf People (now Action on Hearing Loss), which he joined in 1987 as director of public affairs, before taking over as chief executive. Previous roles included director of the charity, Good Practices in Mental Health, and a policy analyst in local government.[9] Etherington was appointed with the dual aim of bringing financial sustainability to the Council and strengthening its role as a membership organisation.

He was also brought in to provide continuity after the turnover of four directors in just over ten years. His vision was that the Council should be seen as the trade body for the sector, analogous to the role of the CBI and the TUC. In his view, the Council 'seemed to have lost its sense of direction over the previous period'. Its reputation with government had suffered and it had neglected its membership.[10] Etherington was brought in to shake things up. An article on his appointment in *The Times* suggested the Council had 'lately been seriously under-performing' and that he had been hired to lead 'the management revolution' that had 'been taking place in the voluntary sector'. He told the paper his priorities were 'a staff structure that works, and a management structure that delivers'.[11]

Etherington kicked off his leadership with a major reorganisation, creating four new departments: membership and advice services, policy, internal services, and public affairs. Staff numbers were significantly reduced, with the aim of putting the Council onto a secure financial footing.[12] Funding had always been an issue. Despite the core grant from government, annual deficits remained a regular feature and by the mid-1980s had reached £250,000.[13] Books were balanced only by drawdowns from the proceeds of the appeal funds, launched at intervals to secure corporate support. By the early 1990s it appeared that it had finally got its finances under control, following a restructure carried out by Prashar, and in 1991–92 it reported a small surplus of £40,000.[14] Any euphoria was short-lived, as it was back in deficit the following year.[15] Income grew significantly during the first 15 years of Etherington's period in office, rising from £4.2 million in 1999–2000 to £13.3 million in 2007–08, largely due to funding from government programmes.[16] Etherington also identified early in his leadership the need to diversify income to guard against a decline in public funding. In 2006 an enterprise department was established to increase earned income 'in order to ensure that our independence is maintained'.[17] Such was the success that, almost alone among the leading umbrella bodies, it could ride out the storm when the Coalition government ended core funding following its election in 2010.[18] Income from CAF continued to be hugely significant, but there was growing resentment at the hefty payments made each year and discussions were opened in 1996 about the possibility of a buyout. The discussions broke down without agreement.[19] Another attempt by CAF to sever the arrangement in 2005 was again unsuccessful.[20] The Council's dependency on the vagaries of CAF's performance was made clear in March 2001 when the Board heard that a downturn in its income had led to a projected annual shortfall of between £200,000 and £400,000. Further restructuring was carried out to meet the deficit.[21]

Etherington's senior colleagues from this time talk admiringly of his strengths as a leader. Adam Gaines, who joined in 1995 as director of public affairs, describes him as 'a brilliant strategist' and 'a great leader and manager'.[22] 'His towering strength', he says, 'is his ability to see the key strategic issues that need taking forward and to develop initiatives and solutions to help meet them.' Janet Morrison, who served as director of policy and research, agrees, saying he brought 'real clarity of purpose' to the role and a sense of 'what our business model was and how we could drive the strategy of the organisation forward'.[23] For Margaret Bolton, Etherington was 'excellent on strategy, gave very clear direction on leadership, and was a very good manager in terms of giving people rein to do their jobs'.[24] Staff remember the Council as an exciting place to work. Gaines says it 'was a great place to work'; the organisation had 'a really big agenda' both for the sector and internally, with 'an increased emphasis on the need of its members'.[25] Morrison recalls a sense of energy about the place: 'I had the feeling it was a place which had given birth to lots of great organisations in its history, it felt like it was a place that spawned new things that were all about social capital and giving people a voice.'[26] The new premises helped. According to Morrison, 'it felt like it was part of a hub for the sector, which I don't think we ever felt at Bedford Square'.[27] The new streamlined strategy, however, had its downsides. As Morrison remembers, the focus on 'future sustainability and financial wellbeing', after Etherington took over, meant the Council 'lost some of the "thousand flowers bloom" approach, so there were less of those just sparking up small projects and funds'.[28]

Etherington was famed for his ability to work constructively with his Board and he was fortunate in the chairs he worked with. Geoffrey Chandler, who appointed him, stepped down in January 1996 after six years in the role. His background was business. He had been director general of the National Economic Development Office and held senior positions in Shell.[29] He was instrumental in reforming the Council's governance and building stronger links with the corporate sector. Morrison remembers him as 'an old school gentleman' with 'great judgement'.[30] Others have suggested that he was overly interventionist in his approach and poor at sticking to the boundaries between chair and director.[31] He was succeeded by Winifred Tumin, who had been Etherington's chair at the Royal National Institute for Deaf People, and they formed a powerful alliance during the first phase of his leadership.[32] Tumin is remembered by people who worked with her with great affection and admiration: 'She was an absolutely amazing lady', recalls Gaines, 'very impressive in her view of the importance of the sector' and with a 'quite extraordinary' drive to push things through.[33] 'A unique force in terms of public life, in public policy and what she saw the role of NCVO to be', agrees Campbell Robb, who was director of public policy at the Council.[34] For Etherington it was her intellect and passion that stands out: 'She was intellectually very able; very good at chairing board meetings, a bit eccentric in the best possible way, and she did all of our work around the reform of charity law and public benefit.'[35] Tumin was replaced in 2001 by Norman Warner, who served just one term before joining the government as minister of health.[36] Etherington remembers him as 'very able, politically astute, and good at reading the political runes'. He was succeeded in 2004 by Graham Melmoth, an interesting appointment as he came from the cooperative movement rather than the mainstream voluntary sector.[37] He was an inspired choice. Not only was he regarded as a superb chair of meetings, he gave legitimacy to the Council's ambition to broaden its sphere of influence to other non-profit organisations within the newly conceptualised *third sector*.[38] According to Julia Cleverdon, Melmoth 'brought a lot' to the Council. 'He was high on integrity, came from the Co-op that cared about the bottom up, knew a bit about how you ran much more complicated organisations, and had a very sharp eye on the money.'[39] Reflecting on his time, Melmoth suggests he might 'have brought a little bit of management discipline and lightened it up a bit as well'.[40] In 2010 he was succeeded by the BBC newsreader, Martyn Lewis.[41] Again the timing was good. Lewis, with close links to senior Conservative politicians, helped ensure the Council retained its political influence following the election of the Conservative-led Coalition government. He was also hugely interested in volunteering and played an important part in brokering discussions with Volunteering England that led to the merger in 2013. Etherington recalls him as a great chairman, 'the world's greatest optimist', and 'a great external ambassador for the organisation'.[42]

GOVERNANCE AND MEMBERSHIP

Despite the changes introduced by Hinton and Prashar, it was clear that further modifications were required to bring the Council's governance up to date. The Executive Committee was too large for purposeful decision-making and the practice of delegating major policy discussions to sub-groups raised concerns that power was leaking away from members. In October 1992, a working party was established to produce recommendations for a new model.[43] The changes, agreed by members the following year, resulted in a radical transformation in the way the Council ran its affairs. Gone was the Executive Committee, which had been in place since it was established, replaced by a new slimmed-down Board of Trustees of 24 members, supported by a finance and general purposes sub-committee.[44] This model, taken from the corporate sector, also saw the re-designation of the role of director to chief executive. Ironically, given one of the drivers behind the changes, there were concerns that the smaller board would reduce the link with the membership as there would be fewer places for elected representatives.[45] To offset such criticism, an advisory council was set up under the president, Sir Campbell Adamson, although membership was composed mainly of business leaders.[46]

More important for the longer term, the review called for a concerted membership drive with the aim of achieving the 'maximum number possible, so that NCVO could properly call itself the representative body and collective voice of the voluntary sector'.[47] For the moment, the Council still sought to recruit only national organisations, although this restriction would soon be lifted. Further tweaking of the governance structure took place in 1996 when, somewhat confusingly, the finance and general purposes sub-committee was replaced by a new executive committee and a new electoral college was set up to increase consultation with members.[48] In 2008 more changes were introduced. The Board was reduced in size to just 12 (since the changes made in

1993 it had grown again to 40) and there was concern that it was not only too 'large and unwieldy', but risked confusing 'governance and representation'.[49] The executive committee was scrapped and in its place an audit and risk committee and remuneration and human relations committee were established. A new members' assembly was set up 'reflecting the breadth and geographical spread' of members as 'a forum for debating sector policy'.[50] The assembly was to meet twice a year, once outside London, with members elected for a three-year term. Finally, it seemed that the Council had come up with a governance structure that worked.

More significant still was the change to the constitution introduced in 2000.[51] For all of its first 80 years, the Council sought only to recruit national organisations into membership. Now for the first time, apart from the concession offered under Prashar to groups focusing on diversity and equality, local organisations were accepted as full members.[52] This was a key turning point in the Council's history.[53] In 2000, membership stood at 1600.[54] The door was opened for a big expansion over the next few years. The change made sense financially and strategically in that it helped soften the blow of the loss of the local networks. But it also raised accusations that the Council was competing unfairly with other umbrella organisations.[55] In 2005, free membership was introduced for small organisations with an income of less than £10,000 per annum, which led to a further significant rise in numbers.[56] Not everyone was convinced that the opening up of membership to local groups was the right decision. Morrison suggests that 'it created a little bit of a split personality' in that the Council still 'spoke in a kind of corporate way, which was driven more by contracting and the contract culture', yet was now trying to embrace smaller organisations for which this agenda 'was less relevant'.[57]

The difficulty of riding these two horses was a perennial challenge. At its annual meeting in February 1998 a special resolution from Community Matters (the new name for the National Federation of Community Organisations) proposed to instruct the Board 'to ensure that, when policy statements are made by NCVO, it is made explicit as to whether they are intended to reflect the interests and views of the professionalised, staff-led voluntary sector, or of the much broader diversity of the voluntary and community sectors'.[58] The resolution was withdrawn after the Board agreed to discuss the matter further, but it was a clear indication that trying to represent large voluntary organisations and small community groups was fraught with difficulties. Despite these concerns, member satisfaction remained high. In 2002 an independent review reported 87 per cent of members felt the Council was effective in representing the sector,[59] while a 2007 internal review reported that members found the Council 'independent', not 'partisan', although some non-members felt it was 'just another layer of bureaucracy' and 'not in the real world'.[60] The Council set about developing a range of services to woo its supporters, including an inquiries help desk, an advice service on employment matters, an online resource 'askNCVO', and a buddying scheme, 'Only Connect', to help members learn from each another.[61] It also negotiated a range of brokered services, offering discounts on such goods and services as IT, printing, and financial advice. By 1999 it was estimated that savings to members totalled over £1 million per year, as well, of course, as bringing a tidy sum to the Council in commission.[62] In 2002, membership had reached 2600 and in 2006 the Council welcomed its 5000th member.[63]

REPUTATIONS

In 1993 the Voluntary Services Unit commissioned a review of the Council.[64] Carried out by Coopers and Lybrand, the terms of reference were to examine the value for money the government was receiving for its grant and the Council's effectiveness in meeting the needs of the voluntary sector. The review had some encouraging things to say, but was also highly critical. It ran concurrently with the internal inquiry set up by Chandler in 1992 and its recommendation for an overhaul of governance echoed the Council's own plans. It highlighted high levels of member and non-member satisfaction, but suggested the Council could do more in 'demonstrating leadership of the voluntary sector and taking the high ground on key issues on behalf of the sector'. In particular, there was felt to be a need to reach out more to large charities, many of which demonstrated 'a lack of commitment' to the organisation and 'a very limited recognition' of its value.[65] Respondents told the reviewers that 'if NCVO didn't exist, it would need to be invented', but the research also pointed to 'an element of disillusionment'. There was a need for greater clarity of vision, measurement of outcomes, and 'sharpening of focus'.[66] The Council, it concluded, was doing adequately but could do better. To ensure value for money, the review recommended that tighter restrictions be placed on the use of the core grant. The government accepted the findings and told the Council it hoped it would make 'a positive response'.[67] On the crucial issue of funding, it agreed that it should give 'a fairly firm steer' on priorities 'to justify the public expenditure involved', although it hoped this could be arrived at through dialogue.[68]

The Council's response was fairly relaxed. It argued that many of the suggested changes had been anticipated and were in process of being implemented. However, it strongly challenged the suggestion that government should have a role in dictating its strategic priorities, arguing that its primary responsibility was to its membership and the wider sector.[69] In 1995 the Voluntary Services Unit announced a cut in the core grant on the grounds that the Council's work didn't fit with the government's focus on volunteering and refugees. The Board expressed itself 'disappointed and alarmed at the extent of the cuts being proposed' and said it found it 'difficult to understand that a vital part of the sector's infrastructure was considered not relevant to the government's volunteering objectives'.[70] It was a sign of the government's determination to exert greater control over its funding. It was also symptomatic of the Council's declining reach and influence, following the loss of its networks and the setting up of the Volunteer Centre.

SETTING THE AGENDA

By the early 1990s there was a feeling within the Council that it needed to set a new agenda. It had become increasingly disillusioned by the coarsening of relations with government and with what it saw as an overemphasis within the sector on service provision at the expense of advocacy.[71] When in 1993, a highly controversial report was published by the Home Office, calling for a formal separation of these two roles, the Council felt the need to act.[72] There is, Chandler wrote in the annual report for 1993–94, an 'urgent need for the sector itself to take stock of its role in a changing world and to influence the debate about itself'.[73]

The Home Office report was not a government publication. It had been written by a team of researchers from the think tank Centris, led by Barry Knight, an ex-Home Office civil servant. Such was the controversy the report generated, the Home Office soon distanced itself from it, and a second edition, released a few months after the first, was published directly by Centris. Much of the content was unremarkable, consisting of a potted history of the sector and of leading philanthropists over the previous 400 years. Its recommendations, however, caused an outcry. In the introduction to the second edition, the authors wryly comment that 'the book has both touched some old sensitivities and identified some new ones'.[74] Most controversial was the suggestion that the sector should be divided for tax relief purposes into two distinct camps: a 'first force' of campaigning and advocacy groups, described as 'authentic voluntary action, prophetic, vision led, reformist, independent of government' and 'pursuing independent energy for moral purposes', which should not receive any public funds but would be eligible for charitable relief; and a 'third force' of larger charities, which act 'philanthropically on sub-contract from the state' to deliver public services under contract to government, and for whom charitable tax breaks would be withdrawn.[75]

The sector, or at least the established part, piled in with criticism, arguing that such a simplistic division between campaigning and service delivery made no sense. Many service delivery agencies saw it as their duty to campaign and their knowledge and legitimacy to do so came from their experience on the front line.[76] The Council joined in the attack, arguing that it took the sector in a backward and unhelpful direction.[77] It had a more specific reason to be irked by the report, which included the radical suggestion that in future there would be no need for intermediary organisations, as any 'residual functions' could be supplied by private consultants.[78] Intermediaries, it concluded, 'belong nowhere'. As bureaucracies, 'they are neither rooted in the cultural traditions of the voluntary organisations they work with' nor 'are they part of the state, which in culture and organisation they resemble and on whose patronage they depend'. It repeated the erroneous claim that the Council was formed in 1919 by 'two civil servants', but its blistering critique was in a long tradition of attacks on the legitimacy of intermediary bodies, particularly those receiving public funds, and it clearly touched a nerve.[79]

The idea of a new inquiry to examine the future of the sector was first mooted within the Council in 1994.[80] But it was not until the following year that work got underway. In addition to providing a corrective to the Centris report, Etherington suggests the Council was keen 'to head off a proposal by Michael Brophy at CAF to establish a Royal Commission'.[81] To chair the inquiry, or commission, the Council turned to the eminent academic, Nicholas Deakin. Deakin had long been associated with the Council, having been both chair of the Council for Voluntary Service—National Association and a member of the Executive Committee. He was ideal for the role. As well as a long involvement with the sector, he had a glittering career in academia and worked within government at both national and local level. 'The job of Chair was hawked around', he recalls, and 'it was widely seen as an opportunity, but also a challenge, to produce a commission report in a short period of time'.[82]

It was the first major review of the sector since Wolfenden 20 years previously and the Council was determined to learn from past mistakes.[83] One of the problems with Wolfenden was timing. When it was published in 1978, it had received a generally favourable response from James Callaghan's Labour administration. But the election of a Conservative government under Margaret Thatcher in 1979, which came to power with a very different vision for the sector, meant there was little follow-through. The Deakin commission similarly reported just before a change of government. However, New Labour's victory in 1997, rather than derailing the new agenda, was crucial to its implementation. The timing was not purely by chance. According to Deakin and Etherington, the commission was banking on a Labour victory and did much to court the shadow charity minister, Alun Michael, in advance of publication.[84] The commission's agenda of partnership matched emerging New Labour philosophy, and Tony Blair's victory ensured many of Deakin's recommendations fell on receptive ears.

The commission was independent of the Council, although it provided funding and acted as the secretariat. It was made up of 12 senior individuals who gathered written and oral evidence throughout the second half of 1995. It published its report, *Meeting the Challenge of Change*, in July 1996.[85] Top of its list was independence. Partnership with government, it argued, was to be desired, but it must be on an equal basis and organisations must be free to campaign irrespective of any funding relationship.[86] There were over 60 recommendations covering three main areas of focus: external relations of the sector (particularly with government), the legal and fiscal environment, and internal management and governance. Deakin said his aim was to increase awareness of the value of voluntary action and create 'a more positive climate within which organisations can operate without putting their independence at risk' and would be 'helped to make their distinctive contribution with the minimum of bureaucracy' and without damaging 'the dazzling variety' which was one of the hallmarks of the sector.[87]

The Conservative government's response was less than enthusiastic. Written by Virginia Bottomley, *Raising the Voltage* was described by one Deakin commissioner as not so much raising the voltage as 'turning the lights out'.[88] Academic reaction was mixed. For the Liberal peer, Lord Dahrendorf, the report recommended 'too much co-ordination and central organization'.[89] Diana Leat and Perri 6 felt it was 'self-referential' and 'backward looking', while Jane Lewis called it 'statesmanlike'.[90] The press was also undecided. The *Economist* felt the report was 'timid', while the *Financial Times* praised it for its radicalism. Polly Toynbee, in The *Independent,* felt it contained 'excellent recommendations for revitalising the sector', but that there was unlikely to be agreement on its common purpose, and she concluded that there was nothing in 'this bunch of nettles' for politicians except a 'guaranteed row of nuclear proportions'.[91]

Looking back, two things stand out. First, the report's lack of a radical edge. Compared to the Centris report, it was rather timid, a 'Consensus document', according to one academic, and there was criticism that its authors were too close to the Council.[92] Deakin himself, reflecting on the report 20 years later, accepts that it had limitations and could have gone further in setting a more positive vision: 'What was not so good in the report', he remembers, 'was that we muted our sharper criticisms of government and we shouldn't have done that. We could have been more radical.'[93] But it was just what was needed at the time. Relations with government had gone sour and there was a need to develop a more positive relationship based on a more equitable partnership. There was also a pressing need to sort out the architecture of the sector—charity law, charity tax, and infrastructure. Deakin might not have come up with eye-catching recommendations to match those of Knight, but at least they were sensible, in tune with the tenor of the times, and held out the promise that, if implemented, they would make a positive difference to the sector. Jeremy Kendall suggests that the report was deliberately 'Big tent' and 'permissive' to allow it to appeal to interests across the political spectrum.[94] The Council overall was delighted with the commission's deliberations. Etherington recalls 'that the narrative was right for the time' and the report was 'massively successful', although he feels in retrospect that it was perhaps 'too government-facing' and didn't have enough to say about 'the emerging dynamics within the sector and the growth of much more informal organisations'.[95] The task of implementing Deakin dominated the work of the Council for the next decade.

NEW LABOUR

For many scholars, the New Labour governments of Tony Blair and Gordon Brown represent the high point of relations between the voluntary sector and the state. Pete Alcock, for example, has argued that 'history may judge the New Labour era to have been a high water mark in partnership between the state and the sector'.[96] Certainly in terms of funding this was true, with more public money going to voluntary organisations than at any other time. But it wasn't just money. New Labour courted the sector like never before, drawing it ever more closely into the policy-making arena as a key agent in its plans for a radical transformation of British society. For New Labour, voluntary organisations were a central component of the *Third Way*. This was a rather vague concept, inspired by the work of the British social scientist, Anthony Giddens, and the American communitarian thinker, Amitai Etzioni, which signalled the government's intention to break with both Labour's statist past and Thatcher's preoccupation with the market.[97] It was also intended to correct what was portrayed as Labour's past hostility to the voluntary sector, although it has been argued elsewhere that this was a partial reading of history that ignored the strong alternative tradition within the Labour movement.[98]

Blair used a speech to the Council's annual meeting in January 1999 to outline his vision for the voluntary movement: 'History shows', he said, 'that the most successful societies are those that harness the energies of voluntary action, giving due recognition to the third sector of voluntary and community organisations.'[99] Partnership between the state and the sector was seen as crucial to harnessing this energy.[100] The Council enthusiastically set about making this vision a reality. Bolton, who was director of policy and research at the Council at the time, recalls the government was very open to the sector and access was good: 'A lot of new MPs in that intake had been voluntary sector workers. We had produced the Deakin report and we'd worked very closely with Alun Michael on that so it felt a bit like the door was open around the government saying what's needed for a really healthy, vibrant voluntary sector because we want to help you achieve that.'[101] By 2002 Etherington was speaking admiringly about 'a growing understanding of, and emphasis on working with, the voluntary sector across government' and proclaiming that 'partnership working has become the norm'.[102]

An enhanced Active Community Unit was established within the Cabinet Office in 2001 to lead the government's work with the sector and replace the largely ineffectual Voluntary Services Unit, and the government embarked upon a major programme of financial support.[103] There had been large-scale funding programmes before, but they had been policy specific. What was different now was the scale of New Labour's support for strengthening the sector, what Kendall has called 'horizontal' policy mainstreaming.[104] A Treasury cross-cutting review in 2002 into the role of voluntary organisations in service delivery was followed by a spate of funding programmes.[105] First, Futurebuilders to help organisations bid for contracts, then Communitybuilders to support community groups, then ChangeUp, which was launched in 2004 with a budget of £150 million, aimed at infrastructure organisations to develop their work to support front-line organisations. A series of hubs were set up to offer advice and support on a range of topics, from information technology to volunteering. The Council secured the lead in running four of these, on IT, workforce development, trustees, and governance and sustainable funding.[106] The hubs were in time replaced by a number of national support services, funded by a new arms-length organisation, Capacitybuilders, and the Council secured a leading role with three of these, covering governance and leadership, campaigning, and social change.[107] 'Never before', Alcock notes, 'had so much public investment been available to the sector.'[108] The Council was criticised by some for monopolising this funding and the long-term value of the work of these 'builder' funds has been questioned.[109] It, however, saw capacity building as very much *its* business and part of its long-running mission to raise standards within the sector. Work and funds were shared, at least to an extent. The Governance Hub, for example, collaborated with Volunteering England on a campaign to recruit trustees, *Get on Board*, which it was estimated reached over 12 million people in the media and registered over 2500 people interested in taking on a trustee position.[110]

Central to the new spirit of partnership was the Compact, a non-binding statement of principle, setting out the values governing relations between the government and the sector. Once again the Council was at the centre of developments. The call for such an agreement had been included both within the Deakin report and New Labour's own pre-1997 general election statement on the sector, *Building the Future Together*, although the idea had originally come from separate work by Deakin with the Treasury.[111] It was rejected by the Conservative government as being neither 'sensible' nor 'usefully achievable'.[112] But after Labour's election victory, the Council worked closely with the new government on the development of the concept, and in November 1998, just over two years after it was first proposed, a Compact for England was launched.[113] It was followed by five topic-specific codes and a separate code for local government. Separate Compacts were also later launched in Wales, Scotland, and Northern Ireland as, following devolution in 1999, responsibility for voluntary sector matters were transferred to the devolved nations.[114] The Council provided administrative support to the Compact Working Group, which had been set up to negotiate with government. Chaired by Sir Kenneth Stowe, it embarked on a consultation exercise involving over 20,000 organisations, representing, according to Stowe, one of the largest consultation exercises ever undertaken with the sector.[115] Compact Voice, the independent voice on the Compact, was housed within the Council, and in 2003 the Council set up the Compact Advocacy Programme to take forward cases of breach of the Compact on behalf of the sector.[116]

How important was the Compact? Kendall has suggested that it was 'completely without precedent in this country or elsewhere' and represented 'an unparalleled step change in the positioning of the voluntary sector in public policy'.[117] Certainly it was hugely important symbolically, containing as it did a statement from the prime minister that the government recognised the independence of the sector and its right to criticise government, irrespective of the funding relationship. After many years of hostile attacks, this was a major advance. 'It was an attempt to set the relationship in a different way', recalls Deakin, 'and whatever one says now about its effectiveness it was at the time an important step forward.'[118] There were also practical benefits, with a number of groups, particularly at a local level, citing successful use of it to influence government policy and funding practice.[119] Results overall, however, were mixed. The lack of resources to support its roll-out, combined with its voluntary nature, meant it was slow to gain traction and often ignored by government. Meta Zimmeck was probably correct, when reviewing the Compact's achievements ten years after its introduction, to argue that 'like so many of New Labour's initiatives, it promised more than it has delivered'.[120]

CHARITY LAW AND TAXATION

If the Compact was the symbol of a new spirit of partnership, the reform of charity law remained perhaps the most pressing priority for the sector. The early 1990s had seen a welcome relaxation by the Charity Commission of the hard-line stance on campaigning during the previous decade. This owed much to the chief charity commissioner, Richard Fries, who was commended by the Council for all he had done 'to facilitate progress in a more liberal direction'.[121] Nevertheless, the restrictive guidelines remained in place, and charity law remained an anachronistic throwback to an Elizabethan regulation introduced at the beginning of the seventeenth century. The main area of controversy concerned the definition of public benefit, which had proved impervious to reform, despite several previous attempts.[122] With relations with government at an all-time high, the Council sensed an opening for change. In 1998 it formed the charity law reform advisory group, which argued for 'a stronger "public benefit" test'.[123] The recommendation was picked up by the government in its 2002 report, *Private Action, Public Benefit*.[124] The Council immediately called for legislation to bring this into law.[125] A charities bill coalition was set up representing the largest UK charities, and the Council embarked on a major lobbying campaign.[126] A new Charities Bill was included in the Queen's Speech in November 2003. In May 2004 the charities bill coalition was relaunched as the coalition for a charities act. In 2006 the new Charities Act reached the statute book. It represented the biggest change to charity law for over 400 years and was widely welcomed by the sector, though it fell short of what the Council had hoped for.[127] Although it included the provision that a public benefit test would apply to all charities for the first time, there was no statutory definition of public benefit and the bar on meeting the public benefit threshold was set so low as to be almost meaningless. But the Act, although a disappointment, was not without merit. Campbell Robb suggests that even 'though it had many failings, the fact that we were able to get the government to take this seriously enough to put it at the heart of government and to have a discussion in the wider public life about the role of charities and what public benefit is, was a huge stepping stone in bringing charity into the modern day'.[128] One outcome that proved to be of significant benefit for many smaller organisations was the introduction of the new status of Charitable Incorporated Organisation, which gave charities protection of incorporation without having to register as a company.

The Council had played its part in the introduction of a range of favourable tax changes during the previous Conservative administrations to stimulate individual and corporate giving. It was to see further success under New

Labour. Concern had been growing since the mid-1970s about a decline in the number of households giving to charity, although the overall amount donated had risen.[129] At the Council's annual conference in 2000, the chancellor of the exchequer, Gordon Brown, announced a number of new tax-efficient ways of giving, including the removal of any threshold limits under the Gift Aid Scheme and the relaunching of payroll giving, as part of a desire to create a 'democracy of giving'.[130] Gift Aid had been introduced by the Conservative government in 1990, replacing the covenants that had been used to support tax-effective giving since 1842 and underpinned the Council's work since 1924.[131] Despite the fact that the Council had been pushing for further reform, the scale of the changes took them by surprise. The challenge was to make people aware of them and get them to use them. A Giving Campaign was launched in 2001 with Lord Joffe as chair, with the aim of creating 'a culture of giving where it is natural for everyone able to do so to give money and time to improve the quality of life for others'.[132] The Council committed £100,000 from reserves. CAF put in £300,000 and over £250,000 was raised from other charities. The government contributed £1 million.[133] The Campaign closed in June 2004 with mixed results. Brown's reforms had stimulated tax-efficient giving from existing supporters. Gift Aid schemes grew from 1 per cent of donors to around a third in 2006, with one survey suggesting the number had increased 12-fold, with £1 billion being given by 2000.[134] However, the changes failed in their primary objective of stimulating new donors. In 2009 Brown, now prime minister, backed another Council campaign, *What do you believe in?*, to try once more to kick-start giving.[135] The campaign had none of the impetus, or resources, of the Giving Campaign and passed largely unnoticed.

INVENTING THE THIRD SECTOR

The Council has been credited with helping to create the *voluntary sector* in the 1970s as a means of strengthening its arm with government.[136] In the same way, commentators have argued that it played a crucial role during the second half of the New Labour era in recasting the voluntary sector as the *third sector*.[137] Such a reconfiguration involved reaching out to groups not usually seen as occupying the voluntary sector terrain: trade unions, mutuals, housing associations, cooperatives, and social enterprises. This work was helped by the presence of Melmoth as chair, who had been a key figure within the cooperative movement, and it linked well with Labour's desire to harness social enterprises for economic growth. In 2001 the government created a Social Enterprise Unit to support such groups, and in 2006 an enhanced Office of the Third Sector was set up within the Cabinet Office, combining the functions of the existing Active Communities and Social Enterprise units.[138] A new minister for the third sector was appointed and a new director general brought in from outside government. The first post holder was Robb, who moved from his position of director of public policy at the Council to take up the role. His appointment represented, according to Alcock, 'a clear indication that partnership between the government and the sector could lead to transfer of people as well as ideas and resources'.[139] To further strengthen links with the sector the government established a group of strategic partners, which included the Council.[140] The group was short-lived and was disbanded by the incoming Coalition government, along with many other aspects of the architecture of partnership.[141]

The *third sector* was always a strained concept, bringing together a disparate group of organisations that had even less in common than the groups that came together to form the *voluntary sector*. Some commentators have suggested it was a deliberate move by government to bring into the policy arena groups that had previously lain outside the 'governable terrain' and make them more amenable to influence and control.[142] But, as with the invention of the *voluntary sector*, it would be a mistake to assume it was all the government's doing. There was much to be gained by social enterprises and mutuals in terms of policy influence and funding by being brought within the *third sector* fold, just as there were advantages for traditional voluntary agencies in being grouped with organisations that were gaining traction within government. The *third sector* was as much the movement's invention as New Labour's and the Council, as always, was at the heart of the action.[143] In 2006 it helped set up a third sector network to offer space for these 'new' forms of social action to meet representatives of the traditional voluntary sector.[144] The experiment was only partially successful and the network was short-lived, although social enterprises remained a permanent feature of the sector landscape and of ongoing interest to the Council.

INDEPENDENCE AND VOICE

In 2002 the Council commissioned external consultants to assess its effectiveness in influencing public policy. It had submitted a response to the Treasury cross-cutting review on the role of the sector in public services, calling for full implementation of the Compact, support for local infrastructure and better procurement, commissioning and contracting practices.[145] The report from the consultants, which was never published, was submitted in April 2003 and provides a fascinating commentary on the Council's performance.[146] It argued that it should take 'much credit' from the results of the cross-cutting review, which were judged as hugely beneficial for the sector, and suggested in some respects the Council could be seen as its originator. It concluded that the organisation 'is generally well regarded in Government' for its 'political acumen' and 'much-respected willingness and ability to help create the political space within which policy initiatives are able to flourish'.[147] However, it was less positive about the extent to which it could be said to be representing the sector in its negotiations with government. It also suggested that tensions could arise when it was seen to be lobbying for the sector and pushing its own agenda, and it concluded that it 'does not protect itself well enough against suspicions from some parts of Government and elsewhere that evidence it provides may be skewed towards areas of self-interest'.[148] Such a concern had been raised before, both between the wars when it used public funds to set up centres for the unemployed and during the 1980s when it accessed Manpower Services Commission funds.[149] So long as the Council saw its role as the voice of the sector and the deliverer of services, such tensions were bound to surface.

The review also addressed the issue of independence. Despite acknowledging criticism from some within the sector that the Council was too close to government, it suggested that it had got its tactics about right: 'There are of course centripetal forces pulling insider organisations towards a prisoner relationship', but the Council was 'too astute to fall into this trap'. It was able, it argued, to operate 'skilfully behind closed doors', but also, when required, 'to criticise its targets'.[150] Such a conclusion was a powerful endorsement of the Council's campaigning strategy. Such a twin-track approach would never satisfy critics who wanted to see it take a more combative approach with government, but this was never going to be the Council's way. It was set up with the belief in the value of partnership. Influence, it believed, was best achieved quietly and behind closed doors, but with a willingness to shift to an external campaigning strategy should the insider track fail to deliver. On many occasions, it proved willing to shift tracks if the situation demanded, although the timing and extent of such shifts were open to criticism.[151]

The issue of independence would not go away. In February 2004 the Council published a thoughtful report on the issue. Written by its head of policy, Ann Blackmore, it suggested that the sector needed at all times to assert its independence, especially when receiving public funding, but it rejected what it saw as a simplistic argument that public funding was an inevitable route to co-option.[152] The claim had come from a variety of sources. Robert Whelan, of the neo-liberal Institute of Economic Affairs, argued that parts of the sector were 'muzzled by contract and neutered by subsidy'.[153] The Baring Foundation said it was hard to find evidence of organisations losing funding as a result of their criticism of government, but that there was danger that 'organisations censor themselves, in fear of reprisal, without any hard evidence that this would be the effect'.[154] Colin Rochester, who would later write a coruscating attack on the Council, was concerned at this time not that organisations would lose their right to campaign by taking government funds, but that producing the programmes government wanted froze out more important activities: 'It is not a question of being censored', he suggested, 'it's a question of your energy being put into delivering services.'[155] Kendall and Knapp argued that there was little evidence to support the co-option thesis, but suggested that the sector needed to 'beat the bounds' a little harder, more often.[156]

Blackmore outlined what the Council deemed necessary to safeguard independence: first, good governance and, crucially, retaining the unpaid nature of trusteeship; second, better support and training for trustees; third, improved transparency and accountability; and, fourth, funding. Organisations, the Council suggested, should seek to avoid overdependence on one form of funding and should be prepared 'to walk away from a grant or contract' if the terms were inappropriate.[157] In 2008 the Council's Board returned to the issue. Concerns, it said, had grown further since the publication of the 2004 report, fuelled by the rise of contracting, the growing divide between large and small charities, and the growing professionalisation of the sector that risked 'a loss of distinctiveness and the capacity to innovate – confusing being business like with being like business'.[158] The remedy was again seen as better governance, a funding mix, and rearticulation of the sector's mission. It ran a debate on the issue at its annual conference in 2008, which included one of its foremost critics, Nick Seddon, who argued in a 2007 report for Civitas that charities were increasingly following the government agenda.[159] What research there was did not support these claims. A report for Centris in 2007, based on a survey of 121 voluntary organisations, found that most felt themselves to be independent. The issue was one of perception rather than hard fact. The authors concluded that public funding 'does diminish the sense of an organisation's independence', though 'freedoms are diminished at the margin, rather than in a wholesale way'.[160]

STRENGTHENING THE SECTOR

The period saw a continuation of the Council's drive to improve standards in the sector. In 1997 the voluntary sector national training organisation was established to improve the skills and training of staff.[161] In 2001 the quality standards task group was set up, an independent project housed within the Council, to raise awareness and usage of quality systems.[162] Concerns had long been expressed that professionalisation ran the risk of undermining core values, especially where it consisted of advocating practices common within the corporate sector. The Council shared these concerns. In November 1994, Etherington warned against aping business practices and argued that the sector should have its own tools 'developed by us and for us'.[163] In 2004 the Council acknowledged that the 'press to be efficient, to focus on performance improvement and to win contracts' could lead to 'managerialism at the top of charities', the squeezing out of volunteers, and a focus 'on funding and targets rather than the core mission'.[164]

It was partly a question of style. Few doubted that there was room for improvement in the way that organisations went about their work. But the constant exhortation that the sector should take lessons from the business community, no paragon of virtue itself, on matters of governance and probity, seemed to many an attack on the sector's core identity. Debra Allcock Tyler, of the Directory of Social Change, wrote that suggestions that the sector should professionalise were 'clumsy and even arrogant' by 'implying that freely associated groups of citizens who volunteer do not know what is best for their own communities, and that more organised 'professionalised' institutions do'.[165] And, as the Council pointed out, it was ironical that all too often those calling for professionalism were the same people who expected voluntary groups to 'be run by amateurs who are either volunteers or poorly paid, and who invest little or nothing in skills and training'.[166] This tension between helping to improve the sector's performance, while retaining the values that made it distinctive, was an enduring one, going back to when the Council was formed. It was a tension that returned with added intensity over the next few years and stretched the Council's resolve to the limit.[167]

The Council's information and research services were also strengthened during this period. In 1996 a third sector foresight programme was set up with the Henley Management Centre to help identify future issues likely to impact on the sector.[168] A new website was launched in 1998 and in 2000 the Council's long-running magazine was relaunched as *Voluntary Sector*.[169] More significant was the launch in 1996 of the Almanac, an annual digest of statistics on the sector, aimed at providing for the first time 'reliable statistics on the whole sector rather than focusing solely on large charities'.[170] This would become one of the Council's most valued services. Some activities proved less successful. GuideStar UK, a charity information website, did not last long, despite enthusiastic support from the Council.[171] And the Council's foray into the lottery world was equally unsuccessful. *Bingo Lotto*, a live television game offering 20 per cent of game-card revenue to good causes, closed within a month due to poor sales.[172] More successful was the Council's lobbying of government over proposals to merge the Community Fund and the New Opportunities Fund to create a new lottery funding body for good causes. The Council argued that any new body should be independent, additional to government programmes and sustainable.[173] The Big Lottery Fund became one of the major funders for the sector in future years, although its independence was on occasions questioned, not least by the Council.

Overseas Work

Most overseas work continued to be focused on Europe. Securing influence within the European Union was never going to be easy, and the Council remained frustrated by the slow pace of change. Attempts to introduce a European Compact came to nothing, with Etherington complaining of the 'Byzantine bureaucracy' that hampered progress.[174] To secure greater leverage it helped establish a new grouping of national voluntary sector umbrella bodies, the European Network of National Civil Society Associations (ENNA), providing it with administrative support before its establishment as an independent organisation in Brussels.[175] Oliver Henman, who headed the international work at this time, suggests that, while 'recent events' may have set back the European project 'for a few years', the Council had some impact over 'what was being shaped'.[176] The Council also helped secure significant European funds for UK groups. In the 1980s and 1990s it distributed European social funds directly to members. This work was now floated off to a separate network, the Third Sector European Network (TSEN), which provided technical assistance to local groups rather than direct funding. The TSEN was later brought back into the Council and rebranded as the European Funding

Network. In 2014 the Council helped secure joint funding from government and the Big Lottery Fund for a sizeable programme from European social funds to support individuals furthest away from the labour market.[177]

Outside of Europe, most of the Council's work focused on the new international network, CIVICUS, which had started in the US in 1993 to support civil society in newly emerging democracies, before moving its headquarters to South Africa.[178] The Council had been active in its establishment and continued to be involved, particularly through the Affinity Group of National Associations (AGNA), which shared information and know-how across countries. Following the Arab Spring Revolutions in 2010, the Council received funding from the Foreign Office to build national infrastructure organisations in Tunisia, Egypt, and Libya.[179] Looking back on the Council's international work during this period, Robb expresses disappointment: 'There were opportunities to create an even stronger alliance across Europe and the world which we never quite managed', he notes. 'There was a chance to forge a kind of global civil society alliance which was probably overambitious and the European work ultimately became about European social funds, as opposed to campaigning and other activities'.[180]

COOPERATION AND COMPETITION

Although relations with other infrastructure bodies were largely cordial, tensions often simmered beneath the surface. Nowhere was this more so than with the newly established umbrella body for charity chief executives, ACENVO (later rebranded as ACEVO), which began to position itself as an alternative voice for the sector on policy matters, particularly following the appointment of Stephen Bubb as chief executive in 2000.[181] In November 1999, the Council accused it of a marketing campaign that seemed to present it as a direct and cheaper competitor.[182] Bubb describes relations between the two organisations during his time as 'varied', 'sometimes they were good, sometimes they were very fraught'. Partly this can be explained by two big personalities jockeying for position. But it was also about organisational alignment. 'There was an immediate clash on policy', recalls Bubb, 'because up to the point of my appointment NCVO was the body that did representation and worked with government on policy development. And when ACEVO started doing that it was seen as a threat.'[183] Informal merger discussions between the two organisations were held on several occasions, but never came to anything, primarily because of Bubb's belief that there was a need for a separate voice for chief executives: 'I took a strong view that chief executives as the leaders of their organisations ought to have a voice, and that sometimes there would be issues on which we as chief executives might have a different view from NCVO as an organisation representative.'[184] For many within the sector, the failure to come together was a missed opportunity. Julia Cleverdon suggests that the 'fight with ACEVO' was not 'helpful' and that a better way should have been found 'in recognising that the senior leaders in the voluntary sector deserved respect, engagement and support'.[185] Relations with the National Association of councils for Voluntary Service (NACVS) were easier, and a new agreement was signed in September 2005 acknowledging NACVS as the lead voice for local councils, while accepting the Council would continue to have a role in supporting local infrastructure bodies in its membership. The Board felt this represented 'a positive step towards more collaborative and effective working on behalf of the sector'.[186]

Attempts were also made to foster closer working between infrastructure bodies. A new resource and umbrella organisations' forum was established in June 2001, serviced by the Council.[187] It was not a great success. Bolton remembers it feeling as if it was 'us telling them what to do'.[188] There was criticism that the Council was using its power and influence to win large contracts for itself rather than for the sector as a whole. Bolton acknowledges that 'there was a view that we were too competitive as an organisation, that we were soaking up a lot of the funding, that we were too powerful and that generally in the work that we did we didn't collaborate enough and that that cut against what might be presumed to be solid voluntary sector values'.[189]

The Council's strategy of floating off its networks continued, with BOND and Urban Forum becoming independent in April 1997.[190] By the mid-2000s, however, the agenda had begun to shift to consolidation and mergers.[191] This was primarily driven by ongoing concerns over funding, but also from a desire by the Council to reclaim lost ground. Over the next decade, merger discussions were opened with a variety of groups, some on the initiative of the Council, some the partner organisation. Several came to fruition, others did not. Most were presented as mergers rather than takeovers, though not everyone was convinced, and there were accusations that the Council was engaged in empire-building, taking advantage of its privileged financial position. This was a reversal of previous complaints that accused the Council of giving away its core assets and abandoning its community roots. The first merger was with a small group, Working for a Charity.[192] The big one came in 2013 with Volunteering England.[193]

CONCLUSION

By the early years of the new century, most of Deakin's recommendations were either completed or near completion. The commission had achieved a lot and was right for its time. It can be criticised for being too much about the architecture of the sector and its relationship with the state and not enough about core values and mission. But in the climate in which it was launched, at the tail end of the Conservative administration, a positive restatement of relations was required. In 2004 the Council set about developing a new agenda for the next decade. Despite continued good relations with the New Labour government, there was concern that the agenda had shifted too much towards public service delivery. Contracts had delivered significant income for some large charities, but many smaller groups had missed out, and, even among those in a position to win contracts, there was a worry that the prime and sub-prime delivery structure had resulted in groups being squeezed out by private contractors, or left to deal with the most difficult cases. The focus moving forward, the Council believed, should be less on relations with government and more on what the sector stood for. Five position papers were commissioned on social enterprise, accountability and regulation, new localism, civil society, and future funding, and meetings were held around the country with members to debate the issues.[194]

The Council's new ten-year strategic agenda, 'NCVO's Vision for the Future', was launched in September 2005, complete with a new corporate brand and logo, but it would be a couple more years before it was fully formed.[195] When it came, it represented a significant break with the recent past and an attempt to recapture the early priorities of the Council, based around the notion of civil society. At its annual meeting in November 2007 a new civil society agenda was unveiled, with a new strapline aimed at *giving voice and support to civil society*.[196] The launch was seen as an opportunity 'to celebrate the richness of civil society'.[197] The focus over the past decade had been on getting the right architecture for the sector. Now, with this largely in place, there was a need 'to refocus to emphasise the sector's role at the heart of civil society and the positive difference that voluntary and community organisations can and do make to individuals and communities'. Civil society was understood as 'the space where people voluntarily come together for mutual support; to pursue shared interest; to further a cause they care about; or simply for fun and friendship'.[198]

Such a reconfiguration was redolent of the language of the Council at its establishment and a conscious move away from the prevailing narrative of the day. 'Action within civil society is driven by people themselves, by their passions and enthusiasms; their needs and a concern for the needs of others', the Council asserted. Identifying ourselves as part of civil society enables us to 'define ourselves, rather than be defined by others – and to do so positively, in relation to those we work with and for, rather than in comparison to, the public or private sector: we are not simply non-governmental and not for profit, we are *for* people and communities'.[199] Etherington, writing in *Voluntary Sector*, emphasised the desire to reclaim the organisation's founding values by suggesting that 'as we move forward we need to go back to our civil society roots'.[200] Just as the Council had anticipated, and in some ways set, the agenda for the incoming New Labour administration, so in its emerging civil society strategy it anticipated elements of the *Big Society* agenda that emerged as the prevailing narrative after the next general election. But there were two significant differences after 2010 that prevented it from making the impact it had made after 1997. The first was the recession and the ensuing period of austerity. The second, and in some ways more worrying for the Council, was a distancing by government from established voluntary organisations. *Big Society* was not only a philosophy juxtaposed against a *Big State*; it was also placed in opposition to the *Big Voluntary Sector*. The Council would find itself, for perhaps the first time in its history, battling for recognition and influence within Whitehall at a time when, also for perhaps the first time, the government had made voluntary action one of its key political priorities. It would not be the only irony. Despite its antipathy towards large professionalised voluntary bodies, the government ramped up the contracting culture, which virtually ensured that only large national organisations (and then only some of them) could enter the arena of public service delivery.[201]

Relations with the Coalition government were not the only concern. The sector's own performance, especially in relation to fundraising, again came under the spotlight and unleashed a barrage of criticism from the press.[202] In responding to what it saw as a major crisis of public trust and confidence, the Council became more critical of the sector's failings and more interventionist in pushing for higher standards than ever before. The approach again divided opinion, between those who backed the Council's stance and recognised its legitimacy to speak on behalf of the sector and those who felt that it had over-reacted and over-reached itself.[203]

Notes

1. This issue is discussed in the conclusion.
2. NCVO, 1996. On the origins and significance of the Deakin Commission, see discussion below.
3. Interview with Sir Stuart Etherington, 25 July 2017. On the sector's *Golden Age*, see Alcock and Kendall, 2011, and Alcock, 2011, 2016.
4. For a discussion of these issues, see below, Chaps. 10 and 11.
5. The *Big Society* is discussed in Chap. 10.
6. Interview with Judy Weleminsky, 27 September 2017.
7. Interview with Judy Weleminsky, 27 September 2017.
8. Interview with Judy Weleminsky, 27 September 2017.
9. NCVO Annual Report 1993–94.
10. Interview with Sir Stuart Etherington, 25 July 2017.
11. *The Times*, 3 November 1994, p. 3.
12. NCVO Annual Report 1994–95.
13. See Chap. 8.
14. Minutes of Executive Committee, 6 October 1992; London Metropolitan Archives (LMA)/4016/IS/A/01/043(2).
15. Minutes of Executive Committee, 12 October 1993; LMA/4016/IS/A/01/043(1).
16. NCVO Annual Report 2007–08.
17. NCVO Annual Report 2006–07, p. 5.
18. See Chap. 10 for a discussion of this issue.
19. Minutes of Trustee Board, 5 March 1996 and 7 May 1996; uncatalogued papers, NCVO.
20. Minutes of Trustee Board, 7 June 2005; uncatalogued papers, NCVO.
21. Minutes of Trustee Board, 7 March 2001; uncatalogued papers, NCVO.
22. Interview with Adam Gaines, 12 October 2017.
23. Interview with Janet Morrison, 10 October 2017.

24. Interview with Margaret Bolton, 2 October 2017.
25. Interview with Adam Gaines, 12 October 2017.
26. Interview with Janet Morrison, 10 October 2017.
27. Interview with Janet Morrison, 10 October 2017.
28. Interview with Janet Morrison, 10 October 2017.
29. Chandler was one of the first business champions of the newly emerging field of corporate social responsibility. In addition to his work with the Council, he was chair of Amnesty International's UK Business Group, the Charities Aid Foundation, and the Council for Charitable Support; industry adviser to the Royal Society of Arts; and director of Industry Year, 1986. He was knighted in 1983 and died in 2011. See *The Guardian*, 10 April 2011, and Marsden, 2015.
30. Interview with Janet Morrison, 10 October 2017.
31. Interviews with Judy Weleminsky, 27 September 2017, Baroness Prashar, 9 October 2017, and Sir Stuart Etherington, 25 July 2017.
32. Lady Winifred Tumin was chair of the Royal National Institute for Deaf People, 1985–92. She played a key role in the Council's work on charity law reform and governance and, after her death in 2009, a memorial prize was established in her honour to recognise excellence by charities in governance.
33. Interview with Adam Gaines, 12 October 2017.
34. Interview with Campbell Robb, 18 September 2017.
35. Interview with Sir Stuart Etherington, 25 July 2017.
36. Norman Warner, a former director of social services for Kent County Council, was a Labour health minister between 2003 and 2007. In 2010 he was appointed chair of the Social Care Funding Commission by the Coalition government. He was made a life peer in 1998 and resigned the Labour Whip in 2015 to join the cross-benches in the House of Lords.
37. After qualifying as a chartered secretary, following two years' National Service, Melmoth had what he describes as a 'polyglot career' as a business manager with BOC, Fisons, and Letraset. He joined the Cooperative Group as corporate secretary in 1975 and was chief executive for six years before taking on the role at NCVO. Interview with Sir Graham Melmoth, 25 April 2018.
38. On the reconceptualisation of the voluntary sector as the *third sector*, see discussion below.
39. Interview with Dame Julia Cleverdon, 16 May 2018.
40. Interview with Sir Graham Melmoth, 25 April 2018.
41. Lewis had a glittering career as a journalist with ITN and the BBC. His philanthropic activities include vice-president of Hospice UK, president of United Response, founder of YouthNet (now The Mix), and chair of the Queen's Awards for Voluntary Service. He was knighted for his services to charity in 2016. He is a champion of the constructive journalism movement and helped establish the Constructive Voices project at NCVO to link charities and journalists.
42. Interview with Sir Stuart Etherington, 25 July 2017.
43. Minutes of Executive Committee, 6 October 1992; LMA/4016/IS/A/043(2).
44. Minutes of Executive Committee, 8 June 1993; LMA/4016/IS/A/01/043(1).
45. Minutes of Executive Committee, 8 June 1993; LMA/4016/IS/A/01/043(1).

46. Minutes of Executive Committee, 12 October 1993; LMA/4016/IS/A/ 01/043(1). Campbell Adamson was director general of the CBI from 1969 to 1976 and chair of Abbey National from 1978 to 1991. In 1984 he founded the Family Policy Studies Centre. He was knighted in 1976, and he died in 2000. See *The Times*, 24 August 2000.

47. Extraordinary General Meeting, 11 November 1993; uncatalogued papers, NCVO.

48. Minutes of Trustee Board, 2 July 1996; uncatalogued papers, NCVO; Minutes of Trustee Board, 1 October 1996; uncatalogued papers, NCVO.

49. Minutes of Board planning event 6–7 June 2006; uncatalogued papers, NCVO.

50. *NCVO Members' Assembly Proposals*, paper to Trustee Board, 17 September 2008; uncatalogued papers, NCVO.

51. NCVO Annual Report 2000–01.

52. On the changes introduced under Prashar, see Chap. 8.

53. Minutes of Trustee Board, 24 November 1999; uncatalogued papers, NCVO.

54. NCVO Annual Report 1999–2000.

55. Similar accusations had been made earlier in the Council's history over the issue of fundraising. See Chaps. 3 and 5 for a fuller discussion.

56. NCVO Annual Report 2004–05.

57. Interview with Janet Morrison, 10 October 2017.

58. Minutes of AGM, February 1998; uncatalogued papers, NCVO.

59. NCVO Annual Report 2002–03. Minutes of Trustee Board, 20 November 2002; uncatalogued papers, NCVO.

60. *NCVO's Biennial Market Research*, paper to Trustee Board, 19 September 2007; uncatalogued papers, NCVO.

61. NCVO Annual Report 2008–09.

62. NCVO Annual Report 1998–99.

63. NCVO Annual Reports 2001–02 and 2006–07.

64. *Review by Coopers and Lybrand: Draft Summary Report*, July 1993; LMA/4016/IS/A/05/026(4).

65. Ibid.

66. Ibid., pp. 18–20

67. Letter from D. Hardwick from the VSU to Judy Weleminsky, 15 September 1993; LMA/4016/IS/A/01/043(1).

68. Letter from D. Hardwick from the VSU to Judy Weleminsky, 15 September 1993; LMA/4016/IS/A/01/043(1). Minutes of Executive Committee, 7 December 1993; LMA/4016/IS/A/01/043(1).

69. Paper entitled *NCVO Review – Response to VSU*, 7 December 1993; Minutes of Executive Committee, 7 December 1993; LMA/4016/IS/A/01/043(1).

70. Minutes of Trustee Board, 5 December 1995; uncatalogued papers, NCVO.

71. This disillusionment had been growing for some time. See Chap. 8 for a fuller discussion.

72. Knight, 1993.

73. NCVO Annual Report 1993–94, p. 2.

74. Knight, 1993, p. viii.

75. Ibid., p. xvii.

76. See, for example, The *Guardian*, 5 November 1993, p. 2.

77. NCVO Annual Report 1993–94.

78. Knight, 1993, p. xviii.
79. For similar criticisms, see the discussion in Chap. 7.
80. NCVO Annual Report 1994–95.
81. Interview with Sir Stuart Etherington, 25 July 2017.
82. Interview with Nicholas Deakin, 4 April 2017.
83. For a discussion of Wolfenden, see Chap. 6.
84. Interviews with Nicholas Deakin, 4 April 2017, and Sir Stuart Etherington, 25 July 2017.
85. NCVO, 1996a.
86. Ibid.
87. NCVO, 1996b, pp. 14–15.
88. Department of National Heritage, 1996. The 'turning the lights out' quip was from Sir Stuart Etherington in his 2017 lecture at Cass Business School; unpublished.
89. *Hansard*, House of Lords Debates, 27 November 1996, Vol. 576, col. 315.
90. Lewis, 1999.
91. Press response was gathered together by NCVO; NCVO, 1996c, p. 8.
92. Kendall, 2003, p. 53.
93. Interview with Nicholas Deakin, 4 April 2017.
94. Kendall, 2009.
95. Interview with Sir Stuart Etherington, 25 July 2017.
96. Alcock, 2011, p. 179.
97. Giddens, 1998; Blair, 1998. Giddens was director of the London School of Economics from 1997 to 2003 and is a life fellow of King's College, Cambridge. Etzioni, an American sociologist, is best known for his work on communitarianism, which influenced politicians and academics on civil society on both sides of the Atlantic. He is director of the Institute for Communitarian Policy Studies at George Washington University.
98. On the myth of Labour's hostility to charity, see Deakin and Davis Smith, 2011.
99. Blair, 1999.
100. Blair, 1998. See also Dickinson, 2014.
101. Interview with Margaret Bolton, 2 October 2017.
102. Etherington, 2002.
103. On New Labour's support for the voluntary movement, see, in particular, Alcock, 2011.
104. Kendall, 2003, p. 12. See also Kendall, 2009a, and Zimmer and Strecker, 2004.
105. H.M. Treasury, 2002.
106. NCVO Annual Report 2004–05.
107. NCVO Annual Report 2008–09.
108. Alcock, 2011, p. 173.
109. See, for example, National Audit Office, 2009, and Harris and Schlappa, 2008.
110. NCVO Annual Report 2006–07.
111. Labour Party, 1997, p. 56, and Kendall, 2003, p. 53.
112. Department of National Heritage, 1996, p. 2.
113. Home Office, 1998.
114. Alcock, 2009.

115. Stowe, 1998. Stowe was principal private secretary to three prime ministers, Wilson, Callaghan, and Thatcher, between 1975 and 1979 and permanent secretary in the Northern Ireland Office and Department of Health and Social Security. He was chair of the Institute of Cancer Research and the Carnegie UK Trust's Inquiry into the Third Age. He was knighted in 1980 and died in 2015.

116. NCVO Annual Report 2002–03.

117. Kendall, 2003, p. 46.

118. Interview with Nicholas Deakin, 4 April 2017.

119. Lewis, 2005.

120. Zimmeck, 2010, and Zimmeck et al., 2011.

121. Minutes of annual general meeting, January 1995, p. 2; uncatalogued papers, NCVO.

122. On attempts to reform charity law, see Morgan, 2012.

123. NCVO, 2001, p. 1.

124. Cabinet Office, 2002.

125. *Government Reviews*, paper to Trustee Board, 2 October 2002; uncatalogued papers, NCVO.

126. NCVO Annual Report 2002–03.

127. See, for example, Morgan, 2012.

128. Interview with Campbell Robb, 18 September 2017.

129. Pharoah and Tanner, 1997.

130. NCVO Annual Report 1999–2000. See also Pharoah, 2010.

131. Davies, 2015.

132. Paper on Giving Campaign submitted to Trustee Board, 22 September 2004; uncatalogued papers, NCVO. Joel Joffe, lawyer and businessman, was the instructing solicitor for Nelson Mandela's defence team in 1963–64, director of Abbey Life Assurance, and chair of Oxfam. He was made a life peer in 2000, and he died in 2017. See The *Guardian*, 26 June 2017.

133. Minutes of Trustee Board, 5 October 2000; uncatalogued papers, NCVO.

134. Pharoah, 2010. Survey quoted in The *Observer*, 25 March 2001, pp. 30–31.

135. Youde, 2009.

136. 6 and Leat, 1997. For a discussion of this issue, see Chap. 7.

137. Kendall, 2009, and Alcock and Kendall, 2011.

138. Alcock, 2011.

139. Ibid., p. 168.

140. Alcock and Kendall, 2011.

141. This is discussed further in Chap. 10.

142. Carmel and Harlock, 2008.

143. Kendall, 2009, and Alcock and Kendall, 2011.

144. NCVO Annual Report 2006–07.

145. Minutes of Trustee Board, 11 June 2003; uncatalogued papers, NCVO.

146. *Assessing the impact of NCVO's work on the Treasury's cross-cutting review of the role of the voluntary sector in public services, April 2003*, paper considered by Trustee Board, 11 June 2003; uncatalogued papers, NCVO.

147. Ibid.

148. Ibid.

149. For a discussion of this issue, see Chaps. 4 and 8.

150. *Assessing the impact of NCVO's work on the Treasury's cross-cutting review of the role of the voluntary sector in public services, April 2003*, paper considered by Trustee Board, 11 June 2003; uncatalogued papers, NCVO.
151. This issue is discussed in detail in Chap. 11.
152. Blackmore, 2004.
153. Whelan, 1999, p. 20.
154. Baring Foundation, 2000.
155. Quoted in 'At arm's length', The *Guardian*, 28 April 1999, p. 35. For his later critique of the Council, see Rochester, 2013.
156. Quoted in Blackmore, 2004, p. 38.
157. Ibid., pp. 36–38.
158. *The Issue of Independence*, paper submitted to Trustee Board, 19 February 2008; uncatalogued papers, NCVO.
159. Seddon, 2007.
160. Knight and Robson, 2007, p. 55.
161. NCVO Annual Report 1997–98.
162. NCVO Annual Report 2001–02.
163. Speech by Stuart Etherington on *Redefining Charity*, CAF Conference, 10 November 1994, quoted in Blackmore, 2004, p. 33.
164. Blackmore, 2004, p. 33.
165. Allcock Tyler, 2007, p. 34.
166. Blackmore, 2004, p. 33.
167. For an early discussion of this tension, see Chaps. 2 and 5. The issue is also discussed in Chaps. 10 and 11.
168. NCVO Annual Report 1996–97.
169. NCVO Annual Reports 1998–99 and 2000–01.
170. NCVO Annual Report 1995–96, p. 3. The Almanac was first published as the *UK Voluntary Sector Statistical Almanac*. It is now published as the *UK Civil Society Almanac*.
171. NCVO Annual Report 2004–05.
172. NCVO Annual Report 2009–10.
173. NCVO Annual Report 2002–03.
174. Etherington, 2007, p. 13.
175. NCVO Annual Report 2009–10.
176. Interview with Oliver Henman, 9 October 2017.
177. Interview with Oliver Henman, 9 October 2017.
178. In 2018, Civicus, which celebrated its 25th anniversary, had 4000 members in 175 countries.
179. NCVO Annual Report 2012–13.
180. Interview with Campbell Robb, 18 September 2017.
181. The Association of Chief Executives of National Voluntary Organisations (ACENVO), later the Association of Chief Executives of Voluntary Organisations (ACEVO), was established in 1987. Its current chief executive, Vicky Browning, took over from Stephen Bubb in 2016, who replaced the first chief executive, Dorothy Dalton, in 2000.
182. Minutes of Trustee Board, 24 November 1999; uncatalogued papers, NCVO.
183. Interview with Sir Stephen Bubb, 19 July 2017.
184. Interview with Sir Stephen Bubb, 19 July 2017.

185. Interview with Dame Julia Cleverdon, 16 May 2018.
186. Minutes of Trustee Board, 23 November 2005; uncatalogued papers, NCVO. NACVS was renamed the National Association for Voluntary and Community Action (NAVCA) in 2006.
187. Minutes of Trustee Board, 7 June 2001; uncatalogued papers, NCVO.
188. Interview with Margaret Bolton, 2 October 2017.
189. Interview with Margaret Bolton, 2 October 2017.
190. Bond, the UK membership body for non-governmental organisations, was established in 1993.
191. Minutes of Trustee Board, 1 October 1996; uncatalogued papers, NCVO.
192. Minutes of Trustee Board, 22 September 2004; uncatalogued papers, NCVO.
193. The merger with Volunteering England is discussed in Chap. 10.
194. Minutes of Trustee Board, 22 September 2004; uncatalogued papers, NCVO.
195. Minutes of Trustee Board, 21 September 2005; uncatalogued papers, NCVO. NCVO Annual Report 2004–05.
196. *Voluntary Sector (VS) Magazine*, December/January 2007/2008, p. 13.
197. Minutes of Trustee Board, 3 and 4 June 2008; uncatalogued papers, NCVO.
198. *NCVO's civil society strategy*, paper to Trustee Board, 17 September 2008; uncatalogued papers, NCVO.
199. Ibid.
200. *Voluntary Sector (VS) Magazine*, December/January 2007/2008, p. 13.
201. These issues are discussed in Chap. 10.
202. Fundraising had been a perennial issue of concern for the Council. See Chaps. 7 and 8 for previous reviews into alleged malpractice.
203. This issue is discussed further in Chaps. 10 and 11.

References

6, P., & Leat, D. (1997). Inventing the British voluntary sector by committee: From Wolfenden to Deakin. *Non-Profit Studies, 1*(2), 33–47.

Alcock, P. (2009). *Devolution or divergence? Third sector policy across the UK since 2000.* Working paper 2, Third Sector Research Centre.

Alcock, P. (2011). Voluntary action, new labour and the "third sector". In M. Hilton & J. McKay (Eds.), *The ages of voluntarism: How we got to the big society* (pp. 158–179). Oxford: Oxford University Press.

Alcock, P. (2016). From partnership to the big society: The third sector policy regime in the UK. *Nonprofit Policy Forum, 7*(2), 95–116.

Alcock, P., & Kendall, J. (2011). Constituting the third sector: Processes of decontestation and contention under the UK Labour governments in England. *Voluntas: International Journal of Voluntary and Nonprofit Organizations, 22*(3), 450–469.

Allcock Tyler, D. (2007, December/January). We are professional enough. *Voluntary Sector (VS) Magazine.*

Baring Foundation. (2000). *Speaking truth to power: A discussion paper on the voluntary sector's relationship with government.* London: The Baring Foundation.

Blackmore, A. (2004). *Standing apart, working together: A study of the myths and realities of voluntary and community sector independence.* London: NCVO.

Blair, T. (1998). *The third way: New politics for the new century.* London: Fabian Society.

Blair, T. (1999, February). *Speech to National Council for Voluntary Organisations annual conference.* London: NCVO.

Cabinet Office. (2002). *Private action, public benefit: A review of charities and the wider not-for-profit sector*. London: Cabinet Office.

Carmel, E., & Harlock, J. (2008). Instituting the "third sector" as a governable terrain: Partnership, procurement and performance in the UK. *Policy and Politics, 36*(2), 155–171.

Davies, R. (2015). *Public good by private means: How philanthropy shapes Britain*. London: Alliance Publishing Trust.

Deakin, N., & Davis Smith, J. (2011). Labour, charity and voluntary action: The myth of hostility. In M. Hilton & J. McKay (Eds.), *The ages of voluntarism: How we got to the big society* (pp. 69–93). Oxford: Oxford University Press for British Academy.

Department of National Heritage. (1996). *Raising the voltage: The government's response to the Deakin Commission report*. London: Department of National Heritage.

Dickinson, H. (2014). *Performing governance: Partnerships, culture and new labour*. Basingstoke: Palgrave Macmillan.

Etherington, S. (2002, October 22). *Delivery: The role of the voluntary sector*. Public Management and Policy Association Lecture.

Etherington, S. (2007, May). A compact for Europe? *Voluntary Sector (VS) Magazine*.

Giddens, A. (1998). *The third way: The renewal of social democracy*. Cambridge: Polity Press.

H.M. Treasury. (2002). *The role of the voluntary and community sector in service delivery: A cross cutting review*. London: H.M. Treasury.

Harris, M., & Schlappa, H. (2008). Hoovering up the money? Delivering government-funded capacity-building programmes to voluntary and community organisations. *Social Policy and Society, 7*(2), 135–146.

Home Office. (1998). *Compact on relations between government and the voluntary and community sector in England*. London: Home Office.

Kendall, J. (2003). *The voluntary sector: Comparative perspectives in the UK*. London: Routledge.

Kendall, J. (2009). *Losing political innocence? Finding a place for ideology in understanding the development of recent English third sector policy*. Working paper 13, Third Sector Research Centre.

Kendall, J. (2009a). The third sector and the policy process in the UK: Ingredients in a hyperactive horizontal policy environment. In J. Kendall (Ed.), *Handbook on third sector policy in Europe: Multi-level processes and organised civil society*. Cheltenham: Edward Elgar.

Knight, B. (1993). *Voluntary action in the 1990s*. London: Centris.

Knight, B., & Robson, S. (2007). *The value and independence of the voluntary sector*. London: Centris.

Labour Party. (1997). *Building the future together*. London: The Labour Party.

Lewis, J. (1999). Reviewing the relationship between the voluntary sector and the state in Britain in the 1990s. *Voluntas: International Journal of Voluntary and Nonprofit Organizations, 10*(3), 255–270.

Lewis, J. (2005). New labour's approach to the voluntary sector: Independence and the meaning of partnership. *Social Policy and Society, 4*(2), 121–131.

Marsden, C. (2015). Sir Geoffrey Chandler. In *Oxford dictionary of national biography*. Oxford: Oxford University Press.

Morgan, G. (2012). Public benefit and charitable status: Assessing a 20-year process of reforming the primary legal framework for voluntary activity in the UK. *Voluntary Sector Review, 3*(1), 67–91.

National Audit Office. (2009). *Building the capacity of the third sector*. London: The Stationery Office.

NCVO. (1996a). *Meeting the challenge of change: Voluntary action into the 21st century: The report of the commission on the future of the voluntary sector*. London: NCVO.

NCVO. (1996b, July). Meeting the challenge of change. *NCVO News*.

NCVO. (1996c, August/September). Plenty of ideas, little agreement. *NCVO News*.

NCVO. (2001). *For the public benefit? A consultation document on charity law reform*. London: NCVO.

Pharoah, C. (2010). Challenges for tax policy towards individual charitable giving: The experience of recent attempts to "reform" the UK gift aid scheme. *Voluntary Sector Review, 1*(2), 259–267.

Pharoah, C., & Tanner, S. (1997). Trends in charitable giving. *Fiscal Studies, 18*, 427–443.

Rochester, C. (2013). *Rediscovering voluntary action: The beat of a different drum*. Basingstoke: Palgrave Macmillan.

Seddon, N. (2007). *Who cares? How state funding and political activism change charity*. London: Civitas.

Stowe, K. (1998). Compact on relations between government and the voluntary and community sector in England and Wales. *Public Administration and Development, 18*(5), 519–522.

Whelan, R. (1999). *Involuntary action: How voluntary is the 'voluntary' sector?* London: Institute of Economic Affairs.

Youde, K. (2009, December 3). Gordon Brown backs NCVO campaign. *Third Sector*.

Zimmeck, M. (2010). The compact 10 years on: Government's approach to partnership with the voluntary and community sector in England. *Voluntary Sector Review, 1*(1), 125–133.

Zimmeck, M., Rochester, C., & Rushbrooke, B. (2011). *Use it or lose it: A summative evaluation of the Compact*. Birmingham: Commission for the Compact.

Zimmer, A., & Strecker, C. (2004). *Strategy mix for nonprofit organisations: Vehicles for social and labour market integration*. New York: Kluwer Academic/Plenum Publishers.

CHAPTER 10

Big Society and Beyond

Introduction

In 2018 the voluntary sector was in a difficult place. It was at last emerging from one of the longest and sharpest economic downturns of the past century, but many organisations still struggled for resources in a hostile funding climate.[1] Eight years on from the end of the New Labour project, relations between the sector and government were increasingly strained. The central government unit with responsibility for the sector had been downgraded and moved from the Cabinet Office to the Department for Digital, Culture, Media and Sport. The Compact, although still in operation, had fallen into disrepute, following repeated infractions by government. The strategic partners programme had been disbanded and central funding to the Council and other leading infrastructure groups withdrawn. Although the Council remained on good terms with ministers, its policy influence was severely curtailed, as in the words of one academic, 'to a large extent the seats were removed from the decision-making tables'.[2] Overlaying these structural changes was a growing sense of mistrust, with the sector accusing the government of disproportionate cuts in funding and attempting to curb its campaigning role. For many organisations, including the Council, relations with government had never been worse.

Such a situation could not have been predicted eight years earlier. When the Conservative-led Coalition government under David Cameron took office in 2010 promising to build a *Big Society*, many within the voluntary movement felt their time had come.[3] Such optimism did not last long. Within two years, the architect of the project, Steve Hilton, had resigned, and the *Big Society* was quietly shelved, undone by its own internal contradictions, public indifference, and Treasury opposition.[4] The Council, which had welcomed the idea as a chance to place voluntary action centre stage in the political process, criticised the wasted opportunity and the long-term damage it feared had been caused.

© The Author(s) 2019
J. Davis Smith, *100 Years of NCVO and Voluntary Action*,
https://doi.org/10.1007/978-3-030-02774-2_10

The period also saw a fall in public trust and confidence in charities, and for this the sector bore some responsibility.[5] A number of high-profile crises hit the sector, from the demise of Kids Company to much-publicised cases of poor fundraising practice, which threatened to bring the sector into disrepute. Some blamed the media for fanning the flames, others argued that the abuses were limited and mainly the preserve of large charities. The Council took a different view and led a robust campaign aimed at helping the sector to put its house in order, arguing that a failure to do so would lead to government stepping in to legislate. This enraged its critics who argued that the professionalisation of the voluntary movement, which the Council had promoted over many years, was the cause of the crisis by encouraging organisations to put money and growth before mission and values. The Council found itself on the receiving end of some of the harshest criticism since its controversial work on unemployment in the inter-war years.[6]

Organisationally the period witnessed some significant changes to the Council. As one of the more financially robust infrastructure bodies, it attracted the attention of a number of groups looking to collaborate. Several successful mergers were negotiated, the most important with Volunteering England in 2013, which meant that, for the first time since the setting up of the Volunteer Centre in 1973, the organisation had strategic responsibility for volunteering. By the end of the period, the Council was in a state of flux. Its chief executive, Stuart Etherington, had been in post for almost 25 years and attention inevitably was turning to his replacement. A new inquiry into the future of civil society had been launched, partly funded by the Council, but over which, in contrast to the Deakin commission, it had little influence.[7] Just as in the 1960s and 1970s, the development of new forms of social action, operating outside the traditional sector, raised questions about its role and legitimacy.[8]

AGE OF AUSTERITY

In 2008, Britain entered what would become the deepest and longest recession since the Second World War. With both the Coalition government of 2010 and the following Conservative government of 2015 prioritising cutting the fiscal deficit by heavy reductions in public expenditure, the country entered a new 'age of austerity'.[9] The impact on the voluntary sector was severe and led to growing tensions between the Council and the government. At first, however, at the end of the New Labour administration, the crisis served to strengthen relations and bolster the Council's position. A series of joint recession summits were organised, resulting in a £42 million bursary scheme to support voluntary groups.[10] The process, according to Pete Alcock, represented the 'high water mark of the deepening interdependence of the state and the sector under Labour'.[11] In 2009 a Cabinet Office document highlighted the crucial role of the third sector 'in delivering real help and support to people from all walks of life who are affected by the recession'.[12] There was a marked shift of direction under the Coalition government. The rhetoric was still about the contribution the sector could make in helping communities affected by the recession, but crucially any such role was to be achieved in the face of severe cuts in public funding.[13] The Council found its influence severely curtailed as the government abandoned what it saw as New Labour corporatism, epitomised by its relationship with a few select strategic partners, in favour of engagement with grassroots groups and social enterprises more in tune with its *Big Society* philosophy.

During previous recessions, in the inter-war years and the 1970s and 1980s, the Council worked closely with government on a range of special employment measures, acting as a conduit for public funds to the wider movement.[14] Largely excluded from the policy-making process this time, the Council adopted a more oppositional stance. With other umbrella groups, it tried to measure the extent of the cuts and the likely impact on local communities, establishing a website to 'crowdsource the cuts'.[15] As before, it argued that the sector could not expect to be immune from austerity but that any cuts should be proportionate.[16] Such a stance led to criticism that it wasn't going far enough in speaking out against government policy. A new ginger group, the National Coalition for Independent Action, argued that the Council and other 'sector leadership bodies' had 'shamefully failed to oppose the discriminatory and disproportionate cuts to poor and vulnerable communities'.[17] Little heed was taken of the Council's exhortations. Figures from the *Counting the Cuts* survey published in 2013 estimated that public funding for charities could be 12 per cent lower by 2017–18, while the 2014 UK Civil Society Almanac found funding had fallen by £1.3 billion in the year and at a faster rate than overall spending cuts.[18] Etherington warned that there was 'a very real and present danger that it will reach breaking point if the gulf between demand and resource continues to widen'. The sector, he said, 'is already doing a lot more with much less, and something has got to give eventually'.[19] The reality of the scale of the cuts during this period has been revealed by recent academic study. David Clifford has shown how over the six-year period from 2008 the sector was affected by a 'sizeable cumulative real income decline' with mid-sized charities and those in deprived areas among the worst hit.[20] In 2014 the Council launched a review into the future of the voluntary sector's finances.[21] In 2015 it was warning that there was still no economic recovery for charities.[22]

THE BIG SOCIETY

In 2010 things had looked very different. The Conservative-led Coalition government came to power with a pledge to build a *Big Society*, in which the voluntary sector was expected to play a significant part. The concept was not new. Its ideological underpinnings owed much to the eighteenth-century Tory Liberalism of Edmund Burke and his *little platoons* and to the rediscovery of active citizenship by a previous generation of Conservative ministers, including Douglas Hurd.[23] 'Little platoons armed with iPads', was the judgement of one commentator keen to dispel the notion that the *Big Society* was a radical departure from earlier Conservative thought.[24] The concept also drew on the work of Phillip Blond and his *Red Toryism* and the libertarian paternalism of the behavioural science, or *nudge school*, which was gaining interest in Conservative circles.[25] It also had links to Tony Blair's *Third Way* philosophy, which had been advanced as a way of reconciling what was seen as a damaging division on the Left between champions of the state and supporters of a voluntary response.[26]

The *Big Society* was launched by the new prime minister in a speech in Liverpool in July 2010.[27] That Cameron chose to unveil it at an event not organised by the Council was telling, given that previous prime ministers as far back as Edward Heath in the 1970s had used the Council's annual conference as an opportunity to launch major new policy pronouncements.[28] In a foreword to the Cabinet Office consultation document, *Supporting a Stronger Civil Society*, the minister for civil society, Nick Hurd, wrote of wanting 'to end top-down initiatives that filter spending through multiple layers'.[29] Stephen Bubb, head of the chief executive's charity, ACEVO, recalls that 'Cameron decided to freeze out' the established voluntary sector and 'never spoke to Stuart, never spoke to me' until it was too late.[30] The snub did not stop the Council from establishing good relations with the new minister, and Etherington speaks highly of Hurd's time in office, describing him as 'very good', even though with austerity 'he didn't have many cards to play with'.[31] The government, however, had clearly signalled that the era of strategic partnership was coming to an end.

For Cameron the purpose of the *Big Society* was to bring about 'the redistribution of power: from state to citizens'. It was made up of three 'strands'—social action, public service reform, and community empowerment—and three 'techniques'—decentralisation, transparency, and finance.[32] A key priority was the National Citizen Service, a personal development and volunteering experience for 16–17-year-olds, introduced in 2011.[33] A commitment was given to train up to 5000 community organisers. There was also a push on social finance, with Cameron calling for the government to 'connect private capital to investment in social projects'.[34] In 2012, Big Society Capital was formed, capitalised with funds from dormant bank accounts, and by 2015, £1.4 billion of social finance had been raised, although problems bedevilled it from the outset. Big Society Capital was largely a rebranding of the idea of a Social Investment Bank championed by New Labour and points to a degree of continuity in policies between the new government and its predecessor.[35] A major focus of the *Big Society* in the early years was the devolution of power to local communities, instituted through a process of *Community Right to Buy* and *Community Right to Challenge*, enshrined in the 'Localism' Bill of 2010.[36] New proposals were also put forward to stimulate the giving of money and time in a *Green Paper on Giving* in 2010 and a *Giving White Paper* in 2011.[37] In 2013 a new charity, Step Up to Serve, was launched, with cross-party support, aimed at stimulating volunteering and service among 10–20-year-olds.[38] Changes were also made to the machinery of government. An Office for Civil Society was established in

May 2010, replacing the Office of the Third Sector, although with significantly reduced resources, and a refreshed Compact was published in December 2010, calling for a renewed push on opening public services to the private and voluntary sectors.[39] In 2013 the government removed the 12-week notice period for consultation under the Compact. The Panel on the Independence of the Voluntary Sector led calls for it to be reinstated and raised concerns about high levels of non-compliance.[40] In 2016 it concluded that 'the Compact has been broken by the Government and is proving ineffective'.[41] The same year, the Office for Civil Society was transferred from the Cabinet Office to the Department for Digital, Culture, Media and Sport, a move largely judged to have been a retrograde step.[42]

At the end of the Coalition government in 2015, the *Big Society* was a distant memory. It left little permanent legacy, with the exception perhaps of the National Citizen Service, the Step Up to Serve campaign, and an ongoing, but reducing, interest in social finance. Few observers judge it a success. A Big Society Audit carried out by Civil Exchange in 2015 concluded that it had 'failed to deliver against its original goals' and 'to establish a strong partnership with the voluntary sector'. Most damning of all, it concluded that 'the voice of the voluntary sector ... and its sense of partnership with the government nationally and locally has been reduced by the Big Society, not strengthened'.[43] Reasons for its failure are not difficult to discern. Despite its high-blown rhetoric, it lacked a detailed strategy for translating vision into reality. Richard Harries, who was working in Whitehall at the time, suggests that 'Cameron's intention was to see the reinvigoration of the third sector and he really did think it was the right thing to do', but 'we ended up with the *Big Society* which was really a slogan, with nothing behind it and the whole thing imploded'.[44] The deliberate freezing out of the larger umbrella organisations did little to win the support of the wider sector, and the concept was perceived not only as an attack on the *Big State* but on the *Big Voluntary Sector*. The government abandoned the strategic partners programme, which had been set up by New Labour, and phased out core funding for the Council and other intermediary bodies.[45] Ultimately, however, the *Big Society* was undone by austerity. Rightly or wrongly, it became equated in the public mind with *the cuts* and an attempt by government to use the sector to prop up struggling public services. Steve Corbett and Alan Walker have suggested that the *Big Society* was 'completely overwhelmed by the neo-liberal ideology of the deficit reduction strategy'.[46] When Cameron resigned in June 2016, following the European Union membership referendum, his successor as prime minister, Theresa May, replaced the rhetoric of the *Big Society* with that of the *Shared Society*.[47] The Council made a plea to put charities and volunteering 'at the heart of our shared society', but, with Britain's decision to leave the European Union dominating the political agenda to an unparalleled degree, there was little chance that the new slogan would gain political traction.[48] If the *Big Society* had suffered an early death by a thousand cuts, the *Shared Society* was still-born.

One of the key ambitions of the *Big Society*, to devolve more public service delivery to the voluntary sector, was not a great success. The policy had also been a priority of New Labour and had earlier roots in the New Public Management-inspired reforms of the 1980s.[49] The new government pushed this approach further, with a greater emphasis on payment by results, which had been introduced by New Labour in the health field and used over 100 years earlier by the Liberal government in the 1860s to raise standards in schools.[50] The results were disappointing. Most voluntary organisations lacked the capital or reserves to operate within such a system. Those that could find a role usually did so as sub-contractors to private sector primes, where all too often they were squeezed on price and given the hardest cases to deal with.[51] This was one of the ironies of the *Big Society*. It eschewed the merits of grassroots action and volunteering, juxtaposing this support with its suspicion of large voluntary organisations, yet it also envisaged a role for the sector in service delivery.[52] However, because of the way the commissioning processes were structured, these opportunities were available only to the largest charities and most were unable to compete with the private sector.[53] The Council remained largely supportive of the principle of involving more voluntary agencies in service delivery, but was increasingly disillusioned by results. In 2012 it published a report showing that 75 per cent of the 150 contractors surveyed felt that their contracts were not financially sustainable.[54] A new code of practice was launched with the private contractor SERCO to improve relations between primes and sub-contractors, but it carried no weight and had little influence.[55] The Council stepped up its criticism of the Work Programme, the Coalition's flagship welfare-to-work scheme, calling for more co-design with the sector and decrying the practice of 'parking and creaming'.[56] By 2017 Etherington was lamenting all that was 'dramatically wrong' with current approaches to commissioning and calling for 'pragmatic solutions' with the sector playing the role of 'constructive partner'.[57] It was all a far cry from the *welfare pluralism* of Hinton and Gladstone, which had argued for the sector taking over the wholesale running of public services.[58]

The Council faced criticism for its timidity in not pushing the contracting agenda further and for dabbling with the principle at all.[59] The National Coalition for Independent Action (NCIA) led the charge. It argued that the Council was complicit in the destruction of public services and in the drift from grants to contracts that threatened the independence of the voluntary movement by placing all the power in the hands of the state whilst shifting all the risk onto the sector.[60] Although acknowledging the Council's criticism of the 'mechanism' and 'process' of specific programmes, it berated it for failing to challenge 'the underlying principle of privatisation' or 'the government belief that services for vulnerable people are best delivered by a commercial model where profit is the key driver'.[61] Colin Rochester, a founder member of NCIA, pushed this criticism further. He claimed that the Council had been responsible over many years for leading the voluntary sector in the wrong direction, away from its roots in the community, towards a highly professionalised model that saw voluntary action primarily as an instrument for the delivery of public ser-vices. He contrasted its history of support for volunteering and community associations with its current preoccupation with contracting and management and issued a heartfelt cry for the sector to 'beat to a different drum'.[62]

CAMPAIGNING AND INDEPENDENCE

In 2010 the new government issued a refreshed version of the Compact.[63] This retained the commitment to safeguard the independence of the sector and its right to campaign, irrespective of its funding relationship with the state.[64] However, doubts had long been expressed about the value of the Compact and within a few years of its relaunch any residual belief in its worth would disap-pear as the government embarked on a fresh assault on the right of charities to campaign. As had been the case under the Thatcher administrations, the gov-ernment was again heavily influenced by a Right-wing think-tank, in this case the Institute of Economic Affairs, which produced a series of polemics attack-ing public funding of charities being used to lobby—a case, it argued, of gov-ernment lobbying itself.[65] The Council, as it had throughout its history, challenged what it saw as a fundamental attack on the sector's mission, although not strongly enough for its critics.

In January 2014 the Transparency of Lobbying, Non-party Campaigning and Trade Union Administration Act was introduced.[66] The legislation was primarily aimed at lobbyists and much of it didn't touch the sector. But in practice it had disproportionate impact on voluntary groups, leaving untouched the vast majority of private sector lobbyists.[67] Charities were to be treated as non-party campaigners, and the Act required them to register with the Electoral Commission if they intended to spend on regulated campaigning activities over a stipulated limit in the 12 months before an election. When the first draft of the Bill was introduced in July 2013, the Council was outraged. It wrote to the minister for political and constitutional reform, Chloe Smith, suggesting that the government was 'at risk of inadvertently making charities and community groups 'collateral damage' in its efforts to regulate election campaigning'.[68] The regulations, it said, were so unclear that charities would not know what to do. Legal opinion obtained by the Council reinforced its concerns. 'Uncertainty about what the law requires', Helen Mountfield QC wrote, 'is likely to have a chilling effect on freedom of expression, putting small organisations and their trustees and directors in fear of criminal penalty if they speak out on matters of public interest and concern.' The restrictions and restraints were so wide and burdensome, she argued, 'as arguably to amount to a disproportionate restraint on freedom of expression'.[69] In September, in an attempt to outflank the gov-ernment, the Council announced the setting up of a group to develop a new set of standards on lobbying and campaigning. The sector, it suggested, 'should be setting a gold standard in transparency and accountability'.[70] Changes secured to the Bill by the Commission on Civil Society and Democratic Engagement were welcomed by the Council, although it said the amendments did not go far enough.[71] In December Etherington wrote to peers asking them to support further changes proposed by the commission.[72] In January, however, the Council appeared to have a change of heart, suggesting that 'much of the risk to charities from this legislation has now been averted' and that the Bill now provided a more 'sensible balance than it did to begin with between creating accountability and transparency in elections while still allowing for charities and others to speak up on issues of concern'.[73] Some felt that the Council had gone too far, given the limited changes made. Stephen Bubb believes that the Council's position was too nuanced for what 'was an appalling piece of legislation' and that it should have been more forthright in its criticism.[74] The Council clearly continued to have major reservations. Once the Act was passed, it announced that it did not believe that it 'strikes the right balance'.[75]

In 2015, in the face of continuing criticism, the government appointed the Conservative peer, Lord Hodgson of Astley Abbotts, a former president of the Council, to review the Act. During the general election that year the concerns of the sector appeared to be borne out. A further report by the Commission on Civil Society and Democratic Engagement suggested that the lack of clarity over what was a regulated activity had led to self-censoring among some charities.[76] The Act, it argued, had a 'chilling effect' on the ability of charities to speak out and called for it to be repealed.[77] Lord Hodgson reported in March 2016. He recommended maintaining a registry and a limit on spending, but applying spending limits only to the costs of campaigning intended to influence voters and reducing the length of time in which the Act was applicable from 12 to 4 months.[78] His report was welcomed by the Council and supported by the House of Lords, whose Charities Committee report in the spring of 2017 warned of 'unnecessary concern and pressure' that 'threatened the vital advocacy role of charities'.[79] An article in the *Guardian* suggested that charities had been 'infantalised by fear' and described it as the year they decided to 'stick to the knitting'.[80] The government rejected Hodgson's recommendations, a decision described by Etherington as 'unacceptable'.[81]

On 17 April 2017 the government called a snap general election for 8 June. The Electoral Commission guidance confirmed that the regulated period would be judged to have begun 12 months before election day on 9 June 2016, highlighting the absurdity of the Act. Actions by charities not in breach at the time they had been undertaken became potentially so once the election had been called. Following the election, the Council, along with other infrastructure bodies, wrote to the first secretary of state, Damien Green, to 'request a meeting to discuss how the sector can work with the Cabinet Office to implement Lord Hodgson's recommendations'.[82] Later the same month, it put its name to another letter to government by the overseas aid umbrella group, BOND, calling for changes to be made following the election confusion.[83] In August over 100 charities, including the Council, wrote to the minister for civil society, Tracey Crouch, calling for full implementation of Hodgson's recommendations.[84] In September the Cabinet Office announced that the legislation would stand unchanged.[85]

ANTI-LOBBYING CLAUSE

Any suggestion that the impact of the Lobbying Act on the voluntary sector was the unintentional fall-out from a wider bill was dispelled the following year. In 2015 the government sought to impose restrictions on the use of public funds for lobbying by charities in complete contravention of the Compact. The first move came from Eric Pickles in February 2015 when he announced the introduction of an 'anti-sock puppet' clause into all standard grant agreements issued by the Department for Communities and Local Government.[86] A year later it was announced that the policy would be rolled out across government.[87] The origins of the move were research from the Institute of Economic Affairs that argued that government funding of voluntary groups engaged in campaigning was tantamount to the government lobbying itself.[88] The first version had been published in 2012 with a follow-up report in 2014. Although it contained no evidence to support the charge, it was picked up directly by the government and used to justify the policy shift. Not only did it fly in the face of one of the key Compact principles, there was no consultation with the sector in advance, which was also in contravention of Compact protocol. The Council slapped down the first report, describing it as 'woefully short-sighted' and suggesting the sector's campaigning work, 'rather than being dragged through the mire', should be 'protected, promoted and celebrated'. The independence of the sector, it argued, was 'paramount in helping voices to be heard and bringing major social issues to public attention'.[89] It responded equally robustly in 2016 to the announcement that the so-called gagging clause was to be extended to all voluntary sector grant agreements, arguing that it was 'tantamount to making charities take a vow of silence'.[90] A joint letter was sent with ACEVO, signed by 140 charities, demanding the clause be repealed.[91] The Cabinet Office took 50 days to reply, providing a clear indication of the declining influence of the Council and other former strategic partners.[92] In his state of the sector address at the Council's annual conference later that year, Etherington argued that the anti-advocacy clause was not only a clear violation of the Compact, but evidence of 'the government closing its ears to experts'.[93] A Civil Exchange report on the independence of the sector claimed that the clause had caused confusion, with organisations unsure what forms of advocacy they were allowed to undertake.[94]

Opposition to the policy came from outside the traditional voluntary sector, with universities claiming it was a direct attack on academic freedom.[95] In April the government announced that it was 'pausing' the roll-out while it took further soundings. The Council welcomed the move, but continued to call for 'full and immediate withdrawal'.[96] In December the clause was replaced by a set of new grant standards dealing with 'eligible expenditure'.[97] The Council was supportive, suggesting that the new directive took 'a substantially more sophisticated approach' to the issue and that the new standards 'have the potential to improve grant-making across government, ensuring public money is fairly awarded and effectively spent'.[98] Etherington said that 'ministers and officials deserve credit for transforming what was initially a very poorly thought out notion into something that has the potential to be a positive tool for quality grant-making'.[99]

It was a major victory for the sector and the Council played a leading part in getting the government to back down. However, some critics argued the Council should have reacted more strongly when Pickles first made his move and not waited until the policy was rolled out. They cite this as an example of the weakness of relying too much on an inside-track strategy. Andrew Purkis says he wrote to the Council when the issue first surfaced suggesting that the clause was 'making an absolute nonsense of the Compact' and that 'years and years of work led by NCVO was in danger of being trashed'. The Council responded that it felt the matter could best be resolved through using its inside contacts in Westminster. It was only, Purkis argues, when these steps failed to deliver, and the government announced its intention to extend the policy throughout Whitehall, that the Council moved to a more campaigning stance. 'At that point', he says, the Council 'became very muscular, and the NCVO lion roared' and succeeded in 'knocking the government off course'. It offered very good leadership, 'but it was in some ways too late because it had allowed this to happen and relied on an inside track that didn't work'.[100] The conclusion, drawn by Purkis, is not that the Council should abandon the inside-track strategy, which he admits has served it well over the years, but that there are occasions when 'it overestimates its influence' and that, when faced with such 'egregious threats to the integrity of the sector', it needs to speak out sooner and louder. Much has been written on the relative merits of the insider and outsider strategies to influence policy and we will return to this debate in the final chapter.

A PERFECT STORM

If the Council was embroiled in an increasingly fractious battle with the government, it was also exercised by what it saw as evidence of growing bad practice within parts of the sector, which it felt was threatening to undermine public trust and confidence and bring the movement into disrepute. This was not a new situation. It had convened groups in the past to examine poor practice in fundraising and governance, but had generally stopped short of publicly criticising individual organisations, preferring to focus on leadership and management development for the sector as a whole. A *perfect storm* of circumstances now arose to convince the Council to take a firmer stance. Many applauded its leadership, but some felt it had gone too far and that it should have aimed its criticism at the government or the media rather than at the sector. For others, the Council was seen as part of the problem. They argued that the drive for professionalisation had caused the current crisis by encouraging organisations to focus too much on the bottom line and put money before mission. The Council was unrepentant and suggested that the crisis had shown up the poor governance and leadership of many charities, and it embarked on a campaign

to raise standards among chief executives and boards. Etherington acknowledges that the Council shifted tack at this time. He says that the sector 'was in
a slightly more defensive mode' following the election of the Coalition government and the Council increasingly saw its role as acting not only as an advocate
for charities but as a challenger of poor practice.[101] The *perfect storm* had three
main elements: revelations of bad fundraising practice within some large charities; fall-out from the demise of the high-profile charity, Kids Company; and a
press campaign against 'excessive' salaries of some charity chief executives. The
Council responded robustly in each case, challenging the sector where it felt
criticism was appropriate and refuting attacks it judged unfair.

The fundraising crisis was sparked by the death, on 6 May 2015, of Olive
Cooke, a 92-year-old grandmother, charity supporter, and poppy seller from
Bristol. A firestorm of press criticism was unleashed when it became clear she
had been on the receiving end of numerous unsolicited charitable requests,
even though her family later said that this wasn't the reason for her suicide. *The
Sun* led with 'Killed by her kindness',[102] the *Daily Mail* chose the headline
'Hounded to death by cold callers',[103] while the *Guardian* said that the 'long-
serving British poppy-seller died after being "tormented" by cold-callers'.[104]
The press scented blood, and over the next few weeks a series of further stories
came to light that painted an unedifying picture of poor and, in some instances,
unethical practice within some large charities.[105] In June the Council announced
that it would be working with ACEVO and the Institute of Fundraising on
new fundraising guidance.[106] On 11 July the government announced that new
provisions to protect vulnerable people from 'rogue fundraisers' would be
included as an amendment to the 2006 Charities Act, which was under review.
It also announced the launch of an independent review into fundraising regulation, to be led by Etherington. A parallel review in Scotland, led by the Scottish
Council for Voluntary Organisations, was announced by the Scottish government, and a week later the Public Administration and Constitutional Affairs
Committee launched its own enquiry.[107]

The Etherington review group was made up of three peers from each of the
main political parties: Lord Leigh of Hurley (Conservative), Baroness
Pitkeathley (Labour), and Lord Wallace of Saltaire (Liberal Democratic).
According to Pitkeathley, speed was of the essence: 'We worked rather inten-
sively with a lot of colleagues from NCVO, we did a lot of consultation, but
actually speed was our driver. We had to come up with something comprehensive
in a relatively short space of time and I think we did that.'[108] The group
reported in September 2015.[109] The previous inquiries into fundraising in the
late 1960s and 1980s found little evidence of wrongdoing to justify taking
action.[110] This was not the conclusion reached by the Etherington group. In
the face of what it argued was shocking behaviour by a small group of charities
and the agencies they had hired to fundraise on their behalf, it concluded that
self-regulation wasn't working. The group called for a new, more robust, and
better-resourced independent Fundraising Regulator to be created to oversee
fundraising standards to replace the existing Fundraising Standards Board, and

the transfer of responsibility for ownership of the Fundraising Code of Practice from the Institute of Fundraising to the new body. It demanded greater transparency and openness from charities, including a statement in annual reports detailing the 'approach to fundraising activity, and whether a professional fundraiser or commercial participator was used'. Most controversially, it called for the establishment of a fundraising preference service to give the public greater control over the fundraising requests they received and the opportunity to opt out of any communications. At the launch, Etherington said that the sector had found itself 'in a position where charities didn't think hard enough about what it was like to be on the receiving end of some of their fundraising methods. They thought too much about the ends and not enough about the means.' The crisis, he said, had been 'a clear wake-up call' and now was 'the time to tighten the standards'.[111] The government accepted the recommendations and in October Etherington co-hosted a meeting with the minister of civil society, Rob Wilson, to discuss implementation.[112] Support was also given by the Public Administration and Constitutional Affairs Committee, although some MPs did not think the review had gone far enough.[113]

Response from the voluntary sector and fundraising community was mixed. Opinion was generally favourable, although the influential fundraising academic, Adrian Sargeant, led the opposition, lambasting the group for overreacting and claiming that the fundraising preference service would deter people from giving.[114] Opinion was divided even within the Council's own Board, with some trustees suggesting not enough had been done to reflect the perspective of small organisations and there was a danger that, by focusing on the poor practice of some large organisations, 'all charities have been tarnished with the same brush'.[115] In Scotland, the Scottish Council for Voluntary Organisations took a softer line, emphasising the need for 'a change of culture' and restating its belief in the importance of self-regulation.[116] In July 2016 the Fundraising Regulator for England, Wales, and Northern Ireland was launched and clauses added to the Charities (Protection and Social Investment) Act 2016, including giving power to the government to establish a statutory regulator if the new body was judged to have failed.[117] In September the Council supported a new commission on the donor experience aimed at giving donors more control.[118] The chair of the new body was Martyn Lewis, outgoing chair of the Council.

At about the same time as the fundraising crisis, another one was unfolding. The Kids Company charity was established by Camila Batmanghelidjh in 1996 to support children in need and by 2011 was working with 36,000 beneficiaries across 11 sites, involving almost 500 paid staff and over 9000 volunteers.[119] Its collapse in August 2015 sparked a major public debate about the health of charities. A highly critical report from a parliamentary committee blamed the collapse on the failings of the charity's governance, but said lessons needed to be learnt by government and the Charity Commission.[120] A National Audit Office investigation found the charity had received over £40 million from seven central government departments, with funding continuing despite concerns expressed within Whitehall over value for money.[121] For the Council, the crisis was symptomatic of wider failings of governance within the sector, and it embarked on a new campaign to raise standards.[122] A governance code for the sector had been created in 2005 and revised in 2010. The Council now involved itself in the production of a new version, which was launched in July 2017, and called, among other things, for more action on Board diversity, stricter adherence to fixed-length terms of office and greater openness and transparency in the ways boards did their business.[123] In November the Council announced that the code was 'winning support from charities', although a report from the Charity Commission and the Centre for Charity Effectiveness at Cass Business School suggested there was still some way to go, especially on diversity.[124]

The third crisis, which also raised issues to do with governance, was a concerted press campaign against what was held to be excessive salaries of chief executives of some major charities.[125] Criticism was not confined to the press and the Council's arch critic, the National Coalition for Independent Action, railed against what it saw as further evidence of professionalisation.[126] This time the Council was more robust in its support of the sector and challenged what it claimed were ill-thought through and inconsistent attacks. It had long argued that, if the voluntary movement was to achieve its full potential, it needed to look after its staff, including reimbursing its senior leaders at an appropriate level. The debate had first been aired as far back as 1915 at the wartime conference organised by the Guild of Help and Charity Organisation Society, which led to the establishment of the Council. Delegates at the conference had drawn attention to the dangers of colluding with the argument that people who worked for a charity shouldn't expect to be paid a decent wage, commensurate with their responsibilities.[127] From its support after the Second World War for a dedicated pension fund for charity staff to periodic reviews into the pay and conditions of employment, the Council had shown itself determined to champion the rights of staff at all levels within voluntary organisations.[128] In 2013 it established a new inquiry into chief executive pay, chaired by Lewis. Its report, published in April 2014, rejected claims that the sector was paying inflated salaries, but called for greater transparency in the way organisations determined and reported on pay levels for their senior staff.[129] The heat was taken out of the issue, although reviewing the matter four years later Etherington expressed disappointment with the sector's response to the recommendations.[130]

Tax Relief and Cornish Pasties

In 2011 the Council welcomed government proposals 'to incentivise philanthropy among wealthy donors' and to simplify Gift Aid, which it said would be 'a huge benefit in bringing in extra funding and reducing bureaucracy'.[131] The following year, however, the chancellor of the exchequer, George Osborne, outlined plans to put a cap on tax relief on charitable donations, along with tax rises on Cornish pasties and caravans.[132] As part of a broad coalition of over 3000 organisations and individuals, the Council worked on a *Give It Back,*

George campaign and, when the government backed down, Etherington said it was 'a great day for philanthropy'.[133] Not everyone agreed. The *Financial Times* argued that 'the case for entirely open-ended relief rests on the curious premise that charitable giving is invariably superior to public spending'.[134] Polly Toynbee agreed, accusing the movement of colluding with tax avoidance.[135] The attack was reminiscent of the criticism of the Council in 1924 when it established a scheme to take advantage of the loophole in the law regarding covenants.[136] In 2011 the Council launched a working group to examine tax incentives and social investment.[137] In 2017 it announced the establishment of a new charity tax commission, chaired by Sir Nicholas Montagu, a former chair of the Inland Revenue, to carry out a wholesale review of the tax system for charities.[138] Charity law remained a priority. The Council contributed to the government's review of the 2006 Charities Act and set up its own review group to run in parallel with the official review.[139] When the group reported in 2012 it gave the Charities Act a 'clean bill of health', declaring that it 'has largely proved to be a good piece of legislation' and that the Charity Commission could be held to be doing 'a respectable job of supporting the sector despite its limited resources'.[140] Over the following years the Council revised this judgement and took an increasingly critical stance towards the Charity Commission, accusing it of political bias and seeking to curb the campaigning work of charities.

Europe and International

The Council retained an active interest in Europe and international affairs, although there is a suggestion that its wider international engagement was reduced during this period.[141] In 2013 the European Network for National Associations (ENNA), an umbrella body for non-profit infrastructure organisations across Europe, was established as an independent body with an office in Brussels.[142] The Council had been instrumental in its establishment in 2009 and provided administrative support since its inception. Its independence showed that the old model of setting up and incubating organisations had not disappeared entirely. In 2014 the Council brokered a match funding agreement between the Big Lottery Fund and the European Union to secure more than £500 million of funding for charities on employability and social exclusion.[143] It remained frustrated by the labyrinthine bureaucracy of the European Union, especially in relation to the European structural funds, and admitted that it could 'feel distant, inaccessible and unresponsive', especially for small charities. But it was convinced that 'the answer is unquestionably reform of Europe, not walking away from it'.[144] On 23 June 2016 the UK voted narrowly in favour of leaving the European Union. In advance of the referendum, the Council put out a discussion paper on the implications of European Union membership for charities.[145] It criticised the Charity Commission for its guidance to charities on engaging in the debate, the tone of which, it argued, was 'negative and prescriptive'.[146] After the decision to leave, it called on charities to play a role 'in healing the divisions' caused by the referendum.[147] In his state of the sector address to the Council's annual conference the following year, Etherington called for the sector 'to set out our vision of what a post-Brexit Britain can and should look like'.[148]

MERGERS AND CONSOLIDATIONS

Lewis replaced Graham Melmoth as chair in November 2010. In taking over he paid tribute to Melmoth for steering the organisation 'through massive structural changes', including the introduction of the members' assembly and the reduction in the size of the Board from 40 to 12.[149] When Lewis handed over the reins to the journalist and broadcaster, Peter Kellner, in late 2016, he too could look back on his period in office with satisfaction. It had not been an easy time, with the sector having to cope with a prolonged recession, internal crises, and a more hostile government.[150] However, he had provided a reassuring and calming presence throughout the period and successfully led the work on chief executive pay. The constructive voices project launched by the Council in 2015, to connect journalists with solutions to everyday problems, drew directly on Lewis' long-standing interest in 'positive journalism'.[151]

In 2009 Etherington celebrated 15 years as chief executive, and in June 2010 he was made a knight of the realm in the Queen's Birthday Honours, following in the footsteps of his predecessor, George Haynes.[152] Organisationally, the period was difficult for the Council, which carried out several restructurings to deal with a significant fall in income following the end of core funding and cuts in public grants. On 31 March 2011 the Council was forced to make a third of its staff redundant following a 27 per cent loss in income, and there was a second major round of job losses in 2016.[153] The Council, however, was in a better position than many other organisations, having diversified its income base earlier than most. By 2014 its trading arm was bringing in over £2.3 million per annum, including over £1 million from its conference facilities.[154] Its refurbished and renamed offices, Society Building, represented the realisation of its long-held dream to provide a hub for the voluntary movement, and in 2012 a new floor was added to the building offering further opportunities for collaborative working and resource generation.[155] Membership was also thriving, and in January 2013 the Council welcomed its 10,000th member, the youth work and homelessness charity, the Foxton Centre in Preston.[156] By 2018 the figure stood at 13,000. In addition, it could rely on over £1.5 million each year from CAF as a result of the agreement signed in 1974 when it became independent. In 2016 CAF raised the question of whether the agreement was out of touch with 'today's standards of charitable governance and good practice', but the Council argued it had been entered into voluntarily, in good faith and was still valid.[157]

Given the Council's relative economic security, it is not surprising that a number of organisations were interested in the possibility of closer working relations. In October 2011 the Centre for Charity Effectiveness at Cass Business

School transferred its KnowHow NonProfit website to the Council, in November 2014 a merger took place with the Charities Evaluation Service, and in April 2015 the core services of the Mentoring and Befriending Foundation were acquired.[158] The big prize, however, occurred in January 2013 when the Council merged with Volunteering England.[159] Formal merger discussions had been announced in June 2012 and a joint working party of the two organisations found a 'compelling case' for merger on grounds of efficiency and sustainability and a belief 'that the new organisation will enhance the work of both agencies and help deliver on a new vision for volunteering and voluntary action'.[160] For most of its history, until the establishment of the Volunteer Centre in 1973, the Council had arguably seen the promotion of volunteering as its number one priority. The establishment of the new centre, much against its wishes, especially when combined with the loss of responsibility for the local networks, dealt a severe blow to its sense of purpose and legitimacy.[161] Gone was the rootedness in local communities that had driven much of its most important early work with village halls and community centres and had underpinned its national campaigning. The Council's response to this loss had been a reformulation of its mission to focus almost exclusively on support for the larger and more professionalised part of the emerging voluntary sector. It achieved much success with this work, but had never quite shaken off the sense that the loss of the volunteering agenda, and the separation of the national from the local, reduced its reach and standing within the voluntary movement.[162]

Following the merger with Volunteering England, a new five-point strategy was developed, 'Together we make a bigger difference', putting volunteering at the heart of the new organisation.[163] Thirty volunteering ambassadors were recruited in 2014 to celebrate the 30th anniversary of Volunteers' Week, and the week was extended in 2016 to encompass the Patrons' Lunch, an event marking the Queen's patronage of UK charities, which Etherington helped organise.[164] The Council supported Cameron's ill-fated call for public bodies and large private sector employers to offer staff three days' paid volunteering leave.[165] In 2017 Etherington called for the sector to be 'bold' about creating more opportunities for volunteering, especially within public services, and in looking at ways to strengthen volunteer management.[166] At the time of writing it is too early to say what the long-term impact of the merger will be. But many within the voluntary sector will look for evidence of a sustained commitment from the Council to back up the assertion from Lewis at the time of the merger that 'NCVO has become, and will continue to be, a powerful advocate for volunteers and volunteering'.[167] For Dame Julia Cleverdon, the merger offers the perfect opportunity for the Council to go back to its roots, 'to recognise that where they had begun was all about the volunteer principle'. You 'can wrap it up' in all sorts of ways, she suggests, 'call it civil society, do anything you like, but in the end it's how do you get free people to care about the passions and the concerns and the issues which are close to them'. The Council, she says, might not yet 'entirely understand the implications of what it has done', but she has no doubt that the merger with Volunteering England was 'absolutely critical' for its future.[168]

Other merger discussions were less successful. Discussions with ACEVO came to nothing, largely because of ACEVO's insistence that a separate body was required to represent chief executives, although the organisation did move into Society Building in 2012 which aided collaborative working.[169] There was frustration that the tense relationship between the two agencies was damaging the sector 'and that some better accommodation between the two agencies would have been good'.[170] The Council's courting of the National Association for Voluntary and Community Action (NAVCA) also failed, with NAVCA insisting that any coming together should be on the basis of a federated model, with both organisations retaining their separate identities, but sharing back office services, a stipulation the Council was unwilling to consider.[171] Such a model was reminiscent of the Council under Haynes, with the central body offering administrative support to a range of quasi-independent agencies, each with a strong separate identity. It is a model that it might wish to consider reviving in future as a means of supporting groups that have an important contribution to make, but lack resources to go it alone. The binary option of merger or independence might not be the only one available.

Conclusion

The period from 2010 was difficult for the sector and the Council. Austerity impacted significantly on many voluntary groups and, with the ignominious demise of the *Big Society*, the government appeared to run out of ideas. The partnership under New Labour was replaced under the Coalition and subsequent Conservative administrations by a policy of *strategic decoupling*. Speaking in 2017, Etherington argued that he could see no clear 'narrative' from the current government concerning the sector and was at a loss to know how to 're-ignite that interest'.[172] In August 2018 the government launched a new civil society strategy, which was welcomed by the Council as an 'encouraging start', although the 'real test' it said would be 'embedding' its aspirations across government.[173] Etherington has been in post a long time, second only to Haynes. Most people judge him to have done an excellent job. Cleverdon, for example, describes his leadership at the Council as 'amazing' and says that 'nobody would ever budge my belief in his clarity, steadfastness, and ability to reinvent and push it forward'.[174] Melmoth concurs and describes him as 'a remarkable individual', a 'polymath, an extraordinarily rounded person and an acute, shrewd and caring manager and team builder'.[175] Baroness Pitkeathley believes he has 'been a good thing'. She suggests that he has managed the line with government very skilfully, 'speaking truth to power, but in a way that is acceptable and which power can hear'.[176] Others have criticised his style and feel that he could have promoted a more cooperative and less competitive culture within the sector.[177] For Perri 6, the Etherington years were characterised by an unhealthy focus on what he calls 'sectional defensiveness' at the expense of a more critical, expansive approach, although he admits that 'he's probably done that as well as anybody could have done if that's what you fundamentally wanted to do rather than to challenge and shake up the sector'.[178] Some feel that he has stayed too long.[179] Campbell Robb claims he will be judged 'as being a driving force over the last 15 to 20 years of putting civil society into the heart of decision making in public life'. He suggests that 'like many in trade body roles he probably feels that at times he could have gone earlier', but feels he has moved into a different role as an 'elder statesman', where 'he can act as an interlocutor between the sector and the government, as he did with the fundraising issues'.[180] Cleverdon agrees, suggesting that 'Stuart's continuity is a very great strength', while also acknowledging the challenge this presents for organisational renewal.[181]

In 2016 it was announced that the former chief executive of the Joseph Rowntree Foundation, Julia Unwin, would lead an inquiry into the future of voluntary action, funded by a consortium of charitable trusts.[182] It was the first major inquiry since the Deakin commission 20 years previously and its focus was on new forms of social action, many operating outside the formal voluntary sector. The Council contributed £100,000 towards its running costs, but, unlike Deakin, was not involved in its administration.[183] It was reminiscent of the 1960s and 1970s when the emergence of new campaigning and self-help groups raised questions about its reach and relevance. In June 2014 the Council's Board discussed its future, and called for it to be more proactive in 'taking the leadership to galvanise the agenda'. The challenge, it argued, was to awaken 'the sleeping giant' and get 'ready to take action' if it was 'not to become irrelevant'.[184]

Notes

1. Evidence suggests that larger charities are doing better than smaller and medium-sized charities. See, for example, NCVO, 2018.
2. Alcock, 2016, p. 99.
3. The *Big Society* concept is discussed below.
4. Hilton was Prime Minister David Cameron's director of strategy from 2010 to 2012. He resigned in 2012 and moved to the US where he currently hosts a weekly show, *The Next Revolution*, on the Fox News Channel.
5. According to the Charity Commission's biennial survey, public trust in charities fell from 6.7 out of 10 in 2014 to 5.5 in 2018. See Populus, 2018.
6. For a discussion of the criticism of the Council during the 1930s, see Chap. 4.
7. Civil Society Futures was funded by a consortium of charitable trusts and chaired by Julia Unwin, former chief executive of the Joseph Rowntree Foundation and Charity Commissioner. See https://civilsocietyfutures.org/. It reported in 2018. For a discussion of the Deakin commission, see Chap. 9.
8. The challenge to the legitimacy of the Council in the 1960s and 1970s is discussed in Chap. 7.
9. Clifford, 2017.
10. Alcock, 2016.

11. Ibid., p. 104.
12. Cabinet Office, 2009.
13. NCVO Annual Report 2010–11.
14. See Chaps. 4 and 8.
15. NCVO Press Release January 2011, *Civil society bodies team up to map intelligence on voluntary sector cuts across the country.*
16. NCVO Press Release 30 June 2011, *Charities put up a good fight for survival.*
17. National Coalition for Independent Action, 2015, p. 2.
18. NCVO Press Release 14 May 2013, *New NCVO analysis shows impact of cuts on charities*; NCVO Press Release 4 April 2014, *Over £1bn of government income wiped from charities.*
19. NCVO Press Release 4 April 2014, *Over £1bn of government income wiped from charities.*
20. Clifford, 2017. See also Jones et al., 2015.
21. NCVO Press Release 12 June 2014, *NCVO review to consider future finances of the voluntary sector.*
22. NCVO Press Release 22 July 2015, *No economic recovery for charities – new report.* NCVO, 2015.
23. Green, 2002, pp. 240–78.
24. D'Ancona, 2013, p. 403. See also Norman, 2010, on the ideological underpinnings of *Big Society.*
25. See Blond, 2009. For a critique of the *Big Society*, see Corbett and Walker, 2013. *Nudge* was popularised in the best-selling book of the same name by Thaler and Sunstein, 2008. It was picked up by the Coalition government and a behavioural insights team, or Nudge unit, was established in the Cabinet Office in 2010, later part-privatised as a mutual joint venture.
26. It was described as 'Blairite dressing' by one observer. Cited in Seldon and Snowdon, 2015, p. 152. For a discussion of the *Third Way*, see Chap. 9.
27. The idea had been outlined in a number of policy documents and speeches both prior to and following the general election, but it was in Liverpool that major policy announcements were made. See Alcock, 2010.
28. Cameron, 2010. On Heath's address to the Council, see Chap. 7.
29. Cabinet Office, 2010a, p. 3.
30. Interview with Sir Stephen Bubb, 19 July 2017.
31. Interview with Sir Stuart Etherington, 25 July 2017.
32. Cameron, 2010.
33. Mycock and Tonge, 2011.
34. Cameron, 2010.
35. Alcock, 2010, and Alcock et al., 2012.
36. The Bill set out to devolve greater powers to councils and neighbourhoods and give local communities more control over housing and planning decisions. It was enacted in 2011.
37. Cabinet Office, 2010b and 2011.
38. The charity was formed following a review into youth social action carried out by Dame Julia Cleverdon and Amanda Jordan for the prime minister in 2012. It is responsible for the #iwill campaign and has the Prince of Wales as patron. See http://www.stepuptoserve.org.uk/
39. Alcock, 2010 and 2016.

40. Baring Foundation, 2013, pp. 27–29, and 2015, p. 13. The panel was established by the Baring Foundation in June 2011 to monitor the independence of the voluntary sector. Chaired by Sir Roger Singleton, chief executive of Barnado's for over 20 years, it produced four *independence audits* between 2012 and 2015. Its work was continued by the think-tank, Civil Exchange.
41. Civil Exchange, 2016, p. 62.
42. Interview with Richard Harries, 11 January 2018.
43. Civil Exchange, 2015, pp. 4, 8, and 27. See also an earlier audit, Civil Exchange, 2013.
44. Interview with Richard Harries, 11 January 2018.
45. Core funding for the Council and other infrastructure bodies was finally phased out in March 2014. NCVO Annual Report 2013–14.
46. Corbett and Walker, 2013, p. 468.
47. May launched the *Shared Society* at a speech on 9 January 2017 at the Charity Commission annual meeting. May, 2017.
48. NCVO Press Release 9 January 2017, *Charities and volunteering are at the heart of our shared society.*
49. Rees, 2014.
50. HM Government, 2011. Midgley, 2016.
51. Carter and Whitworth, 2014.
52. See, for example, Lamb, 2014.
53. On government support for small over large voluntary groups, see Lamb, 2014.
54. NCVO, 2012. See also NCVO Press Release 30 October 2013, *Payment by results implementation "seriously flawed"* – new report, and Sheil and Breidenbach-Roe, 2014.
55. NCVO Press Release 11 April 2013, *NCVO and SERCO launch code of practice to raise standards.* SERCO Group plc, a public services provider based in Hampshire, has been described as 'the company that is running Britain'. The *Guardian*, 29 July 2013.
56. NCVO Press Release 29 July 2014, *Next work programme must involve charities in design to succeed.* The Work Programme ended in April 2017.
57. NCVO Press Release 20 April 2017, *Sir Stuart Etherington's 2017 state of the sector address to NCVO annual conference delegates.*
58. For a discussion of Hinton and Gladstone's vision of *welfare pluralism*, see Chap. 8.
59. ACEVO was critical of the Council for not pushing the agenda further. Interview with Sir Stephen Bubb, 19 July 2017.
60. NCIA, 2014. The National Coalition for Independent Action was formed in 2006 by Penny Waterhouse and Andy Benson to 'defend the whole terrain of citizen action' or, what they called, 'ungoverned space'. It produced a series of research reports, position papers, and case studies on funding, commissioning, volunteering, the rise of managerialism, and the 'largely supine and ineffective role of infrastructure groups'. It closed in 2016.
61. NCIA, 2014, p. 6.
62. Rochester, 2013.
63. Cabinet Office, 2010c.
64. The new Compact included a commitment from government 'to respect and uphold the independence of CSOs [civil society organisations] to deliver their

mission, including their right to campaign, regardless of any relationship, financial or otherwise, which may exist'. Cabinet Office, 2010c, p. 8.

65. See below for details.

66. Parliament, 2014.

67. Parvin, 2016.

68. NCVO Press Release 23 August 2013, *NCVO seeks urgent legal advice over government campaigning proposals; Re: non-party campaigning letter to Chloe Smith MP*, blogs.ncvo.org.uk/wp-content/uploads/2013/08/Chloe-Smith-non-party-campaigning-final.pdf

69. NCVO Press Release 2 September 2013, *Lobbying bill puts charities in fear of criminal prosecution, says top QC*.

70. NCVO Press Release 26 September 2013, *Campaigning and lobbying standards group announced*.

71. NCVO Press Release 7 October 2013, *Lobbying bill amendments do not go far enough. Joint statement from NCVO and ACEVO*. The commission was established in 2013 following the concerns expressed by Helen Mountfield QC that the Bill was likely to have a 'chilling effect' on campaigning. Chaired by Lord Harries of Pentregarth, former Bishop of Oxford, it secured a number of amendments but failed to get the Act repealed.

72. NCVO Press Release 16 December 2013, *NCVO in "Christmas appeal" to peers on lobbying bill*.

73. NCVO Press Release 9 January 2014, *Government to amend lobbying bill following pressure from charities*.

74. Interview with Sir Stephen Bubb, 19 July 2017.

75. NCVO Press Release 13 November 2014, *NCVO responds to the lobbying act consultation*.

76. Commission on Civil Society and Democratic Engagement, 2015. See also Commission on Civil Society and Democratic Engagement, 2014.

77. Morris, 2016.

78. Hodgson, 2016.

79. House of Lords Select Committee on Charities, 2017, p. 133.

80. A Singh 2017 'Charities muzzled by gagging law? No, we've embraced a culture of silence' www.theguardian.com/voluntary-sector-network/2017/jul/10/charities-muzzled-lobbying-act-gagging-law-no-embraced-fear-apathy-silence

81. K. Liam (2017) 'Government to reject Lord Hodgson's proposals to reform the lobbying act' *Third Sector*, https://www.thirdsector.co.uk/government-reject-lord-hodgsons-proposals-reform-lobbying-act/policy-and-politics/article/1444725. Weakley, K. (2017) 'Charities 'outraged' after government rejects calls to amend Lobbying Act', *Civil Society*, https://www.civilsociety.co.uk/news/charities-outraged-after-government-rejects-calls-to-amend-lobbying-act.html

82. Weakley, K. (2017) 'Charities call for 'urgent' review to the Lobbying Act', *Civil Society*, https://www.civilsociety.co.uk/news/charities-call-for-urgent-revisions-to-the-lobbying-act.html

83. NCVO Press Release 19 June 2017, *Charities call for quick government action on lobbying act*.

84. Barton et al., (2017) 'Letter to Tracey Crouch MP', 30 August 2017, BOND; https://www.bond.org.uk/news/2017/08/uks-charities-and-campaigners-strengthen-call-on-government-to-overhaul-lobbying-act

85. The *Guardian*, 15 September 2017, *Charities condemn rejection of changes to Lobbying Act.*

86. Department for Communities and Local Government and The Rt Hon Sir Eric Pickles (2015) 'Eric Pickles cracks down on wasteful spending of government lobbying government' *Press Release* 23 February.

87. Cabinet Office and the Rt Hon Matt Hancock (2016) 'Government announces new clause to be inserted into grant agreements', Press Release 6 February.

88. Snowdon, 2012 and 2014.

89. NCVO Press Release 11 June 2012, *Lobbying report is 'woefully ignorant' of charities right to campaign.*

90. NCVO Press Release 6 February 2016, *NCVO statement on government announcement of anti-advocacy clauses.*

91. NCVO Press Release 11 February 2016, *Charities' letter to the Prime Minister on anti-advocacy clauses in grant agreements.*

92. Weakley, K. (2016) 'Charities angered by government failure to address anti-advocacy concerns', *Civil Society*; www.civilsociety.co.uk/news/charities-angered-by-government-failure-to-address-anti-advocacy-concerns.html

93. NCVO Press Release 18 April 2016, *Sir Stuart Etherington's state of the sector address to NCVO annual conference delegates.*

94. Civil Exchange, 2016.

95. *Nature*, 26 February 2016, *Confusion reigns as UK scientists face government 'gagging' clause.*

96. NCVO Press Release 27 April 2016, *Joint statement from NCVO, ACEVO and SEUK on anti-lobbying 'pause on implementation'.*

97. Cabinet Office Press Releases 2016, *Update on a new clause to be inserted into grant agreements; New standards announced for government grants.*

98. NCVO Press Release 2 December 2016, *Charities welcome new grants standards.*

99. Etherington S (2016) 'A resolution to the anti-lobbying clause' NCVO Blog 2 December 2016; https://blogs.ncvo.org.uk/2016/12/02/a-resolution-to-the-anti-lobbying-clause/

100. Interview with Andrew Purkis, 23 August 2017.

101. Interview with Sir Stuart Etherington, 25 July 2017.

102. The *Sun*, 14 May 2015, p. 1.

103. The *Daily Mail*, 15 May 2015, p. 1.

104. The *Guardian*, 14 May 2015.

105. Hind, 2017.

106. NCVO Press Release 29 June 2015, *Sector bodies come together to create fundraising guidance.*

107. UK Parliament (2015), Fundraising in the charitable sector inquiry launched, Press Release.

108. Interview with Baroness Pitkeathley, 24 April 2018.

109. Etherington et al., 2015.

110. See Chaps. 7 and 8 for a discussion of the earlier fundraising inquiries.

111. NCVO Press Release 23 September 2015, *Tough new fundraising regulator to ensure high standards – review.*
112. NCVO Press Release 15 October 2015, *Charity fundraising self-regulation meeting.*
113. Public Administration and Constitutional Affairs Committee, 2015. On MPs concerns, see Birkwood, S. (2016) 'Etherington review "did not go far enough", MPs conclude', *Third Sector*, https://www.thirdsector.co.uk/etherington-review-did-not-go-far-enough-mps-conclude/policy-and-politics/article/1380627
114. Sargeant A (2015) 'Opinion: Shame on those who are supporting the fundraising preference service' *Critical Fundraising – Plymouth University Blogs* 26 October 2015; http://blogs.plymouth.ac.uk/criticalfundraising/2015/10/26/opinion-shame-on-those-who-are-supporting-the-fundraising-preference-service/. For a more supportive viewpoint, see Pidgeon, S. (2015) 'Blog: I welcome the findings of Sir Stuart Etherington', *Third Sector* 22 October 2015; https://www.thirdsector.co.uk/stephen-pidgeon-i-welcome-findings-sir-stuart-etherington/fundraising/article/1368897
115. Minutes of Trustee Board, 14 December 2015; uncatalogued papers, NCVO.
116. SCVO, 2015.
117. Quoted in Hind, 2017.
118. NCVO Press Release 27 September 2016, *Leading charities commit to put donors in control of fundraising.*
119. National Audit Office, 2015.
120. Public Administration and Constitutional Affairs Committee, 2016.
121. Ibid., pp. 6–7.
122. NCVO Press Release 1 February 2016, *Kids Company took 'reckless' approach to finances.* See also Grierson, J. (2017) *Kids Company insolvency,* The *Guardian,* 31 July 2017, for a discussion of the governance failures.
123. NCVO Press Release 13 July 2017, *Larger charities should undergo external reviews every three years, new governance code recommends.* Charity Governance Code Steering Group, 2017.
124. NCVO Press Release 20 November 2017, *New charity governance code winning support from trustees.* Charity Commission and Centre for Charity Effectiveness, 2017.
125. For example, Hope, C. (2013) '30 charity chiefs paid more than £100,000', The *Daily Telegraph,* 6 August 2013, and Stevenson, C. and Preskey, N. (2013) 'Charities chief's £653,000 pay ignites row', The *Independent,* 20 October 2013.
126. NCIA, 2014, pp. 10–11.
127. See Chap. 2 for a discussion of the 1915 conference.
128. The establishment of the Social Workers' Pension Fund is discussed in Chap. 6.
129. NCVO Annual Report 2013–14. NCVO, 2014.
130. NCVO (2018) Sir Stuart Etherington's 2018 State of the Sector address to NCVO Annual Conference Delegates, 16 April; https://www.ncvo.org.uk/about-us/media-centre/press-releases/2236-sir-stuart-etherington-s-2018-state-of-the-sector-address-to-ncvo-annual-conference-delegates
131. NCVO Press Release March 2011, *NCVO responds to the budget.*
132. Breeze and Lloyd, 2013.

133. NCVO Press Releases 29 May 2012, *After caravan and pasty tax climbdowns, charity tax needs to follow suit*; 31 May 2012, *Victory for the give it back, George campaign*.

134. 'Philanthropy is no alternative to paying tax', *Financial Times*, 16 April 2012.

135. 'On charity George Osborne must stand up to the self-interested super-rich', The *Guardian*, 16 April 2012.

136. See Chap. 3 for details.

137. NCVO Press Release June 2011, *NCVO launches social investment working group*.

138. NCVO Press Release 6 November 2017, *Charity tax commissioners announced*.

139. NCVO Press Release September 2011, *New group to review charity law*.

140. NCVO Press Release 16 May 2012, *Charity law system gets a clean bill of health*.

141. Interview with Oliver Henman, 9 October 2017.

142. NCVO Press Release 30 January 2013, *Charities to have stronger voice in Europe*.

143. NCVO Annual Report 2014–15.

144. NCVO Press Release 23 January 2013, *EU is crucial for Britain and the voluntary sector, but reforms are overdue*.

145. NCVO Press Release 5 April 2016, *NCVO discussion paper explores implications of EU membership for charities*.

146. Minutes of Trustee Board, 14 December 2015; uncatalogued papers, NCVO.

147. NCVO Press Release 24 June 2016, *Charities must help bridge divisions in society*.

148. NCVO Press Release 20 April 2017, *Sir Stuart Etherington's 2017 state of the sector address to NCVO annual conference delegates*.

149. NCVO Annual Report 2010–11, p. 6.

150. Kellner, journalist and political commentator, is a former chair of the YouGov opinion polling company and the Royal Commonwealth Society.

151. NCVO Annual Report 2015–16.

152. Haynes was knighted in 1962. See Chap. 8.

153. NCVO Annual Reports 2011–12 and 2016–17.

154. NCVO Annual Report 2013–14.

155. NCVO Annual Report 2012–13.

156. NCVO Annual Report 2012–13.

157. Minutes of Trustee Board, 16 December 2016; uncatalogued papers, NCVO.

158. NCVO Annual Reports 2011–12 and 2014–15.

159. NCVO Press Release 11 December 2012, *Free NCVO membership extended as merger with Volunteering England is confirmed*. Volunteering England was the same charity as the Volunteer Centre, which had been established in 1973, having gone through several name changes and mergers of its own.

160. NCVO Press Release 21 June 2012, *NCVO and Volunteering England merger talks*.

161. On the establishment of the Volunteer Centre, see Chap. 7.

162. This issue is discussed further in the conclusion.

163. NCVO Press Release 31 March 2014, *Campaigning, volunteering and public trust among NCVO's priorities in new five-year strategy*.

164. NCVO Press Release 1 June 2014, *Thirty ambassadors chosen to mark thirtieth anniversary of volunteers' week*; NCVO Annual Report 2016–17.

165. NCVO Press Release 10 April 2015, *Conservative party volunteering proposal – NCVO comment*. On the ignominious demise of the plan, see Davis Smith, 2017.

166. NCVO Press Release 20 April 2017, *Sir Stuart Etherington's 2017 state of the sector address to NCVO annual conference delegates*.

167. NCVO Annual Report 2012–13, p. 9.

168. Interview with Dame Julia Cleverdon, 16 May 2018.

169. Interview with Sir Stephen Bubb, 19 July 2017. ACEVO has since moved out of Society Building.

170. Interview with Bharat Mehta, 27 July 2017.

171. Minutes of Trustee Board, 3 March 2011; uncatalogued papers, NCVO.

172. Interview with Sir Stuart Etherington, 25 July 2017.

173. NCVO Press Release 9 August 2018, *Civil society strategy: Encouraging start, but implementation will be key*. Cabinet Office, 2018.

174. Interview with Dame Julia Cleverdon, 16 May 2018.

175. Interview with Sir Graham Melmoth, 25 April 2018.

176. Interview with Baroness Pitkeathley, 24 April 2018.

177. Various interviews conducted for the book.

178. Interview with Perri 6, 30 April 2018.

179. Interviews with Richard Harries, 11 January 2018, Sir Graham Melmoth, 25 April 2018, and Campbell Robb, 18 September 2017.

180. Interview with Campbell Robb, 18 September 2017.

181. Interview with Dame Julia Cleverdon, 16 May 2018.

182. See note 8 for further details.

183. NCVO Press Release 11 February 2015, *NCVO devotes £100 K to commission on future of the voluntary sector.*

184. Minutes of Trustee Board, 18 June 2014; uncatalogued papers, NCVO.

REFERENCES

Alcock, P. (2010). Building the big society: A new policy environment for the third sector in England. *Voluntary Sector Review, 1*(3), 379–389.

Alcock, P. (2016). From partnership to the big society: The third sector policy regime in the UK. *Nonprofit Policy Forum, 7*(2), 95–116.

Alcock, P., Kendall, J., & Parry, J. (2012). From the third sector to the big society: Consensus or contention in the 2010 UK general election. *Voluntary Sector Review, 3*(3), 347–363.

Baring Foundation. (2013). *Independence under threat: The voluntary sector in 2013*. London: The Baring Foundation.

Baring Foundation. (2015). *An independent mission: The voluntary sector in 2015*. London: The Baring Foundation.

Blond, P. (2009). *The ownership state: Restoring excellence, innovation and ethos to the public services*. London: NESTA.

Breeze, B., & Lloyd, T. (2013). *Richer lives: Why rich people give*. London: Directory of Social Change.

Cabinet Office. (2009). *Real help for communities: Volunteers, charities and social enterprises*. London: Cabinet Office.

Cabinet Office. (2010a). *Supporting a stronger civil society*. London: Cabinet Office.

Cabinet Office. (2010b). *Giving Green Paper*. HMSO.

Cabinet Office. (2010c). *The Compact*. HMSO.

Cabinet Office. (2011). *Giving White Paper*. HMSO.

Cabinet Office. (2018). *Civil society strategy: Building a future that works for everyone*. London: HMSO.

Cameron, D. (2010, July 19). Big Society speech. *Cabinet Office*.

Carter, E., & Whitworth, A. (2014). Creaming and parking in quasi-marketised welfare-to-work schemes: Designed out of or designed into the UK work programme? *Journal of Social Policy, 44*(2), 277–296.

Charity Commission and Centre for Charity Effectiveness. (2017). *Taken on trust: The awareness and effectiveness of charity trustees in England and Wales*. London: Charity Commission.

Charity Governance Code Steering Group. (2017). *Charity governance code for larger charities*. London: Charity Governance Code Steering Group.

Civil Exchange. (2013). *The Big Society audit 2013*. London: Civil Exchange.

Civil Exchange. (2015). *Whose society? The final Big Society audit*. London: Civil Exchange.

Civil Exchange. (2016). *Independence in question: The voluntary sector in 2016*. London: Civil Exchange.

Clifford, D. (2017). Charitable organisations, the great recession and the age of austerity: Longitudinal evidence for England and Wales. *Journal of Social Policy, 46*(1), 1–30.

Commission on Civil Society and Democratic Engagement. (2014). *The Lobbying Act: Analysis of the law, and regulatory guidance recommendations*. London: Commission on Civil Society and Democratic Engagement.

Commission on Civil Society and Democratic Engagement. (2015). *Non-party campaigning ahead of elections: Consultation and recommendations relating to part 2 of the Transparency in Lobbying, Non-party Campaigning and Trade Union Administration Bill, report 4*. London: Commission on Civil Society and Democratic Engagement.

Corbett, S., & Walker, A. (2013). The Big Society: Rediscovery of the social or rhetorical fig-leaf for neo-liberalism. *Critical Social Policy, 33*(3), 451–472.

D'Ancona, M. (2013). *In it together: The inside story of the Coalition government*. London: Viking.

Davis Smith, J. (2017). David Cameron's three-day volunteering initiative: Genuine proposal or electoral sham? *Voluntary Sector Review, 8*(2), 219–229.

Etherington, S. S., Lord Leigh of Hurley, Pitkeathley, B., & Lord Wallace of Saltaire. (2015). *Regulating fundraising for the future: Trust in charities, confidence in fundraising regulation*. London: NCVO.

Green, E. (2002). *Ideologies of conservatism*. Oxford: Oxford University Press.

HM Government. (2011). *Open public services: White paper*. London: Stationery Office.

Hind, A. (2017). New development: Fundraising in UK charities – Stepping back from the abyss. *Public Money and Management, 37*(3), 205–210.

Hodgson, Lord of Astley Abbotts. (2016). *Third party election campaigning – Getting the balance right: Review of the operation of the third party campaigning rules at the 2015 general election (Cm 9205)*. London: The Stationery Office.

House of Lords Select Committee on Charities. (2017). *Stronger charities for a stronger society*. London: House of Lords.

Jones, G., Meegan, R., Kennett, P., & Croft, J. (2015). The uneven impact of austerity on the voluntary and community sector: A tale of two cities. *Urban Studies, 53*(10), 2064–2080.

Lamb, B. (2014). Is charity campaigning under threat from the Coalition government? *Voluntary Sector Review, 5*(1), 125–138.

May, T. (2017). *The Shared Society: Prime Minister's speech at the Charity Commission annual meeting.* London: Prime Minister's Office.

Midgley, H. (2016). Payment by results in nineteenth-century British education: A study in how priorities change. *Journal of Policy History, 28*(4), 680–706.

Morris, D. (2016). Legal limits on political campaigning by charities: Drawing the line. *Voluntary Sector Review, 7*(1), 109–115.

Mycock and Tonge. (2011). A big idea for the Big Society? The advent of national citizen service. *The Political Quarterly, 82*(1), 56–66.

National Audit Office. (2015). *Investigation: The government's funding of Kids Company.* London: Department for Education and the Cabinet Office.

National Coalition for Independent Action. (2014). *NCIA inquiry into the future of voluntary services: Working paper 1: The position and role of national infrastructure bodies concerning the cuts to and privatisation of public services.* London: NCIA.

National Coalition for Independent Action. (2015). *Our last word: Fighting for the soul of voluntary action.* London: NCIA.

NCVO. (2012). *Open public services: Experiences from the voluntary sector.* London: NCVO.

NCVO. (2014). *Report of the inquiry into charity senior executive pay and guidance for trustees on setting remuneration.* London: NCVO.

NCVO. (2015). *A financial sustainability review: Change and adaptation in the voluntary sector as the economy recovers.* London: NCVO.

NCVO. (2018). *The UK Civil Society Almanac.* London: NCVO.

Norman, J. (2010). *The Big Society: The anatomy of the new politics.* Buckingham: University of Buckingham Press.

Parliament. (2014). *Transparency of Lobbying, Non-party Campaigning and Trade Union Administration Act 2014.* London: Stationery Office.

Parvin, P. (2016). Silencing the critics: Charities, lobbyists, and the government's quiet war on dissent. *Renewal, 24*(3), 62–75.

Populus. (2018). *Trust in charities, 2018.* London: Charity Commission.

Public Administration and Constitutional Affairs Committee. (2015). *The 2015 charity fundraising controversy: Lessons for trustees, the Charity Commission, and regulators.* London: The Stationery Office.

Public Administration and Constitutional Affairs Committee. (2016). *The collapse of Kids Company: Lessons for charity trustees, professional firms, the Charity Commission and Whitehall.* London: HMSO.

Rees, J. (2014). Public sector commissioning and the third sector: Old wine in new bottles? *Public Policy and Administration, 29*(1), 45–63.

Rochester, C. (2013). *Rediscovering voluntary action: The beat of a different drum.* Basingstoke: Palgrave Macmillan.

SCVO. (2015). *The effectiveness of the self-regulation of fundraising in Scotland: An informal review.* Scotland: SCVO.

Seldon, A., & Snowdon, P. (2015). *Cameron at 10.* London: William Collins.

Sheil, F., & Breidenbach-Roe, R. (2014). *Payment by results and the voluntary sector.* London: NCVO.

Snowdon, C. (2012). *Sock puppets: How the government lobbies itself and why*. London: Institute of Economic Affairs.

Snowdon, C. (2014). *The sock doctrine – What can be done about state-funded political activism?* London: Institute of Economic Affairs.

Thaler, R., & Sunstein, C. (2008). *Nudge: Improving decisions about health, wealth and happiness*. Yale: Yale University Press.

CHAPTER 11

Conclusion: Idealists and Realists

SURVIVAL OF THE FITTEST

How are we to judge the Council's performance over one hundred years? First, it should be congratulated on its longevity and sticking power. Not many charities survive that long. It was not always an easy journey and there was no guarantee, or even expectation, when it was established in 1919 that it would live to celebrate its centenary. Its financial situation remained tight for most of its early history, and it was only after the onset of core funding in the early 1960s that a measure of sustainability was assured. Even then, annual deficits remained an all too familiar reality for many years. The problem it faced was that its main work, supporting other organisations and championing voluntary action to government, what later became known as infrastructure, was never fashionable or easily fundable. That it survived and flourished, when other infrastructure bodies at national and local level fell by the wayside, is a tribute to the enduring value of its work and the foresight and ingenuity of its leaders. Special mention should be made of Judy Weleminsky, for her role in purchasing premises for the Council for the first time in the early 1990s, and Stuart Etherington, for pursuing a highly successful membership drive and resource diversification strategy in the first decades of the twenty-first century. Tribute should also be paid to the negotiators behind the spin-off discussions with the Charities Aid Foundation in 1974, which secured a regular flow of unrestricted income. This currently amounts to over £1.5 million per annum, although the settlement has not been without its critics. When austerity bit in 2008 and the Coalition government terminated core funding, threatening to decimate the landscape of support agencies in the sector, the Council not only survived but strengthened its position by merging with a number of strategically important organisations. From the vantage point of 2018, the Council's financial position looks robust and its future secure, even though like many other charities it remains burdened by a large pension fund deficit.

© The Author(s) 2019
J. Davis Smith, *100 Years of NCVO and Voluntary Action*,
https://doi.org/10.1007/978-3-030-02774-2_11

A GLORIOUS HISTORY

But survival for its own sake has little merit, and the Council can look back on a long life well spent, with much to celebrate. One of its greatest achievements has been to support the development, and ultimate independence, of a range of household name charities, which have gone on to make a major contribution to the voluntary sector in the UK. Many of these successes have been documented in this book and this list is not exhaustive. Key organisations that stand out include young farmers, the Youth Hostels Association, village halls and community associations, citizens' advice bureaux, and Age Concern. The Council can't claim sole credit for initiating these groups, but in all cases the administrative support and guidance provided was an important part in their growth and success. It is not possible to say that they wouldn't have found another way to emerge and thrive if the Council hadn't been there, but it is indisputable that it was instrumental in giving support, and often sustained assistance, to a number of organisations that have gone on to play key roles in British society.

Another major achievement was to act as a focal point for the development of voluntary action at a local level, particularly in the first half of its history. The Council was founded with this aim and, for its first 60 or 70 years, it sought to build a network of support agencies in towns and villages across the country to promote voluntary action. Such an ambition was never going to be easy to realise, especially in towns, where funding wasn't as readily available as rural areas, but overall it did a good job under difficult circumstances. The abandonment of the federal model in the late 1960s left a hole in its work that needed to be filled. The choice taken was to turn away from the local and focus almost exclusively on the national, particularly on generic policy issues, research and the professional development of the movement. This book suggests something important was lost in the process, although the switch was not absolute. The Council was involved in policy work and research from the outset and continues to promote voluntary action at a local level. But there was a definite change of focus in the 1970s, which left it open to the charge of elitism and being out of touch with grassroots opinion. It sought to answer this criticism by a major push on membership and can claim some success, increasing numbers from a few hundred in the early 1990s to almost 13,000 today. However, with the total charity sector approaching 200,000 organisations and a voluntary sector of some three quarters of a million, any claim to representativeness is difficult to make. In contrast, in its early years, when it was responsible for the local networks and numerous associated groups, it claimed reach into tens of thousands of local agencies and millions of volunteers. The loss of strategic responsibility for volunteering, around the same time that the groups were going independent, served to highlight this deficit.

POLICY INFLUENCE

The Council can also point to many successes in the policy arena. Key areas of successful intervention run throughout its history: reform of charity law, improved tax treatment of charities, and, particularly under New Labour, support for infrastructure. The Council was instrumental in raising issues, bringing groups together, and lobbying government for change. It did not always get what it wanted and disappointments include failure to secure more profound change in the treatment of public benefit in charity law and greater government recognition of the value of infrastructure. Overall, however, it is an impressive record, which has made a significant difference to the health and vitality of the voluntary movement. And there is much more. For its first 60 years, it was heavily involved in social policy of all kinds, from housing and unemployment to support for older people, citizen's advice, women's issues, faith matters, and youth. Many achievements were secured through the work of the associated groups and the Council made a crucial contribution in supporting and facilitating this work. A case can again be made that the loss of the groups diluted its impact in the policy arena, but with many determined to push for independence, and the federated model creaking at the seams, it is perhaps unrealistic to expect it to have been able to hold the model together, even if it had so desired. Its replacement strategy focusing on core, cross-cutting issues important to the movement as a whole, has brought considerable success, but has not been without challenges.

For much of the second half of its history, large charities were suspicious of the Council and doubtful of the value it could add to their often well-resourced functions. This is a paradox that has confronted the organisation in recent years, when its main area of focus has been to support the work of larger charities, where its work arguably is less needed, rather than smaller, less well-resourced community groups, to which it devoted most of its energy in its early life. A second challenge of such an approach is that it only works when the government is willing to support the sector. Under New Labour, as Kendall has suggested, the growth of 'horizontal' support enabled the Council to stake a claim as a key, perhaps, the key, strategic partner.[1] The return under recent governments to a 'vertical', incremental approach to supporting voluntary action leaves the Council vulnerable to being sidelined, as most policy discussions take place between individual government departments and policy-specific charities.[2]

SPREADING THE WORD

It is not just at home that the Council can claim credit for spreading the word about the value of voluntary action and for securing policy and institutional changes beneficial to its development. From its inception, it saw the advance of voluntary action overseas as a fundamental part of its mission. This was perhaps most pronounced during the inter-war years, when the growing threat of a second world war gave added impetus to building international alliances. But the Council was also heavily involved in post-war international peace building through the United Nations and the revitalised International Conference on Social Work. Haynes, who did so much to set the federal direction of the Council in its domestic work, was also pivotal in advancing its international mission, and he helped position it as a major force on the international scene. The Council later took an active interest in Britain's European project, although its influence here was more limited. It can look back with some success on efforts to influence policy formulation in Brussels and in helping voluntary groups access funding from the European Commission. When Britain voted to leave the European Union in June 2016, the Council expressed major concerns about the financial impact on the voluntary sector and called for voluntary groups and volunteers to play their part in rebuilding a fractured nation. But for some commentators, the Council's impact on the international stage in the past 20 years has been a disappointment and they detect a narrowing of its horizons. Perhaps this is an inevitable consequence of the austerity that has decimated large parts of the sector and led to a tighter focus on domestic priorities. 'It is astonishing', Perri 6 suggests, 'how domestically oriented we were and how little we understood the wider international trends.'[3]

BUILDING AN EVIDENCE BASE

A further success has been in building a body of evidence about voluntary action and its contribution to society. Early attempts to map the sector were curtailed by the onset of the Second World War and the untimely death of the movement's chief researcher, Dr. Henry Mess. But the vision of the Council as a centre for research was revived on several occasions after the war. Many important studies were undertaken often, like so much of the Council's most important work, under the auspices of the associated groups. An extensive repository of books and pamphlets on voluntary action was built up and several quality journals were published, most notably *Social Service Quarterly*, which for more than two decades served as the intellectual organ of the movement. It would take the end of the federated model, and the shift of direction under Nicholas Hinton and Usha Prashar, before the research function really began to take shape. Francis Gladstone was recruited by Hinton and given a free rein to trial new ideas, and his landmark book on *welfare pluralism* set the agenda for the Council for more than a decade. Both Prashar and Etherington invested heavily in the function, and the Council forged close links with the burgeoning academic research community studying the voluntary sector in the UK and overseas. Margaret Harris has traced the development of the voluntary sector as an academic field of study and rightly pays tribute to the work of the Council from the 1980s.[4] Perri 6, however, suggests that too much of its research has been focused on 'boosting' the role of the sector, rather than critically examining its contribution.[5] In 2013, following the merger with Volunteering England, the Council inherited the Institute for Volunteering Research, which pioneered much of the research in the UK on volunteering. It was a disappointment to many in the academic and practitioner community when the Council disbanded the Institute in 2018.

CONTESTED TERRAIN

Despite the many successes, it is important to examine the criticisms that have been levelled against the Council over the years. The first charge is that it has been too close to government, resulting in a timidity in its campaigning and, ultimately, leading the sector down the wrong path towards incorporation. In assessing the justice or not of this charge, we first need to return to the reasons for its establishment. The Council was born out of a desire within the voluntary movement for greater cohesion at a national and local level and for a stronger voice to represent it with government. It wholly accepted the emerging philosophy of the *New Philanthropy*, which was circulating at the time.[6] This rejected the notion of *separate spheres*, which had characterised relations between the state and the voluntary movement for much of the nineteenth and early twentieth centuries, in favour of closer partnership. Indeed, one could argue that the Council, rather than reacting to the *New Philanthropy*, actively helped to invent it through its work in towns and villages and on new estates in the inter-war years. It was never a creation of the state as some historians have claimed.[7] It was always independent and owed its existence to the vision and energy of a small number of reformers who were determined to bring together the disparate strands within the voluntary movement active in the years leading up to the First World War.

First and foremost, it was established to promote and champion voluntary action, but, from the outset, it advocated a policy of close cooperation with the state as essential to achieving its goal. It would be disingenuous, therefore, to judge its work against the criteria of its closeness to government. Developing close relations with government was what it was set up to do. A well-respected alternative philosophy, advanced by writers including Ralph Dahrendorf, argues that the sector and the state should remain at arms-length, but this was not the ideology that drove the formation of the Council.[8] We need to judge its performance not against a philosophy that it never intended to follow but according to the values it espoused and the vision it was set up to deliver. In the process we should examine any unintended consequences that might have arisen from its chosen path and any lessons for the Council and the wider movement.

First, can the Council claim success for its chosen strategy? We have suggested it can point to many policy advances it has helped bring about that have aided the development of voluntary action and the strengthening of voluntary organisations. The close relations developed with the state, at both national and local level, undoubtedly raised awareness within government of the value of voluntary action and led to many favourable policy interventions. A crucial step towards achieving its goal of closer partnership was its work in bringing together a broad and disparate group of agencies that could only nominally be seen as sharing the same institutional forms and values under the umbrella, first of the *voluntary sector* in the late 1970s, and then the *third sector* in the late 1990s. Such a construct was unavoidably unstable given the diversity of the voluntary movement and, following the austerity policies of the 2010 Coalition and successor Conservative administrations, this strategic unity looks increasingly fragile.[9] Moreover, even at its height, some argued that unity never stretched very far and mainly encompassed larger organisations, without permeating to the majority of smaller community groups.[10] But by helping to create *the sector*, the Council could argue more forcibly within government for voluntary action to be taken seriously and make the case for why it should be supported and financed. Etherington suggests that a major achievement of the Council has been to provide 'a positive environment for voluntary action' and use its 'enormous convening power' to 'bring organisations together in a way that doesn't feel threatening, in order to make a case to government'.[11] For Nicholas Deakin, the Council's achievements 'have been to do with the growth of confidence and the ability to address government with a degree of conviction about the interests of the sector as a totality'.[12] For Prashar, the Council has acted as a 'flagship' for voluntary action, 'safeguarding the interests of voluntary organisations so they do not get stifled by government policy'.[13]

Was there more the Council could have done to push government to achieve change? Throughout its history its chosen approach to influencing policy has been to take the inside track and there is little evidence to support the claim that its closeness to government has resulted in its co-option.[14] There are numerous examples of it speaking out against government policy, especially in defence of what it has held to be the historic right of the movement to campaign. But on other occasions, it has been reluctant to put its head above the parapet, inviting accusations of timidity. There is a growing literature on the pros and cons of different approaches to political influence and the consensus appears to be that a binary distinction between insider and outsider strategy is too simplistic and not supported by empirical research.[15] Grant identifies three types of insider groups: 'prisoners', who find it difficult to exert their independence; 'low profile' insiders, who place emphasis on 'behind the scenes' interaction; and 'high profile' insiders, who aim to persuade government through appeals to public opinion.[16] The Council has switched over the course of its history between low- and high-profile insider status and has managed the tension quite well. It has also played the role of a 'mediating organisation', which Lune and Oberstein suggest involves facing inside and outside at the same time, acting as a connector between government and the sector.[17]

Many organisations, it is suggested, operate simultaneously on both tracks, or move between the two at different times as a deliberate strategic choice.[18] Virginia Berridge and Alex Mold claim that in the 1960s Action on Smoking and Health, representing one of the new breed of social movements, used both approaches in its campaigning and its outsider image was crucial to its insider status: government was more willing to consult with it because of its image as a fearless campaigner.[19] There are lessons here for the Council. In its early history, its outsider image was boosted by its connection to the community through its plethora of local networks and associated groups. The separation of these groups reduced its claim to legitimacy and dented this image. It was forced to base its policy-influencing strategy more on its reputation as a body of expertise and professional competence, rather than as a representative of grassroots action. Arguably, its influence suffered as a consequence and the power of its insider status was lessened. Strengthening its outsider image thus appears crucial for the success of its insider strategy, especially given the onset of a more fractured relationship with the state in which it no longer occupies a position of strategic partner. How could it do this? First, by seeking to build a base within local communities through revitalisation of some version of the Haynes model of federation, connecting the national with the local again as had been the vision for its first 60 years. But it could also seek to boost its outsider image by more fearless campaigning and moving faster to the outside track when the inside track fails to deliver. The Council will never be a deliberate outsider group, which is at odds with its aim of building closer links with the state. Nor will it be a 'prisoner' group, trading influence for independence. But a more fearless approach to campaigning might paradoxically strengthen its insider status and deflect criticism that it has been slow to stand up against fundamental assaults on the rights of the voluntary movement. Colin Rochester argues that the Council needs to reclaim its 'outsider' associational roots to counter the drift towards managerialism and co-option, while Stephen Bubb suggests it 'needs to be more in the public domain, and more outspoken than it has been'.[20] For Bharat Mehta, the Council needs, 'on occasions', to 'bare its teeth' more.[21]

The Council has always located itself as a body of expertise. During the inter-war years it could be seen, along with think-tanks such as Political and Economic Planning, as an example of 'middle opinion', which drew its authority from expertise rather than mass support.[22] But, although not a mass membership organisation, through its networks and groups, it could claim reach into local communities as some others could not. Anthony Sampson identified a similar trend in the early 1960s with the growth of 'new institutes', such as think-tanks and umbrella bodies, that provided politicians with 'a kind of shadow civil service' based once more on expertise.[23] Hilton and colleagues argue that modern charities have become deeply embedded in the policy-making process, although they reject the accusation that they 'have become mere stooges of the liberal state'.[24] In the 'modern expert-based and technocratic state', they write, 'the NGO is at one and the same time a wing of the state, and an agent acting against it', although they suggest that the closeness of the state means that alternative approaches have 'been diluted in the pragmatism of cooperation'.[25] It is possible that occupying a position as a body of professional competence will be increasingly uncomfortable in the world of post-truth and growing antipathy to experts.[26] Countering such bias, and hitting back against accusations of being out of touch and divorced from the everyday experience of community life, provides another powerful justification for the Council to reconnect with its founding ideals and rediscover its federal roots.

Pillar of the Establishment

One further criticism needs to be addressed on the subject of legitimacy. The Council has long been criticised for being part of the establishment and harbouring an inherent conservatism that has worked against the development of more radical solutions.[27] It is certainly the case that from its inception it has been able to call on the support of the great and the good. Its early sponsors, patrons, and Executive Committee members were drawn from the worlds of high politics, business, and academia. In its early years the post of president was passed from one Speaker of the House of Commons to the next. Its chair for the first 30 years of its life was W.G.S. Adams, Gladstone professor of politics at Balliol, Oxford University, and head of Lloyd George's wartime private office. Even locally, much of its early work was guided by the elite, especially in the countryside, where the rural community councils drew upon the support and patronage of the landowning aristocracy.[28] The leadership of the Council for much of its early history consisted of a web of closely connected individuals active in business, academia, politics, charity, and the arts. Adams, for example, alongside his marathon stint at the Council, was also a long-standing trustee of the Carnegie UK Foundation and the Development Commission, both major supporters of the Council. And of course for much of its history, it could count on the active patronage of the British royal family. This establishment bias became less pronounced in the latter half of its history, reflecting the more democratic nature of society and the world of charity, although it still exists.

Paradoxically, it is professionalisation, which the Council has done so much to promote, and which has been the subject of such intense criticism, that played a key part in the democratisation of the movement. So long as the leadership of charities was the sole preserve of unpaid volunteers, it was inevitable that individuals of private means would dominate. The growth of a salaried professional cadre opened opportunities for a broader cross-section of society to get involved and take on leadership roles. Such developments would not prevent the Council from losing touch with the radical changes taking place in the movement in the 1960s and 1970s, and it would take the arrival of Prashar as director in the mid-1980s before it could claim some measure of connectivity with the new forms of self-help and campaign groups that had emerged over the previous couple of decades. The Council was never able to claim to represent the more radical end of the movement, but it gradually began to shake off its establishment image and draw in a more diverse range of members and supporters.

We should not, however, overstress these developments. The Council remains supremely well connected at its upper echelons, with chairs and presidents continuing to be drawn from the worlds of politics and business, helping to oil the wheels of influence on the inside track when negotiating with government and furnishing the periodic appeals to industry required to keep the organisation afloat. But even in its formative years, it was not solely a body of the establishment. Through its extensive local networks, it could connect to numerous community and grassroots groups and millions of volunteers, representing a broad swathe of interest and orientation. Its work with community associations on the new estates in the 1920s and with the occupational clubs in the 1930s gave prominence to local ownership and representation and broke from the traditions of noblesse oblige, which had dominated much formal charity work in the nineteenth and early twentieth centuries. Critics have questioned the extent to which such initiatives challenged these orthodoxies, pointing to the presence of many volunteer leaders recruited from outside the new estates and the tendency of the occupational clubs to ignore the traditions of working-class literature and culture in their educational work.[29] But the models advanced were trying out something new, not replicating what had gone before and were imbued with an Idealist spirit that was not simply aimed at perpetuating the status quo.

The Council's record on diversity is mixed. Some of its work during the inter-war years pushed the issue of women's leadership, and the activity of the Women's Group on Public Welfare during and after the Second World War facilitated the involvement of tens of thousands of women volunteers. However, most of the work privileged more traditional forms of voluntary action, and the Council was not linked to any significant degree to the more radical women's movement of the 1960s and 1970s. Similarly on race and ethnicity, it undertook some important work on integration following the first wave of immigration from the Commonwealth in the 1960s, but it failed to connect to the new social movements at the time pushing for greater equality. Under Prashar, the Council finally began to embrace the issue of exclusion and diversity, but progress was slow.

IDEALISTS AND REALISTS

Some of the philosophies that underpinned the councils early work clearly had a conservative bent. Idealism, with its emphasis on individual service and active citizenship, which inspired so many of its pioneers, carried with it a distrust of the state that was at odds with more progressive thought at the turn of the twentieth century. Critics have also suggested that some of its early views on constructive leisure carried a whiff of the paternalistic and patronising, being concerned as much with keeping working men out of the pubs and race tracks as developing a spirit of active, democratic engagement in local communities.[30] But again we should be careful not to push this argument too far. Jose Harris has argued that Idealism spanned a wide range of political opinion, with many of its adherents advocating a stronger role for the state in social provision alongside voluntary action.[31] Several of the Council's early champions and most influential thinkers, including Adams, Lindsay, and Barker came from this Liberal or Left-leaning tradition, which chimed well with calls for greater partnership between the voluntary movement and the state. And, although many criticisms of the useful leisure movement might be justified, it also underpinned much of the Council's most creative work with the community associations and village halls. Such work laid the foundations for local community action that was to be the bedrock for the more radical tenants association and community development movement later in the century.[32]

The Council found a way for most of its history to encompass a broad range of political opinion. Few organisations, perhaps, could have given an intellectual home to figures with such diverse views as the Communist-leaning, Dorothy Keeling, and the future Conservative cabinet minister and intellectual inspiration for Thatcherism, Sir Keith Joseph.[33] This desire to spread its umbrella reflects the contested ideological basis of voluntary action that continues to divide and unite thinkers across the political spectrum, from Sir Stanley Baldwin and Clement Attlee at the beginning of this story, through Douglas Hurd and David Blunkett in the 1980s, to Tony Blair and David Cameron in the early twenty-first century. One of the Council's greatest achievements is that for most of its history it has managed to hold this diverse coalition together. It has also been one of its greatest challenges, leaving it open to accusations of fudge and of failing to develop a clear and distinctive ideological position of its own.

For some critics, the problem is not so much that the Council has never had a strong ideological position, but that it has shifted positions over time. According to Rochester, the Council has moved during the course of its history from a philosophical approach that sees voluntary action largely as a good in its own right, in terms of its ability to build strong local active communities, to one that views it in instrumental terms, as a means of getting things done and delivering services with state money.[34] There is no doubt such a shift occurred and that the timing can be traced to the end of the federated model in the late 1960s and the establishment of the Volunteer Centre in the early 1970s. This fracture of the national from the local demanded a new approach to which the Council was initially slow to respond, with the result that its reputation was badly damaged and it lost ground for over a decade. It took the appointment of a radical new director, Hinton, in the late 1970s to produce a replacement strategy that was based on increasing the movement's role in service delivery as part of a new dream of *welfare pluralism*.[35] In order to deliver this agenda the sector, the Council argued, needed to raise its game, so it embarked on a process of supporting organisations to improve their leadership and management. Such work was not altogether new. Through its associated groups, the Council had long paid attention to the training of staff and volunteers, and it had launched early enquiries into pay and conditions and established a pension scheme for social service workers after the Second World War. But support for the professional development of voluntary organisations and its staff and trustees now became one of its main areas of focus. For critics, this was a mistake, a wrong path chosen, which represented the end of ideology for the Council.[36] The result they argue is a sector that has become overly professionalised and formalised and has lost the values and energy that were present in the looser, less formal tradition of civic association. Offer has suggested that the shift in direction came under Thatcher. For Idealists 'in a sense practical outcomes of charity were secondary'. After 1979, voluntary organisations were increasingly seen in more instrumental terms.[37]

Others take a different view. They suggest that the Hinton revolution was long overdue and that he helped bring the Council and the wider movement into a new era of professionalism. For Hinton, there was nothing romantic about informality. If voluntary organisations and volunteers were to make the biggest impact possible, they needed to be at the front line of delivering services. To do this they needed to prove that they were competent, efficient, and effective. The Hinton/Gladstone dream of a bottom-up, grassroots *welfare pluralism* was never fulfilled. As Martin Knapp has argued, it was never viable and was based on an overestimate of the movement's capacity to deliver.[38] It was replaced by a top-down, competitive, contractual model in which voluntary organisations were invited to compete alongside commercial companies to run a range of public services. Over the next 30 years the Council focused much of its energy on trying to influence the new contract culture to provide an entry route for voluntary groups. This largely ended in failure. The focus on professionalisation, however, continued unabated, and the Council redoubled its efforts to strengthen the leadership and governance of voluntary organisations. Critics are right to argue that the Council has shifted its ideological focus over the course of its history, and that in doing so it has played a part in shifting the voluntary movement away from its associational roots towards more professionalism. The question is not whether this occurred but what the impact has been and whether anything has been lost in the process.

MANAGERIALISM AND PROFESSIONALISATION

Much recent writing has suggested that professionalisation and managerialism has had a negative effect. Writers such as Linda Milbourne and Mike Hemmings argue that the sector has been too quick to adopt management systems drawn from the worlds of New Public Management and business, which have undermined the sector's claim to distinctiveness and squeezed out volunteers in favour of professional staff.[39] They draw on the work of writers such as Di Maggio, Powell, and Billis, who have pointed at the potential for institutional isomorphism, hybridisation, and loss of identity due to increasing professionalisation and dependency on state funding.[40] The Council, as the standard-bearer for professionalisation, has received particular criticism.[41] There are some grounds for this attack. Since the 1980s, the Council has unashamedly pushed an agenda of professionalisation. From early on, some expressed concern about this direction of travel. For Marilyn Taylor, there was a danger that the adoption of a 'more competitive ethos' would 'put at risk traditions of collaboration and cooperation'.[42] Wilson suggests that the sector was slow to embrace alternative cooperative strategies as a way out of 'the seemingly deterministic logic of resource dependencies, or enterprise-driven competition'.[43] The Council claimed it was never about aping business practice, but was searching for a voluntary sector solution. Tim Dartington, who led much of the early work, was clear that the private sector was not always an appropriate model as it did not fit the sector's values and mission.[44] The Management Development Unit established to take forward the agenda is remembered by some contemporaries as experimenting with a range of organisational models.[45] Such innovation, however, appears to have stalled, and the Council's failure to build on this early promise and develop an approach more in keeping with the ethos of the sector, was a missed opportunity.

But we can push this critique too far. A recent systematic review of the literature on professionalisation has found no consensus on its impact. Some studies suggest that it damages advocacy and causes mission drift, while others point to the opposite. The authors conclude that impact is determined by context and has more to do with governance and leadership than professionalisation per se.[46] The same goes for evidence on the impact of government funding. Academics such as Hemmings argue that increased reliance on state funding, coupled with growing managerialism and professionalisation, has blunted the sector's voice.[47] But hard evidence is lacking, a point acknowledged even by those advancing the claim.[48] There is some evidence that the opposite may be true. Berridge and Mold, for example, have argued that in the 1960s 'taking money from the state actually seems to have enhanced the reputation of some agencies and allowed them access into policy-making circles'.[49]

The Council has consistently pushed back against attempts to muzzle the sector. However, it has acknowledged the dangers of resource dependency, arguing that organisations need a diverse funding base to avoid becoming over-reliant on government. In the absence of evidence pointing one way or the other, assertions about professionalisation and government funding have become articles of faith. For some, the Council's work in strengthening the sector's governance, leadership, and management and in securing state funding has been among its most important achievements. For others, its drive for professionalisation and acceptance of state funding was the point in its history when things began to go wrong, when it abandoned its commitment to its associational roots and local civic endeavour, in favour of a contracts-funded, corporately inspired, managerial model of voluntary action.

Highs and Lows

What were the Council's most and least successful periods? It is not easy to judge, as most periods saw both successes and disappointments. The early years were marked by the struggle to get established, when funds were extremely tight and members of the Executive Committee were forced to guarantee their own contributions to keep the organisation afloat. But it also saw some notable successes, especially with the village halls and community associations. The 1930s saw the Council increase its public profile with its unemployment work and much closer relationship with government, but it was an era fraught with controversy. The Second World War can stake a claim for being the most productive period. The organisation played an important role in mobilising volunteering for the war effort. One could perhaps also claim, as Peter Grant has done for the First World War, that by building social capital it gave the country an edge in the war, boosting morale and keeping citizens informed through the network of citizens' advice bureaux, although we should be careful not to buy into the Myth of the Blitz.[50]

In the immediate post-war years, amid fears of the demise of the voluntary movement that were largely dispelled, the Council can take credit for mapping out a new role for voluntary action in the ever-shifting frontier with the state. New national charities were established, and the Council's international work expanded significantly, although it is probably fair to conclude, as Wolfenden later did, that the period saw the movement marking time after the creativity and vitality of the war years.[51] The same was true for the Council. The 1960s and 1970s were the most barren time. Not for the wider movement, as new organisational forms emerged imbued with the spirit of self-help and mutuality. But the Council lost energy and found itself increasingly out of touch. The 1980s and early 1990s were a difficult time in terms of relations with the government, which took a more instrumental approach to voluntary action and sought to restrict the right of voluntary organisations to campaign. The Council repositioned itself under the inspirational leadership of Hinton, with a new focus on *welfare pluralism*, although the dream never materialised and it became disillusioned with the marketised direction of the contract revolution. Under Prashar, it began to connect with the new forms of voluntary action, but the process of independence for the associated groups was speeded up and led to a growing separation from the grassroots. New Labour was the high point in the century-long search for a productive partnership between the voluntary movement and the state and marked the realisation of much of what the Council had been striving for: recognition of the value of voluntary action, significant investment, a new charity law, and significant new tax benefits. However, it also saw growing concerns about the unintended consequences of the shifts taking place and fears that the movement was trading its independence for influence and funding. The most recent period, following the election of the Conservative-controlled Coalition government in 2010, has seen an end of partnership and a strategic decoupling by the government, which the Council was powerless to stop. We finish the story with it searching for a new role, in the absence of a supportive state, and with a question mark over how well attuned it is to the new forms of social action that have emerged over the past decade. Over the course of its 100-year history, the 1930s, 1940s, 1990s, and early 2000s stand out as the most dynamic periods, with the least successful being the 1960s and 1970s.

THE SECOND CURVE

Such an analysis raises the question of stages of organisational development and how successful the Council has been in reinventing itself. We can turn to Charles Handy, who led the management development work in the 1980s, to inform our thinking. Handy has popularised the notion of the *Second Curve*, arguing that organisations need continually to reinvent themselves before they reach their peak to avoid stasis.[52] Like many organisations, the Council has struggled with this process. It reached the zenith of its influence during the war, but a failure to reinvent itself in the post-war years meant it was unable to respond to the changes of the 1960s and 1970s. By the time Hinton and Prashar began the process of revitalisation it was behind the curve. One could argue that this phenomenon is at risk of repeating itself. The organisation has enjoyed significant success under Etherington's leadership, but a failure to anticipate and respond to the emergence of new forms of less formal, net-worked social movements, many driven by the digital revolution, means it is again in danger of being left behind. In Handy's terms, the Council missed the pre-peak renewal point in the late 1950s and again in the early 2000s. It lagged behind the development of the voluntary movement in the 1960s and 1970s and is in danger of having to play catch-up once more in connecting with the new voluntary sector.[53] It may not be an easy task, as Handy argues that when 'income, productivity or reputation is falling it is hard to contemplate anything new'.[54] Hemmings suggests there is little evidence of the established sector 'supporting or building new associational social movements'.[55] Margaret Bolton agrees: 'Rightly or wrongly', she suggests, the Council 'is perceived as about established traditional charities and voluntary organisations, and as time moves on that's where less of the action is'. There is a perception, she says, 'NCVO is not ahead of the curve'.[56]

Another way to look at the changes that have taken place with the Council over its 100 years is to draw on Brian Harrison's distinction between *cause* and *interest* groups. Cause groups, he sees, as driven by the ideal of the 'active citizen', 'by the energetic and often prickly reformer who readily breaks off from parent organisations to create a splinter group'. Within such groups, 'spontaneity and diversity of ideas and opportunity were the ideal, with leaders responding to initiatives that bubbled up from below'. Such groups, he argues, 'actually encourage such people to hive off into a useful, more specialist, and nominally independent offshoot'.[57] This is as a good description of the Council for its first 70 years. Constantly refreshing itself through its plethora of associated groups, starting new initiatives and hiving them off, but always with roots in the *cause* through its local networks. In contrast, its last 30 years are more analogous to Harrison's *interest* group, with a focus on representing the sector and providing it with a range of high-quality services. Much was achieved as a result of this transition, but some of the early innovation and spontaneity was lost.

THE FUTURE

What does the future hold for the Council as it begins its second century? Some commentators have called for a revival of its early culture of experimentation and incubation. Janet Morrison, for example, suggests that, although it continues to be regarded as 'a professional, solid and competent organisation', it has moved 'a long way from the organisation that had all these different projects and consortia growing up, and it may have lost a little bit of its creativity'.[58] Julia Cleverdon agrees and argues for 'better partnerships between NCVO and others' and a return, 'in a funny way', to 'the chaos it had built up with all those networks'.[59] Deakin suggests that it needs to 'reach out' and build 'coalitions of interest with other groups in civil society'.[60] Prashar calls for 'a revival of community action', bringing people together 'so they don't feel so isolated and are able to cope with the pressures of globalisation'.[61]

A return to the Council's associated group structure is unlikely to be feasible; financial and governance constraints rule it out. But a move away from its centralised structure towards a federal model, using its power and influence to nurture quasi-independent networks and enterprises, should be considered. The Council should look to reclaim its early pioneering spirit and reinvent itself as a *cause* group, moving away from its role as trade body to the established voluntary sector and reconnecting to its roots in local communities. This would require a major shift of strategy, to match that led by Haynes at the end of the Second World War, and it is by no means clear that it is well enough connected with the new world of voluntary action to make it work. Etherington is honest about the challenge, admitting that the organisation currently 'hasn't really got a grasp on the informal civil action that's going on, the new developments, the new networks that are taking place'.[62] There are some positive signs. The merger with Volunteering England in 2013 has reconnected the organisation to the individual and the network of local Volunteer Centres, although, like most infrastructure bodies, they are struggling to survive in an increasingly difficult funding climate. It has also invested heavily in its digital strategy, an essential pre-requisite for connecting to the looser, networked forms of voluntary action. But this is unlikely to be sufficient, and for the organisation to retain its relevance and leadership a radical rethink of mission and structure is required. History is an uncertain guide to the future, but if the past 100 years tell us anything, it is that the Council is never short of new ideas.

NOTES

1. Kendall, 2000.
2. Alcock, 2016.
3. Interview with Perri 6, 30 April 2018.
4. Harris, 2016.
5. Interview with Perri 6, 30 April 2018.
6. The term was popularised in the 1930s by Elizabeth Macadam in her book of the same name. Macadam, 1934.
7. For example, Flanagan, 1991, p. 202, and Lowe, 1995, p. 373.
8. See, for example, Dahrendorf, 2001.
9. Alcock, 2016.
10. See, for example, Milbourne, 2013, and Rochester, 2013.

11. Interview with Sir Stuart Etherington, 25 July 2017.

12. Interview with Nicholas Deakin, 4 April 2017.

13. Interview with Baroness Prashar, 9 October 2017.

14. On claims that the sector has been co-opted by government, see Carmel and Harlock, 2008.

15. See, for example, Maloney et al., 1994.

16. Grant, 1999.

17. Lune and Oberstein, 2001.

18. For example, Craig et al., 2004, and McGhee et al, 2016.

19. Berridge and Mold, 2011, p. 117.

20. Rochester, 2013. Interview with Sir Stephen Bubb, 19 July 2017.

21. Interview with Bharat Mehta, 27 July 2017.

22. Marwick, 1964. See also Hilton, 2011, and Hilton et al., 2013.

23. Sampson, 1962, pp. 242–3.

24. Hilton et al., p. 16.

25. Ibid., p. 16.

26. On the growing aversion to experts, see Hay, 2007.

27. See, for example, Snape, 2015, on accusations of elitism during the inter-war years.

28. Burchardt, 2012.

29. For criticism of the work on the new estates, see Garside, 2004, and Olechnowicz, 1997. For criticism of the occupational club movement with the unemployed, see Flanagan, 1991.

30. Snape, 2015.

31. Harris, 1992, p. 126.

32. See, for example, Shapely, 2011.

33. The future Labour foreign secretary, David Miliband, also worked at the Council for a short time as a political analyst.

34. Rochester, 2013.

35. The dream was based on a book by Francis Gladstone, director of policy at the Council under Hinton. Gladstone, 1979.

36. Rochester, 2013.

37. Offer, 2003, p. 232.

38. Knapp, 1984.

39. Milbourne, 2013; Hemmings, 2017.

40. DiMaggio and Powell, 1983; and Billis, 2012.

41. See the various reports from the National Coalition for Independent Action, in particular, NCIA, 2014.

42. Taylor, 1996, p. 23.

43. Wilson, 1992.

44. Dartington, 1991.

45. See Chap. 8.

46. Maier et al., 2014.

47. Hemmings, 2017.

48. Ibid.

49. Berridge and Mold, 2011, p. 132.

50. Grant, 2014. Calder, 1992.

51. Wolfenden Committee, 1978.

52. Handy, 2015.

53. On the changing shape of civil society, see the final report of the inquiry into Civil Society Futures, 2018.
54. Handy, 2015, p. 24.
55. Hemmings, 2017, p. 62.
56. Interview with Margaret Bolton, 2 October 2017.
57. Harrison, 2003, p. 87.
58. Interview with Janet Morrison, 10 October 2017.
59. Interview with Dame Julia Cleverdon, 16 May 2018.
60. Interview with Nicholas Deakin, 4 April 2017.
61. Interview with Baroness Prashar, 9 October 2017.
62. Interview with Sir Stuart Etherington, 25 July 2017.

References

Alcock, P. (2016). From partnership to the Big Society: The third sector policy regime in the UK. *Nonprofit Policy Forum, 7*(2), 95–116.

Berridge, V., & Mold, A. (2011). Professionalisation, new social movements and voluntary action in the 1960s and 1970s. In M. Hilton & J. McKay (Eds.), *The ages of voluntarism: How we got to the Big Society* (pp. 114–134). Oxford: Oxford University Press for British Academy.

Billis, D. (Ed.). (2012). *Hybrid organisations and the third sector: Challenges for practice, theory and policy.* Basingstoke: Palgrave Macmillan.

Burchardt, J. (2012). State and society in the English countryside: The rural community movement, 1918–39. *Rural History, 23*(1), 81–106.

Calder, A. (1992). *The people's war: Britain 1939–1945.* London: Pimlico.

Carmel, E., & Harlock, J. (2008). Instituting the "third sector" as a governable terrain: Partnership, procurement and performance in the UK. *Policy and Politics, 36*(2), 155–171.

Civil Society Futures. (2018). *The story of our times: Shifting power, bridging divides, transforming society.* London: Civil Society Futures.

Craig, G., Taylor, M., & Parkes, T. (2004). Protest or partnership? The voluntary and community sectors in the policy process. *Social Policy and Administration, 38*(3), 221–239.

Dahrendorf, R. (2001). *Challenges to the voluntary sector. Arnold Goodman Lecture.* London: Charities Aid Foundation.

Dartington, T. (1991). Professional management in voluntary organisations: Some cautionary notes. In J. Batsleer, C. Cornforth, & R. Paton (Eds.), *Issues in voluntary and non-profit management.* Wokingham: Addison Wesley.

DiMaggio, P., & Powell, W. (1983). The iron cage revisited: Institutional isomorphism and collective rationality in organisational fields. *American Sociological Review, 48*(2), 147–160.

Flanagan, R. (1991). *'Parish-fed bastards': A history of the politics of the unemployed in Britain, 1884–1939.* Westport: Greenwood Press.

Garside, P. (2004). Citizenship, civil society and quality of life: Sutton model dwellings estates, 1919–39. In R. Colls & R. Rodger (Eds.), *Cities of ideas: Civil society and urban governance in Britain, 1800–2000* (pp. 258–282). Aldershot: Ashgate.

Gladstone, F. (1979). *Voluntary action in a changing world.* London: Bedford Square Press.

Grant, W. (1999). *Pressure groups and British politics*. Basingstoke: Macmillan.

Grant, P. (2014). *Philanthropy and voluntary action in the First World War: Mobilizing charity*. London: Routledge, Taylor & Francis Group.

Handy, C. (2015). *The second curve: Thoughts on reinventing society*. London: Random House.

Harris, J. (1992). Political thought and the welfare state, 1870–1940: An intellectual framework for British social policy. *Past and Present, 135*, 116–141.

Harris, M. (2016). Where did we come from? The emergence and early development of voluntary sector studies in the UK. *Voluntary Sector Review, 7*(1), 5–25.

Harrison, B. (2003). Civil society by accident? Paradoxes of voluntarism and pluralism in the nineteenth and twentieth centuries. In J. Harris (Ed.), *Civil society in British history: Ideas, identities, institutions* (pp. 79–96). Oxford: Oxford University Press.

Hay, C. (2007). *Why we hate politics*. Cambridge: Polity.

Hemmings, M. (2017). The constraints on voluntary sector voice in a period of continued austerity. *Voluntary Sector Review, 8*(1), 41–66.

Hilton, M. (2011). Politics is ordinary: Non-governmental organisations and political participation in contemporary Britain. *Twentieth Century British History, 22*(2), 230–268.

Hilton, M., McKay, J., Crowson, N., & Mouhot, J. (2013). *The politics of expertise: How NGOs shaped modern Britain*. Oxford: Oxford University Press.

Kendall, J. (2000). The mainstreaming of the third sector into public policy in England in the late 1990's: Whys and wherefores. *Policy and Politics, 28*(4), 541–562.

Knapp, M. (1984). *The economics of social care*. Basingstoke: Macmillan.

Lowe, R. (1995). Welfare's moving frontier. *Twentieth Century British History, 6*(3), 369–376.

Lune, H., & Oberstein, H. (2001). Embedded systems: The case of HIV/AIDS nonprofit organisations in New York City. *Voluntas: International Journal of Voluntary and Nonprofit Organizations, 12*(1), 17–33.

Macadam, E. (1934). *The New Philanthropy: A study of the relations between the statutory and voluntary social services*. London: Allen and Unwin.

Maier, F., Meyer, M., & Steinbereithner, M. (2014). Nonprofit organisations becoming business-like: A systematic review. *Nonprofit and Voluntary Sector Quarterly, 45*(1), 64–86.

Maloney, W., Jordan, G., & McLaughlin, A. (1994). Interest groups and public policy: The insider/outsider model revisited. *Journal of Public Policy, 14*(1), 17–38.

Marwick, A. (1964). Middle opinion in the thirties: Planning progress and political "agreement"'. *The English Historical Review, 79*(311), 285–298.

McGhee, D., Bennett, C., & Walker, S. (2016). The combination of "insider" and "outsider" strategies in VSO-government partnerships: The relationship between Refugee Action and the Home Office in the UK. *Voluntary Sector Review, 7*(1), 27–46.

Milbourne, L. (2013). *Voluntary sector in transition: Hard times or new opportunities?* Bristol: Policy Press.

National Coalition for Independent Action. (2014). *NCIA inquiry into the future of voluntary services: Working paper 1: The position and role of national infrastructure bodies concerning the cuts to and privatisation of public services*. London: NCIA.

Offer, J. (2003). Idealism versus non-idealism: New light on social policy and voluntary action in Britain since 1880. *Voluntas: International Journal of Voluntary and Nonprofit Organizations, 14*(2), 227–240.

Olechnowicz, A. (1997). *Working-class housing in England between the wars: The Becontree Estate*. Oxford: Clarendon Press.

Rochester, C. (2013). *Rediscovering voluntary action: The beat of a different drum*. Basingstoke: Palgrave Macmillan.

Sampson, A. (1962). *Anatomy of Britain*. London: Hodder and Stoughton.

Shapely, P. (2011). Civil society, class and locality: Tenant groups in post-war Britain. In M. Hilton & J. McKay (Eds.), *The ages of voluntarism: How we got to the Big Society* (pp. 94–113). Oxford: Oxford University Press for British Academy.

Snape, R. (2015). The new leisure, voluntarism and social reconstruction in inter-war Britain. *Contemporary British History, 29*(1), 51–83.

Taylor, M. (1996). What are the key influences on the work of voluntary agencies. In D. Billis & M. Harris (Eds.), *Voluntary agencies: Challenges of organisation and management* (pp. 13–28). Basingstoke: Macmillan.

Wilson, D. (1992). The strategic challenges of cooperation and competition in British voluntary organisations: Towards the next century. *Non-profit management and leadership, 2*(3), 239–254.

Wolfenden Committee. (1978). *The future of voluntary organisations: Report of the Wolfenden Committee*. London: Croom Helm.

APPENDIX

APPENDIX 1: KEY FIGURES IN THE HISTORY OF THE COUNCIL

Patrons
The Prince of Wales, later King Edward VIII
   King George VI
   Queen Elizabeth II

Presidents
1919–21 James Lowther (Viscount Ullswater)
Conservative politician and Speaker of the House of Commons, 1905–21.
1921–28 and 1932–35 John Henry Whitley
Liberal politician and Speaker of the House of Commons, 1921–28.
1928–32 Edward Fitzroy
Conservative politician and Speaker of the House of Commons, 1928–43.
1935–38 Viscount Bledisloe
Conservative politician and governor-general of New Zealand, 1930–35.
1938–39 Baron Snell
Labour politician and Labour leader in the House of Lords in the late 1930s.
1939–51 Sir Percy Malcolm Stewart
Industrialist, appointed special commissioner by Ramsay MacDonald in 1934, to develop schemes to reduce unemployment.
1951–54 Earl of Halifax
Conservative politician, viceroy of India, 1925–31, and foreign secretary, 1938–40.
1954–57 Sir Edward Peacock
Canadian banker, director of the Bank of England and receiver-general to the Duchy of Cornwall.

© The Author(s) 2019
J. Davis Smith, *100 Years of NCVO and Voluntary Action*,
https://doi.org/10.1007/978-3-030-02774-2

1957–70 Lord Heyworth
Industrialist, chair of Imperial Chemical Industries and Unilever and the committee that led to the establishment of the Social Science Research Council.

1970–73 The Duke of Edinburgh
Husband and consort of Queen Elizabeth 11

1973–81 Sir John Partridge
Industrialist, chair of the Imperial Tobacco Group, and president of the Confederation of British Industry, 1970–72.

1981–86 Sir John Greenborough
Industrialist, deputy chair of Shell UK, and president of the Confederation of British Industry, 1978–80.

1986–91 Sir Kenneth Durham
Industrialist, chair of Unilever and Kingfisher and deputy chair of British Aerospace.

1991–97 Sir Campbell Adamson
Industrialist, director general of the Confederation of British Industry, 1969–76, and chair of Abbey National.

1997–2002 Lord Plant
Labour peer and academic, master of St Catherine's College, Oxford, 1994–2000.

2002–07 Baroness Rawlings
Conservative politician and member of the European Parliament, 1989–94.

2007–12 Lord Hodgson
Conservative politician and peer, chair of the National Conservative Convention 1998–2000.

2012–17 Baroness Grey-Thompson
Athlete, cross-bench peer, and chancellor of Northumbria University.

2017–Baroness Pitkeathley
Labour peer, former chief executive of Carers National Association (now Carers UK).

Chairs

1919 Sir Aubrey Symonds
Civil servant, assistant secretary at the Local Government Board.

1919–49 Dr W.G.S. (William) Adams
Academic and public servant, head of Lloyd George's wartime secretariat, and Gladstone professor at Balliol College, Oxford.

1949–53 Sir Keith Murray (Lord Murray of Newhaven)
Academic and public servant, rector of Lincoln College, Oxford, and chair of the University Grants Committee.

1953–60 Sir John Wolfenden (Lord Wolfenden)
Academic and public servant, headmaster of Uppingham and Shrewsbury schools, vice-chancellor of the University of Reading, and chair of the University Grants Committee.

1961–73 Dr Leslie Farrer-Brown
Lawyer, economist and charity administrator, founder and first secretary of the Nuffield Foundation, and chair of the University of London.
1973–77 Sir Philip Allen (Lord Allen of Abbeydale)
Civil servant, permanent under-secretary of state at the Home Office.
1977–81 The Hon Sara Morrison
Businesswoman and Conservative politician, vice-chair of the Conservative Party, 1971–75.
1981–86 The Hon Peter Jay
Journalist, broadcaster and diplomat, British ambassador to the US, 1977–79.
1986–89 The Reverend Alan Morgan
Cleric, Archdeacon of Coventry, and suffragan Bishop of Sherwood.
1989–96 Sir Geoffrey Chandler
Businessman, director general of the National Economic Development Office, and senior director at Shell.
1996–2001 Lady Tumin
Campaigner and philanthropist, chair of the National Institute for Deaf People (now Action on Hearing Loss), Foyer Federation, and Forum on Children and Violence.
2001–04 Norman Warner (Lord Warner of Brockley)
Public administrator and Labour politician, health minister, 2003–2007.
2004–10 Graham Melmoth
Businessman, senior roles at BOC and Fisons, and corporate secretary and chief executive of the Co-operative Group.
2010–16 Sir Martyn Lewis
Journalist, broadcaster and philanthropist, vice-president of Hospice UK, founder of YouthNet (now The Mix), and chair of the Queen's Awards for Voluntary Service.
2016–Peter Kellner
Journalist and political commentator, chairman of YouGov opinion polling company, 2001–2007, and former chair of the Royal Commonwealth Society.

Secretaries/Directors/Chief Executives
The title general secretary was used from 1919 to 1945, secretary from 1945 to 1956, and director from 1956 to 1993. From 1993 chief executive has been used.

1919–36 Lionel Ellis
1936–40 Leonard Shoeten Sack
1940–67 George Haynes (Sir George Haynes)
1967–77 John Kenneth (JK) Owens
1977–84 Nicholas Hinton
1985–85 William Griffiths
1986–91 Ushar Prashar (Baroness Prashar)
1991–94 Judy Weleminsky
1994–Present Stuart Etherington (Sir Stuart Etherington)

APPENDIX 2: SELECT LIST OF ORGANISATIONS SUPPORTED
BY THE COUNCIL

Not all the organisations were established by the Council, but all received support, either financial or administrative, in their early days and often much longer. Many no longer exist, but several have gone on to be household name charities, albeit often under different names. To avoid repetition and confusion, I have used the most recent name, rather than the founding name.

Action with Communities in Rural England
Age Concern (now Age UK)
Amateur Music Association
Association for Research into Restricted Growth
BOND (British Overseas NGOs for Development)
British Association for Counselling
British Association for Local History
British Committee for the International Exchange of Social Workers and
    Administrators
British Council for Aid to Refugees
British National Conference on Social Work
British Volunteer Programme
Central Churches Group
Central Council for Amateur Theatre
Central Council for the Disabled
Charities Aid Foundation
Community Care Alliance
Community Matters (National Federation of Community Organisations)
Council for the Preservation of Rural England
European Council for Voluntary Organisations
European Network for National Associations
European Network of National Civil Society Organisations
Family Forum
Festival Welfare Services
International Council on Social Welfare
National Agency on Alcohol Misuse
National Alliance of Women's Organisations
National Association for Voluntary and Community Action
National Association of Boys' Clubs
National Association of Citizens' Advice Bureaux
National Association of Parish councils
National Association of Women's Clubs
National Association of Young Farmers' Clubs
National Bureau for Cooperation in Child Care
National Children's Bureau
National Council for Voluntary Youth Services

National Council on Gambling
National Food Alliance
National Playing Fields Association
National Self-Help Support Centre
National Television Advisory Group
Neighbourhood Energy Action
Northern Ireland Council for Voluntary Action
Pre-Retirement Association of Great Britain and Northern Ireland
Rural Industries Loan Fund
Rural Voice
Scottish Council for Voluntary Organisations
Self-Help Alliance
Sia (Organisation Development Unit)
Social Work Advisory Service
Standing Conference for Drama
Standing Conference of British Organisations for Aid to Refugees
Standing Conference of Women's Organisations
The Pensions Trust for Charities and Voluntary Organisations (now TPT
    Retirement Solutions)
Third Sector European Network
United Funds
Urban Forum
Wales Council for Voluntary Action
Waste Watch
Women's Group on Public Welfare
World Assembly of Youth
Youth Hostels Association

BIBLIOGRAPHY

6, P., & Leat, D. (1997). Inventing the British voluntary sector by Committee: from Wolfenden to Deakin. *Non-Profit Studies, 1*(2), 33–47.

Alcock, P. (2010). Building the big society: A new policy environment for the third sector in England. *Voluntary Sector Review, 1*(3), 379–389.

Alcock, P. (2016). From partnership to the big society: The third sector policy regime in the UK. *Nonprofit Policy Forum, 7*(2), 95–116.

Alcock, P., & Kendall, J. (2011). Constituting the third sector: Processes of decontestation and contention under the UK Labour governments in England. *Voluntas, 22*(3), 450–469.

Andrews, M. (1997). *The acceptable face of feminism: The Women's Institute as a social movement.* London: Lawrence & Wishart.

Aves, G. (1969). *The voluntary worker in the social services: Report of a committee jointly set up by the National Council of Social Service and the National Institute for Social Work Training under the chairmanship of Geraldine M. Aves.* London: Allen & Unwin.

Beaumont, C. (2013). *Housewives and citizens: Domesticity and the women's movement in England, 1928–64.* Manchester: Manchester University Press.

Beaven, B., & Griffiths, J. (2008). Creating the exemplary citizen: The changing notion of citizenship in Britain, 1870–1939. *Contemporary British History, 22*(2), 203–225.

Beveridge, W. (1948). *Voluntary action: A report on methods of social advance.* London: George Allen & Unwin.

Bingham, D. (Ed.). (2005). Margaret Simey. *From rhetoric to reality: A study of the work of F.G. D'Aeth, social administrator.* Liverpool: Liverpool University Press.

Bourdillon, A. (Ed.). (1945). *Voluntary social services: Their place in the modern state.* London: Methuen & Co.

Braithwaite, C. (1938). *The voluntary citizen: An enquiry into the place of philanthropy in the community.* London: Methuen.

Brasnett, M. (1969). *Voluntary social action.* London: NCSS.

Brenton, M. (1985). *The voluntary sector in British social services.* Harlow: Longman.

J. Davis Smith, *100 Years of NCVO and Voluntary Action,*
https://doi.org/10.1007/978-3-030-02774-2

Burchardt, J. (1999). Reconstructing the rural community: Village halls and the National Council of Social Service, 1919 to 1939. *Rural History, 10*(2), 193–216.

Burchardt, J. (2011). Rethinking the rural idyll: The English rural community movement, 1913–26. *Cultural and Social History, 8*(1), 73–94.

Burnett, J. (1994). *Idle hands: The experience of unemployment, 1790–1990*. London: Routledge.

Cahill, M., & Jowitt, T. (1980). The new philanthropy: The emergence of the Bradford City Guild of help. *Journal of Social Policy, 9*(3), 359–382.

Carmel, E., & Harlock, J. (2008). Instituting the "third sector" as a governable terrain: Partnership, procurement and performance in the UK. *Policy and Politics, 36*(2), 155–171.

Charity Commission and Centre for Charity Effectiveness. (2017). *Taken on trust: The awareness and effectiveness of charity trustees in England and Wales*. London: Charity Commission.

Clifford, D. (2017). Charitable organisations, the great recession and the age of austerity: Longitudinal evidence for England and Wales. *Journal of Social Policy, 46*(1), 1–30.

Committee on Voluntary Organisations. (1978). *The future of voluntary organisations: Report of the Wolfenden Committee*. London: Croom Helm.

Craig, G., Taylor, M., & Parkes, T. (2004). Protest or partnership? The voluntary and community sectors in the policy process. *Social Policy and Administration, 38*(3), 221–239.

Crowson, N., Hilton, M., & McKay, J. (Eds.). (2009). *NGOs in contemporary Britain: Non-state actors in society and politics since 1945*. Basingstoke: Palgrave Macmillan.

Crowson, N., Hilton, M., McKay, J., & Marway, H. (Eds.). (2011). Witness seminar: The voluntary sector in 1980s Britain, abridged. *Contemporary British History, 25*(4), 499–519.

Davies, R. (2015). *Public good by private means: How philanthropy shapes Britain*. London: Alliance Publishing Trust.

Davis Smith, J. (2017). David Cameron's three-day volunteering initiative: Genuine proposal or electoral sham? *Voluntary Sector Review, 8*(2), 219–229.

Davis Smith, J., Rochester, C., & Hedley, R. (Eds.). (1995). *An introduction to the voluntary sector*. London: Routledge.

Den Otter, S. (1996). *British idealism and social explanation: A study in late Victorian thought*. Oxford: Clarendon.

Finlayson, G. (1994). *Citizen, state, and social welfare in Britain 1830–1990*. Oxford: Clarendon Press.

Flanagan, R. (1991). *'Parish-fed bastards': A history of the politics of the unemployed in Britain, 1884–1939*. Westport: Greenwood Press.

Garside, P. (2000). *The conduct of philanthropy: William Sutton Trust, 1900–2000*. London: The Athlone Press.

Gladstone, F. (1979). *Voluntary action in a changing world*. London: Bedford Square Press.

Goldman, L. (2002). *Science, reform, and politics in Victorian Britain*. Cambridge: Cambridge University Press.

Grant, W. (1999). *Pressure groups and British politics*. Basingstoke: Macmillan.

Grant, P. (2014). *Philanthropy and voluntary action in the First World War: Mobilizing charity*. London: Routledge, Taylor & Francis Group.

Grimley, M. (2004). *Citizenship, community and the Church of England: Liberal Anglican theories of the state between the wars*. Oxford: Oxford University Press.

Hall, P. (1992). Inventing the nonprofit sector. In P. Hall (Ed.), *Inventing the nonprofit sector and other essays on philanthropy, voluntarism, and nonprofit organisations* (pp. 13–84). Baltimore: Johns Hopkins University Press.

Harris, J. (1992). Political thought and the welfare state, 1870–1940: An intellectual framework for British social policy. *Past and Present, 135*, 116–141.

Harris, J. (1997). *William Beveridge: A biography*. Oxford: Clarendon Press.

Harris, J. (Ed.). (2003). *Civil society in British history: Ideas, identities, institutions*. Oxford: Oxford University Press.

Harris, B. (2010). Voluntary action and the state in historical perspective. *Voluntary Sector Review, 1*(1), 25–40.

Harris, M. (2016). Where did we come from? The emergence and early development of voluntary sector studies in the UK. *Voluntary Sector Review, 7*(1), 5–25.

Harris, M., & Rochester, C. (Eds.). (2001). *Voluntary organisations and social policy in Britain*. Basingstoke: Palgrave.

Harris, R., & Seldon, A. (1987). *Welfare without the state: A quarter-century of suppressed public choice*. London: Institute of Economic Affairs.

Hatch, S. (1980). *Outside the state: Voluntary organisations in three towns*. London: Croom Helm.

Hayburn, R. (1971). The voluntary occupational centre movement, 1932–9. *Journal of Contemporary History, 6*(3), 156–171.

Hedley, R., & Davis Smith, J. (Eds.). (1982). *Volunteering and society: Principles and practice*. London: Bedford Square Press.

Hemmings, M. (2017). The constraints on voluntary sector voice in a period of continued austerity. *Voluntary Sector Review, 8*(1), 41–66.

Hilton, M. (2011). Politics is ordinary: Non-governmental organisations and political participation in contemporary Britain. *Twentieth Century British History, 22*(2), 230–268.

Hilton, M., & McKay, J. (Eds.). (2011). *The ages of voluntarism: How we got to the big society*. Oxford: Oxford University Press.

Hilton, M., Crowson, N., Mouhot, J., & McKay, J. (2012). *A historical guide to NGOs in Britain: Charities, civil society and the voluntary sector since 1945*. Basingstoke: Palgrave Macmillan.

Hilton, M., McKay, J., Crowson, N., & Mouhot, J. (2013). *The politics of expertise: How NGOs shaped modern Britain*. Oxford: Oxford University Press.

Hinton, J. (1998). Volunteerism and the welfare state: Women's Voluntary Service in the 1940s. *Twentieth Century British History, 9*, 274–305.

Hinton, J. (2002). *Women, social leadership, and the Second World War*. Oxford: Oxford University Press.

Humphreys, R. (2001). *Poor relief and charity, 1969–1945: The London Charity Organisations Society*. Basingstoke: Palgrave.

Jenkins, J. (2001). The organisation man: George Haynes at the National Council of Social Service. In L. Black et al. (Eds.), *Consensus or coercion?: The state, the people and social cohesion in post-war Britain* (pp. 151–168). Cheltenham: New Clarion Press.

Jones, S. (1986). *Workers at play: A social and economic history of leisure, 1918–1939*. London: Routledge & Kegan Paul.

Keeling, D. (1961). *The crowded stairs: Recollections of social work in Liverpool.* London: NCSS.

Kendall, J. (2000). The mainstreaming of the third sector into public policy in England in the late 1990s: Whys and wherefores. *Policy and Politics, 28*(4), 541–562.

Kendall, J. (2003). *The voluntary sector: Comparative perspectives in the UK.* London: Routledge.

Kendall, J., & Knapp, M. (1996). *The voluntary sector in the UK.* Manchester: Manchester University Press.

Knight, B. (1993). *Voluntary action in the 1990s.* London: Centris.

Kramer, R. (1990). Change and continuity in British voluntary organisations, 1976 to 1988. *Voluntas, 1*(2), 33–60.

Laybourn, K. (1994). *The Guild of Help and the changing face of Edwardian philanthropy: The Guild of Help, voluntary work and the state, 1904–1919.* Lampeter: The Edwin Mellen Press.

Lent, A. (2001). *British social movements since 1945: Sex, colour, peace and power.* Basingstoke: Palgrave.

Lewis, J. (1995). *The voluntary sector, the state and social work in Britain: The Charity Organisation Society/Family Welfare Association since 1869.* Aldershot: Edward Elgar.

Lewis, J. (1996). The boundary between voluntary and statutory social service in the late nineteenth and early twentieth centuries. *The Historical Journal, 1,* 155–177.

Lewis, J. (1999). Reviewing the relationship between the voluntary sector and the state in Britain in the 1990s. *Voluntas, 10*(3), 255–270.

Lewis, J. (2005). New labour's approach to the voluntary sector: Independence and the meaning of partnership. *Social Policy and Society, 4*(2), 121–131.

Lowe, R. (1995). Welfare's moving frontier. *Twentieth Century British History, 6*(3), 369–376.

Macadam, E. (1934). *The new philanthropy: A study of the relations between the statutory and voluntary social services.* London: Allen and Unwin.

Maier, F., Meyer, M., & Steinbereithner, M. (2014). Nonprofit organisations becoming business-like: A systematic review. *Nonprofit and Voluntary Sector Quarterly, 45*(1), 64–86.

Maloney, W., Jordan, G., & McLaughlin, A. (1994). Interest groups and public policy: The insider/outsider model revisited. *Journal of Public Policy, 14*(1), 17–38.

Marwick, A. (1964). Middle opinion in the thirties: Planning progress and political "agreement". *The English Historical Review, 79*(311), 285–298.

Marwick, A. (1998). *The sixties: Cultural revolution in Britain, France, Italy and the United States, c1958–1974.* Oxford: Oxford University Press.

McBriar, A. (1987). *An Edwardian mixed doubles: The Bosanquets versus the Webbs, a study in British social policy 1890–1929.* Oxford: Clarendon Press.

McCarthy, H. (2007). Parties, voluntary associations, and democratic politics in interwar Britain. *The Historical Journal, 50*(4), 891–912.

McCarthy, H. (2008). Service clubs, citizenship and equality: Gender relations and middle-class associations in Britain between the wars. *Historical Research, 81*(213), 531–552.

McCarthy, H., & Thane, P. (2011). The politics of association in industrial society. *Twentieth Century British History, 22*(2), 217–229.

McKibbin, R. (1988). *Classes and cultures: England, 1918–1951.* Oxford: Oxford University Press.

Mess, H. (Ed.). (1947). *Voluntary social services since 1918*. London: Kegan Paul.

Milbourne, L. (2013). *Voluntary sector in transition: Hard times or new opportunities?* Bristol: Policy Press.

Moore, M. (1977). Social work and social welfare: The organisation of philanthropic resources in Britain, 1900–1914. *The Journal of British Studies, 16*(2), 85–104.

Morgan, G. (2012). Public benefit and charitable status: Assessing a 20 year process of reforming the primary legal framework for voluntary activity in the UK. *Voluntary Sector Review, 3*(1), 67–91.

Nathan Committee. (1952). *Report of the committee on the law and practice relating to charitable trusts*. London: HMSO.

National Coalition for Independent Action. (2014). *NCIA inquiry into the future of voluntary services: Working paper 1: The position and role of national infrastructure bodies concerning the cuts to and privatisation of public services*. London: NCIA.

NCVO. (1984). *The management and effectiveness of voluntary organisations*. London: NCVO.

NCVO. (1996). *Meeting the challenge of change: voluntary action into the 21st century: The report of the Commission on the Future of the voluntary sector*. London: NCVO.

Norman, J. (2010). *The big society: The anatomy of the new politics*. Buckingham: University of Buckingham Press.

Offer, J. (2003). Idealism versus non-idealism: New light on social policy and voluntary action in Britain since 1880. *Voluntas, 14*(2), 227–240.

Olechnowicz, A. (2005). Unemployed workers, "enforced leisure" and education for "the right use of leisure" in Britain in the 1930s. *Labour History Review, 70*(1), 27–52.

Oppenheimer, M., & Deakin, N. (Eds.). (2011). *Beveridge and voluntary action in Britain and the wider British world*. Manchester: Manchester University Press.

Owen, D. (1964). *English philanthropy, 1660–1960*. London: Oxford University Press.

Prochaska, F. (1988). *The voluntary impulse: Philanthropy in modern Britain*. London: Faber and Faber.

Prochaska, F. (1995). *Royal bounty: The making of a welfare monarchy*. New Haven: Yale University Press.

Prochaska, F. (2008). *Christianity and social service in modern Britain: The disinherited spirit*. Oxford: Oxford University Press.

Pugh, M. (2008). *We danced all night: A social history of Britain between the wars*. London: Bodley Head.

Rochester, C. (2013). *Rediscovering voluntary action: The beat of a different drum*. Basingstoke: Palgrave Macmillan.

Rooff, M. (1972). *A hundred years of family welfare: A study of the Family Welfare Association (formerly Charity Organisation Society), 1869–1969*. London: Michael Joseph.

Rose, S. (2003). *Which people's war?: National identity and citizenship in wartime Britain, 1939–1945*. Oxford: Oxford University Press.

Simey, M. (2005). In D. Bingham (Ed.), *From rhetoric to reality: A study of the work of F.G. D'Aeth, social administrator*. Liverpool: Liverpool University Press.

Smith, H. (Ed.). (1986). *War and social change: British society in the Second World War*. Manchester: Manchester University Press.

Snape, R. (2015). Voluntary action and leisure: An historical perspective, 1830–1939. *Voluntary Sector Review, 6*(1), 153–171.

Stapleton, J. (1994). *Englishness and the study of politics: The social and political thought of Ernest Barker*. Cambridge: Cambridge University Press.

Stevenson, J. (1984). *British society, 1914–1945*. Harmondsworth: Penguin.

Thane, P. (2012). The "big society" and the "big state": Creative tension or crowding out? *Twentieth Century British History, 23*(3), 408–429.

Thane, P., & Davidson, R. (2016). *The Child Poverty Action Group, 1965–2015*. London: Child Poverty Action Group.

Thane, P., & Evans, T. (2012). *Sinners? scroungers? saints?: Unmarried motherhood in twentieth-century England*. Oxford: Oxford University Press.

Tumin, W. (1992). *On trust report: Increasing the effectiveness of charity trustees and management committees*. London: NCVO.

Vincent, A., & Plant, R. (1984). *Philosophy, politics and citizenship: The life and thought of the British idealists*. Oxford: Blackwell.

Willmott, P. (1992). *A singular woman: The life of Geraldine Aves, 1898–1986*. London: Whiting & Birch Ltd.

Wolfenden Committee. (1978). *The future of voluntary organisations: Report of the Wolfenden Committee*. London: Croom Helm.

Zimmeck, M. (2010). The compact 10 years on: government's approach to partnership with the voluntary and community sector in England. *Voluntary Sector Review, 1*(1), 125–133.

Index

© The Author(s) 2019
J. Davis Smith, *100 Years of NCVO and Voluntary Action*,
https://doi.org/10.1007/978-3-030-02774-2

9 783030 027735